The Afterlife of Character, 1726–1825

MATERIAL TEXTS

A complete list of books in the series is available from the publisher.

The Afterlife of Character, 1726–1825

David A. Brewer

PENN

University of Pennsylvania Press
Philadelphia

Printed in the United States of America on acid-free paper

10 9 8 7 6 5 4 3 2 1

Published by
University of Pennsylvania Press
Philadelphia, Pennsylvania 19104-4011

Library of Congress Cataloging-in-Publication Data

Brewer, David A. (David Allen), 1969–
The afterlife of character, 1726–1825 / David A. Brewer.
p. cm. — (Material texts)
Includes bibliographical references and index.
ISBN 0-8122-3864-8 (cloth : alk. paper)
1. English literature—18th century—History and criticism. 2. Characters and characteristics in literature. 3. Intellectual property—Great Britain—History—18th century. 4. Intellectual property—Great Britain—History—19th century. 5. Authors and readers—Great Britain—History—18th century. 6. Authors and readers—Great Britain—History—19th century. 7. English literature—19th century—History and criticism. 8. Influence (Literary, artistic, etc.) 9. Sequels (Literature) I. Title. II. Series.

PR448.C52B74 2005
820.9'27'09033—dc22

2004061217

For Rebecca,
a more-of-the-same girl,
and for Charlotte and Lucian,
whose first word was, in each case, "more"

Contents

I have said somewhere it is the unwritten part of books that would be the most interesting.

— William Makepeace Thackeray

Cottagers upon the Textual Commons, an Introduction

I began with the desire to read with the dead. Or, more accurately, with the desire to read one book with one dead person, to understand how and why Lady Mary Wortley Montagu read *The Adventures of Peregrine Pickle* in the way in which she did. In a letter to her daughter, Lady Mary wrote that she was "sorry not to see more of P. Pickle's performances."[1] I was struck by this desire for "more" of a literary character, and puzzled by why it should be couched in theatrical terms (after all, Smollett's work is generally regarded as a novel). As a child, I had been a voracious reader of series fiction and had frequently wished a story might go on longer, but I had always regarded this desire as simply a mark of my own reluctance to accept closure of any sort. With Lady Mary, however, I was confronted by a clearly sophisticated and clever reader who nonetheless shared my interest in "more" and did so in ways that defied explanation as simply "a deep unconscious nostalgia for a past reading experience," a "wish to read the 'unforgettable' text once more, yet as if [she] had forgotten it."[2] As I began to read the rest of Lady Mary's correspondence, along with some of the traces of reading left by her contemporaries in the form of letters, diaries, and marginalia, I came to realize that, eccentric as she was in many ways, Lady Mary's desire "to see more" was hardly unique. Indeed, as my research progressed, I discovered a sizable number of readers who not only pined for "more" but actually sat down and invented additional performances for some of the most celebrated characters in eighteenth-century British literature: Lemuel Gulliver, Captain Macheath, Inkle and Yarico, Sir Roger de Coverly, Pamela Andrews, Tristram Shandy. Indeed, some readers went beyond the productions of their own time to devise lives off-page for older characters, especially Sir John Falstaff. Lady Mary thus may well be unusual in her desire for more Peregrine Pickle (which has always been something of a specialty taste), but she can nonetheless be taken as exemplary, for through her desire "to see more" she was engaging in the provocative and deeply revealing reading practices which are the subject of this book: what I would like to collectively term "imaginative expansion."[3]

I use "imaginative expansion" as an umbrella term for an array of reading practices in eighteenth-century Britain by which the characters in broadly successful texts were treated as if they were both fundamentally incomplete and the common property of all. Far from being the final word on the subject, the originary representation of these characters was, for readers engaged in these practices, merely a starting point—a common reference, but one perpetually inviting supplementation through the invention of additional details and often entirely new adventures. Consider, for a moment, George Saville Carey's *Shakespeare's Jubilee, A Masque,* in which Falstaff is "charm-call'd from his quiet grave" in order to attend the 1769 Stratford Jubilee.[4] En route, "fat old Jack" is taunted by Oberon and Puck—who "talk of sack, but . . . remain unseen"—and kidnapped by the witches from *Macbeth,* who "force him across" a broom "and fly away with him," even as he upbraids them as "old carl-cats," "imps of old Satan, made up all of rags," and "faggots of filth" (14, 18). Once they have reached Stratford, though, all has been forgiven, and the "witches descend in thunder" as part of a grand procession "and introduce Falstaff, Caliban, Pistol, and all of Shakespeare's favourite Characters," who "walk two and two down the temple" of Apollo to great applause (20–21). As even this brief description should suggest, Carey's masque revolves around the invention of more adventures in heaven and earth than were dreamt of in Shakespeare's philosophy. Nowhere does Carey betray even the slightest sense that the Falstaff scenes in *1 Henry IV, 2 Henry IV,* and *The Merry Wives of Windsor* (much less his reported death in *Henry V*) provide "all / Ye know . . . and all ye need to know" about Plump Jack. Nor does Carey seem to worry in the least that the "Genius of Shakespeare" (who also puts in an appearance) might resent this appropriation of what we have been trained to regard as his characters. If anything, Carey presumes that the best way to promote "great Shakespeare's matchless fame" is to conjure up "such sprites as owe / To his creative boundless muse, / Their existence, birth, and name" and set them loose in a series of additional performances which echo, but hardly replicate, their assorted Shakespearean originals (10, 23).

I dwell upon the sheer unfamiliarity of Carey's presumptions because they, like Lady Mary's wish for "more," pose such an intriguing challenge to our usual ways of thinking about the relationship between authors, readers, and literary characters and signal how my investigation of imaginative expansion participates in—and, I hope, usefully extends—the broader reconsideration of the use of character which has been one of the real highpoints of eighteenth-century studies over the past decade. For most of the twentieth century, serious studies of literary character conceived of their project as one of demystification. Countering what they saw as a naïve and pernicious tendency on the part of nonacademic readers and earlier critics to talk about characters as if they were actual people, these scholars insisted, in L. C. Knights's words, that a character "is merely an abstraction from the total response in the mind of the reader or spectator, brought into being by written or spoken words."[5] Because she never really existed, Lady Macbeth necessarily had no children, so enumerating them was at best a patent fallacy. Harry Berger Jr. offers perhaps the most thoroughgoing of these critiques, insisting that

> speakers are the effects rather than the causes of their language and our interpretation: in the unperformed Shakespeare text there are no characters, no persons, no bodies, no interiorities; there are only dramatis personae, the masks through which the text speaks. . . . Speakers don't have bodies, age, insomnia, corpulence, or illness unless and until they mention them, and when they do it is usually in the service of some discourse in which states of the body are signifiers used to mystify moral effects as physical causes. Speakers don't have childhoods unless and until they mention them. If, for example, John of Gaunt never mentions his youth, then he has and had no youth, no childhood whose critical events the analytical dialogue may recuperate and revise by the light of the future anterior.[6]

Psychoanalysis or any other form of character criticism is thus, for Berger, a fundamentally misguided effort. What Knights and Berger and countless others have argued seems both irrefutable and commonsensical. Of course "speakers don't have childhoods"; they don't even have adulthoods. Yet to presume that readers who have pretended otherwise were just willfully blind to the obvious truth does them a grave disservice and simply perpetuates what E. P. Thompson has termed "the enormous condescension of posterity."[7] Whatever else George Saville Carey and Lady Mary Wortley Montagu may have been, they were hardly idiots running around in an ontological fog unable to distinguish fiction from reality.

What most distinguishes the recent work on character from the tradition which Knights and Berger represent is its willingness to take seriously the apparent desire of many readers to imagine characters as in full possession of a deep interiority and a life which extends off-page, despite the patent counterfactuality of it all. That is, this recent work takes the desire to talk about characters as if they were real people as evidence of what that fantasy allowed readers to do, rather than as rope with which to hang them for their methodological felonies. Where these scholars part company, of course, is in their respective accounts of what the consideration of characters in this way did for those who so suspended their disbelief. Catherine Gallagher, following David Hume, has argued that "fictional characters were uniquely suitable objects of compassion" because of their immateriality: since they have no bodies, fictional characters pose no barriers to "the process by which someone else's emotion becomes our own," a process which cannot occur so long as those emotions are "conceiv'd to belong to another person."[8] Accordingly, fictional characters were peculiarly well suited to help "women conform their emotional lives to the exigencies of property exchange" by giving them "practice in the various modes of having emotions, trying them out, holding them in a speculative, tentative, and above all temporary way" (193–94). By engaging in this sort of "emotional practice," readers could better prepare themselves for the constraints and indignities of life in a world increasingly dependent upon speculation of all sorts.

Deidre Lynch, on the other hand, is interested in how "people used characters . . . to renegotiate social relations in their changed, commercialized world" and "to derive new kinds of pleasure from these changes."[9] For Lynch, readers "accommodated themselves to their increasingly commercial society" in two principal ways: either they plumbed "characters' hidden depths" in order to furnish evidence of "their own interior resources of sensibility" or they ostentatiously cultivated their enjoyment of finely wrought characters as "a way of asserting that [they] did not belong to the sort of undiscriminating audience that would take pleasure" in "illegitimate modes of inscribing character," such as caricature or burlesque (1, 10, 57). That is, "people's transactions with books came to be connected in new ways, first, to their endeavors to find themselves as 'individuals' and to escape from their social context, and, second, to their endeavors to position themselves within an economy of prestige in which cultural capital was distributed asymmetrically and in which not all who read were accredited to 'really read' literature" (6). Either way, valuing characters "for their indescribability, their exceptionality, and their polyvalence" could serve as a means of distinguishing oneself from the relentless world of exchange and universal equivalence (76).

Lisa Freeman has recently challenged these accounts as being far too devoted to "the novel's version of the modern subject when it was neither the inevitable nor the only configuration of identity in circulation at the time."[10] For Freeman, "the rise of the subject," with its putative depth, independence, and continuity across time, "enforced" an "ideological conformity," which contemporaries, as well as modern theorists, found troubling (1). In order to resist "that identity formation," playwrights and other social commentators championed a counter-conception of character which refused "the illusory consolations offered in the novel through the figure of the transparent subject" and "highlighted" instead "the multiple, contradictory, and opaque surfaces of character," "the contingencies and contexts that shape perception and recognition" (1, 8). Far from affording readers a safe haven from market culture, the novelistic version of the subject simply interpellated them more securely in its grasp. Only by embracing "the culture's general anxieties over the instability of identity" and "staging" them "precisely as a competition in which actions, words, figure, and reputation could all be weighed against one another" could Britons hope to produce "a way to apprehend identity and locate value that was not dependent on an illusion of interiority" (16, 27, 237). Only by "understanding [the] identity" of a character "not as an emanation of a stable interiority, but as the unstable product of staged contests between interpretable surfaces," could audience members resist subjection (27).

I have learned a great deal from each of these accounts and I wholeheartedly share their impulse to focus upon what characters allowed readers and viewers to do, rather than upon what those characters might mean in and of themselves. My own project differs from this work, however, in three important ways. First of all, Gallagher, Lynch, and even Freeman (somewhat surprisingly given her focus upon the theater) all presume that eighteenth-century readers and viewers are fundamentally operating in alienated solitude. For them, whatever a reader does with a character proceeds first and foremost from an underlying sense of anomie brought about by the wrenching transformations of commercial culture. Accordingly, anyone engaging in emotional practice, attempting to distinguish herself from the marketplace, or resisting subjection is always already attempting to compensate for what Freeman calls "the culture's general anxieties over the instabilities of identity" (16). I do not doubt that this was often the case. Anxiety and modernity seem to go hand in hand. But most of the readers with whom we shall be concerned seem remarkably calm and even playful in their invention of various characters' lives off-page. Perhaps they were just whistling in the dark, but their tone consistently suggests a pleasure not ordinarily associated with coping mechanisms. Moreover, far from being essentially alone, many of these readers seem to have readily imagined themselves as part of larger virtual—and occasionally actual—communities devoted to the sharing and circulation of these further adventures. Reading, for someone like Carey, may well have begun in solitude, but it was hardly a solitary activity. Indeed, these readers went out of their way to emphasize how much their inventions could forge new sociable ties with a broad range of their fellow readers.

Additionally, these recent scholars have all located the compensatory power of characters in their respective materiality or immateriality. For Gallagher and Lynch, the heroes and heroines of novels could serve as objects for emotional practice or proof that one had that within which passeth show precisely because of their disembodiment. Conversely, Freeman attributes the resistance to subjection afforded by theatrical characters to the ways in which the "bodies of actors and actresses" mimicked "the kinds of epistemological confusion experienced over identity in everyday life" (18–19). My own research suggests that what readers found attractive about characters was neither their materiality nor their immateriality per se, but rather the ways in which one enabled the other in a perpetual feedback loop. As we shall see, the characters for whom further adventures were invented tended to be those whose immateriality was paradoxically guaranteed by the sheer material proliferation of different and differing editions, formats, and performances.

Finally, as my opening with Lady Mary should suggest, I am far more devoted than my predecessors have been to reconstructing the specific practices of actual readers in all their puzzling eccentricity. As a result, my inquiry has been conducted much closer to the ground, which has necessarily required what Jacques Revel terms "a change in the scale of analysis."[11] This, in turn, has allowed me to notice interconnections and patterns which have escaped previous, more overarching observers. None of my departures from this recent (and for the most part extremely valuable) scholarship necessarily undermines that work—although I have my doubts about Lynch's chronology and Freeman's stark division between the novel and theater—but it does, I hope, suggest that this is still very much an emerging field, one in which a premature consensus would be both counterproductive for the living and unjust to the dead.[12]

* * *

Obviously, not all readers in eighteenth-century Britain engaged in imaginative expansion any more than all readers in any era read the same way. The century's single most famous reader, Samuel Johnson, once pointedly dismissed the desire for "more": "Alas, Madam! . . . how few books are there of which one ever can possibly arrive at the *last* page! Was ever yet any thing written by mere man that was wished longer by its readers, excepting Don

Quixote, Robinson Crusoe, and the Pilgrim's Progress?"[13] But in this respect, as in so many others, Johnson cannot be treated as fully representative (indeed, alarm bells should go off whenever Johnson makes one of these blanket pronouncements). Robert DeMaria Jr.'s contention that "Johnson was a great reader and read in so many different ways . . . that the categories I use to describe his life of reading are adequate for describing any other life of reading" simply cannot be sustained, no matter how tempting it might be to have the Great Cham as our model.[14] In the course of this study, we shall encounter many readers wishing many texts longer, fuller, and richer. And most of the originary texts with which we shall be concerned were never continued by their authors, and so seem to most modern readers self-contained and complete—unlike the three titles Johnson singles out as exceptions, each of which received an authorial sequel or two, as well as augmentations by other hands.

Yet DeMaria's example of Johnson begs an important methodological question for a project like this one. If Johnson is not representative—and hence DeMaria's categories are not in fact "adequate for describing any other life of reading"—then how can we claim with any certainty that George Saville Carey or any of the other readers with whom we shall be concerned are illustrative of larger trends? The problem is simply the paucity of evidence: the vast majority of readers do not leave any sort of trace and so those who do are necessarily going to be atypical, at least in this area. We are in possession, of course, of what Robert Darnton describes as "a great deal of information about the external history of reading," but John Brewer is quite right to note that such sources—"inventories, library catalogues and salesroom lists"—tend to be "inert" and "exceptionally difficult to animate." Conversely, the surviving commentary of individual readers, like Lady Mary, can often seem "perfunctory and elliptical," not to mention wildly eccentric.[15] What possibilities remain reasonably open for antiquarian souls like myself who want to read with the dead? Must we choose only from the rather stark menu which Darnton and Brewer present to us? Must, as Janusz Sławinksi wonders, "the history of readers, somehow counter to its own nature, . . . be practiced mainly as a history of eminent readers?" or else simply as a history of what, rather than how, people read?[16] And if the former, must "eminent" necessarily mean unrepresentative?

Most histories of reading seem caught in this bind, albeit often brilliantly so. Historians like Darnton, Brewer, and Roger Chartier have reconstructed the cultural significance of reading and reading matter largely through the judicious sifting and interweaving of what Darnton would call "external" evidence: probate inventories, publishers' records, library catalogs, and the like. When their accounts required a more vivid example, they pluck a supposedly representative reader, like Brewer's Anna Larpent, out of the archive. But well aware of the infrequency with which such readers have come down to us, most of these historians draw upon other kinds of evidence, including the hints given within texts as to their intended readers and the clues yielded by the scrutiny of books as bibliographic objects. Chartier, for example, has made a number of intriguing suggestions concerning the reading practices of the French peasantry based upon the kinds of abridgments made for those readers by the publishers of chapbooks.[17] Efforts like Chartier's are both noble and necessary—otherwise, we could have no access whatsoever to those peasants—yet, given their mediation by both the necessity for deciding what various bibliographic features mean and by the presumption that we can then infer reading practices from those features, they are at least as conjectural as anything based upon more ostentatiously "elliptical" evidence.

Other historians have eschewed these macroscopic accounts, choosing instead to focus upon reconstructing individual readers from the past in all their particularity and (oftentimes) peculiarity. Carlo Ginzburg's meticulous recreation of the inner life of the heretical sixteenth-century Friulian miller Domenico Scandella (Menocchio) is perhaps the best-known example of this kind of work, although Darnton, Brewer, Lisa Jardine, Anthony Grafton, and Kevin Sharpe have all written fascinating explorations of the practices of particular readers.[18] Individually, these accounts are quite intriguing and persuasive, but—as perhaps they should—they resist synthesis: the leap made in the subtitle of Ginzburg's book from Menocchio to "the cosmos of a sixteenth-century miller" is a rather large one. Menocchio seems so wacky that it is hard to believe that he is at all representative, yet surely he must have something in common with his fellow millers, fellow Friulians, fellow heretics. Pinning down what exactly that common ground is, however, seems an impossible endeavor, given that most of his fellows never had to face the obsessively record-keeping Holy Office. Accordingly, trying to write a history of reading based upon case studies like Ginzburg's seems hopelessly fraught: not only would it be at best only a "history of eminent readers," but it is not even clear what that "eminence" would tell us about any readers other than those specifically selected for study.[19]

In striving to avoid the methodological pitfalls of both macro- and microscopic approaches to the history of reading, I have tried—in good eighteenth-century fashion—to carve out a middle way, a kind of analysis attentive to individual eccentricity and caprice, yet not limited by it. I want to preserve the ways in which attention to individual cases can usefully undercut grand theorizing, yet I hope to show the larger significance of those cases without simply presuming their exemplarity, for the traces left by individual readers are never going to be wholly exemplary, if only because most readers do not leave traces. In trying to define my quest for explanatory relevance through particularity, I have been heartened by a concept central to Italian microhistory: "the normal exception." I would like to hypothesize that the eccentric reading practices I group together under the rubric of imaginative expansion constitute a kind of "normal exception" and so deserve a form of historiographic attention which, as Giovanni Levi argues, "tries not to sacrifice knowledge of individual elements to wider generalization . . . but, at the same time . . . tries not to reject all forms of abstraction since minimal facts and individual cases can serve to reveal more general phenomena."[20] That is, imaginative expansion is far from representative behavior per se, but it is nonetheless quite revealing. Indeed, such reading practices may be all the more revealing because of, not despite, their "anomalous" character: one of the chief insights of microhistory has been Ginzburg's contention that "the more improbable sort of documentation" is "potentially richer," because, as Levi reminds us, "in a weak science [such as cultural history] in which, if experimentation itself is not impossible, that aspect of experimentation involving the ability to reproduce the causes is excluded, even the smallest dissonances prove to be indicators of meaning which can potentially assume general dimensions."[21] This seemingly paradoxical situation obtains because it is precisely "those traces, those clues, those details previously overlooked"—or dismissed as merely whimsical or opportunist—"which upset and throw into disarray the superficial aspect of the documentation" upon which the standard histories have drawn. Once we recognize "the decisive importance" of these normal exceptions, "it is possible to reach a deeper, invisible level, the one comprising the rules of the game, 'the history that men do not know they are making.'"[22]

In pursuing my microhistorical *via media*, then, I hope to show how a sustained attention to the apparently eccentric practice of imaginative expansion can "assume general dimensions" and reveal "the rules of [a] game" whose players extended well beyond those specifically involved in the practices I am describing. By focusing upon the paradoxes inherent in these practices—lack stemming from plenitude, the seemingly teeming ever in need of more, the privately owned being treated as if it were common to all—we can discover an entire constellation of more broadly held readerly presumptions concerning literature, publicity, and property, the traces of which still shape our experience of cultural community. Indeed, our investigation of imaginative expansion can substantially complicate and revise three of the most pressing issues in literary and historical study today: namely, the emergence of proprietary authorship, the processes by which canonical texts gain their canonicity, and the related practices through which virtual communities are invented.

Evaluation is, of course, inescapable, but I have purposely striven to take my evidence on its own terms, employing what Ginzburg describes as a "flexible rigor," rather than reject or distort it, no matter how alien or wrongheaded it might seem.[23] Indeed, I cannot imagine doing otherwise with this kind of project, for if we were to confine ourselves to those few traces of past reading that "coincide with the rights of the text," as Umberto Eco puts it, then we would exclude almost everything that makes a historical investigation interesting and simply confirm our own prejudices concerning what those textual rights comprise.[24] This, then, will be a story not of good readers or bad readers, misreaders or proper readers, much less of readers who are types (in the sense of typology) of ourselves; it will simply be a tale of past readers who, like Oliver Twist, wanted some more.

* * *

Yet in order to understand how an investigation of eighteenth-century readers' desire for more might "assume general dimensions" and so productively complicate some of our current ways of thinking about the field, we need first to survey the underlying presumptions of imaginative expansion, beginning with what we have already noticed in the case of Carey's treatment of Falstaff: namely, a persistent fantasy that literary characters were both fundamentally inexhaustible and available to all. Their alleged inexhaustibility stemmed from what I would like to term their felt immateriality, which in turn seems to have been the paradoxical consequence of the sheer extent of their material dissemination. In an ontological puzzle which will recur throughout this study, the more copies or performances of a text there were in circulation, the more the characters who inhabited that text came to be regarded as what Carey describes as disembodied "sprites" (23). That is, they seemed to be simultaneously everywhere and nowhere, in the hands of countless strangers and yet never wholly reducible to any particular manifestation. The extent to which characters appeared to "transcend" their textual origins (to adopt Gérard Genette's terms) was thus directly proportionate to the sheer number of sites in which they seemed to be "immanent."[25] Falstaff was no more (or less) present in any of, say, James Quin's performances of *1 Henry IV* than he was in Carey's own copy of that play, but by virtue of those hundreds of performances and tens of thousands of printed copies—not to mention his additional iteration in texts like *Shakespeare's Jubilee*—he could seem exempt from the ordinary laws of physics: "we nor pay, or tax, or toll / No mortal law can us controul" (9). As such, he could be envisioned as ultimately inexhaustible: one cannot wear out a "sprite" capable of appearing in thousands of places at the same time any more than one can deplete an "immortal spirit" by conjuring it up yet another time (7).

If characters were unconstrained by "mortal law," then they could also be regarded as perpetually available through what Simon Stern has usefully termed an "economy of abundance." This way of thinking about literary property postulates that "any future use becomes a form of increase," that value is added merely by additional iteration and circulation.[26] Needless to say, this is just a fantasy, a conjecture concerning the supposed fundamental nature of literary property, not a description of the actual material conditions of the book trade, which, like any sector of the economy, involved finite resources. But for our purposes, and those of the readers with whom we are concerned, the accuracy of this fantasy was irrelevant. The important thing was the way in which it could provide a compelling alternative to the (equally far-fetched, but to us far more familiar) "economy of scarcity, driven by the logic of an inelastic marketplace," which many booksellers promulgated in their attempts to secure perpetual copyright.[27] In an economy of scarcity, literary property was conceived as a zero-sum game: a reader's gain must mean an author's loss. In an economy of abundance, on the other hand, no such dispossession could occur, since "with respect to Intellectual Labours, we may improve the Discoveries of others without invading their Property."[28] By imagining themselves as participants in an economy of abundance populated by inexhaustible "sprites," readers could feel free to invent whatever additional performances struck their fancy without having to worry that they were being unjust or larcenous.

Like most pseudolegal discourse, this way of thinking about literary property proceeded more through metaphor and analogy than rigorous argument. Perhaps the single most readily available metaphor was that of the traditional village commons, albeit with the caveat that these commons, unlike the actual wastes and Lammas lands, were in no danger of overuse. Consider only the analogy as it was formulated by William Kenrick (to whom we shall return in Chapter 3—indeed, he is one of the heroes of this book). In the epilogue to the 1766 version of *Falstaff's Wedding*, Kenrick compares a reader's relation with literary characters to the common right of cottagers. In order to counter a trumped-up charge of plagiarism, Kenrick asserts that "Dramatic sprites" "as mere ideal characters exist, / And stand as cyphers mark'd on Nature's list." Accordingly, figures like Falstaff are "free to range in fancy's pimlico: / . . . . *Ferae naturae* there, their preservation / Is purchas'd by no game association: / The poaching plagiary alone denied / A privilege, granted to each bard beside; / Who' tho' a cottager, to try his skill, / May shoot, or course, or hunt them down at will; / In his own paddock may the strays receive, / And scorn to ask a lordly owner's leave." Let us take a moment to unpack Kenrick's tangle of metaphors. He first asserts that dramatic characters are immaterial ("mere ideal . . . cyphers") and hence "are free to range" like "*ferae naturae*": wild beasts incapable of becoming the objects of absolute property. Then, in a conflation of the game laws with common right, he claims that "each bard," "tho' a cottager," has the right to receive stray characters "in his own paddock," thereby gaining a qualified property through the labor of confining them, despite the existence of "a lordly owner"—presumably of the commons upon which "the strays" were being shot, coursed after, or hunted. Consequently, so long as "each bard"—which, for Kenrick, means "each reader"—does not claim an absolute property right in a character, as a "poaching plagiary" would do, he need not worry about the propriety of his actions, for they are part of the same customary tradition as grants cottagers common right.

Clearly Kenrick's analogy has no legal authority. Nonetheless, it richly captures the underlying economic logic of imaginative expansion. For Kenrick, readers have a traditionary right to use characters, just as cottagers have the right to use the commons, and in both cases that right extends from the peculiar status of its object vis-à-vis conventional property. As *ferae naturae* grazing on the commons, characters are doubly forms of what Carol Rose terms "inherently public property."[29] Accordingly, they pose a significant challenge to our usual ways of thinking about property as the right to exclude the public. For example, William Blackstone famously defined property as "that sole and despotic dominion which one man claims and exercises over the external things of the world, in total exclusion of the right of any other individual in the universe." Yet common right undermined that dominion by allowing a "kind of possession without ownership, a profit which a man hath in the land of another."[30] Herein, presumably, lay part of the analogy's appeal: if readers were cottagers exercising their common right, then their "possession" of a character could be regarded as not only innocent but profitable and productive. And since the textual commons, unlike the actual commons, were manifestly inexhaustible, those profits could be enjoyed without any more risk of injury to the "lordly owner" than was incurred by *The Spectator*'s "Man of a Polite Imagination," who "often feels a greater Satisfaction in the Prospect of Fields and Meadows, than another does in the Possession." Indeed, as Addison's language suggests, pinning down absolute ownership was a bit irrelevant in the economy of abundance; what mattered was use and the satisfactions it could afford, satisfactions which, like common right, somehow mysteriously translated into "a kind of Property in everything he sees."[31]

Of course, if readers were cottagers exercising their common right, then they were necessarily bound together by their shared use of the same property. After all, cottagers do not have the right to graze their cattle upon just any waste: their right is tied to a specific locale and so too is their sense of felt commonality with other cottagers. They were not just cottagers in the abstract but rather, say, the "Cottagers, Day Labourers, Shopkeepers, and other little Housekeepers" of Sutton Coldfield.[32] Yet as the sheer bagginess of this list testifies, the collective entity thus formed is impossible to delimit with any real precision: common right attaches to anyone who can persuasively claim to be one of "the other little Housekeepers." Carol Rose insists that this ambiguity is inherent in the very notion of "customary rights," as "custom is the means by which an otherwise unorganized public can order its affairs" by vesting "property rights in groups that are indefinite and informal yet nevertheless capable of self-management" (124). No census of little housekeepers could capture for more than a moment who was entitled to use the commons of Sutton Coldfield, any more than a catalog of likely readers could delimit who had the authority to receive stray characters in "fancy's pimlico." Yet far from translating into "a wasteland of uncertain or conflicting . . . claims," this demographic imprecision was precisely what marked the commons as common in the first place, since "indefiniteness of use—abstracted from numbers or intensity of use—count[s] as the essential measure of 'publicness.'"[33] Public property and the public are thus mutually constitutive, since, as Michael Warner has shown, the thing which most characterizes a public as such is that it "can be . . . participated in by any number of unknown and *in principle unknowable* others."[34] Accordingly, public property is simply that which is used by a public.

Moreover, given the logic of scale returns, which we have already seen vis-à-vis the issue of felt immateriality, the attractiveness of treating characters as if they were public property increased in direct proportion to how public they already felt, which is to say, how large their public seemed to be. Additional use could only enhance a character's felt publicity by further strengthening his or her public's imagined self-identity as a public: "as with festive activities generally, the more members of the community who participate, the more they come to feel as one. . . . Activities of this sort . . . have value precisely because they reinforce the solidarity and fellow-feeling of the community as a whole; thus the more members of the community participate, even only as observers, the better for all."[35] With greater scale come greater returns, such that "one values one's own" interest in, say, the afterlife of a given character "all the more because others do so as well": like other "practices that enhance the sociability of the practitioners . . . one cannot get too much of them."[36] Granted, the sociability afforded by the textual commons was almost wholly virtual, but that seems to have only sped up the cycle of scale returns: readers would invent further adventures for a particular character, see that strangers were apparently doing the same (as evidenced by publications like *Falstaff's Wedding*), and so conclude that both they and the strangers were far from alone, that there were still others, yet unknown, with whom they all shared a desire for "more." Here, in a nutshell, we have the central link between publicity, canonicity, and virtual community which both underpins imaginative expansion and drives this book: namely, that readers who imagine characters as common, and hence available to the public, also imagine themselves as part of a public, a virtual community interested in the same things as they are, which in turn requires a common object to rally around even as it enhances that object's felt value—what we will call its social canonicity—by making it the commons around which the virtual community organizes itself.[37]

These practices thus set up a feedback loop or bandwagon effect in which they reinforce one another: characters came to seem more socially canonical and desirable as they came to seem more common and used by all, which in turn enhanced their value and publicity that much more. This process of increasing collective value and publicity through repeated individual use is neatly formulated by another one of the heroes of this book: Charles Churchill. Churchill spoke for many when he proclaimed, in defense of his *Rosciad,* "The Stage I chose—a subject fair and free— / 'Tis yours— 'tis mine—'tis Public Property. / All Common Exhibitions open lye / For Praise or Censure to the Common Eye."[38] The apposition here is actually an equation: for Churchill, the stage was public property precisely because it was both "yours" and "mine" and so defied any pretensions to absolute ownership. "Exhibitions" were "Common" because all who attended (in theory, all who could scrape together a shilling or two for admittance) could stake a proprietary claim "meerly by employing more Labour on them."[39] And this felt commonness or publicity was what in turn ensured not only the availability of the stage as a "subject" but also its attractiveness: it is, after all, both "fair and free." The textual commons—what Sir Joshua Reynolds would term "a magazine of common property, always open to the publick, whence every man has a right to take what materials he pleases"—thus paradoxically stems from the proliferation of private claims upon the same artwork, from the oscillation between individual appropriation and imagining the individual appropriations of others.[40] As with the roads, the mere fact of repeated public use could transform private property into a public benefit.[41]

* * *

I dwell upon the paradoxical logic of the feedback loop because it helps to illuminate several important ways in which the phenomenon of imaginative expansion might challenge our usual ways of thinking about authorship, canonicity, and the public. The full force of these challenges will emerge in the course of my narrative; for now it will suffice to catalog them. First of all, the pattern of scale returns which we have been tracing offers an implicit justification for my use of not only the letters, diaries, and marginalia to which I have already made reference but also a wide array of materials originally intended for publication (including *Falstaff's Wedding* and *Shakespeare's Jubilee*). Some historians of reading would reject the latter kind of evidence as inauthentic or overly mediated. DeMaria, for example, rather puzzlingly insists that "a real reader is not a writer," which means that, since "writing about reading is writing," it is illegitimate to consider "the history of remarks about reading" as anything other than "contributions to" "a branch of literary criticism" (xii). What DeMaria is after is "evidence of reading that is unsullied by being part of the history of writing," that is "a part of personal rather than public life" (xiii, 2).[42] Yet the logic of the feedback loop suggests that the publicity of something like *Shakespeare's Jubilee,* far from being an obstacle to regarding it as part of the history of reading, is in fact its greatest contribution. By making his masque available to hundreds or thousands of strangers, Carey could enhance the felt commonness and value of Falstaff and company that much more, even as that commonness and value justified his project in the first place. Indeed, it would not be too much to say that the practice of imaginative expansion not only relies upon the publicity of beloved characters, it aspires to bolster that publicity through making its own additional iterations as public as possible. Accordingly, it would be not only counterproductive to exclude published evidence from an inquiry into imaginative expansion, it would obscure the very motives driving the practice in the first place, motives which call into question the sustainability of DeMaria's distinction between "personal" and "public life."

The logic of the feedback loop can also help us to recognize and begin to theorize the rather different sense of canonicity at work here and to see how it might complicate our current accounts of what John Guillory has termed "the problem of literary canon formation." In recent years, we have been taught—chiefly by Guillory—to consider canon formation as ultimately a matter of "the social function and institutional protocols of the school," "which regulates and thus distributes cultural capital *unequally*" as a means of reproducing "the social order, with all of its various inequities."[43] For Guillory, assessments of value "are necessary rather than sufficient to constitute a process of canon formation. An individual's judgment that a work is great does nothing in itself to preserve that work, unless that judgment is made in a certain institutional context, a setting in which it is possible to insure the *reproduction* of the work, its continual reintroduction to generations of readers" (28). Accordingly, the culture wars of the late 1980s were fundamentally misguided when they cast the issue of canon formation as one of blinkered aesthetics, rather than the institutional regulation of linguistic and symbolic capital. There is much to recommend Guillory's analysis of the recent past, just as there is much to be learned from the literary historians who have followed his lead and credited various eighteenth-century institutions—most notably antiquarian scholarship, Scottish reprint publishing, and the House of Lords—with the invention of the vernacular canon.[44] However, the phenomenon of imaginative expansion challenges the adequacy of these accounts by presenting us with a host of individual readers whose supposedly impotent value judgments nonetheless uncannily anticipate those of generations to come. That is, with the possible exception of Falstaff, Sir Roger de Coverly, and Inkle and Yarico, none of the characters for whom further adventures were invented were part of the curricula of English literature introduced into the primary schools in the mid-eighteenth century, nor were many of them championed by influential orderers of the arts like Thomas Warton. Yet one would be hard pressed to find characters who were more familiar to and valued by "generations of readers" than, say, Lemuel Gulliver or Pamela Andrews.[45] All this suggests that what we are dealing with is a form of canonicity which exists both prior to and outside the institutions which have been so central to recent accounts of canon formation.

Following Franco Moretti, I would like to describe this other form of canonicity as the "social canon": that unwritten list of texts kept alive in the hearts and minds of myriad individual readers from generation to generation.[46] Obviously, the social canon is a much broader phenomenon than imaginative expansion. Nonetheless, I would like to propose that the normal exceptionality of imaginative expansion can lay bare some of the underlying presumptions of the social canon and so reveal the radical incompleteness of accounts like Guillory's.[47] Perhaps the most obvious difference between the social canon and what we could term the academic canon lies in their respective relation to popularity. For most academic canon makers, beginning in the eighteenth century, value was inversely proportionate to a text's current number of avid readers. Indeed, it is hard to imagine how it could be otherwise and still serve as a mode of distinction. Reading Spenser would cease to be an accomplishment if all could both readily and eagerly do so. With the social canon, on the other hand, popularity—especially what Moretti describes as "steady survival from one generation to the next" (210)—was not only compatible with canonicity, it was in large part constitutive of it. As the logic of the feedback loop suggests, what marks the characters who populate the social canon as desirable is precisely that others have already desired them. Their felt value, that is, resides in the possibilities they provide for forging a sense of ongoing kinship with one's fellow readers, rather than in the opportunities they afford for polite self-fashioning or philological one-upmanship. Taste is here demonstrated by commonality, rather than distinction.

Closely related to its embrace of popularity was the social canon's devotion to beloved characters, rather than authorial voice, as its chief "principle of textual classification."[48] Socially canonical characters were presumed to be, in Maurice Morgann's famous distinction, "Historic" rather than "Dramatic beings," and so were credited with what Tony Bennett and Janet Woollacott term "a semi-independent existence that is capable of working . . . even for those who are not directly familiar with the original texts in which they first made their appearance."[49] As such, they were not bound by the temporal confines of their originary text but rather could "acquire the validity of historical figures" whose "entire lives, from birth to death, are sources of interest."[50] This matters because the very act of presuming that the "entire life" of a character was what lent that character interest and value requires abandoning any strict notion of "correctness." The off-page life of Pamela Andrews cannot be pinned down with the same exactitude as, say, the metrical refinement of a couplet by Edmund Waller or even the sublimity of Milton's description of Sin and Death. As such, it cannot nearly as readily serve as a means of demonstrating one's own distinction and refinement: potentially anyone could imagine what Pamela did before she went into service, whereas it takes a certain amount of specialized training to appreciate the ways in which Milton's account grimly parodies the birth of Athena. The social canon's attachment to characters' entire lives is thus part of what disqualifies it from the school (unless those lives could be reconfigured as evidence of authorial genius): it too easily permits an equitable distribution of cultural capital, its "reproduction" is insufficiently grounded within a gate-keeping "institutional context."

All this lends credence to Moretti's seemingly hyperbolic insistence that the social canon almost always precedes the academic canon: "readers, not professors, make canons: academic decisions are mere echoes of a process that unfolds fundamentally outside the school: reluctant rubber-stamping, not much more" (209). Not everything embraced by the social canon ends up in the school, of course, but comparatively few texts which were not initially socially canonical have ever ended up part of the academic canon, albeit toward rather different ends. Indeed, the belatedness of the academic canon may help illuminate why the social canon has gone so curiously uninvestigated. That is, it might be useful to consider the ways in which academic canon makers have traditionally almost instinctively positioned themselves against anything still popular as something of a reaction formation, an anxious attempt to dismiss as mere vulgarity what was in fact a competing and prior conception of canonicity. Similarly, it might be profitable to consider the academic canon's attachment to distinction as evidence of an underlying desire to redefine as an economy of scarcity what the social canon had presumed was an economy of abundance, in which cultural capital was available to all who could read or even simply attend a performance. At the very least, the historical priority of the social canon should serve as a reminder that despite the widespread desire to provide a genealogy for "the present crisis" in the humanities, we should not willfully disregard the ways in which canon formation has operated over time as first and foremost an extracurricular activity.

Yet comprehending the ways in which the social canon emerged "from below" poses a significant challenge to another of our customary ways of thinking: namely, the embattled but still widespread presumption that the eighteenth-century public is best understood by recourse to Jürgen Habermas's influential analysis of it as a sphere devoted to "rational-critical" debate. In recent years, a number of social and cultural historians have attempted to adapt Habermas's model to better account for the actual complexities of the eighteenth-century public. Some have attempted to chart out what Habermas has himself conceded as "the coexistence of competing public spheres," most notably the plebian public spheres of political radicals and the gendered public spheres of bluestockings and early feminists.[51] Others have tried to contend that the public sphere encompassed modes of expression which went well beyond strict rationality: festivals, toasts, parades, huzzahing at the election hustings, and the like. As descriptions of the sheer range of kinds of publicity which were invoked in the period, these accounts have been invaluable. But as Harold Mah has powerfully argued, the findings of these historians cannot ultimately be reconciled with Habermas's theory: "the universality of the public sphere requires what Habermas calls 'abstract' individualism," which cannot accommodate dissenting social groups whose identity stems precisely from their status as, say, the disenfranchised poor.[52] Similarly, since the broader "repertoire of public expression" which these historians have recovered "derive[s] from the specific character of different social groups and [its] use always foregrounds that group's character," it must "necessarily appear as the 'other' to the public" as formulated by Habermas, "as the particularity . . . against which it defines itself" (164, 167). For Mah, this means that we should recognize that "the public sphere is a fiction, which, because it can appear real, exerts real political force": accordingly, our task should be to "figure out why and how certain groups are able to render their social particularity invisible and therefore make viable claims to universality" (168). But surely a simpler and more historically satisfying conclusion would be that we just need to disentangle our understanding of the public from Habermas's model. Habermas has proved deeply attractive to historians for reasons that would no doubt prove professionally revealing, but the sheer amount of tinkering his theory has required is more than a little reminiscent of pre-Copernican astronomers devising more and more elaborate epicycles to preserve their Ptolemaic cosmology. It is high time that we stop trying to squeeze the wealth and diversity of our evidence into the Procrustean bed of a model which can only conceive of the public as a body devoted to impartial rational-critical debate in the hope of reaching consensus. This may be good political theory, but it makes for rather dubious historiography.

What the normal exceptionality of imaginative expansion can help us to see is that the concept of the public in the eighteenth century was far broader than Habermas and some of his devotees have allowed and was not necessarily wedded to any of the things which they see as defining. For example, the virtual communities invented through imaginative expansion could hardly be described as engaged in rational-critical debate, yet, for all that, they are nonetheless behaving like a public in the ways in which they both rely upon and promote "a reflexivity in the circulation of texts among strangers who become, by virtue of their reflexively circulating discourse, a social entity."[53] The principal reason why readers like Carey or Kenrick cannot be described as rational-critical (in addition to the manifest playfulness of their contributions) is that the collective project in which they are engaged does not aspire to consensus and so need not ever end. Indeed, as the logic of the feedback loop should suggest, what guaranteed a character's "semi-independent existence" was the ongoing proliferation of attempts to sketch out various aspects of that existence: Morgann, for example, thought that Falstaff's landing in "the *Fleet* might be no bad idea of further amusement," while Samuel Foote looked forward to "spending an Evening with that merry Mortal," and Corbyn Morris could not wait to see his "future Embarrassments."[54] Similarly, Carey busied himself with imagining how Falstaff would react when mugged by Puck, while Kenrick envisioned the means through which a boisterous, yet tearful reconciliation with the newly crowned Hal might still be brought about. Each of these readers takes Falstaff in a different direction: there is both no chance of consensus and no apparent desire for it. Rather, they are all engaged in what Robert Newsom calls "probabilistic talk," which in its endless speculation about what a character might "probably" or "possibly" do in his life off-page both testifies to that character's felt inexhaustibility and further contributes to it. Since such speculation can never be gotten right (who's to say what Falstaff's boyhood was like?), it has no necessary endpoint: to modify Frank Kermode's famous pronouncement about canonicity, "there will always be something else and something different to say" about what form those "future Embarrassments" might take.[55] At the same time, much of the pleasure to be had from "probabilistic talk" derives from comparing competing possibilities with other readers and so "letting the game of fiction go on, and, in particular, . . . letting it go on in some public and communal fashion—not just within individual readers, but among an audience as the game called criticism. Probabilistic talk about fictions provides a way for players to compare games or even conjoin private games into larger public ones."[56] As fellow players of the "game called criticism"—what we could call the game of imaginative expansion—these readers cite and so necessarily reproduce what Morgann terms the "common fame" (156) of the Shakespearean Falstaff who serves as their collective point of reference, thereby ensuring his "semi-independent existence." Yet in so doing, they also invent a virtual community, a "social entity" in which because "we all like *Old Jack*," "we" can feel a commonality with one another, even if we are otherwise divided by barriers of class, gender, religion, politics, or anything else.[57]

Clearly the "we" who "like *Old Jack*" are hardly what Mah describes as the Habermasian ideal of "a unitary mass subject" speaking with a single voice (167). Nor do they need to be. One of the most intriguing challenges posed by the phenomenon of imaginative expansion is the way in which it shows how a public can suspend its social differences while still showcasing its interpretative differences. All of these readers present themselves as unmarked by any particularity other than their shared affection for a given character, yet they manifestly do not have any ambitions of transforming their social abstraction into a monologic *vox populi*. If anything, these readers seem to regard their lack of consensus as a sign of their strength, a token that they too constitute an "exhaustless fund of wit and humour."[58] All of this is simply to make explicit what much recent scholarship has left unsaid in its desire to hang on to the Habermasian schema: namely, that while the public sphere described by Habermas may have represented "a powerful political fiction" in certain eighteenth-century circles, it was hardly the dominant discourse—especially within literary culture—nor was it the ideal to which everyone aspired.[59] Far more representative are what David Shields has termed "communities of appetite and feeling," publics whose publicity did not depend upon a collective suspension of individual hobbyhorses.[60]

* * *

Why should virtual participation in a "community of appetite and feeling" have been so attractive to readers in eighteenth-century Britain? In some ways, this is an unanswerable question: there are, no doubt, as many explanations as there are readers, if not more. For many readers the sense of belonging to a larger community of fellow readers—particularly one whose felt value was ever increasing through the logic of the feedback loop—may have assuaged the existential anxieties prompted by urbanization, commercialization, and all of the other historical processes transforming the social fabric of Britain. J. Paul Hunter has argued that the novel was invented in large part to "substitute for communality," to provide compensation for the world we have lost.[61] Imaginative expansion may well have offered many of the same compensations, whether or not they were practiced upon novels. Such claims, however, are almost impossible to prove. Just as the middle class seems to have been rising ever since the Fall, so too one can always find nostalgia for lost community. Like cannibalism, organic community seems to be something that always happens over there or back then.

If an explanation for why readers found imaginative expansion particularly psychologically satisfying in the eighteenth century is beyond my abilities, I can offer instead a few suggestions as to what made the textual commons particularly imaginable in this period. Obviously, imaginative expansion of one sort or another has been with us since antiquity: classical epics and medieval romances are full of characters who migrate from text to text, while even today devotees of various books and television programs are busy devising further adventures (so-called fan fiction) for their favorite characters. Indeed, more than a full century before the start of my story, Don Quijote and Sancho Panza encounter rumors that rival versions of themselves were gallivanting about the countryside. But two factors seem to have come together in the early decades of the eighteenth century to make the virtual communities of imaginative expansion especially compelling and central, insofar as anything eccentric can ever be central: (1) the comparative domestic political stability of Britain, especially England, during the mid-eighteenth century, which cleared a space for nonpartisan textual play, and (2) an increasing propensity for conceiving of texts as property, which had not yet fully coalesced into our modern notions of proprietary authorship.

In the later seventeenth century and into the very first decades of the eighteenth century, authorship was still largely regarded as an inherently political act. Both authors and readers were presumed to be participants in the rage of parties and so the ways in which a text could be read depended largely upon a reader's stance toward its (and its author's) inferred politics. Seemingly fictitious characters were generally understood to possess extra-textual reference and an author's denial that a text was *à clef* only heightened most readers' suspicions of topicality—often rightly so. Yet as the Civil Wars passed from living memory and the Whig Ascendancy entrenched itself in the wake of the failed Jacobite uprising of 1715, the stakes of writing *à clef* seemed to many observers to be in decline, despite the proliferation of Opposition writings throughout the 1720s and 1730s. The habits of reading which decades of partisan squabbling (and several dramatic changes and attempted changes in government) had engendered were still current in the 1720s, but the impact of learning about the secret affairs or backstairs influence peddling of ministers seemed less of a life-and-death affair and more of a game than it had, say, forty years previous in the Exclusion Crisis.

This comparative political calm made it possible to imagine the reading public as a potentially coherent entity, something other than always already riven by the legacy of the regicide. This is not to deny the presence of domestic strife (one need only remember the '45), but compared to the previous century or to the class tensions, radicalism, and suppression of radicalism that marked the decades leading up to the First Reform Bill, the mid-eighteenth century was comparatively tranquil, especially between the mid-1720s and the early 1760s: the central period with which we shall be concerned.[62] Or at least, contemporaries could imagine their time as comparatively tranquil: "the national settlement" seemed "to allow" for "what Hobbes [had] denied; a stable, nonpolitical realm, not a private world of the self, but a leisure space for reading and writing which could" remain largely untroubled "by questions of power." Most mid-eighteenth-century readers seemed able to assure themselves that "someone else [was] taking reasonably good care of things, looking after the state" while they rode their hobbyhorses.[63] Such assurance had not been possible during the Civil Wars and Restoration (when the prevailing presumption was that the nation was always already divided into us and them, regicide and royalist, Whig and Tory) and it would become quite arduous again in the face of the palpable discontent surrounding the American War, the wars against revolutionary and Napoleonic France, and the deeply felt campaigns for reform which followed in their wake. This is not to say that politics vanished from literature in the mid-eighteenth century, only that the relationship between the aesthetic and the political took on a different shape, one more congenial to the imagining of the public as a coherent whole and to the playful proliferation of further adventures for beloved characters.[64]

In addition to this newfound awareness of the possibilities for textual play which the comparative stability of the nation might afford, most eighteenth-century readers shared a somewhat inchoate sense that texts were best regarded as a form of property, but not one necessarily subject to strict authorial control. As a number of recent scholars have shown, the very notion of literary property was in flux throughout the period, with the result that the linkages between authorship, ownership, and the copyright statutes which now seem so self-evident were at the time both highly contested and widely disregarded.[65] Moreover, the social function of property itself was undergoing a massive reconsideration, what J. G. A. Pocock has identified as the running debate between "a conception . . . which stresses possession and civic virtue" and "one which stresses exchange and the civilisation of the passions."[66] Given such a milieu, it is not surprising that many readers should have convinced themselves that texts were property capable of acquiring "value through [their] circulation within a dynamic market economy," even if it was unclear to whom they might ultimately belong.[67] In large part, it is this notion that "if the printed book was being cautiously tied to its author . . . , the knot was not yet secure" that allows us to account for the peculiar availability of imaginative expansion in the mid-eighteenth century and to distinguish it from earlier forms of the practice.[68] That is, readers like Carey or Kenrick are not simply drawing upon an already extant fund of traditional materials (as medieval *chansons de geste* or the nameless creators of ballads about Robin Hood or Dick Whittington might do); rather, they are knowingly appropriating the creations of another in the hope that they could further increase the felt value of those creations for all who delighted in them. Yet their knowingness almost never translates into a self-conscious delight in their own transgression: they are cottagers exercising their common right, not "nomads poaching their way across fields they did not write, despoiling the wealth of Egypt to enjoy it themselves."[69] Indeed, the sheer ease with which readers engaged in imaginative expansion underscores how much of an act of historical imagination it requires to go back to a time when copyright meant just that: the right to mechanically reproduce copies of a particular text for a certain length of time, not the fuzzier and more metaphysical assertion of absolute dominion into which it has since transmuted. The blithe facility with which readers invented further adventures should remind us of just how strenuously authors had to solicit and cajole readers into granting them that proprietary authority over their own creations which now goes largely without saying. It should help us remember that the origins of modern literary culture lie not so much in a heroic "Age of Authors" asserting their sovereignty as in an age of perpetual negotiation between readers and writers over, among other things, the afterlife of character.

Chapter 1
The Invention of the Fictional Archive

We begin with a sustained look at a key moment in the transformation of British reading practices: the later 1720s. The first decades of the eighteenth century saw a decisive reduction in domestic political tensions compared with those that had gripped the nation for most of the previous century. Certainly not even the most Whiggish of historians would deny the presence of real divisions and resentments in the years leading up to 1730—tensions perhaps best exemplified by the abortive Jacobite uprisings of 1715 and 1719—but these paled in comparison to those surrounding the Popish Plot, the expulsion of James II, and, of course, the Civil Wars themselves. One of the principal consequences of this comparative political stability was that it became possible to imagine oneself as part of a community of readers not always already marked by the legacy of the regicide. This is not to say that the divisions of Whig and Tory or Dissenter and High Church did not still play a significant part in the everyday life of literate Britons after the Hanoverian succession; they certainly did. But they could be imaginatively suspended in a way which had previously seemed impossible, in large part because partisanship itself seemed less of a life-and-death affair than it had been a few decades before. As Steven Zwicker has argued, "the stakes" of political argument

> had begun to change by the close of the seventeenth century. A sea change took place when the civil wars had to be reconstituted wholly as secondary effect. Dryden knew this . . . as did Pope when he invented a triumphant epic not of empire but of dullness. There is no regretting the astonishing diminutions of *The Dunciad;* but the apocalypse that Pope imagined was very different from the one that Marvell hoped might suffuse the world and transform time at the close of *The First Anniversary.* No one was yawning when the angel of the commonweal stirred the healing waters in 1654 or when, at the height of Exclusion, Locke allowed himself to imagine the dissolution of civil society. Dullness is one kind of cultural demise; civil war, quite another.[1]

With the stakes of partisanship thus reduced—especially after the essentially uncontested accession of George II—it became increasingly possible to envision aesthetics and politics as potentially separable entities and so to recognize some of the limitations and shortcomings of politicized reading, especially the commonplace that even the most seemingly apolitical narrative was best read for its "application" (and likely coded reference) to contemporary politics.[2]

In this chapter we will examine how the declining attractiveness of application, in conjunction with readers' increasing ability to imagine themselves part of a virtual community not inevitably divided against itself, created an opening for a new reading practice—imaginative expansion—which could seize upon the same liminal features of a text as reading *à clef* had done, but turn them into an opportunity for communal play, rather than partisan strife. That is, we will investigate how hitherto politicized readers transformed what Catherine Gallagher has termed their "desire to open every book to some extra-textual reality" into a means of imagining those books as but installments from a larger *fictional* reality: what I would like to term "the fictional archive."[3] By tracing this shift in the desirability of different reading practices, we can account for the otherwise deeply puzzling phenomenon with which my story begins: the unprecedented proliferation of afterlives for Lemuel Gulliver, which began in late 1726 and was followed, less than two years later, with a similar explosion of off-page adventures for Captain Macheath and Polly Peachum. This chapter, then, details the origins and first efflorescence of imaginative expansion in eighteenth-century Britain. Subsequent chapters will explore its varieties, consequences, and ultimate transformation over the course of the next hundred years.[4]

* * *

One of the most striking aspects of the decreasing appeal of application in the first decades of the eighteenth century was the proliferation of attempts to theorize the place of topicality within the text itself. By "topicality" I mean not only specific extratextual referents for particular characters—the figures for whom a "key" would be supplied—but also what Leah Marcus has termed "localization": the "fierce desire for decoding more generally."[5] As with many other cultural phenomena, these self-conscious efforts to pin down what had previously gone without saying indicate something of "a crisis in faith" regarding the utility of application.[6] What strikes me as peculiar to this particular historical juncture, though, is the way in which readers and writers consistently figured topicality as liminal, both of and not of the text itself, somehow paratextual and textual at the same time. In so doing, they unwittingly set the terms within which imaginative expansion would flourish. Joseph Addison, for example, repeatedly tried to distinguish between what he called the "essential standing Beauties" of a text and "those accidental Circumstances that at first help'd to set it off" through allusions to contemporary persons and events.[7] Despite his evaluative adjectives, however, the "accidental Circumstances" of topicality seem, for Addison, to provide most of the pleasures of reading. Thus once a topical allusion has been identified, "the Reader can't but be pleas'd to have an Acquaintance thus rising by degrees in his Imagination, for whilst the Mind is busy applying every Particular, and adjusting the Several Parts of the Description, it is not a little delighted with its Discoveries and feels something like the Satisfaction of an Author from his own Composure" (6–7). Without the ability to make such identifications—as is necessarily the case with texts from classical antiquity, all of which Addison does not "question but" were "secret Histor[ies]"—our pleasure is imperfect (3, 2). And a century hence, the same will be true of the topicality of, say, *Absalom and Achitophel.* Despite the primacy of these pleasures, though, Addison strives to preserve his distinction between the "essential" and the "accidental," figuring the latter as but "a Comment on the Story," distinct from "the Writing" itself (8). Yet if these "Comments" provide a text's principal appeal—and Addison asserts that "nothing can be more delightful" (7)—and if, in their absence, the supposedly primary "Graces" left to a text are equally accidental—namely, those "that arise merely from the Antiquity of an Author" (2)—then it seems as if Addison's distinction is ultimately one without a difference. The "accidental" and paratextual turn out to be as "essential" as any other part of the text. Indeed, if we strip a text of both its "Comments" and the "Graces" arising merely from antiquity, it is unclear whether anything is left as the putatively "essential" core.

Other efforts to theorize the work of art in the age of reading *à clef* ran into similar difficulties in defining the bounds of a text. In the 1720s, topicality was repeatedly figured as marginal and dispensable; yet once dispensed with, the remaining "essential" text invariably proved lacking. In a 1729 sermon in memory of Charles I, for example, Edward Young claims to have preached "with an entire abstinence from *party,* without which, most modern compositions would be famish'd."[8] Topicality is here figured as food: not of the body and yet necessary to it; apart from it, yet convertible into it (and, Swift no doubt would add, ultimately excretable by it). As with Addison, the more topicality gets figured as marginal, the less separable and dispensable it seems to become, the more it seems—in a telling phrase of Pope's—"secretly insinuated through the whole," with the result that the bounds of a given text were perpetually capable of being redefined.[9] Indeed, for partisans in the age of reading *à clef,* any invocation of what Addison describes as "something foreign to [an author's] Subject" (8) could be taken as a sign of veiled topicality. By their very superfluity and representational excess, such moments supposedly called readerly attention to an "extra-textual reality" that was nonetheless always already inscribed within the text.

But, of course, the definition of what constituted "something foreign to [an author's] Subject" depended upon individual judgment and so could vary quite widely from reader to reader, none of whose interpretations would necessarily correspond with an author's intentions. As Steven Zwicker reminds us, readers in this period made it quite clear that "the meaning of texts would be delimited neither by the moment of their creation nor by the antiquity of their idiom."[10] As the Civil Wars passed from living memory and the Whig Ascendancy came to seem unassailably entrenched—if nonetheless a perennially good topic for complaint—these variations, and the textual liminality which enabled them, came, for many, to feel like a game, an opportunity for a reader to "exert . . . his own Talents" and thereby "come . . . in for half the Performance."[11] Consider, for example, the reader who annotated the Clark Library's copy of the second edition of Eliza Haywood's *Memoirs of a Certain Island Adjacent to the Kingdom of Utopia.* When confronted with an account of how the incestuous Gloatitia had a child with "a certain Duke" (44), whom the key identifies as the D. R——d, this reader tried out the various possibilities, writing "Rutland" above the dash and "Richmond" in the margin. While the Duke of Richmond is a more likely bet, the marginalia betrays no anxiety about having potentially libeled an innocent. Such collateral damage was simply the price one paid for admission to the game.[12] Zwicker has described such readings as a "trivializing of annotation, a reduction to puzzle and enigma of what is in other settings a fuller, more impassioned polemical and ideological engagement." And perhaps they are, when compared to "that powerful drama of partisanship that constituted the world of popery and Exclusion."[13] But the reduction of the identity of "a certain Duke" to "puzzle and enigma" also testifies to a certain readerly fatigue with partisanship, a desire for gossip and play, rather than constant caballing. I suspect that it was this collective desire to relax a little which prompted the always market-savvy John Durant Breval to couch his identification of various figures in Colley Cibber's *The Non-Juror* with phrases like "generally attributed"; "either" x, y, or z; "is suppos'd to be"; or "is said to be." While "the Town" might still "be curious enough to enquire," it seems that there was a newfound lack of urgency when it came to decoding Cibber's quite patently topical play.[14] And with this reduction in urgency came a broadening readerly awareness of the potential pleasures afforded by all sorts of hitherto politicized texts.

* * *

For the Scriblerians, though, the inclination of many 1720s readers to treat application as a game marked a dangerous loss of authorial control. Over and over, their letters betray an anxiety that their carefully wrought satire might be misapplied. Thus Gay and Pope went out of their way to assure Swift that "the Politicians to a man agree, that [*Gulliver's Travels*] is free from particular reflections . . . not but we now and then meet with people of greater perspicuity, who are in search for particular applications in every leaf; and 'tis highly probable we shall have keys publish'd to give light into Gulliver's design."[15] Indeed, Pope confirmed this state of affairs a week later, writing that he had found "no considerable man very angry at [*Gulliver's Travels*] . . . none that I hear of accuse it of particular reflections (I mean no persons of consequence, or good judgment; the mob of Criticks . . . always are desirous to apply Satire to those that they envy for being above them)."[16] Meanwhile in the more duncical milieu of Dublin, "the general opinion is, that reflections on particular persons are most to be blam'd," but such readings were as self-discrediting as the (most likely apocryphal) bishop who "said, that book was full of improbable lies, and for his part, he hardly believed a word of it."[17] Nor was this concern with misapplication an exclusively Gulliverian phenomenon: two years later Gay was insisting that "I am sure I have written nothing that can be legally suppress, unless the setting the vices in general in an odious light, and virtue in an amiable one may give offence."[18] Clearly these letters are united in their desire to dismiss readers bent upon the discovery of libelous "particular reflections" as either fools or knaves. Yet the ridiculousness and impotence of such readings are not nearly as self-evident as the letters would like to suggest. Swift and Gay understood that they were writing in a world in which they and their agents could still be held responsible for the reflections which readers found in their work, whether or not such reflections were actually intended (although few would dispute that *Gulliver's Travels, The Beggar's Opera,* and *Polly* contain at least some personal jabs).[19] Thus Swift follows up his announcement to Pope that his "Travells" were "intended for the press when the world shall deserve them" with the qualification "or rather when a Printer shall be found brave enough to venture his Eares."[20] Similarly, Gay apparently felt it necessary not only to publicly protest (perhaps disingenuously) that "I am as loyal a subject and as firmly attach'd to the present happy establishment as any," but also to insist that "particular passages which were not in [*Polly*] were quoted and propagated in support" of the charge that "it is fill'd with slander and calumny against particular great persons."[21] Indeed, even when official prosecution was not a threat, the Scriblerians seemed to worry about the ways in which their readers might misdirect the intended satire: Swift was concerned that "the persons and facts [of *The Dunciad*] will not be understood" in Dublin, since "twenty miles from London no body understands hints, initial letters, or town-facts and passages." Accordingly, he insisted, "you must have your Asterisks fill'd up with some real names of real Dunces."[22] Names had to be named, if satire was to be both understood and properly applied. In a world in which application had become a game, the Scriblerians were confronted by the prospect of losing their authority while still being liable for the uses to which their texts might be put. Clearly something had to be done.

In their somewhat different ways, *Gulliver's Travels* and *The Beggar's Opera* each exemplify a broader Scriblerian campaign to reverse this state of affairs by soliciting what Paul Hammond has termed "a way of reading which allows the author control without responsibility."[23] That is, the Scriblerians sought to reassert authorial control by turning the game of application into a series of traps that would thwart the inventions of independent-minded readers while still permitting authorized satiric jabs to pass through. In Swift's case, these traps took the form of an extended hoax. *Gulliver's Travels* begins by offering itself as a fantastic travel narrative of the sort frequently employed for partisan ends. Just as Astrea and Virtue escorted Delarivier Manley's readers around "the New Atalantis," a hitherto unknown "Island in the Mediterranean," so too, it would seem, Lemuel Gulliver was traveling into "Several Remote Nations of the World" in order to recount the secret history underlying recent domestic politics. At the very least, most of the standard conventions for such writing are in place within the first few chapters of Part I. Thus we get the extravagant claims for the narrator's credibility, the echoes of previous satiric or utopian travel writing, the foreign lands whose exoticism turns out to uncannily resemble the situation at home, the persistent use of islands more generally. Indeed, "Richard Sympson" even provides the pro forma denunciation of "the common Scribbles of Politicks and Party" that typically serves to invite reading *à clef* in this period.[24] And yet, repeatedly, just as the scandalous allegory seems to get going, the details refuse to map, with the result that the fruits of application come off as at best banal or ridiculous. Consider, for example, the quarrel between the Big Enders and Little Enders in Part I. In general terms, it seems to refer quite clearly to the ongoing battle between Catholics and Protestants and some of the episodes can be readily translated into their English counterparts: "his present Majesty's Grand-father" seems to stand in for Henry VIII, and the Emperor who "lost his Life" and the one who lost "his Crown" no doubt represent Charles I and James II (40–41). But why eggs? Why specify that the cause of the rift was a boyish accident? Why insist that the doctrinal divide between the two factions hinges upon "the fifty-fourth Chapter of the *Brundecral*," which turns out simply to read "*That all true Believers shall break their Eggs at the convenient End*" (41)? Application-minded readers might be tempted to allegorize all this, perhaps seeing a jab at Henry VIII's willingness to cause a schism across Christendom simply in order to get a divorce, or a sly insistence that the differences between Catholicism and the Church of England were really just a matter of taste or convenience "to be left to every Man's Conscience, or . . . the Chief Magistrate" (41). But such decodings immediately lead to a position that almost any reader of the 1720s would have found both ridiculous and heretical: namely, that the Reformation was but a tempest in a teapot and so the "bloody War[s]" waged against the threat of French and Jacobite invasion were a pointless waste of "thirty thousand of our best Seamen and Soldiers" (41). The result of this trap is that readers keen on application are left with either a self-evidently preposterous allegory or else a set of ostentatiously opaque details that seem equivalent only to themselves (as in the proverbial "as sure as eggs are eggs"). Similar traps recur throughout the *Travels,* each time offering an alluring glimpse of topicality which leads only to a dead end. Swift's apparent invitations to allegory would thus seem to be a hoax or wild-goose chase aimed at sending readers upon what one rather annoyed contemporary, the Reverend James Hume, described as "the hunt for Mysteries where nothing at all was intended."[25]

Yet at the same time, the parallels between Britain and the "Several Remote Nations of the World" to which Gulliver travels are undeniable, even if no strict allegory can be sustained. Amid the ludicrous exoticism of Lilliput (such as the contortionist postures in which they swear oaths) may be discerned a series of insistent, if loose comparisons which collectively score a number of quite savage points. For example, while efforts to read Gulliver as simply standing in for a particular figure quickly tie themselves in knots, his account of the ministerial ingratitude he experienced after he had saved the palace and brought about a peace with Blefuscu strongly suggests that the roughly analogous prosecution of Oxford and Bolingbroke after the death of Queen Anne was every bit as petty, vindictive, and ultimately self-defeating.

Similarly, the description of how Lilliput has fallen away from its utopian past in which "Fraud" was "a greater Crime than Theft" and "the Disbelief of a Divine Providence renders a Man uncapable of holding any Publick Station" (48–49) invites readerly speculation as to which "original Institutions" at home have similarly declined into "the most scandalous Corruptions" "by the gradual increase of Party and Faction" (50). Attempts to line up one-to-one correspondences almost invariably fall flat, but the general thrust of the critique seems hard to avoid.

No doubt some readers previously intent on application were entrapped by the rhetoric I have been describing and dutifully confined themselves thereafter to noting only the overarching satiric parallels authorized by Swift. But as Claude Rawson has argued, "with Swift, we are always on our guard from the beginning (I believe this is true of sensitive *first* readings as well as later ones), and what surprises us is not the fact of betrayal, but its particular form in each case."[26] This suggests, quite rightly, that readers are independent agents and that while we may take pleasure in the "particular form" of entrapment Swift employs, we are not nearly as bound by his rhetoric as many modern critics have presumed. Indeed, one of the chief contributions of the history of reading has been its persistent concern with "the fault lines that . . . separate the readers or readings imagined, designated or targeted in specific works from the plural and successive publics those works actually had."[27] It should thus come as no surprise that some readers were undeterred by Swift's rhetorical traps and continued to delight in "puzzle and enigma" at authorial expense: the Reverend Hume, for example, playfully speculated that the giant eagle that snatched up Gulliver's traveling-box at the end of Part II might be "a handsome way of rallying the Famous Legend of the Chapel of Loretto . . . for the Sancta Casa is suppos'd to have been transported by Angels, & so the Effect is not disproportioned to the cause."[28] Still others sidestepped those traps altogether by redirecting their "desire to open every book to some extra-textual reality" into a means of imagining Swift's account of Gulliver as but the first installment from a larger archive.

The notion that Lemuel Gulliver's life extended beyond what his *Travels* record seems to have been the inadvertent result of Swift's desire to parody the prolixity of travelers' tales. From the very beginning of the *Travels*, Gulliver calls attention to all that he has not included in the present text and thereby suggests that "more" is somehow "out there" to be discovered. Consider, for example, Richard Sympson's letter from "The Publisher to the Reader," which prefaces Part I. In it, Sympson explains—at considerable length—that the original manuscript of the *Travels* was "after the Manner of

Travellers . . . a little too Circumstantial" (5). Accordingly, he "made bold to strike out innumerable Passages relating to the Winds and Tides, as well as to the Variations and Bearings in the several Voyages; together with the minute Descriptions of the Management of the Ship in Storms, in the Style of Sailors: Likewise the Account of the Longitudes and Latitudes; wherein I have Reason to apprehend that Mr. *Gulliver* may be a little dissatisfied: But I was resolved to fit the Work as much as possible to the general Capacity of Readers. . . . And if any Traveller hath a Curiosity to see the whole Work at large, as it came from the Hand of the Author, I shall be ready to gratify him" (6). The joke, of course, is that there is no more, that the prolixity which had supposedly been edited out is still there in all of its antiglory (just as it is in the work of William Dampier and other travel writers). Yet in setting up the *Travels* as but a selection from a longer manuscript, Sympson inaugurates a recurrent pattern in the text whereby Gulliver refers to portions of his life and observations which did not make it into the published narrative, whether it be the "Maligners" who have questioned his "Character in point of Cleanliness"—in answer to whom Gulliver explains his defecation procedures (24)—or the "Opinions of [the King of Lilliput's] learned Men" concerning his watch "although indeed I could not very perfectly understand them" (30) or his plan to "reserve" "farther Descriptions" of his ingenuity in moving about Mildendo for "a greater Work, which is now almost ready for the Press, containing a general Description of this Empire, from its first Erection, through a long Series of Princes, with a particular Account of their Wars and Politicks, Laws, Learning, and Religion; their Plants and Animals, their peculiar Manners and Customs, with other Matters very curious and useful; my chief design at present being only to relate such Events and Transactions as happened to the Publick, or to myself, during a Residence of about nine Months in that Empire" (39). As with the letter from Sympson, the joke hinges upon the inclusion of the supposed omissions: Part I is about little but Lilliputian wars, politics, laws, customs, and the like.[29] Much as in Addison's or Young's efforts to theorize topicality, Gulliver's allegedly supplementary foray into ethnography cannot be distinguished from his putative core narrative. Gulliver's life extends beyond the published text to include these supposedly extraneous additional episodes, even as it recasts his hypothetically pared-down text as but a long "particular Account" with which to "trouble the Reader." For readers schooled in the habits of application, such liminal fuzziness could only indicate one thing: a world of extratextual reference ripe for the plucking.

Perhaps the first reader to realize the ludic possibilities of exploring

Gulliver's life off-page was William Hogarth, who published his *Punishment Inflicted on Lemuel Gulliver* (Figure 1) a scant two months after the initial appearance of the *Travels.* This engraving claims to have been "intended as a Frontispiece to [Gulliver's] first Volume but Omitted." Few viewers then or since have taken the claim of accidental omission seriously, but as a belated frontispiece, however unauthorized, the print playfully embraces the editorial logic we have been tracing, for it depicts a scene not recounted in the *Travels,* yet plausible: an enema administered to Gulliver as punishment "for his Urinal Profanation of the Royal Pallace at Mildendo." By Lilliputian standards, the punishment makes a certain sense: it is cruel and demeaning, like the proposed blinding of Gulliver, and in its liquid-for-liquid retribution—a point highlighted by the Lilliputian relieving himself on Gulliver's hat—it might well be the sort of thing which Gulliver's prudery would cause him to omit (although, to be sure, some of the crudest passages in the *Travels* are marked out by Gulliver's protestations of modesty).[30] Hogarth even pays homage to the pride Gulliver takes in his own outsized excrement by providing an obviously inadequate bedpan.

What is most striking about the print for our purposes, however, is how, by virtue of depicting a scene regarding which Gulliver has told us nothing, it engages with him as a fictional character, rather than a thinly veiled stand-in for Oxford or Bolingbroke or Swift himself. That is, it plays up the less obviously topical aspects of Part I, delighting in the disparity in size between Gulliver and the Lilliputians: thus the enema syringe is "a Lilypucian fire Engine," the pulpit a chamber pot, and a thimble serves as sedan chair. To highlight these disparities of size, Hogarth brings in the similar proportions of Part II: a Lilliputian child is being mauled by a giant rat. The visual impact of the print, accordingly, seems far more akin to Samuel Johnson's dismissive reduction of the *Travels* to "big men and little men" than it does to the relentless topicality identified by some of the keys.[31] Indeed, a 1727 pamphlet suggests as much in its announcement of a follow-up image: "*Hogarth* the Engraver is making a print" of the "nine beautiful Pigs . . . about the Bigness of a Ladybird" recently born to "a *Lilliputian* Sow," "which will give a juster Idea of them than I can."[32] Presumably, this sow was brought back from Lilliput, along with "the black Cattle and Sheep" that Gulliver explicitly mentions (65). None of this is to suggest that savvy readers like Hogarth had wholeheartedly abandoned application; it is only to underscore the ways in which the invention of a fictional archive from which further adventures for a character could be putatively drawn was beginning to become a more compelling arena for a reader interested in "exerting his own Talents."

Some of the other ways in which one could imagine a life off-page for Gulliver were soon inadvertently modeled for readers by the "Several Copies of Verses Explanatory and Commendatory" which appeared in May 1727. Written by some combination of the Scriblerians, these poems each offer a dramatic monologue by a character who either appeared in the published *Travels* or else could seem a semi-plausible supplement from the fictional archive (such as Titty Tit, Esq., Poet Laureat of Lilliput, whose lines are only three syllables long). Perhaps the most intriguing of these verses are "The Lamentation of Glumdalclitch for the Loss of Grildrig. A Pastoral" and "Mary Gulliver to Capt. Lemuel Gulliver; An Epistle." As their subtitles should suggest, these are first and foremost exercises in mock-pastoral and mock-heroic epistle. But in typical Scriblerian fashion, the "mock" in their mock-form functions not only as mockery but also as surrogacy (as in mock-turtle soup).[33] And this surrogacy works to displace not only pastoral and heroic epistle but also (perhaps unintentionally) the *Travels* themselves—an effect nicely enhanced by the inclusion of the poems in most post-1726 editions of *Gulliver's Travels*, as if to bibliographically guarantee the existence of the very archive from which they supposedly stem.

Figure 1. William Hogarth, *The Punishment inflicted on Lemuel Gulliver*, 1726. Copyright The British Museum.

Thus, for example, Mary Gulliver's lament provides something of an epilogue to the *Travels* which recasts Gulliver's misanthropic repulsion toward his wife as bawdy farce. Gulliver claims that he simply rejected her in horror "when I began to consider, that by copulating with one of the *Yahoo*-Species, I had become a Parent of more" (244). The lament insinuates that her husband may prefer "that dirty Stable-boy" and "the *Sorrel Mare*" for less principled reasons—they are simply less sexually demanding than Mary, who is apparently incapable of hearing about Gulliver's extinguishing of the palace fire in Lilliput without becoming aroused: "But when thy Torrent quench'd the dreadful Blaze, / King, Queen and Nation, staring with Amaze, / Full in my View how all my Husband came, / And what extinguish'd theirs, encreas'd my Flame."[34] She is also wholly willing to "call thee *Houyhnhnm* . . . / So might I find my loving Spouse of course / Endu'd with all the *Virtues* of a *Horse*" (279). Furthermore, the lament hints at what Mary may have been doing all that time Gulliver was at sea. Referring to "my Bed, (the Scene of all our former Joys, / Witness two lovely Girls, two lovely Boys)," she insists that "they are thy own: / Behold, and count them all; secure to find / The honest Number that you left behind" (276–77). Tellingly, though, the *Travels* mention only three children. The point here, no doubt, is to parody the conventions of heroic epistle, especially the ways in which it ventriloquizes the chaste anguish of abandoned women through the recounting of their former lovers' exploits. But in so doing, the authors of this poem, like Hogarth, treat Gulliver and Mary as if they were coherent fictional beings whose lives extend off-page in ways that could be playfully imagined by persons other than the originary author.

A similar scenario is operating in Glumdalclitch's lamentation, in which we learn of Gulliverian adventures which never made it into the published text of Part II: fishing in the vinegar cruet, dodging children's marbles, turning her watch-key like a capstan, walking with a dish of tea on his head as if it were a milk-pail, chasing "the Mite that bore thy Cheese away" (273).[35] All these are presented as memories of a lost age of joy when Glumdalclitch and her Grildrig were inseparable and so, in their clumsy banality, they parody the conventions of pastoral. Even more than with Mary's lament, however, the specific memories invoked suggest that the Gulliverian archive extends beyond what has been published to date and that even supporting characters, like Glumdalclitch, have ongoing lives off-page which may be fleshed out by readers in search of an opportunity to exert their talents: Glumdalclitch, for example, is still busy "search[ing] each Cranny of the House, / Each gaping Chink impervious to a Mouse" (270), fearing all the while that

Gulliver may "bewilder'd wander all alone, / In the green Thicket of a Mossy Stone" (272).

For the next several years (and more intermittently for the rest of the century), readers busied themselves with the invention of further installments from the fictional archive, often justifying them by reference to the porous boundaries of the *Travels* or the precedent set by the "Verses Explanatory and Commendatory." Thus, for example, *An Account of the State of Learning in the Empire of Lilliput* claims on its title page to be "Faithfully Transcribed out of Captain Lemuel Gulliver's General Description of the Empire of Lilliput, mention'd in the 69th Page of the First Volume of his Travels." It goes on to detail Gulliver's interactions with Bullum, a Lilliputian librarian so vain that he insists that Gulliver sign a testimonial to his "vast Erudition and Learning" before he will hand over any books and even then he will only surrender "the five worst Books in the Library," rather than the five hundred requisitioned by the Emperor (19–20). The books in question have supposedly been "brought safe . . . to England" either to be published or presented to Gulliver's alma mater: Emmanuel College, Cambridge (22). Thus this additional installment from the fictional archive playfully guarantees its own veracity by alluding to still other, yet unseen installments from that same archive—which may or may not in turn resolve the various pressing questions left hanging by Gulliver in the *Account of the State of Learning*, such as whether Bullum was lying when he claimed to be "so far from hating [Eggs] that he had a Dish at his own Table every Day" (30).

Similarly, *Travels into Several Remote Nations of the World. By Capt. Lemuel Gulliver. Vol. III*, opens with Gulliver determined "once more to bear the Fatigues of the Sea, with the charming Hope" of returning to Houyhnhnm-Land. His resolve is redoubled when one of his horses "discover'd a criminal Conversation between my Wife and Groom, and their Scene of Guilt the Stable" (1:14). It would seem that the innuendoes of Mary Gulliver's lament were but the lashing-out of a guilty conscience. Gulliver's "charming Hope" is dashed, however, when a storm drives his ship off course and wrecks it upon the Brobdingnagian coast. Once back in Brobdingnag, in what can only be a nod to "The Lamentation of Glumdalclitch," one of Gulliver's sailors "fell into a Sawcer of Vinegar" (1:41), while Gulliver himself, upon being reunited with Glumdalclitch, gets as drenched by her tears "as if I had tumbled into the Sea" (1:45). The further adventures at which the "Verses Explanatory and Commendatory" hinted are here fleshed out and extended well beyond anything the Scriblerians could have anticipated—although, given Swift's meticulous accounting practices and general skepticism toward paper credit, he might well have enjoyed the description of how Gulliver "came off a Loser no more than ten thousand five hundred" pounds after investing in the Mississippi Bubble (2:158). Tellingly, though, the author of the *Travels . . . Vol. III* does not draw any distinction between the material derived from the "Verses Explanatory and Commendatory" and that taken from *Gulliver's Travels* per se. Both were but installments from the same fictional archive, no different in kind from one another.

Indeed, as this last example should suggest, there were no necessary bounds to the fictional archive for readers interested in exerting their talents. Consider only the ways in which a contributor to *Applebee's Original Weekly Journal* implicitly folds the entirety of the unauthorized *Vol. III* into his conception of the *Travels,* describing Gulliver's "whole Life" as but "a continued Series of the most surprising Adventures, which perhaps ever happen'd to any Man living; some Part whereof I have in the Three Volumes of my Life already entertain'd the Publick with." Not surprisingly, given all this, *Applebee's* "Gulliver" defines what he has to offer as but "the remaining Part being indeed more Curious than any I have yet usher'd into the World." Alas, even "the remaining Part" proves incomplete, for it promises all sorts of adventures which are never again mentioned, such as a voyage to "the Empire of *Angambri,* where the Inhabitants . . . are of such unhappy Disposition, that they are continually murthering and pulling one another to Pieces."[36] In order to get his "whole Life," still further installments from the archive would be warranted, which, in turn, would no doubt allude to yet other episodes from that life. The Gulliverian archive, it would seem, is inexhaustible—a prospect which appears to have troubled Swift enough to have included rumors of "his *Travels,* part the third; / A lie, at every second word" among the ways in which his reputation would be posthumously destroyed.[37]

I have been arguing that imaginative expansion came to seem more attractive than application to readers interested in exerting their own talents and opening their books to a world beyond the bounds of the originary text. The examples I have just detailed should suggest, however, an important ontological distinction between the two practices, which can help to account for why imaginative expansion should have lent itself to communal play rather than partisan polarization. As opposed to topical writing, the accuracy of which can (at least in theory) be verified—"a certain Duke" either did or did not have a child with the woman cloaked by the pseudonym "Gloatitia"—there is no apparent way to confirm or refute the "truth" of imaginative expansion. There is no actual story behind the bulk of Gulliver's plot. Or rather, there are as many stories as there are readers. The *Punishment Inflicted on Lemuel Gulliver* need not agree with the *Account of the State of Learning in the Empire of Lilliput*, nor with the Scriblerians' insinuations regarding Gulliver's post-Houyhnhnm domestic life; all it needs to do is not to contradict the *Travels* themselves too egregiously. As Gary Saul Morson notes, these expansions all operate within the realm of *possibilities*: "they appeal as sideshadows, as indications of what a character might have done."[38] And as possibilities, they need not cancel one another out. This holds true even for those expansions which purport to set the record straight—within which category we could put Swift's own "Letter from Capt. Gulliver to his Cousin Sympson," which complains about Gulliveriana "not agreed among themselves," even as it purports to correct the ways in which "your Printer hath been so careless as to confound the Times, and mistake the Dates of my several Voyages and Returns; neither assigning the true Year, or the true Month, or the Day of the Month" (255–56). Hence, for example, while both *Memoirs of the Court of Lilliput* and David Garrick's *Lilliput. A Dramatic Entertainment* seize upon Gulliver's prevarication regarding his relationship with Lady Flimnap as evidence of some sort of illicit liaison between the two of them, the very fact that they contradict one another suggests that the tale of Gulliver's stay in Lilliput cannot be gotten "right" in the way that most contemporaries presumed that, say, the last years of Queen Anne could be definitively narrated. Court and Country might not agree on how to tell the latter, but both would insist that it could be pinned down in a way that the off-page lives of Gulliver and Lady Flimnap could not be. Accordingly, it could be a source of pleasure, rather than partisan strife, when a reader like Garrick counters his "critics," who are supposedly "angry . . . that I make Fripperel talk of firing a broadside, when it may be seen in Gulliver's Travels, that the People of Lilliput had not the use of gunpowder. In answer to which, I shall quote a passage from a Lilliputian manuscript, which was brought over by Gulliver, and shown to me by the gentleman to whom he left all his Curiosities. The passage is this: *Udel mis Aleph penden tipadel quif menef duren.* This, I think, will satisfy . . . and stop the mouth of the most voracious critic of them all."[39] In political disputes, the flourishing of such a document might serve as a coup de grâce; here, it only extends the fictional archive that much further.

The sheer delight with which readers of the late 1720s invented apparently contradictory further adventures for Lemuel Gulliver suggests that they were neither thwarted nor even particularly bothered by the manifest inconsistencies of his character as initially published. Indeed, these expansions proleptically counter a wide range of modern scholarship that would deny Gulliver the minimal coherence necessary to be regarded as a freestanding narrative being. Claude Rawson, for example, has been insisting for decades that "we do not . . . think of [Gulliver] as a 'character' at all in more than a very attenuated sense: the emphasis is so preponderantly on what can be shown through him . . . than on his person in its own right, that we are never allowed to accustom ourselves to him as a real personality despite all the rudimentary local colour about his early career, family life and professional doings."[40] As a description of how Swift employed Gulliver, there is much to recommend Rawson's account. But given his perhaps unavoidable implication in a postnovelistic world, Rawson's sense of what constitutes a character is rather different from that of the readers with whom we are concerned. Readers like the author of "A Lilliputian Ode on the Engine with which Captain *Gulliver* extinguish'd the Flames in the Royal Palace" (which invents an array of microscenarios of Lilliputian awe, desire, and envy at "thy Great Tool") were apparently untroubled by Gulliver's inability to "grow, develop, change, or 'learn' from his experiences" and his utter lack of any "consistency of attitude or, despite his protests, integrity of character."[41] They did not require "any systematic Jamesian manipulation of consciousness" in order to regard the "changes and counterchanges" of "Gulliver's voice" as potentially those of a fictional being coherent enough to have a life which extended off-page.[42] Rather, they seem to have considered Gulliver, like many of the characters with whom we shall be concerned, as but a bundle of possibilities held together by what Roland Barthes has termed the "magnetic field" of the proper name.[43]

The perception that many readers of the late 1720s had of Gulliver as more the intersection of his various adventures than the embodiment of a deep interiority was aided and abetted by the sheer material variety which resulted from the *Travels'* commercial success: three advertised (and five actual) London editions in the first decade, plus two serializations, an abridgment, three Dublin editions, and George Faulkner's 1735 collected *Works of J.S., D.D., D.S.P.D.*[44] This array included both octavo and duodecimo editions; some of the former were also available in both large and small paper. Within these editions there was often considerable variation with respect to the frontispiece portrait of Gulliver: not all copies in a given edition seem to have included the frontispiece and those which did did not always include it in the same state. Similarly, while most copies printed after 1726 include the Scriblerian "Verses Explanatory and Commendatory," not all do. And, of course, the contents of individual copies could differ significantly from one another, depending on whether or not any other texts were bound into the same volume: Edmund Curll's keys and the *Travels into Several Remote Nations of the World . . . Vol. III* were both popular addendums. I rehearse these bibliographic details because their pattern of conflicting and heterogeneous variation around a shared core text neatly doubles (and, I suspect, further licensed) readers' propensity for conceiving of Gulliver as a bundle of potentially contradictory but not ultimately self-canceling possibilities. That is, readers who were attentive to their books as material objects—as most eighteenth-century readers seem to have been—were also likely to note the differences between the particular copy in hand, the edition of which it was part, and the broader textual phenomenon of *Gulliver's Travels.*[45] When coupled with the widespread perception that "Gulliver is in every body's Hands," this process of distinguishing between what Gérard Genette has termed the material contingent, the ideal contingent, and the ideal constitutive properties of a work (roughly speaking, the book, the edition, and the text) could produce a sense that the work exceeded any given manifestation, just as any given manifestation exceeded the work that was supposedly immanent in it.[46] By virtue of the sheer extent and variety of its distribution, that is, *Gulliver's Travels* could seem to be simultaneously everywhere (because "from the highest to the lowest it is universally read, from the Cabinet-council to the Nursery") and yet, at the same time, curiously nowhere—because no particular copy could really *be* the work, if any other copy could do more or less as well.[47] If, as Genette insists, "what defines the allographic state is not actual (selective) iteration, but iterability—in brief, the possibility of distinguishing between [contingent and constitutive] properties," then it stands to reason that the more a reader dwells upon the possibility of iterability (of different and differing copies in the hands of other readers), the more he or she will regard the work at hand as allographic and so oddly placeless, yet potentially omnipresent.[48] In conjunction with Gulliver's "considerable . . . Share in almost every Conversation both in Town and Country," this felt iterability seems to have convinced many readers that the "delightful . . . Entertainment" he afforded was a worthy object upon which to exert their talents.[49]

Gulliver's capacity to serve as an inexhaustible public resource upon which all might draw is neatly exemplified by a curious episode with which I would like to close my account of his afterlife. A survey of Westminster court records from the 1730s and 1740s shows that one Lemuel Gulliver was the plaintiff in a series of proceedings designed to circumvent older procedures for establishing title to pieces of real estate. As a legal fiction (like John

O'Nokes or John O'Styles), Gulliver could serve as a means of "examin[ing] titles to property" without having to go through the process of getting an actual lessee to agree to be nominally ejected from a lease, as would otherwise be required.[50] Luke Wilson has attributed the invention of figures like these to "the law's constant need to adjust and redistribute liabilities within a common-law system plagued by a procedural ossification that often necessitated the maintenance of subject positions despite an absence of persons to occupy them."[51] With Gulliver as plaintiff (and one Peter Swift as defendant) the lawyers could discover all that they needed to know through the "positing [of] an imaginary lessee, an imaginary ejector, and an imaginary deed of violence."[52] As the "magnetic field" holding together disparate and potentially contradictory adventures off-page, whether in Brobdingnag or Westminster or both at once, Gulliver was uniquely suited, it would seem, to become a legal fiction, what Wilson cleverly formulates as "a name without a man."[53] Gulliver's assorted exploits might not cohere into a single biography any more than those of O'Nokes or O'Styles (who could be charged with committing simultaneous crimes at opposite ends of the kingdom), yet they constituted a recognizably stable point of reference. If, as Lady Bolingbroke declared, one could "recommend the worst pieces to the public" merely by "putting Gulliver's name to them," it was because each "piece," regardless of its perceived quality, could be viewed as further testimony to the "open-ended maze of possibilities" that Gulliver had become for many readers of the late 1720s.[54]

* * *

John Gay adopted a somewhat different strategy than Swift when it came to thwarting independent-minded readers *à clef*, but, as with Swift, his traps seem to have done more to inadvertently encourage the invention of a fictional archive than to actually block application. These traps hinge upon the ways in which *The Beggar's Opera*, like Peachum himself, "acts in a double Capacity, both against Rogues and for 'em."[55] That is, the opera functions simultaneously as both a parody of and a surrogate for the objects of its satire, subjecting the rage for playful application, criminal biography, Italian opera, and heroic romance to a thoroughgoing ironic critique even as it offers up somewhat transmuted versions of those forms for its audience's pleasure. Such doubleness is characteristic of mock-form more generally, of course. But in most instances of mock-form one can readily distinguish an allusion from the figure or text to which it alludes. Pope's Belinda is in no danger of being conflated with the Virgin Mary, Adam, Aeneas, Achilles, Jehovah, Minos, Dido, Othello, or Berenice, even though her actions and speech recall various exploits of those figures. *The Beggar's Opera,* on the other hand, allows for no such interpretative stability, in large part because its "double Capacity" is a function of the overlapping and competing doubleness of Gay's dramatis personae themselves, rather than their place in a larger mock-heroic plot.

Consider, for example, the ways in which the figure of Macheath both alludes to Sir Robert Walpole and undercuts such allusions. Lucy proclaims, on the verge of Macheath's intended execution, that "there is nothing moves one so much as a great Man in Distress" (3.15.63). Given that Macheath has already been called "a great Man" by Peachum, in the context of being "take[n] off" (1.11.19), and that his entire career has been devoted to enriching himself at the public expense while carrying on simultaneous liaisons with multiple women, this scene appears to be soliciting audiences to recall the well-established Opposition jibe that Walpole, like Jonathan Wild, was a "great Man" who took "*Times and Opportunities*" to lay "hold of Things he never could have come at, if that Opportunity had been slipp'd."[56] The implication, it would seem, is that this scene—especially as it is framed by the Beggar's intended "poetical Justice" which "'twould have shown that the lower Sort of People have their Vices in a degree as well as the Rich: And that they are punish'd for them" (3.16.63–64)—shows what, in a just world, would happen to Sir Robert. Certainly that is the way in which it was taken by a writer for *The Country Journal,* who contends "that Captain *Macheath,* who hath also a *goodly Presence,* and hath a tolerable *Bronze* upon his Face, is . . . drawn to asperse *somebody in Authority*" and to "inculcate the . . . *Moral* . . . by an *Example* of a *Great Man,* and a *notorious Offender,* who escapes with *Impunity.*"[57] Yet no sooner is the equation between Macheath and Walpole made than it begins to fall apart. Macheath and his accomplices operate at the mercy of Peachum—"for the moment we break loose from him, our Gang is ruin'd" (2.2.25)—whereas one of the principal charges against Walpole was that he had put himself and his friends beyond the reach of any authority, legitimate or otherwise. Similarly, for all his alleged profligacy, Macheath is renowned for getting what he wants—escape from prison, the company of "free-hearted Ladies" (2.3.26)—without spending any money. Walpole, on the other hand, was infamous for his lavish expenditures and his insistence that every man had a price. And, of course, Macheath prides himself upon his "Honour and Truth to the Gang" (2.2.24) and appears to be genuinely "surpriz'd" "that *Jemmy Twitcher* should peach me" (3.14.62), while it was a commonplace of Opposition discourse that "*great Statesmen frequently betray their Friends.*"[58]

Collectively, these irreconcilable differences between Macheath and Walpole begin to suggest that the references to a "great Man" worthy of immediate execution may be a red herring and that the real target is not Walpole so much as it is those habits of application which prompt readers and viewers to prick up their ears every time the words comprising an Opposition cliché happen to be uttered. That is, it seems as if the satire might actually directed toward those members of the audience that instinctively convert generalized irony into libelous particular reflections. These include not only the "Courtiers" whom Lockit insists take offense "when you censure the age" and cry "that was levell'd at me" (2.10.36), but also people like the writer for *The Country Journal* who are equally quick to presume that "that was levell'd at" Walpole. Indeed, a later writer for *The Country Journal* suggests as much in his insinuation that taking offense at *The Beggar's Opera* simply reveals one's own paranoia: "If *Macheath* you should name, in the midst of his *Gang, fa la, /* They'll say 'tis an Hint you would *Somebody* hang; *fa la. /* For *Macheath* is a Word of such evil Report, *fa la, / Application* cries out, *That's a Bob for the C——t, fa la.*" Application, here, would seem to be overreaching, operating more "by Guess-work" and "chance" than shrewd readerly insight.[59]

Yet despite Gay's parody of application and the myriad ways in which the Macheath-Walpole equation falls apart—not to mention the similarly self-consuming parallels between Peachum and Walpole or "*Robin* of *Bagshot* . . . alias *Bluff Bob* . . . alias *Bob Booty*" and Walpole (1.3.6)—the political topicality of *The Beggar's Opera* cannot be wholly explained away, as Calhoun Winton hopes to do, as simply "a creation of the Opposition writers, well after the fact."[60] Even if no consistent identification can be sustained and any efforts to make such identifications can be dismissed as the feverish imaginings of either fools or knaves, the fact remains that after two-and-a-half hours of performance insisting that "the World is all alike, and that even our Gang can no more trust one another than other People" (3.14.62), the "great Man" on-stage will necessarily seem kin to the one off-stage. Macheath cannot "be drawn" merely "for the sake of representing a Highwayman," as one government paper insisted he was, if only because the relentless comparisons between highwaymen and courtiers throughout the play ensures that the two categories can no longer be kept wholly distinct from one another.[61] Each is always *like* the other, even if they can never be satisfactorily conflated.[62] It is thus quite fitting that one of the moments in which the opera most strenuously parodies its audience's penchant for application should have ended up providing them with a surrogate form of topicality. According to William Cook, Lockit's "When you censure the Age" "had such an effect on the audience, that, as if by instinct, the greater part of them threw their eyes on the stage-box, where the Minister was sitting, and loudly *encored* it. Sir Robert saw the stroke instantly, and saw it with good humour and discretion; for no sooner was the song finished, than he *encored* it a second time himself, joined in the general applause, and by this means brought the audience into so much good humour with him, that they gave him a general huzza from all parts of the house."[63] So in the very moment in which "the greater part" of the audience step into Gay's trap and reveal themselves to be the sort of viewers who seize indiscriminately upon anything "so pat to all the Tribe" (2.10.36), Walpole, in an effort to deny he was the sort of courtier targeted by the song, confirms the audience's suspicions that a "stroke" was intended. Yet in so doing, he "brought the audience into . . . good humour with him" and thereby not only blunted the "stroke," but converted it into "a general huzza." Thus topicality is denied only to be affirmed only to have that affirmation turn out not to matter. As an operation of Gay's "total irony," this must have been both delicious and devastating to those who got the joke.[64] But it didn't leave much room for politically minded readers and viewers to maneuver. As with *Gulliver's Travels,* the options Gay presents to would-be topical readers and viewers are rather bleak: one could confine one's applications to the ironized and self-consuming moments solicited by the text (and simply "pray," like Swift, that Walpole saw "an affront to him in [the] opera") or one could blithely press ahead, like *The Country Journal,* and open oneself up to the charge that one had "explained" an "innocent" author "into a *Libel.*"[65] Or, as had been happening with *Gulliver's Travels* for the past eighteen months or so, one could seize upon Gay's other ironic oppositions and convert them into a means of exerting one's talents through the invention of a fictional archive of adventures off-page.

I suggested earlier that the characters of *The Beggar's Opera* act "in a double Capacity" not only in the political realm but in every sphere that the opera touches, with the result that nothing feels exempt from Gay's "total irony." Hence, for example, Peachum and Macheath parody the public's obsession with celebrity criminals like Jonathan Wild and Jack Shepherd by showing how their alluring alterity is but a generic convention of criminal biography: the Peachums are as devoted to double-entry bookkeeping and social advancement as the most respectable of middling families, while Macheath's much-vaunted "Honour" and "Courage" in the face of danger (2.2.24) turn out to be artificially induced: "But Valour the stronger grows, /

The stronger Liquor we're drinking. / And how can we feel our Woes, / When we've lost the Trouble of Thinking / . . . So I drink off this Bumper.—And now I can stand the Test. / And my Comrades shall see, that I die as brave as the Best" (3.13.61). Yet at the same time, Peachum and Macheath offer their audience a peek into a world of stolen jewels and prostitutes exchanging trade secrets that must have seemed fascinatingly exotic indeed. As we saw with the opera's politics, parody and surrogacy are here working at apparent loggerheads without ever wholly canceling one another out. In much the same way, Macheath's actions belie his protestations of undying fidelity and so parody the even more high-flying pledges of "Play-books" and opera (1.10.19). Within three short scenes of his insisting that Polly should "suspect my Honour, my Courage, suspect any thing but my Love.—May my Pistols miss Fire, and my Mare slip her Shoulder while I am pursu'd, if I ever forsake thee!" (1.13.21), he is cavorting with the likes of Jenny Diver and Suky Tawdry. Clearly, Polly is mistaken if she thinks, on the basis of reading "the Romance" Macheath lent her, that since "none of the great Heroes were ever false in Love," her "Dear" will be similarly faithful (1.13.21). Yet the duet with which they pledge their troth is so sweet and memorable that their mutual assurances of fidelity come off as at least momentarily sincere: whether the lovers end up "laid on *Greenland*'s Coast" or "sold on *Indian* Soil," Macheath seems wholly earnest in his promise that "I would love you all the Day, / Every Night would kiss and play, / If with me you'd fondly stray / Over the Hills and far away" (1.13.21). Their love may not be the chaste monogamy of romance, but it seems as close to such love as one can achieve beneath the shadow of the gallows. By themselves, each of these instances of the opera's "double Capacity" yields an exquisite but ultimately self-consuming paradox. Collectively, however, they "merge bizarrely together, continually awakening ironical memories of other kinds of literary experience yet nevertheless forming a whole which is in some ways curiously life-like."[66] It was at the interstices of these juxtapositions of ironic juxtapositions all supposedly subject to "the Taste of the Town" (3.16.64) that independent-minded readers and viewers seem to have discovered that they could flourish.

As in the case of Lemuel Gulliver, many readers and viewers interested in exerting their talents simply sidestepped the traps Gay laid for them, choosing instead to revel in the "open-ended maze of possibilities" which those traps had inadvertently created. The author of *Memoirs Concerning the Life and Manners of Captain Mackheath*, for example, momentarily seems to embrace *The Country Journal*'s position in his account of how Macheath has recently turned to stealing quart and pint pots from public houses and ransoming them back to their owners at a penny a pot (a fairly transparent allegory for Walpole's efforts to shift the basis of the government's income from property to excise taxes). Yet these parallels quickly run out of steam, as the author pauses to pursue some of the opera's other targets, such as the generic conventions of criminal biography. Hence we learn that, as a youth, Macheath was more sinned against than sinning: having lost his patrimony in the South Sea Bubble, he grew outraged at social inequity and set out, Robin Hood–like, to "remit himself to the original State where all Men had a Right to all Things" (16). No doubt the very inclusion of this plan scores points against Walpole, who had no such youthful idealism and who prospered greatly from the Bubble. Far more obviously, though, this invented boyhood undercuts any sustainable political allegory, highlighting instead a conception of Macheath as a highwayman who, like many of his compatriots, was "forced on to the road and into a life of crime through personal misfortune or because the times are out of joint."[67] The result is what purports to be an account of "a living Highway-man" who "has robb'd many whom I know, and goes on still publickly to plunder" (19, 6). Indeed, as these hitherto undocumented robberies of the author's acquaintances should suggest, the *Memoirs* ground their authority in the very archive they are inventing: the proof of their author's having "set out with no personal Prejudice against Captain *Mackheath*" is that "he has never taken a Shilling from me or mine upon the Road" (5–6). Similarly, "if [Macheath] has had any criminal Amours, I never heard him charg'd with Perfidy to a Woman; and *Betty Flareit,* with whom the Captain has sometimes deign'd to amuse himself . . . has often declar'd he was a very innocent Lover. Neither would the Captain's Constitution . . . bear any sort of Debauch in Brandy. . . . Here again the Dramatist has wrong'd him, to make way for a drunken Sonnet or two at his going off" (19–20). Passages like these, which playfully reject the "Poetical License" of the originary text (19) even as they ostentatiously indulge their own, nicely encapsulate the ways in which the *Memoirs* transform the self-consuming ironies of *The Beggar's Opera* into a celebration of the possibilities afforded by those ironies. The Macheath of the *Memoirs* is every bit as contradictory as Gay's hero (it is hard to imagine Betty Flareit's "innocent Lover" ransoming pint pots), but those contradictions are embraced as the sign of his "uncommon Vigour of Mind and Body" (20). That is, despite the author's jestingly coy refusal to "let [his readers] into the more minute Particulars of [Macheath's] Life and Conversation," the entire pamphlet does little but detail "as many Circumstances concerning the Life and Manners of Captain *Mackheath* as have occurr'd to me," with the result that their overall impact is far more a matter of "mark[ing] the Character of this Man's Mind" (60) than anything else. For the author of the *Memoirs,* it would seem, Macheath's "curiously life-like" qualities can be best realized through the invention of additional "Circumstances" to flesh out "the Poet's imperfect Draught of him" (19). Total irony here gives way to the fictional archive.

Much the same dynamic may be seen in miniature in the *Letters in Prose and Verse to the Celebrated Polly Peachum,* which "were dropt as the famous Polly Peachum took Coach to meet his ———" (4). Consider only the epistle from Sulivan Slaver, a law student who purports to be so smitten by Polly that he commits "a Thousand tender Extravagances" after she has visited his room, including kissing "the Chair on which you sat" and drinking what he takes to be the "Coffee left in your Dish" (7), but turns out to be ink. He also encloses "the key of my Chambers" in the hope that she will return for another, less interrupted interlude (8). Slaver apparently expects to seduce his "Most Unaccountable Charmer" merely by rehearsing the "Disasters" he has undergone for her sake, not least of which was "almost resolv[ing] to Sacrifice *Cook upon Littleton*" (8, 7). This may betray an ignorance of what kinds of rhetoric are most likely to succeed with Polly, but it also suggests that Slaver understands quite well that Polly's claims to shrewdness are not all that they seem. She may insist that "I know as well as any of the fine Ladies how to make the most of my self and of my Man too. . . . A Girl who cannot grant some Things and refuse what is most material, will make but a poor Hand of her Beauty, and soon be thrown upon the Common" (1.7.11–12). And yet the ease with which Macheath manipulates her affections belies her allegedly "mercenary" nature and recasts her instead as a gullible child "ruin[ed]" by "those cursed Play-books she reads" (1.10.19). In the opera, Polly's knowing innocence is a self-conscious oxymoron aimed at both parodying the impossible chastity of operatic and romance heroines and providing a surrogate form of such chastity—witness only the moving and lyrical way in which she sings about the inevitable demise of both virgins and flowers "when once pluck'd" (1.7.12). In Slaver's letter, though, Polly's knowingness, far from holding her innocence in a self-consuming dynamic tension, may simply be whetting his appetite. If Polly was drawn in by Macheath's teasing and pleasing, despite all her claims to sophistication, then surely she might be similarly captivated by Slaver's account of his plight as "an unfortunate Lover" (7). As with the *Memoirs,* the letter from Slaver sidesteps Gay's elaborate paradoxes by treating their contradictory possibilities as pointing toward a life off-page.

The social canonicity of Macheath and Polly was hardly inevitable, though. A similarly complex and self-consuming heterogeneity could be pointed out in the principal characters of any of Gay's plays, yet Squire Thomas of *The What D'Ye Call It* is hardly a popular hero. As with Lemuel Gulliver, the felt iterability of Macheath and Polly was doubled and implicitly licensed by the ways in which their widespread dissemination could create the sense that they were somehow simultaneously everywhere and nowhere, that both they and their opera existed curiously "outside of the modes by which it was perceived."[68] Like *Gulliver's Travels, The Beggar's Opera* was available in a range of different and differing printed versions: the first decade saw at least eight advertised Dublin and London editions in formats varying from quarto to large- and small-paper octavo to duodecimo. One could read the opera either with or without an accompanying score, with varying cast lists (including "The Names of the Lilliputians," about whom more below), and, at least in one edition, with an additional "Song on *Polly Peachum.* To the Tune of, *Sally in our Alley.*" For readers attentive to their books as artifacts, such material proliferation could only enhance their sense that "you must sing it everywhere *but at church,* if you have a mind to be *like the polite world.*"[69]

The opera also appeared in a host of varying and variant stage productions, beginning in the very first season. Five months after the play's astonishing debut (an unprecedented sixty-two performances), for example, the Little Haymarket offered *The Beggar's Opera* "as it is perform'd at the Theatre in Lincolns'-Inn-Fields."[70] As with anything claiming to be an exact replica, the Little Haymarket's production necessarily differed from that of Lincoln's Inn Fields, if only by virtue of its cast, its setting, and its ambition to replicate how "it is perform'd" elsewhere, which introduced a self-conscious fidelity not present in the original production. Even before the Little Haymarket production, though, non-London audiences could see performances in Bath, Bristol, Dover, Dublin, Glasgow, Norwich, Wales, and even Minorca—all of which were widely reported both in the newspapers and by the Scriblerians themselves and so further enabled the sense that "All *Ranks, Parties* and *Denominations* of Men [were] either crowding to see [the] *Opera,* or reading it with delight in their Closets."[71] In 1732, the London patent houses complicated matters still further by abandoning their "*de facto* agreement to let each company retain exclusive rights to successful new plays" in order to stage the first in a series of competing simultaneous productions at Drury Lane and Covent Garden.[72] Similar contests would recur in both London and Dublin throughout the century. Moreover, one could sometimes even take one's pick of performers at a given theater: in the first two seasons, for example, both the London and Dublin theaters offered productions starring "Lilliputians" (read "children") as a respite from the usual adult casts, while the 1736–37 season saw a very public feud between Kitty Clive and Susanna Cibber over who had the moral right to play Polly, with one commentator suggesting that "*the Rivals should alternately perform the character contested for*."[73] Indeed, as the century progressed, *The Beggar's Opera* became a perennial favorite for novelty and drag performances and virtuosic doubling: Peg Woffington made her London debut playing Macheath, Mrs. Peachum, and Diana Trapes, while George Colman produced a "topsy-turvy" version: "the Ladies characters being all acted by men, and the men represented by Ladies."[74]

The cumulative effect of such a proliferation of variant versions was, as we shall see in greater detail in the next two chapters, that Macheath and Polly took on a life of their own exclusive of any particular material manifestation. No sooner would, say, Polly get intertwined with a given performer—most notably Lavinia Fenton, who played her in the first season—than that entanglement would be undercut by a similar intertwining with another performer, with the result that no single actress could be said to wholly claim her or provide the definitive performance. Thus while Fenton was "called Polly Peachum in the newspapers," so too were Maria Warren, Fenton's successor in London, and the actress who played Polly in Dublin.[75] Indeed, *Mist's Weekly Journal* was able to turn these competing entanglements and the off-stage lives of the actresses into evidence for Polly's off-page life in the fictional archive, joking that "perhaps their *Polly Peachum* may go to the Congress as well as ours."[76] In the face of so many competing editions and performances, each of which helped viewers to further distinguish between the contingent and constitutive properties of the opera, it is not surprising that Polly and Macheath should have come to feel curiously free-floating and immaterial, possessed of that same placeless omnipresence which overtook Lemuel Gulliver.

Both intrigued and distressed by the ways in which his heroine had come into "so high vogue, that I am in doubt, whether her fame does not surpass that of the Opera itself," Gay attempted to reassert control over his characters by writing a sequel, *Polly*, in which Polly pursues the transported Macheath to the West Indies only to learn that he has "robb'd his master, ran away from the plantation . . . turn'd pyrate" and married Jenny Diver.[77] Once there, she rejects the advances of a lascivious colonist and flees into the bush, where she helps a virtuous native prince escape from the now wholly corrupt Macheath and his gang. For her pains, she is rewarded with Cawwawkee's hand in marriage, while the defeated but unrepentant Macheath is executed (Polly successfully pleads for his life, but the reprieve comes too late). As even this brief sketch should suggest, Gay is here pursuing one of the off-page possibilities at which *The Beggar's Opera* had hinted: namely, Macheath's advice to Lucy and Polly that "if you are fond of marrying again . . . Ship yourselves off for the *West-Indies,* where you'll have a fair chance of getting a Husband a-piece; or by good Luck, two or three, as you like best" (3.15.62–63). In the context of the opera, this seems primarily a jab at the ways in which sentencing convicts to transportation simply reproduced and amplified the vices of the metropolis in the colonies: if one man's bigamy could cause so much trouble in London, Lucy and Polly's getting themselves "two or three" husbands apiece in the Caribbean was unlikely to set matters right, especially considering that most of their likely prospects would be transported felons like Macheath. By treating Macheath's advice as if it were a glimpse into the fictional archive, however, Gay could emulate the reading practices to which his work had been subjected and thereby attempt to take advantage of the "prepossession" which "the customs and taste of the town" had for his characters as a result of their felt iterability, what Gay termed their capacity to be brought "once again upon the Stage."[78] The gambit proved enormously profitable: after the Lord Chamberlain suppressed the planned stage production, perhaps at Walpole's behest, William Bowyer "printed two large editions, 10,500 copies in all" and at least four other printers produced pirated editions, totaling upwards of an additional 3,500 copies, almost all of which were sold within the year.[79] In terms of the market, clearly *Polly* was "deny'd Admission, on the Stage in vain, / Macheath shall still invite the Town again."[80] Yet Gay's apparent hope of regaining control over his characters was not to be. Even the Cervantine gesture of executing Macheath, so that no one else could "think of raising [him] up, against all Death's laws," could not constrain readers from continuing his career off-page, as the very title of *Macheath in the Shades* should attest.[81]

In many ways, the late 1720s shift in the comparative desirability of reading practices that we have been tracing is neatly encapsulated by *The Flying Post*'s description of how "the Town is now entertain'd with the Reading" of *Polly*: "as 'tis not allow'd to be acted, we shall have it in Miniature in a thousand little Circles, over a Bottle, as soon as our merry Fellows have gotten some of the Songs by heart, which they are now very studiously humming over."[82] By virtue of their "prepossession" toward Polly (which stemmed from their varying and competing senses of her possibilities), these "thousand little Circles" will necessarily produce upwards of a thousand different conceptions of Miss Peachum. Yet the widespread dissemination of the printed play (not to mention the clamorous public reports of that dissemination in papers like *The Flying Post*) made it hard for a given circle to ignore the fact that other circles were devising their own Pollys, each of whom would represent a different path through the same maze of possibilities and so further enhance their sense of her as both inexhaustible and common to all. At the same time, if these "merry Fellows" could share a love of Polly, then it was not too difficult to presume that they might well share a more general commonality with one another. That is, while they would probably never meet and if they did meet they would no doubt find themselves differing over many things, the mere fact that they could "very studiously hum" over the same beloved character made it possible to imagine, as it had not been for many decades, that their other differences could be suspended "over a bottle" as they collectively devised what one reader of *Gulliver's Travels* termed *A little more of that Same.*

Chapter 2
Visualization, Theatricality, Fame

My next two chapters trace the principal forms taken by imaginative expansion in the generous half-century following the invention of the fictional archive. In this chapter, we will investigate what I would like to term "visualization," a practice in which readers devised quite elaborate gestures and expressions for literary characters in order to make them appear so vivid to the mind's eye that the readers could imagine themselves as witnesses to the action—a condition Lord Kames would term "ideal presence." Most of these gestures and expressions were drawn from a stock repertoire of modes for representing the passions and so allowed other readers to compare them to their own imaginings of the scene in question. Collectively, these visualizations, along with the awareness that other readers were engaged in the same practice, helped make these characters seem ever more valuable and socially canonical. Often, though not always, readers self-consciously modeled their inventions after what they saw in the theater, where analogous practices could be witnessed on an almost daily basis. Even when the theater was not specifically invoked, however, it still remained something of an absent presence marking how a public could be united across time by its shared attention to the different ways in which a beloved character might be brought to life. The work of this chapter, then, is not only to reconstruct a fascinating reading practice whose significance has gone largely unrecognized; it is also to reconsider the place of the theater in the constitution of the public more generally.

The bulk of the following discussion will be concerned with the afterlife of Inkle and Yarico, two figures whose "story was among the most popular and widely retold" of the entire eighteenth century.[1] While the ways in which Inkle and Yarico were visualized are not identical to every other instance of the practice I have been able to trace, they can nonetheless usefully stand in for the practice as a whole by virtue of how they collectively endow the couple with both commonness and fame through the devising of appropriate gestures for key moments in the story. We will investigate some further examples of—and authorial twists upon—the practice in Chapters 4 and 5.

To demonstrate some of the complexities and paradoxes of visualization, consider only the ways in which "Philypsus" intensely imagines the death of Agamemnon in Joseph Spence's *An Essay on Pope's Odyssey.* According to Spence, this pseudonym disguises a gentleman of his acquaintance whose "enlarged Genius . . . always led him to dwell upon the most beautified Parts of a Poem with the greatest Pleasure."[2] Yet in response to the scene in which Agamemnon's ghost describes his death at the hands of Clytemnestra, Philypsus insists that "we see the Hero weltring on the Floor, all cover'd with Blood, and in the last agonies of Death . . . expiring as he was, he endeavours to raise up his Arm, and at last gets his Hand upon the hilt of his Sword; which he had strength only to grasp, with a look full of Rage, Compassion, and Revenge. Methinks . . . I see him now expired, and dropt upon the Floor: but tho' expired, there is still that Rage and Passion in his Countenance; he still grasps his Sword, and seems to threaten the Traytors and the Adultress with his looks" (45–46). None of these details are to be found in the text which Philypsus has supposedly just read aloud to his friend: Pope's Agamemnon merely describes how "we groan, we faint; with Blood the dome is dy'd, / And o'er the pavement floats the dreadful tide— / . . . Then, tho' pale death froze cold in ev'ry vein, / My Sword I strive to wield, ——but strive in vain" (45). One could certainly infer that in such a situation Agamemnon would welter about and give "a look full of Rage, Compassion, and Revenge," but neither Pope's English nor Homer's Greek specifies anything of the sort. Agamemnon's threatening eyes and struggling limbs are not merely Philypsus's idiosyncratic creations, though. Rather they are clearly derived from a stock repertoire of ways of representing the passions through "their outward visible . . . signs."[3]

This repertoire had been widely available for many decades, both through the highly conventionalized poses of history painting and the equally conventionalized gestures of oratory and the stage, with the result that "audience[s] and . . . viewers knew exactly how anguish and rapture looked because they had seen so many clear episodes of them—on walls and stages, as well as on the faces of those with whom they lived and dealt."[4] Indeed, one did not even need to have seen any paintings or plays in order to recognize these passions, for their signs were repeatedly codified through the broadly circulating handbooks of visual artists like Charles Le Brun and Gérard de Lairesse and theatrical theorists like Samuel Foote, Aaron Hill, and Thomas Wilkes. One could also consult printed commonplace collections like the *Thesaurus Dramaticus,* which conveniently collected various exemplary instances of the passions from "the Body of English Plays, Antient and Modern . . . under Proper Topics" like "Despair" or "Enjoyment." In texts like these, one could learn how Anger "gives a savage wildness to the eye" and can "sometimes excite a trembling in the whole frame," especially "when it swells into an extreme rage." Revenge, on the other hand, is expressed "with the most violent paroxisms of rage and regret, when disappointed." And, of course, the dying were known for their "cold / And shaking Hand[s]."[5]

Given Philypsus's repeated emphasis on sight ("we see the Hero," "I see him now expired"), surely his placement of Agamemnon into a "weltring" and agonized posture with a threatening countenance is more than coincidental. Indeed, his invocation of the glaring eyes and bodily paroxysms that conventionally signify "these last Efforts of dying Heroes" (46) suggests that he is trying to make Pope's translation still more vivid in his mind's eye by replacing Agamemnon's verbal pauses (marked in Pope's text by dashes) with what Wilkes termed "that undisguised natural eloquence [of proper and just action] which only is universally intelligible."[6] In so doing, he can lend the scene what Lord Kames would call "ideal presence": an imagined vivacity sufficient to allow the reader to "conceive . . . every incident as passing in his presence, precisely as if he were an eyewitness."[7] Only by visualizing the scene so intensely as to block out any awareness of the myriad intermediaries between him and Agamemnon—the translation, the heroic couplets, the printed page, the intervening millennia—can Philypsus pronounce that "nothing in Nature can be conceived of greater Strength and Emotion" than this episode (45). That is, only by embellishing "the Variety of Beauties" (45) already extant in this scene can Philypsus derive "the greatest Pleasure" from "the most beautified Parts of [this] Poem." The proof of Book 11 of *The Odyssey*'s supreme pathos—"can any thing be more Pathetick than this whole Book? especially the latter part, when *the Heroes* come to make their Appearance" (44–45)—thus lies not in any of Homer's or Pope's lines per se but rather in their conjunction with Philypsus's own visualizations, which allows him to raise "complete images" and so transport himself "as by magic into the very place and time of the important action, and be converted, as it were, into a real spectator, beholding every thing that passes."[8]

* * *

The traces of a far more extensive array of readerly visualizations may be discerned in the afterlife of Inkle and Yarico, who seem to have come to most readers' attention through their inclusion in the eleventh number of *The Spectator.* One day, while visiting Arietta, Mr. Spectator listens to the endless inanity of "a Common-Place Talker" pestering her with misogynist clichés regarding the inconstancy of women.[9] As his coup de grâce, the talker "repeated and murdered the celebrated Story of the *Ephesian* Matron" (1:48). In response to this provocation, "an Outrage done to her Sex," Arietta condemns the ways in which men have monopolized the means of literary production and so ensured that women would be "unable to return the Injury" (1:48–49). Arietta then offers a counter-narrative, one neither "two thousand Years Old" nor by a writer with any "Ambition or Capacity to embellish [his] Narrations with any Beauties of Imagination": namely, "the History of *Inkle* and *Yarico,*" as given in Richard Ligon's *A True and Exact History of the Island of Barbados* (1:48–49). A young Englishman, Thomas Inkle, having been bred up as a merchant with "an early Love of Gain" (1:50), is shipwrecked on a Caribbean island and rescued from its savage inhabitants by a native woman, Yarico, who becomes his lover. Soon afterward, the couple are taken off the island by an English ship. To recoup the financial losses occasioned by this interlude, Inkle sells Yarico into slavery as soon as they reach Barbados, despite the fact that she is pregnant with his child. Indeed, he "only made use of that Information, to rise in his Demands upon the Purchaser" (1:51). As told by Richard Steele, it is a fairly spare narrative, comprising only a third of the number's total text. And in the context of *The Spectator,* this tale was but one of many—touching to be sure (Mr. Spectator leaves "the Room with Tears in [his] Eyes" [1:51]), but not presented as particularly central or significant. Its impact upon the culture at large, however, extended far beyond what Steele could have had any right to expect.

Frank Felsenstein has cataloged at least twenty-five distinct Anglophone reworkings of the tale in the century after its appearance in *The Spectator,* several of which were widely reprinted and sometimes recombined with one another. I have traced several others and strongly doubt that the archive has been exhausted. Collectively, these augmentations and retellings—along with the incessant reprinting of *The Spectator* itself—transformed Steele's star-crossed lovers into a "great folk epic."[10] By century's end, they were sufficiently part of the vernacular that Mary Wollstonecraft could casually refer to the way in which to "make an Inkle" out of a child and expect her readers to catch the allusion, just as Thomas Bellamy could blithely assert that the "tale" of "the faithful Yarico" is "known to all."[11] Inkle had become a byword for male treachery in search of profit, just as Dick Whittington had long been one for the good fortune which could come to the industrious apprentice. Indeed, two decades before Wollstonecraft, John Gabriel Stedman had held up Inkle as a vivid example of what he was *not* doing in his courtship of a young mulatto woman, and clearly anticipated that his readers would be able to deduce his own good intentions from the negation.[12]

Like Dick Whittington or Jeanne d'Arc, Inkle and Yarico had come to occupy the curious quasi-historical status of folk heroes. And as folk heroes, "anyone was at liberty to add new items of fact, subject to the approval of the reader."[13] But even a figure like Yarico, who so echoed a long tradition of abandoned women (Dido, Ariadne, Pocahontas), could not become a folk heroine immediately, although her similarities to those figures probably helped to "crystallise" aspects of their stories around her.[14] Her story had to be "told again and again until it passed into the collectivity of our culture" and became "common property, at the disposal of anyone."[15] Not surprisingly, the form of choice for most of these tellings and retellings was the heroic epistle, which had been used to ventriloquize abandoned women ever since Ovid's *Heroides.* Unlike the *Heroides* and most of their eighteenth-century imitators, however, Yarico's epistles are as concerned with their heroine's postures as with her voice and so, like Spence, are intensely engaged in visualizing the outward signs of her passions in order to render her ideally present.

Consider only Frances Seymour, Countess of Hertford's "An Epistle from Yarico to Inkle, after He had Sold Her for a Slave." In Hertford's version, Yarico recalls that at their initial meeting she was so "charm'd with thy face, like polish'd iv'ry fair, / Thy beauteous features and enticing hair, / How did I tremble, lest thy bloom of life / Shou'd fall a prey to some barbarian's knife!"[16] Similarly, "when I beheld thee leave the fatal coast, / And every hope to move thy soul was lost, / How did I my neglected bosom tear, / With all the fury of a wild despair! / Then on the sands a stupid corpse I lay, / Till (by my Master's order) dragg'd away" (97). None of these corporeal responses are specified in Steele, who confines himself to mentioning that Yarico "grew immediately enamoured of [Inkle], and consequently sollicitous for his Preservation" (1:50), and does not give her reaction to his departure at all. But they are precisely what a reader schooled in the legible passions would expect from these situations. According to Wilkes, "the apprehension of an approaching evil, or of being deprived of our happiness in any shape, creates fear," whose "symptoms" include "a tremor."[17] "A wild despair," on the other hand, is marked by breast-beating and throwing one's "abandon'd Body on the Ground."[18] In both instances, it would seem, Hertford is augmenting Steele's tale in order better to "unfold [Yarico's] grief" by making it seem ideally present, despite the time which has elapsed since she fell victim to Inkle's "destructive scorn" (96).[19]

Similarly, in "The Story of Inkle and Yarico from the Eleventh *Spectator*" (written by a 1734 contributor to *The London Magazine*), the lovers' initial meeting quickly modulates into a situation in which, with "speaking eyes" and a plea for pity, Inkle "seiz'd her hand, with tender passion prest, / While copious tears both love and fear confest. / The pitying maid view'd him with yielding eyes, / And from each bosom mutual sighs arise" (103–4). As with Hertford, none of these corporeal details are in Steele, despite the poem's titular invocation of *The Spectator*'s authority. They are, however, wholly commonplace ways of expressing the passions that such a situation would conjure up. Those who felt compassion, for example, "mix[ed] their pitying Tears with those that weep," while those who were falling in love spoke little and "in speaking, sigh[ed]."[20] Indeed, one needs only glance at the postures struck by Hannah Pritchard and David Garrick in a circa 1750 production of William Whitehead's *The Roman Father* (Figure 2) to see that, although the genders are reversed, they are drawing upon the same stock set of gestures: like Inkle, Pritchard, "low at [his] feet, in suppliant posture laid" tenderly presses Garrick's hand and sighs, while Garrick, like Yarico, in turn "look'd a kind reply" (103). Despite the plumed helmet and buskins, their "mutual sighs" come through loud and clear. This is not to say that Pritchard and Garrick were self-consciously modeling themselves after *The London Magazine*'s version of "The Story of Inkle and Yarico" (we have no evidence that either of them even knew the poem). It is, however, to underscore the widespread availability of this repertoire of ways in which to convey the signs of, say, Grief and Astonishment, both of which seem to figure in this poem's version of Yarico's final parting from Inkle: "Amaz'd and trembling, silently she mourn'd, / While speaking tears her radiant eyes adorn'd. / Low at his feet, the lovely mourner lay; / Nor would to words her swelling heart give way. / She grasps his knees, in vain attempts to speak, / At length her words in moving accents break" (106).[21]

Similar moments could be pointed out in almost all of the extant contributions to the afterlife of Inkle and Yarico.[22] For the purposes of demonstrating these readers' reliance upon the stock repertoire of the passions, however, one further set of examples will probably suffice. In *Yarico to Inkle. An Epistle*, Yarico reminds her faithless lover how, "pale with . . . fears" at their initial meeting, he "on the bare ground . . . lay o'erwhelm'd in tears; / Your speaking looks, and stifled groans confest / A wretch, with more than common ills opprest. . . . There I beheld you, trembling as you lay, / And, e'er

I knew it, look'd my soul away. / You saw me, and the sight encreas'd your fear, / You rose, and wou'd have fled—but knew not where! / Returning, at my feet your self you threw, / And did by earnest signs, for pity sue" (114). As might by now be expected, none of these postures are in Steele's account; he alludes only to "the first Surprize" which preceded the pair's "appear[ing] mutually agreeable to one another" (1:50). Yet Inkle's pallor, "stifled groans," "speaking looks," and confused desire to flee are wholly in keeping with the conventional modes of designating Fear: in addition to the "trembling" that we have already seen in the case of Hertford, Wilkes notes that Fear is accompanied by a "pale countenance" and an "abject, meek, and contracted" voice, while Aaron Hill insists that "an actor . . . will most effectually represent" Fear by "a starting apprehensive, and listning alarm to his look; keeping . . . his steps light and shifting, —yet his joints unbrac'd, faint, nerveless."[23]

Later in the same epistle, Yarico recalls "that morn, when on the beach I stood, / And saw the bark at anchor in the flood; / Strait to your cave with

Figure 2. Hannah Pritchard, David Garrick, et al. in *The Roman Father*, circa 1750. By permission of the Folger Shakespeare Library.

eager haste I ran" to tell Inkle the news of their rescue: "Pleasure in your eyes / Flash'd like a shooting blaze in evening skies; / Your eager arms around my neck you flung, / And on my lips in silent transport hung; / The mighty joy, too great to be exprest, / Glow'd on your cheeks, and struggled in your breast" (117–18). Steele, of course, does not describe Inkle's reaction to the arrival of the ship at all. But Wilkes suggests that "when our affairs take an unforeseen happy turn," "the vivacity of the spirits gives a brilliancy to the eye, the forehead is calm and serene, the lips moist and smiling, and the whole countenance . . . becomes ruddy and affable."[24] Le Brun confirms these symptoms: the pupils of the joyful are "lively and shining," while their "Cheeks and Lips [are] of a vermilion colour."[25] And as soon as "the mighty joy, too great to be exprest" bursts forth, Inkle's "words flow" with what Wilkes termed "the most pleasurable facility": "'Adieu,' you cried, 'ye friendly shades adieu,' / (As in embraces to the shore we flew) / 'And thou, my cave! thou ever kind retreat, / Scene of our pleasures, and my safety's seat, / Farewel! Ye cruel savages adieu! / Adieu to all, my *Yarico,* but you!'" (117–18).[26] Indeed, Inkle's exuberant repetitions, not to mention his inclusion of the "cruel savages" in his farewells, nicely underscores Hill's contention that "if [a man] attempts to speak *joy,* all the spirit of the passion will ascend in his accents, and the very tone of his voice will seem to out-rapture the meaning."[27]

My rehearsing of how these readers drew upon the stock repertoire of legible passions in their reworkings of the tale begs several important questions, though. First of all, why should the heroic epistle have been the genre of choice for most of these readers?[28] It was, as we have already noted, the traditional form used to ventriloquize abandoned women as they recalled past pleasures, reproached their faithless lovers, and engaged in "unintended autoincrimination," but it was hardly known for its sustained attention to its heroines' gestures (indeed, most putative epistle writers seem to have had bodies only insofar as we can infer them as a source for their tears).[29] The rare exceptions to this tendency seem only to prove the rule. For example, the body of Ovid's Dido appears only in the subjunctive and even then her materiality is called into question: "shou'd some avenging storm thy Vessel tear . . . Then, in thy face thy perjur'd Vows would fly; / And my wrong'd Ghost be present to thy eye. / With threat'ning looks, think thou beholdst me stare, / Gasping my mouth, and clotted all my hair."[30] If Aeneas relents, no such corporeal display will become necessary and so Dido's body need never enter the frame of representation. Similarly, while Pope's Eloisa pulls away from her imagining of Abelard's castration with "I can no more; by shame, by rage supprest, / Let tears, and burning blushes speak the rest," her epistle quite pointedly never fleshes these gestures out, despite her avowed interest in getting Abelard to "see in her Cell sad *Eloisa* spread, / Propt on some tomb, a neighbour of the dead!"[31] Why then should readers have been drawn to the heroic epistle as a form through which they might visualize key scenes from the story of Inkle and Yarico?

I suspect that much of the answer lies with the ways in which, as Gillian Beer puts it, the heroic epistle "transforms the statuesque into the flux of emotion and language. . . . We are elected to intimacy with the great."[32] This intimacy in turn stems from the fact that "the characters are mythical or historical. We can be assumed already to know roughly what happened to them before we begin to read" and so can fully savor the access we are given to the anguish and inner life of a figure like Dido or Heloise.[33] In effect, heroic epistles offer readers the secret history which underpins (and often slyly discredits) the grand public narratives—say, *The Aeneid*—in which these characters have made their best-known previous appearances. Heroic epistles, that is, make the often forbidding figures of official myth seem both fallible and human. Yet in the 1720s and 1730s, when the first of the epistles we have been examining were being written, Inkle and Yarico were only "statuesque" insofar as anything in *The Spectator* was. Accordingly, I propose, what we are dealing with is a series of heroic epistles (and their generic fellow travelers) which were written not so much to elect us "to intimacy with the great" as to thrust greatness upon Inkle and Yarico in the hope that it would enable them to "claim . . . a heroic equality" with the heroes of classical myth.[34]

This at least would explain readers' otherwise deeply puzzling and repeated emphasis upon what the author of *Yarico to Inkle: An Epistle* describes as the inability of the "story to live" without augmentation (112). For this reader, the tale possesses an inherent interest and "will as long as either [Ligon or *The Spectator*] lasts, be mention'd in competition with the blackest, most incredible pieces of ingratitude, that history, or romance can furnish" (112). Yet the mere prospect of a futurity into which these writers will not last underscores, at least for this reader, the urgency of "suppos[ing]" Yarico's epistles (112): in order for her prophecy that "the rememb'rance of my wrongs shall live, / Your treachery whole ages shall survive, / People, unborn, shall my sad tale relate / And curse your cruelty, and weep my fate" (117) to be realized, Inkle will need to become more than just a character in a piece of travel writing or a popular periodical. "The living story of my woe" will need to follow him "and exclaim where'er you go; / . . . 'Behold the wretch, whose breast to nature steel'd, / For kindness hated, for compassion kill'd!'" (122). That is, in order for Inkle's "shame" to "live thro' each abhorring age" and "thus gibbetted enjoy a blasted fame, / While virtuous tongues pour curses on thy name," it will require that his story not only be read in *The Spectator* but "taken from" it and amplified along the lines we have been discussing.[35] And for these readers, it would seem, the most obvious way in which to elevate Inkle and Yarico to the status of bywords for treachery and betrayed innocence was through the writing of heroic epistles, whose effect largely hinges upon the potential pleasures and ironies opened up by a situation in which "the writers experience . . . their stories . . . as open and contingent, whereas the external reader . . . sees them as working out a sequence of events already determined, and . . . to which . . . [they have] been directed all along."[36]

These assertions of the need to ensure that the story of Inkle and Yarico will "live" run counter to what we might expect, considering the sheer omnipresence of *The Spectator* in literate British households. After all, according to Vicesimus Knox, "there is scarcely an individual, not only of those who profess learning, but of those who devote any of their time to reading, who has not digested the Spectators." Indeed, "the Spectators are . . . every where read through the British empire, and much of the learning and the good qualities, which have appeared among us since their publication, has been derived from them."[37] Similarly, Hugh Blair famously claimed that "the Spectator . . . is a book which is in the hands of every one."[38] Surely if any eighteenth-century text could be thought to be able to take care of itself, it would be *The Spectator*, with its innumerable and immediate reprints, widespread anthologizing, and extensive adoption into school curricula. Yet the contributor to *The London Magazine* thought his efforts necessary "to save this story from devouring fate" (102), a task for which he is lauded by another contributor to the same journal two years later. As a result of "The Story of Inkle and Yarico," G. O. insists, the tale "shall live on ev'ry virgin's tongue, / And every youth shall own the cruel wrong." Moreover, G. O.'s poem directs readers not previously familiar with Yarico and Inkle to "See their Story" in "Vol. III" of *The London Magazine*, rather than *The Spectator* itself.[39]

All this suggests that *The Spectator*'s being "in the hands of every one" was a necessary but not sufficient precondition for keeping its stories and characters safe "from devouring fate." Mere widespread dissemination and reproduction of the paper was not enough; readers needed to value its individual stories and characters and to know that other readers were doing the same. Its social canonicity could not go without saying, especially once the paper had ceased to serve as a means of binding readers together through a shared diurnal ritual. Post-1714 readers could, of course, discover what they had missed by reading number 10, in which Mr. Spectator describes himself as the center of a virtual community: "my Publisher tells me, that there are already Three Thousand [copies] . . . distributed each Day: So that if I allow Twenty Readers to every Paper, which I look upon as a modest Computation, I may reckon about Three-score thousand Disciples in *London* and *Westminster*, who I hope will take care to distinguish themselves from the thoughtless Herd of their ignorant and unattentive Brethren" (1:44). Moreover, they could see that almost half of the paper's original series contained letters sent in by various apparently real readers. They might even have known about some of the additional letters which never saw print or have read contemporary testimonies to the paper's cultural centrality, such as John Gay's 1711 claim that it was "in every one's Hand, and a constant Topick for our Morning Conversation."[40] It would thus have been readily apparent to latter-day readers that the original audience for *The Spectator* constituted a rich and vibrant virtual community populated by what Stuart Sherman terms "the real-life avatars of a wholly fictional creation."[41]

Yet that community could not be sustained after the paper ceased publication and became an almost compulsory tool of polite education, rather than a daily "communication" with and "mirroring" of its readership.[42] The disciplinary ends toward which *The Spectator* was often directed in the years after 1714 are aptly captured in one of Joseph Collet's admonishments to his daughter: "Instead of enlarging on the instructions I have already given for your conduct, I enjoyn you to study the Spectators, especially those which relate to Religion and Domestick Life. Next to the Bible you cannot read any writings so much to your purpose for the improvement of your mind and the conduct of your Actions."[43] We have no record, alas, of how Miss Collet responded to this injunction, but it is not difficult to imagine that she, like the boys whose reading Vicesimus Knox hoped to monitor some sixty years later, chafed at the forced imposition of a text that, in other circumstances, she might well have found intriguing and pleasurable.[44] In order to maintain "the punctual time of circulation" which "is crucial to the sense that discussion is currently unfolding" and so of current value, post-1714 readers needed to invent a new sort of virtual community for *The Spectator*, one which could be sustained across a broader expanse of time than diurnal form would allow and which would permit readers to exert their talents in a more expansive fashion than polite pedagogy would generally sanction.[45]

Of course, this just begs the question, why should Inkle and Yarico have been so compelling to so many readers in the first place? Peter Hulme has argued that the story served as something of an ideological screen, "interpretable [like *The Aeneid*] as an unfortunate clash between passion and duty and therefore only an infringement of the laws of hospitality, rather than the complete overturning of such laws through the extirpation of the native population."[46] By pitying Yarico and execrating Inkle even as they deplored the treatment of his shipmates by Yarico's countrymen, readers could displace any anxiety that they felt about the costs of colonization: the two forms of inhospitality cancelled one another out, leaving only a single Dido-like victim to mourn as the tragic but necessary casualty of imperial expansion. There is much to recommend this theory, not least the startling absence of any real concern with slavery as an institution in almost every version of the story I have encountered. Given the sheer extent of growing concern over the slave trade, I do not doubt that some of the readers with whom we are concerned were impelled to write by their emerging abolitionism. Nonetheless, Inkle's selling Yarico into bondage seems to have been seen almost exclusively as an instance of individual cruelty and ingratitude. There are sometimes movements toward a genealogy for Inkle's behavior: after all, Steele tells us, Inkle's father, "an eminent Citizen," had prevented "the natural Impulses of his Passions, by Prepossession towards his Interests"(1:50). But even these antimercantile gestures are fairly circumscribed. What gave the story its power, apparently, was its focus upon Inkle's individual violation of the laws of hospitality and the pathetic spectacle it afforded of an abandoned woman.

Despite its many virtues, though, Hulme's theory cannot account for why a reader like G. O. should praise his predecessor in terms that sound so proprietary and devoted to experiencing the text as if it were ideally present: "so well the injur'd innocent complains, / Or now upbraids in such pathetic strains, / That sharers in the sad distress you show, / We feel his cruelty, and mourn her woe." Nor can Hulme explain why G. O. should regard the 1734 poet's project as one of "giv[ing]" Inkle's crimes "glaring to succeeding times." In order to understand the form taken by the afterlife of Inkle and Yarico—with its heroic epistles, visualized passions, and persistent concern with the couple's place in cultural memory—we need to supplement Hulme's theory with a description of the ways in which individual readers transformed the lovers into a new sort of folk heroes around whom the literate and polite public brought up on *The Spectator* might rally.

Let us then return for a moment to the framing of the tale in *The Spectator*, where Steele makes much of the fact that Arietta offers the story of Inkle and Yarico "in Answer to" the Common-Place Talker's murder of "the celebrated Story of the *Ephesian* Matron" (1:48–49). Indeed, Mr. Spectator leaves convinced that the tale of Inkle and Yarico "should be always a Counterpart to the *Ephesian* Matron" (1:51). Significantly, however, Steele does not reproduce this "celebrated Story" or even give a citation. Rather, readers are expected to know it and if they do not, they presumably should (it is, after all, "celebrated"). However, the canonical version of the story was that which appeared in Petronius's *Satyrica;* hardly suitable reading for the "Tea-tables" of Addison and Steele's "Three-score thousand Disciples." Readers with the benefit of a classical education (those who could parse the Latin mottoes at the head of each paper) were no doubt acquainted with Petronius's version, as were those libertine enough to be familiar with the various translations of the tale.[47] Those who had not received such an education, however (which would include aristocratic women, dissenters, and many of the Anglican middling sort of both genders), would have to rely upon the sketchier versions of the story which trickled down into the vernacular, unless they were so forward as to ask an Etonian and so indecorously betray their ignorance.

In other words, this number of *The Spectator* stages one of the persistent internal divisions of eighteenth-century cultural literacy: the gap between the stock of classical allusions flogged into young gentlemen and the ad-hoc alternatives to such a stock accumulated by those who did not go to the great public schools. Polite readers without a classical education were, in effect, presented with three options. They could accept the position of cultural and social inferiority to which their lack of Latin had traditionally consigned them (and so grudgingly acknowledge that one of the things that identified their betters as such was a more exact knowledge of figures like the Ephesian Matron). Or they could strive to acquire classical literacy and in so doing ratify the very structures which had previously relegated them to the margins. Or they could attempt to erect their own alternative to classical literacy, one which was better suited to their own particular needs and desires and so could resolve what John Guillory has described as "a linguistic ambivalence" among the polite "which takes the form of suspicion toward the classical languages as useless knowledge, and envy of the social distinction they represent."[48] For the readers we have been considering, the alternative of a polite—but pointedly not classical—literacy seems to have been a particularly welcome option, in part because it could allow them to sidestep the traditional hierarchy and so maintain a sense of their own independence (a sense in which knowing the details of the Ephesian Matron's story ultimately mattered far less than knowing those surrounding the tale of Inkle and Yarico).

Indeed, if we consider the augmentation and retelling of the Inkle and Yarico story as part of a larger endeavor to form a vernacular social canon which could rival that handed down from classical antiquity, the selection of this particular tale takes on considerably more resonance. For most eighteenth-century readers, it came already bearing the imprimatur of *The Spectator*, which could enable it to be regarded as at least potentially common to all (*The Spectator* was, after all, "in the hands of every one"). At the same time, in most of the collected reprints of the paper, the tale appeared immediately on the heels of number 10's description of how "this great City inquir[ed] Day by Day after these my Papers, and receiv[ed] my Morning Lectures with a becoming Seriousness and Attention" (1:44). If, as I suspect, this glowing description of the centrality of *The Spectator* to the daily lives of its "Disciples" only underscored to post-1714 readers their own belatedness and inability to participate in this charmed circle, then the opportunity to forge a new sort of virtual community by virtue of which Inkle and Yarico "whole ages shall survive" may have proved almost irresistible. Moreover, the tale's heroine clearly possessed the generic complexity which was so attractive to the readers we considered in Chapter 1: Yarico manages to be simultaneously a latter-day Dido entertaining her shipwrecked foreign lover in a cave and a "Naked *American*" ethnographic curiosity decked out "every day . . . in a different Dress, of the most beautiful Shells, Bugles, and Bredes" (1:50). And perhaps most significantly, by doing their best to ensure that the tale will "live," readers could feel some control over the prospect that one day the story of Inkle and Yarico would be even more "celebrated" than that of the Ephesian Matron.

Unlike those steeped in either classical tradition or popular ballads, polite readers had no preexisting "joint stock" of traditional motifs and heroes "for the common use."[49] Rather, they had first to postulate and then endow Inkle and Yarico with commonness in order for the couple to begin to constitute such a stock. And as this process was repeated again and again, Steele's star-crossed lovers passed over into the never-never-land of public property inhabited by the likes of Dick Whittington. The reason why Wollstonecraft could so confidently and casually refer to the way in which to "make an Inkle" was that Inkles had been made for decades. There was Steele's Inkle, and the Countess of Hertford's Inkle, and Paul Hiffernan's Inkle, and Isaac Bickerstaff's Inkle, and dozens of other Inkles appropriated by various, often nameless readers who have left us the traces of their visualizations.[50] The cumulative weight of these proprietary claims upon the tale yielded "our" Inkle: the Inkle known to and despised by all, a latter-day shabby Aeneas whose fame was "blasted" and yet would "live thro' each abhorring age."

All of this still begs the question, though, of why these readers should have chosen to flesh out the key moments in Inkle and Yarico's story by visualizing the outward signs of their passions, especially since such corporeal gestures were not a standard convention of the heroic epistle. For an answer, we will need to take a detour to consider some of the peculiar practices of the institution where most of these readers learned those signs in the first place: namely, the patent theater.

* * *

One of the most counterintuitive practices of the eighteenth-century theater was its widespread presumption that despite its being primarily a repertory theater, with a limited number of well-known plays as its main offerings, individual parts somehow belonged to a given actor. As Cecil Price notes, "it was taken for granted that actors had possession of certain parts and, while others might occasionally take these roles as a novelty or at a benefit, they were otherwise the property of the people who had been engaged to play them."[51] Thus Thomas Davies, for example, could describe how Colley Cibber "made himself master of the part [of Shallow, in *2 Henry IV*], and performed it so much to the satisfaction of the public, that he retained it as long as he remained upon the stage," while Kitty Clive could cite as "a receiv'd Maxim in the Theatre, *That no Actor or Actress shall be depriv'd of a Part in which they have been well receiv'd, until they are render'd incapable of performing it either by Age or Sickness.*"[52] Indeed, as late as 1800, performers protective of their interests were still asserting "the right to the possession of his cast of characters" as "the most important privilege which appertained to the Actor."[53] Parts, in short, were looked upon "as a kind of *Property, not to be taken away without Injustice.*"[54] Indeed, George Anne Bellamy went so far as to claim that they were "as much the *property* of performers, as their weekly salary."[55] As Clive's language should suggest, though, this was a wholly customary right: actors had no legal protection and theater managers were in principle free to cast a play as they pleased.

In some ways, of course, the ownership of parts was simply an offshoot of the division of the repertory at the Restoration. From the 1660s through the late 1720s, certain plays simply belonged to a given company, either out of continuity with a Caroline forebear or by order of the Lord Chamberlain.[56] Within a given company, a particular part would be quite literally passed on from one actor to his designated successor, typically with the goal of preserving a tradition often dating back to the Elizabethan theater.[57] This system broke down in the face of the fabulous success of *The Beggar's Opera*, which Drury Lane was not content to leave to Covent Garden. Yet for the remainder of the century, certain roles continued to belong primarily to one performer or another, if only out of audience preference. Davies describes (with respect to a 1746 production of *1 Henry IV* at Drury Lane) how "the public could not more bear to see another Falstaff, while Quin was on the stage, than they would now flock to see another Shylock, so long as Macklin continues to have strength" (1:232). Similarly, "Tate Wilkinson's servant would not go to watch the young John Philip Kemble perform Hamlet as 'it is Mr. Cummin's part.'"[58] And the presumption of a proprietary claim could linger for quite some time after an actor ceased regular performance. Sylas Neville, for example, refers to Richard III as one of Garrick's "very capital characters which he has not done these 7 or 8 years."[59] Indeed, audiences would sometimes resort to violence to express their indignation at perceived trespassing upon an actor's property, as happened when Charles Macklin tried to play Macbeth, a traditional preserve of David Garrick's and the current perquisite of William Smith.[60]

Yet despite these riots (which might seem evidence of the audience's desire for property in a part to be restricted to a single owner), both audiences and actors were actively involved in keeping the customary system from becoming a monopoly. Beginning with the debut of *The Beggar's Opera* in 1728, rival productions and competing interpretations came to be a perennial feature of the theatrical scene, each one undercutting the exclusive possession of both plays and parts. Robert Hume notes, for example, that "of the fifty-eight plays offered at Lincoln's Inn Fields [in 1731–32], twenty-three were in the active repertory at Drury Lane this season—an increase of 50 per cent over the average for duplicated plays" prior to the collapse of the traditional system.[61] These included new plays—*The Beggar's Opera, The Provoked Husband, The London Merchant*—which would have previously been off-limits. Similarly, James Lynch describes how of the "seventy different full-length plays . . . performed at the two patent houses [in the 1751–52 season], sixteen . . . were given performance at both," including both perennial favorites like *Macbeth, The Recruiting Officer,* and *Tamerlane,* and successful recent plays, such as *The Suspicious Husband*.[62] And while managers like Colley Cibber might gripe about it, the competing houses were well within their legal rights: as Hume notes, "once published [a] play was in the public domain for any performers to use."[63] Nor was this an exclusively metropolitan phenomenon. West Digges could monopolize Macheath in Edinburgh while John Beard was celebrated for his interpretation at Covent

Garden, just as John Henderson could be "the Bath Roscius" and dominate resort theater in the same roles as those played by Garrick in London. Hence even as roles were owned, they were owned by multiple actors in the same city or the same kingdom at the same time, and so represented a very curious and immaterial sort of property indeed.

As a result of these competing productions—and the challenge to interpretive monopolies which they implied—attention to the theater seems to have markedly increased in the 1730s and 1740s, especially in the wake of the Licensing Act of 1737. Matthew Kinservik has argued that the rapid reduction in the number of new plays staged in the decade after the passage of the Licensing Act, along with the temporary suppression of the non-patent houses and the excising of political content from plays, encouraged a situation in which "audiences and critics began to pay more attention to the performers than ever before. . . . While the law was not intended to create a star system, it did alter the theatre world in such a way that the representation of a text became more important than its content."[64] The fairly narrow but widely shared repertory that emerged in the 1740s encouraged audience members to become connoisseurs of acting, skilled observers of what an actor brought to a role.[65] So, for example, the "war of the Romeos" which held the stage for twelve consecutive nights in the autumn of 1750 encouraged audience comparison of the two lead actors' respective merits to such a degree that "some spectators . . . made a practice of leaving Covent Garden after Act III to catch the wind-up at Drury Lane" so that they could see both Spranger Barry's "Romeo in love" and "Garrick's Romeo die."[66] Given world enough and time, Francis Gentleman would have shuttled back and forth between the theaters even more frequently in order to see each actor in "those scenes in which they most evidently rose above each other": "Mr. Barry the Garden scene of the second act—Mr. Garrick the friar scene in the third—Mr. Barry the garden scene in the fourth—Mr. Garrick in the first scene, description of the Apothecary, &c. fifth act—Mr. Barry first part of the tomb scene, and Mr. Garrick from where the poison operates to the end."[67] Similarly, a commentator for *The Gentleman's Magazine* thought that while Susannah Cibber, "when she gives herself the mortal stab, has introduced a shudder that affects the whole audience . . . she has no claim to superiority" over George Anne Bellamy "in all other parts of the distress upon the body of *Romeo*." Accordingly, while he "shed more tears in seeing Mrs. *Cibber*," he was "more delighted in seeing Miss *Bellamy*."[68] And, of course, habitual playgoers had frequent "opportunities for comparison, not only of Garrick with Barry, but of Garrick with himself" in earlier performances.[69] The very existence of such efforts to weigh the merits of differing approaches to a role marked the death knell for the Restoration presumption that there was "one correct way to play a character" which was encapsulated in "the acting tradition handed on from actor to actor since the days of Shakespeare."[70] Indeed, even those firmly convinced of the superiority of a particular approach might find themselves "discover[ing] *Blemishes,* where they saw only *Beauties* before" as a result of making comparisons and thereby "*incurr*[ing]" a "*refined Nicety*" of theatrical taste.[71]

The establishment in the 1750s of theatrical reporting as a regular part of metropolitan journalism further spurred on audience comparison of various actors' approaches to a given role. As John Brewer notes, "published criticism focused on the actor . . . revelling in the particularities of individual performances."[72] So, for example, in an essay for *The London Chronicle,* Arthur Murphy compares Henry Woodward's version of Marplot—from Susannah Centlivre's *The Busy Body*—to that of Garrick, deciding that Woodward plays the role as one of "characteristic goodness": "he does mischief so innocently that we all forgive him from our hearts. And whenever he goes wrong, they who suffer from it see plainly that his meddling disposition carries its atonement along with it." Garrick's Marplot, on the other hand, "cannot look undesigning; nor can his curiosity be thought to have its source in a total inattention to his own affairs and the good-natured principle of helping others. It looked to me as if he had a sly intention to mar the projects of his friends."[73] In each case, the fundamental motive driving (and hence explaining) Marplot is a product of the performance, rather than Centlivre's script. That is, the truth of the character seems to lie less in the playtext per se than in what Roland Barthes would call its "theatricality": its "theater-minus-text . . . a density of signs and sensations built up on stage starting from the written argument . . . that ecumenical perception of sensuous artifice—gesture, tone, distance, substance, light—which submerges the text beneath the profusion of its external language."[74] The significance—and ultimately, the value—of Marplot thus resides in what an actor brings to the role, rather than in the role itself. And what Woodward and Garrick brought to the role were two competing arrays of legible passions, one signifying self-punishing innocence, the other sly malice.

That is, the way in which actors distinguished themselves from one another was through their differing combinations of the legible signs of the passions—what were known around the playhouse as "points" or "hits." The elements within a given hit or sequence of hits were almost exclusively drawn from the "conventional series of facial, gestural, and vocal postures" that we have been examining, but those elements were assembled and juxtaposed in novel ways so as to draw "attention not so much to the 'character' portrayed as to the *portrayal* of the character by the actor."[75] Accordingly, hits emphasized "technique rather than meaning" and so "naturally provided the opportunity to compare the talents of various actors in the same part."[76] Woodward's "busy but foolish" looks conveyed an impression of Marplot as "innocent of an idea, till some present object . . . lead him . . . blundering . . . into sense, but ever mistaking his path and running into absurdity." Every look of Garrick's Marplot, on the other hand, "seems to carry with it a degree of cunning and of sharp discernment." Even "when he would appear undesigning . . . something of a counterfeit thoughtfulness . . . seems to gleam but faintly over features generally fixed in habitual intenseness of thought." Neither of these versions of what one correspondent of Garrick's termed the "silent eloquence of gestures, looks, and pauses" was necessarily superior to the other or truer to Centlivre's script.[77] Both could "mark to the audience" "such sentiments as are not deliver'd in the play, yet are not only agreeable to, but necessary to be understood of the character they represent."[78] But, of course, the two were wholly incompatible with one another, which meant that what was most "characteristic" about Marplot—what "calls [him] from the Grave, to breathe, and be [himself] again, in Feature, Speech, and Motion"—was not part of the script at all, but rather the product of Woodward's and Garrick's various hits.[79]

I rehearse all this not so much to make a contribution to theater history per se, though, as to underscore the consequences of that history and these practices for readers like the ones we have been considering. The theater presented such readers with a familiar and compelling model with which to think through many of the issues we have been tracing. First and foremost, the theater represented a realm in which proprietary claims were routinely made upon immaterial characters in ways which tacitly acknowledged the implausibility of such claims when weighed against commonsensical notions of property as the right to exclude all others. That is, when actors asserted their ownership of particular roles, they did so by invoking custom, rather than any sort of Lockean theory of appropriation. Given the nigh inescapability of Lockean conceptions of property in the period, this seems a rather telling omission, one which implicitly acknowledges that ordinary notions of property as that which has been removed from the state of nature and mixed with an individual's labor so as to "exclude . . . the common right of other Men" do not really work when it comes to the possession of parts.[80] While performance certainly involves labor, it requires a more than a little special pleading to argue that a role in a stock play is in "the State that Nature hath provided."[81] Consider only the contortions that the author of *The Present State of the Stage in Great-Britain and Ireland* must go through in order to insist that "many Admirers of theatrical Entertainment lament with me the not seeing [Luke Sparks] in the *Old Batchelor*, the *Plain Dealer*, &c. a Walk which we hoped he would have filled, when the Retirement of Mr. *Quin* left it unoccupied" (44). Given that *The Old Batchelor* had been staged at Covent Garden the previous December, with Roger Bridgwater in Quin's role of Heartwell, it is far from clear in what sense these roles could possibly be regarded as "unoccupied." It makes much more sense to imagine one's right to such a role as a matter of custom, like the common-right of cottagers or the perquisites of skilled laborers, neither of which denies that the land or materials in question may already have an owner: they just insist upon their right to use them too. Indeed, as with other forms of seemingly inexhaustible customary property, it is hard to see how a Lockean system of scarcity—in which "another can longer have any right to [an object], before it can do [its owner] any good"—could even apply to the possession of parts.[82] Certainly the practice of competing performances did not seem to cause the theaters any obvious material injury, since "the managers encouraged" such productions so that "the audience had to see both . . . in order to adjudicate between the actors."[83] And as far as immaterial consequences went, well, "one might as well pretend to exclude all others from the Benefits of a refreshing Breeze, or the View of a beautiful Prospect."[84] Readers could thus find in the theater a well-articulated set of precedents for how to regard their own claims upon literary characters: so long as the performance rights to a role were in the public domain as the result of an authorized publication, the "*Character* . . . became *open* to any body that pleased to *take it up*."[85]

At the same time, such readers could see that the way in which actors laid their customary claims upon their roles was precisely through their invention of an appropriate array of hits "to keep up the life and spirit of the action."[86] And as we have already seen, actors devised their hits in full knowledge that others were (or might well in the future be) doing the same, a practice which paradoxically locates the essence of a character in his or her mutability. The result was a situation in which a character's felt iterability was directly proportionate to his or her apparent range of possibilities.

Finally, and perhaps most importantly for our purposes, readers could see that the theatrical public (to which most of them also belonged) was actively engaged in furthering these practices for its own benefit. After all, as Aaron Hill pointed out to Barton Booth, "the *town* has [your *oldest* stock Plays] as much, by *heart,* as the players."[87] Among other things, this meant that the audience regarded stock roles as their customary property too. Charles Churchill nicely captures this sentiment in a passage we glanced at back in the Introduction:

The Stage I chose—a subject fair and free—
'Tis yours—'tis mine—'tis Public Property.
All Common Exhibitions open lye
For Praise or Censure to the Common Eye. . . .
Actors, a venal crew, receive support
From public bounty, for the public sport.
To clap or hiss, all have an equal claim,
The cobbler's and his lordship's right the same.
All join for their subsistence; all expect
Free leave to praise their worth, their faults correct. . . .
Each, or as judgment, or as fancy guides,
The lively witling praises or derides.
Actors, as Actors, are a lawful game;
The poet's right; and Who shall bar his claim?[88]

As I have already suggested, the stage, for Churchill and many others, was "Public Property" precisely because of the competing claims upon it. Anything capable of being simultaneously "yours" and "mine" was necessarily "Common" to all who "join[ed] for [its] subsistence." Accordingly, whatever game the commons supplied was "lawful" for all to hunt "as judgment, or as fancy guides": "all [had] an equal claim."

In order to sustain this fantasy, however, playgoers needed to imagine themselves as part of a community united around their shared experience of the stage as a sort of commons. Michael Warner has argued that "without the idea of texts that can be picked up at different times and in different places by otherwise unrelated people, we would not imagine a public as an entity that embraces all the users of that text, whoever they might be."[89] The converse, however, seems equally important: without the ability to imagine oneself as part of a public embracing all the users of a text, we would be unable to conceive of myriad individuals picking up texts "at different times and in different places" as fellow claimants and so fellow commoners. Luckily, there were a host of collective fictions that "in the whole catalogue of public professions, none have engaged general curiosity so much as the theatre: . . . the stage, like a game of chance, engages the attention of all."[90] If the entire nation could not fit within Drury Lane or Covent Garden, those who could might be regarded as representative. Just as King, Lords, and Commons stood in for the nation in the political realm, so too did Box, Pit, and Gallery in the theatrical world.[91] Nor were these pronouncements simply puffery for the theaters. However one quantifies the social composition of theater audiences in the eighteenth century, one conclusion seems inescapable: the public of the theater—those included in Churchill's "yours" and "mine," those in whose "Service" Cibber claimed to have been "employ'd . . . since many of their Grandfathers were young Men" (7)—was imagined as both representative and inclusive. As Cibber's son put it, "the Town," to whose taste the players submitted themselves, "may be supposed to include all Degrees of Persons, from the highest Nobleman, to the lowly Artisan, . . . who in their different Stations, are Encouragers of dramatic Performances:—Thus all persons, who pay for their Places, whether Noble, Gentle, or Simple, who fill the Boxes, Pit, and Galleries, in a theatrical Sence, form the Town."[92] Accordingly, whatever could be thought of as belonging to "the Town" could also be regarded as "Public Property." After all, "the Stage is the Creature of the Public."[93]

Of course, to imagine the theatrical public as a community united by its shared use of "Public Property" is also to impute a value to that property as what binds the community together. Here again, we can see what Carol Rose terms the "Comedy of the Commons" at work, for not only did the public use of stock characters enhance their felt iterability by making them seem common, it also helped further their social canonicity. James Boaden nicely formulates this phenomenon: the consequence of the audience's "freely confess[ing]" that "there might be endless varieties in the representation of . . . a character; justifiable, too, by very plausible reasonings" is that new "performances . . . would never disgust them by common place, but would at all times tend to make [the playwright] better known, by the necessity for his being more studied."[94] Arthur Murphy hailed Macklin's performance of Macbeth in similar terms by welcoming "as many editions . . . on the stage, as the commentators have given us off the stage": Macklin's version "is not so white and glossy a paper as Garrick's; but the text is as good in general; the punctuation is more exact; and the reading in many places improved."[95] Like scholiasts, these actors, along with members of the audience like Murphy, served as guarantors of the character's underlying value to the community: no one went to the bother of either preparing or reading competing editions of a text that didn't matter.

* * *

By now it should be clear how the "'tis yours—'tis mine—'tis Public Property" logic of the theater might have proved attractive to readers interested in elevating Inkle and Yarico to the rank of polite folk heroes. By treating Steele's account of the couple as "but [the] faint outlines of this striking piece of Barbarity," readers could lay claim to the characters in much the same way as actors did: namely, by augmenting the familiar published text with an array of hits drawn from the stock repertoire of legible passions.[96] At the same time, they could appeal to their fellow readers to witness their particular versions of Yarico as if she were ideally present: "—A thousand things my loaded heart wou'd say, / But Oh! my trembling hand will not obey; / Then let your fancy image my distress, / And yet—Oh yet, while you have power—redress!" (123). And by appealing to those fancies, which would presumably vary from their own at least as much as Churchill's "yours" and "mine" differed from one another, these readers could, in effect, constitute themselves as a public bound together by its shared proprietary interest in Inkle and Yarico.

The ways in which readerly visualization could function as a virtual surrogate for theatrical hits are nicely underscored by Austin Weddell's published but unperformed *Incle and Yarico: A Tragedy*. In this play, the key moments of the story—Inkle and Yarico's first falling in love, their departure together, Yarico's protracted death—all rather curiously take place offstage. Thus, for example, when Inkle and Yarico go to board the English ship that will carry them to Jamaica, the scene is filtered through a messenger, who informs us that "these Eyes have seen" how

Gladly at first she pointed to the Main;
Then stop'd, and paus'd a-while; again went on,
Then stop'd, and paus'd: while her unknown Conductor
Was earnest for her Flight, and strove to haste
Her half-reluctant Steps, beyond the Limits
That Inclination gave them: again she paus'd;
Again he urg'd her Flight.——When on the Verge
Of the tempestuous Sea, her tender Heart
Shrunk back to Land, and her o'erflowing Eyes
Wept, longing to return: amidst the Conflict,
He clasp'd her in his Arms, flung her on board,
And hasted from the Shore.[97]

Yarico's pauses and shrinking back are, not surprisingly, among the conventional modes of designating Reluctance and no doubt an actress at Covent Garden would have come up with something along these lines had the play been staged. What is interesting, though, is how little sense it makes to filter this particular scene through a messenger. There is nothing in it that might violate theatrical decorum and Yarico's hesitation could just as readily be conveyed in a printed stage direction.

It is as if Weddell wished to revenge himself upon the managers of the Covent Garden Theatre, who "promised faithfully [the play] should be act'd" (sig. A2), by substituting a virtual array of gestures for the actual hits he was denied. This at least might explain his otherwise puzzling emphasis upon the "Circle of . . . griev'd Spectators" who, unlike both Inkle and the audience at Covent Garden, had the opportunity to witness Yarico's demise and feel "half her Woes" (63–64). Yet the way in which Yarico's death is reported—complete with tears, shuddering, and "beat[ing] the suppliant Earth"—allows it to be conjured up by Weddell's readers with ideal presence, thus enabling them to expand that circle into a virtual community whose "Fancy / Still keeps her in [their] Sight" (64–65). By thus transforming the key moments of his play into legible passions like those in Yarico's epistles, even as he solicits his readers to see those moments with ideal presence, Weddell could have his cake and eat it too. He could take advantage of the self-conscious community across time that theatrical habitués regarded themselves as constituting, while avoiding the myriad distractions of the actual playhouse (no reader of *Incle and Yarico* was at risk of having his or her contemplation disrupted by an errant orange or a call for "Hearts of Oak"). And in so doing, Weddell could offer up a potentially superior form of theater, one in which he can exploit the same ironies of fame as the epistle writers were trying to create: hence Inkle, whom we discover has already seduced and abandoned a woman back in England, can heighten his own pending ingratitude by predicting to Yarico that their "*Love, / Will be each constant Virgin's Song*" (26), while Yarico's father can blindly insist that her harboring Inkle "agrees not with the Name of *Yarico*" (31). In each case, readers could savor the ways in which they, unlike the dramatis personae, already knew how the story would come out and so could appreciate how, to adopt Roberto Calasso's terms, the "variants" introduced by Weddell not only kept "the mythical blood in circulation," but got it going in the first place, thereby giving the lie to a Barbadian captain's confidence that Yarico's "whining Tale / Will scarcely overtake us" once he and Inkle have sailed to England (57).[98]

Indeed, the far more dramatic variants which characterize the most commercially successful post-*Spectator* version of the tale—George Colman's *Inkle and Yarico: An Opera*—provide unwitting testimony to the sheer success of the efforts of readers like Weddell to thrust greatness upon the couple.

Colman pays remarkably little attention to those moments of the story that so preoccupied the other readers we have been examining, but that seems only to signal that they can now go without saying. That is, Colman's extensive additions only become resonant against the backdrop of Inkle and Yarico's newfound stature as folk heroes. For example, the subplot in which Trudge, Inkle's clerk and valet, refuses to repudiate his courtship of Yarico's maid, Wowski, would make little dramatic sense unless one already knows that Inkle has become "a name which every man of honesty ought to be ashamed of" (226). Similarly, the romance which blossoms between Inkle's intended bride, Narcissa, and a dashing young captain could come off as scandalous and illicit unless one comes to the play with an understanding of how Inkle's "always [having] advantage in view" (175) renders him unworthy of such a wife. Indeed, even the twists which Colman introduces into "the stale narration" depend upon a preexisting familiarity with Inkle's reputation as "all guilt" (173): in the opera, no Englishmen are ever harmed by any of the natives, which implicitly removes any justification Inkle might have had for his ingratitude, as does his meditation, before he has even met Yarico, on "how much [natives] might fetch at the West Indian markets" if they "could be caught" (177). Given such heightenings of his guilt, it is all the more pointed when Inkle repents at the end, renouncing his father's "principles" and clasping Yarico to his heart to "mingle tears of love and penitence" (228). Ultimately, then, what allowed Colman's "little change" (173) to be not only comprehensible but wildly successful for upwards of a quarter century was the way in which it could comically play off the greatness previous readers had thrust upon the couple. In other words, the reason *Inkle and Yarico: An Opera* could join the ranks of what John Downes used to call "living play[s]" was that Steele's "stale narration" had already come to "live" in the hearts and minds of most Britons as the result of visualizations like the ones we have been tracing—which is to say, as the result of being repeatedly and simultaneously claimed as both "yours" and "mine."[99]

Chapter 3
Character Migration, Detachability, Old Friends

If some devotees of imaginative expansion busied themselves with visualizing the passions involved in key moments of an originary text, other readers took a cue from a different aspect of theater (the revival of popular characters in new plays) and invented further adventures for beloved characters which stepped outside the chronological bounds of that text. In this chapter we will investigate this second principal form of imaginative expansion, what I would like to term "character migration."[1] Through this practice, readers imagined characters' lives as extending off-page in ways which suggested their fundamental independence and detachability, their capacity to migrate both into new texts and into the lives of the readers themselves. Despite the origins of this practice in the theater—which is also the origin for most of the characters in question—the vast majority of the character migrations I have discovered take advantage of the allographic logic of print, its ability to make characters take on a placeless omnipresence. So where my second chapter concerned itself with readers expanding nontheatrical texts along theatrical lines, my third investigates how readers invented further adventures for theatrical characters as if they were fundamentally akin to the figures in a novel or newspaper sketch. Of course, as my last chapter argued, print and the theater, for all their manifest differences, are complementary modes of iterability when it comes to the creation of the textual commons. Accordingly, we will see how, by virtue of their familiarity through both theater and print, characters like Sir Roger de Coverly, Falstaff, and Ranger (from Benjamin Hoadly's *The Suspicious Husband*) could not only be sent on further adventures but also regarded as readers' "old friends," figures who could serve as the rallying point for a virtual sociability modeled upon more traditional modes of embodied social interaction. Indeed, even when such characters were not being sent upon further adventures, their newfound status as "old friends" fully *capable* of embarking upon such adventures nonetheless served to underscore their social canonicity (or at the very least their authors' ambition to attain such canonicity). Hence, this chapter not only reconstructs a fascinating and hitherto largely ignored reading practice; it also sheds light upon an important and underconsidered aspect of eighteenth-century canonicity more generally.[2]

A single example should suffice for the purposes of introducing the practice. In 1740, a Mr. Dorman of Hampstead published an afterpiece entitled *Sir Roger de Coverly: or, The Merry Christmas.* As its title suggests, Dorman's "Dramatic Entertainment of Two Acts" stars the foxhunting squire of the *Spectator* papers, along with Will Wimble and Mr. Spectator himself. The plot itself is rather slight, but that does not seem to have mattered much. The important thing, Dorman tells us in his preface, is that through this "Entertainment" we get to see yet another aspect of Sir Roger: namely, how he deals with the rustics on his estate when they try to put on a mildly satiric Christmas review for him and his guests. Presumably, these events are a fleshing out of his fleeting allusion in number 269 of *The Spectator* to how, at Christmas time, his "Tenants pass away a whole Evening in playing their innocent Tricks, and smutting one another" (2:550). By giving us more Sir Roger, Dorman claims that he is conducting the squire "quietly, into the Mansions of his Friends, where he will be treated with all the Gentleness, Candour, and Good-Nature he can possibly wish for."[3] That is, he is reuniting Sir Roger with his "Friends" through the writing of a text into which he could migrate, by creating additional adventures for him beyond those recounted in *The Spectator.*

I begin with this example, despite the atypicality of Sir Roger's origins, because it neatly encapsulates two of the principal concerns of this chapter: the ways in which print and theater, as complementary modes of iterability, could make a character seem detachable from his originary context and the desire to figure the virtual community which forms around such a character as a network of friends bound together through that character. Let us consider these points in turn.

Sir Roger de Coverly began, of course, as a print fiction. We are first introduced to him as a member of Mr. Spectator's club who ensures "that nothing may be written or publish'd to the Prejudice or Infringement of [Country Squires'] just Rights and Privileges."[4] Beginning with number 106 readers encountered him on an almost daily basis for over a month, as Addison, Eustace Budgell, and Steele took turns describing his various adventures at home in the country. By the midst of this run, Budgell was able to presume that his readers were "at present pretty well acquainted" with Sir Roger's "Character."[5] And this acquaintance seems to have only improved with time. According to John Aikin at the end of the century, "the papers in which Sir Roger appears have ever been among the most popular in the Spectator"—high praise indeed, if one recalls the claim of Vicesimus Knox that "there is scarcely an individual . . . of those who devote any of their time to reading, who had not digested the Spectators."[6]

What this social canonicity means for our purposes, however, is that through his widespread dissemination Sir Roger took on the curious ontology of highly successful print itself, what I described in Chapter 1 as its placeless omnipresence. Like many paradoxical cultural phenomena, this condition of being simultaneously everywhere and nowhere is best captured by jokes—in this case, the quips proffered by the editorial personae of *The Spectator* and its myriad imitators. Benjamin Franklin's Poor Richard, for example, defends his ontological reality by asking "if there were no such Man as I am, how is it possible I should appear publickly to hundreds of People, as I have done for several Years past, in print?"[7] Similarly, the first number of *The Jacobite's Journal* turns upon John Trott-plaid's having "contrived a Method of appearing in my *Scotch* Plaid all over the Kingdom at one and the same time."[8] And Arthur Murphy's eidolon for *The Gray's-Inn Journal*, one Charles Ranger, flatters himself "with the Hopes of conversing with many Hundreds of my Countrymen every *Saturday*."[9] The simultaneous appearance to "many Hundreds" "all over the Kingdom at one and the same time" which print enabled meant that Sir Roger could seem everywhere and yet oddly nowhere, for no single material manifestation could be said to adequately contain him if every other copy could serve just as well. That is, by virtue of the omnipresence of the material artifacts in which he appears, Sir Roger could seem to have an existence which sprawled beyond any particular copy or set of *The Spectator*.

At the same time, as the result of his seriality, Sir Roger could also exceed any given number or run as a textual entity. At the very least, Sir Roger is the sum of his thirty-eight appearances in *The Spectator*. George Justice describes him as a "product of the practice of serial publication": he "grows through addition, and not through plumbing the depths of his consciousness."[10] Yet, as befits a character written serially by several hands, there are a number of inconsistencies between the various numbers, each of which necessarily invites further readerly speculation. Indeed, Sir Roger's heir, Captain Sentry, went out of his way to highlight one such discrepancy: in number 544, he attempts to counter the lurid conjectures which were circulating concerning Sir Roger's motives in "enquir[ing] into the private Character of the young Woman at the Tavern" (4:445) back in issue 410. These suppositions had arisen in response to the seeming disparity between Sir Roger's discomfort in the presence of the widow (in numbers mostly written by Addison) and his suave confidence when dealing with this young woman—in a piece authored by Steele. Captain Sentry attempts to resolve the issue by insisting that Mr. Spectator "mentioned that Circumstance as an Instance of the Simplicity and Innocence of [Sir Roger's] Mind, which made him imagine it a very easy thing to reclaim one of those Criminals, and not as an Inclination in him to be guilty with her. The less Discerning of your Readers cannot enter into that Delicacy of Description in the Character" (4:445–46). Yet, as Captain Sentry's language should suggest, any effort to resolve or explain away the disparities endemic to serial publication has to invoke a larger conception of Sir Roger's "character," one which necessarily stands apart from and so exceeds the sum of his manifestations in the text of *The Spectator.* If Sir Roger is fundamentally simple and innocent, yet "the less Discerning of [Mr. Spectator's] Readers" cannot perceive that simplicity and innocence, then clearly it is not as self-evident as Captain Sentry would have it, but rather relies upon a conception of Sir Roger as having a moral character—and so an existence—prior to and apart from the text. That is to say, it relies upon a sense of Sir Roger as fundamentally detachable from any or all of his appearances in *The Spectator.*

I would like to propose that it was the interplay between this detachability—which could make Sir Roger seem perpetually more than the sum of his parts (if only because of the need to reconcile those parts which apparently contradicted one another)—and the sheer material omnipresence of the *Spectator* papers themselves that enabled readers like Dorman to regard Sir Roger as an old friend. The labor and ingenuity which individual readers invested in working out their own solutions to the disparities engendered by serial publication encouraged readers to feel proprietary toward their own particular conceptions of Sir Roger, all of which both presumed and underscored his felt detachability from the text of *The Spectator* itself. Addison's response to Steele's alterations dramatizes what many readers must have felt, although perhaps to lesser degrees: "Sir Roger . . . was Mr. Addison's favourite character; and so tender was he of it, that he went to Sir Richard, upon his publishing a Spectator, in which he made Sir Roger pick up a woman in the temple cloisters, and would not part with his friend, until he promised to meddle with the old knight's character no more."[11]

Dorman went similarly out of his way in order to champion his version of Sir Roger as not only an upholder of traditional hospitality but also a polite and genteel companion, the sort of man who advises his servants to "be sure you remember, in the midst of your Jollity, to keep within Bounds" (12–13). This conception of Sir Roger is a far cry from the living fossil represented in the early numbers of *The Spectator.* Indeed, if anything, it seems a rebuke to Captain Sentry's recollection of Sir Roger's "little Absurdities and Incapacity for the Conversation of the politest Men" (4:445). Nonetheless, Dorman stakes his claim on precisely this conception of Sir Roger's character and in so doing he, like Captain Sentry, implicitly disparages those who do not share his conception: "whether or not such a Character will please the Generality of People, I am, indeed, at a Loss to guess" (5). Yet at the very moment that Dorman is repudiating those who do not take pleasure in his version of Sir Roger, he is also relying upon the widespread material dissemination of *The Spectator*'s version of him in order to conjure up a virtual community of those who *are* "please[d]," those who might be styled Sir Roger's "Friends." Notice how Sir Roger's ontological status as a widely disseminated—and therefore indisputably disembodied—print fiction works hand-in-hand with Dorman's conception of him as nothing if not polite in order to allow the claim that "many a pretty Lady will be closeted with the Knight . . . without the least Reflection on their Conduct, for he's full as harmless as a Child in the Month, and wou'd not, for the World, attempt to make them laugh, at the Expense of either Morality or Good-Breeding." The very possibility of pretty ladies being closeted with Sir Roger stems from his status as a print fiction, which eliminates the chance of inappropriate behavior on his part. But the politeness with which Dorman endows him—the possibility that he could make ladies laugh without any loss of propriety—is what makes being closeted with him a desirable prospect in the first place. In other words, the friendship for Sir Roger that gives Dorman the ability to conduct him "quietly . . . into the Mansions of his Friends" hinges not only upon his prior entrance into those mansions in the form of *The Spectator* but also upon a shared conception of his character as fundamentally polite, despite the apparent counterevidence in number 2 of his having formerly been "what you call a fine Gentleman," who "had often supped with my Lord *Rochester* and Sir *George Etherege,* fought a Duel upon his first coming to Town, and kick'd Bully *Dawson* in a publick Coffee-house for calling him Youngster" (1:8). Conversely, of course, this means that any readers willing to at least entertain this conception of Sir Roger are free to regard themselves as both among his friends and the potential friend of his other friends, including Dorman. Sir Roger's detachability, then, is what enables him to serve as the friend joining together otherwise disparate readers into a virtual community. And this detachability was, in turn, best demonstrated through the invention of further adventures which could underscore the ability of a particular conception of Sir Roger to "please the Generality of People."

* * *

The peculiar, yet compelling logic which links together detachability, character migration, and a virtual community united around "our mutual friend" is codified and implicitly theorized in one of the most often cited (and, I suspect, least considered) instances of a literary character's being treated as if he had a life which extended off-page: Maurice Morgann's *Essay on the Dramatic Character of Sir John Falstaff.* In a lengthy footnote (the single most quoted passage from the entire essay), Morgann proposes that "if the characters of *Shakespeare* are thus *whole,* and as it were original . . . it may be fit to consider them rather as Historic than Dramatic beings; and when occasion requires, to account for their conduct from the *whole* of character, from general principles, from latent motives, and from policies not avowed."[12] By this he means that "there is a certain roundness and integrity in the forms of *Shakespeare,* which give them an independence as well as a relation, insomuch that we often meet with passages, which tho' perfectly felt, cannot be sufficiently explained in words, without unfolding the whole character of the speaker" (167n). According to Morgann, this appeal to the "whole character" is necessarily at odds with "the Understanding" which "seems for the most part to take cognizance of *actions* only, and from these to infer *motives* and *character*" (147). In the absence of passages which would "sufficiently explain" a conundrum, one must either throw up one's hands or else proceed "in a contrary course; and determine . . . of *actions* from certain *first principles of character*" (147). The latter method offers a superior means of dealing with the conflicting emotions which a character like Falstaff inspires: "we often condemn or applaud characters and actions on the credit of some logical process, while our hearts revolt, and would fain lead us to a very different conclusion" (147). Hence, while "we all like *Old Jack;* yet by some strange perverse fate, we all abuse him and deny him the possession of a single good or respectable quality" (148). What Morgann terms Falstaff's "*first principles of character*" is but another name for the phenomenon I was describing above. Morgann, like Dorman, seems to regard Falstaff as existing prior to and apart from his originary texts. Accordingly, the sum of a character's originary appearances (Falstaff's scenes in the *Henry IV* plays and *The Merry Wives of Windsor,* plus his reported death in *Henry V*) can be regarded as but a sketch "taken at that period of his life in which we see him" (152). Moreover, in the case of Falstaff at least, those scenes which constitute the supposedly originary sketch might best be taken with a grain of salt, since "the fact seems to be . . . that there is a real consequence about Sir *John Falstaff* which is not brought forward": as "we see him only in his familiar hours" and so are "witnesses only of *Falstaff*'s weakness and buffoonery; our acquaintance is with *Jack Falstaff, Plump Jack,* and *Sir John Paunch;* but if we would look for *Sir John Falstaff,* we must put on, as *Bunyan* would have expressed it, the spectacles of observation" (158).

With those spectacles, and a sense of Falstaff's "*first principles of character,*" we can envision those periods and aspects of Falstaff's life which lie beyond the edges of the Shakespearean sketch. Thus Morgann confidently invents Falstaff's youth, in which, as a result of his "high degree of wit and humour, accompanied with great natural vigor and alacrity of mind," he was "highly acceptable to society; so acceptable, as to make it unnecessary for him to acquire any other virtue" (151). Given such a beginning, it only stands to reason that as "he found himself esteemed and beloved with all his faults; nay *for* his faults" he "seems to have set, by degrees, all sober reputation at defiance" until "thro' indulgence, he acquires bad habits, becomes an humourist, grows enormously corpulent, and falls into the infirmities of age" which plague him "at that period of his life in which we see him" (151–52). Somewhat curiously, Morgann wants to restrict this imagining of Falstaff's life off-page to those portions which demonstrate his "*Constitutional Courage*": "with respect to every [other] infirmity . . . we must take him at the period in which he is represented to us. If we see him dissipated, fat,—it is enough;—we have nothing to do with his youth, when he might perhaps have been modest, chaste, '*and not an Eagle's talon in the waist*'" (153). Nonetheless, Morgann is willing to violate his own rules when it suits his purpose, as it evidently does when he wishes to infer an inherited fortune sufficient to maintain "apartments in town," "a regular table," and a "house in the country," all of which "necessarily imply . . . some funds which are not immediately under our notice" (165).

This begs the question, though, of why Falstaff should have seemed a detachable "Historic being" in the first place. As with Sir Roger, the answer seems to lie with the peculiar ontology lent to characters by widespread dissemination. As "a stage-character," Falstaff is necessarily "but an Impression; an appearance which we are to consider as a reality; and which we may venture to applaud or condemn as such, without further inquiry or investigation. . . . But if we would account for our Impressions, or for certain sentiments or actions in a character, not derived from its apparent principles, yet appearing, we know not why, natural, we are then compelled to look further, and examine if there be not something more in the character than is *shewn;* something inferred, which is not brought under our special notice" (203). We must, in other words, deduce Falstaff's "*first principles of character*" to supplement the "apparent principles" which are staged. Yet in the case of Falstaff at least, many of those inferred principles are quite unattractive and "become still more intolerable by an excess of unfeeling insolence on one hand, and of base accommodation on the other" (210). The Falstaff of logical inference is no longer "the jovial delightful companion . . . the favourite and the boast of the Stage" (210). He is, however, "the *Falstaff* of Nature; the very stuff out of which the *Stage Falstaff* is composed; nor was it possible, I believe, out of any other materials he could have been formed. From this disagreeable draught we shall be able, I trust, by a proper disposition of light and shade, and from the influence and compression of external things, to produce *plump Jack,* the life of humour, the spirit of pleasantry, and the soul of wit" (211). That is, the stage Falstaff is not only a selection from a larger fictional archive but a carefully crafted selection, one which turns his "vices . . . into incongruities" in order to give him "that appearance of perfect good-nature, pleasantry, mellowness, and hilarity of mind, for which we admire and almost love him": "it is the artificial condition of *Falstaff* [that is, his theatricality] which is the source of our delight" (211–12). But, of course, as with the other stock roles which we examined in Chapter 2, each actor who took up the part selected different elements from the archive in order to produce his own particular "artificial condition" for Plump Jack. Hence James Quin highlighted the "satire," "sarcasm," and "impudent dignity" of Falstaff, while James Love "laughed with ease and gaiety," and Ned Shuter "enjoyed the effects of his roguery with a chuckle of his own compounding, and rolled his full eye, when detected, with a most laughable effect."[13] Similarly, John Henderson called particular attention to Falstaff's "high impudent roguery" and "the loose, easy, merry, ludicrous, gay, and elbow-chair situations and attitudes" in which he so often found himself.[14] I have been unable to discover any records of how Mr. Punch approached the role in Charlotte Charke's puppet versions of the *Henry IV* plays, but one can readily imagine, given her casting, that she would have taken the character in yet another direction and played up the slapstick elements.[15] Thus each new production elicits "Impressions" which "if we would account for" require yet another set of inferences as to what "principles" may be "not brought under our special notice." As with Sir Roger, then, although in a different medium, the sheer number of iterations of "the *Stage Falstaff*"—not to mention the patent differences between the Falstaff of *The Merry Wives of Windsor* and that of the *Henry IV* plays—creates a sense among audience members and readers that no single actor's interpretation can adequately contain him, that as a result of his dissemination he has come to constitute what Thomas Davies termed an "exhaustless fund of wit and humour."[16]

Indeed, Morgann seizes upon this very inexhaustibility to justify his own project. Tracing, as he does, those "talents and qualities" of Falstaff "which were afterwards obscured, and perverted to ends opposite to their nature" serves to highlight Falstaff's status as "a Stage buffoon of a peculiar sort; a kind of Game-bull which would stand the baiting thro' a hundred Plays and produce equal sport, whether he is pinned down occasionally by *Hal* or *Poins*, or tosses such mongrils as *Bardolph*, or the Justices, sprawling in the air" (212). That is, the proof of Falstaff's detachability and inexhaustibility lies in his capacity to migrate into new texts. As a result of his "distinct and separate subsistence" (212), he could carry an additional "hundred Plays" and still be ready for more, as would we. Indeed, according to Morgann, the "we" who "all like *Old Jack*" cannot get enough of him: even after the close of *2 Henry IV*, "we wish to know what course he is afterwards likely to take: He is detected and disgraced, it is true; but he lives by detection, and thrives on disgrace; and we are desirous to see him detected and disgraced again" (215). Thus Morgann, through his speculative invention of further adventures, is offering his readers what he has insisted all along is their heart's desire. He is providing an opportunity for the readerly equivalent of "a morning's ride" where "the real object is Exercise, and the Delight which a rich, beautiful, picturesque, and perhaps unknown Country, may excite from every side" (144). And by accompanying him "in a leisure hour" on this ride "we return . . . to converse with this jovial, this fat, this roguish, this frail . . . companion" (188). By partaking of his exercise in character migration, "we" join together in a virtual community imagined as a shared conversation with the Falstaff that we love—which is to say, despite the medium in which Morgann works, "the *Stage Falstaff*." Through reading the *Essay on the Dramatic Character of Sir John Falstaff*, readers can enter into "possession of the whole man, and [be] ready to hug him, guts, lyes and all, as an inexhaustible fund of pleasantry and humor" (195). Hence, it would seem, the best way in which to share and further disseminate "the *Stage Falstaff*" is not, as one might expect, to set about staging those "hundred Plays" but rather to read and write "Experiments" (144) like Morgann's and thereby take advantage of the ways in which the placeless omnipresence of print can enable additional "conversations" with one's favorite companion. The virtual community of friends of "*Old Jack*" is thus constructed not only through habitual attendance at the theater but also (and perhaps even more importantly) through the invention and printed dissemination of further adventures for him, a practice which, as we have seen, both relies upon and contributes to the collective sense of Falstaff as a "distinct and separate subsistence" in whose "nature" "there is nothing perishable" (212–13).

One of Morgann's most ardent admirers was William Kenrick, whom we met briefly back in the Introduction. Kenrick hailed Morgann as "a very masterly critic," and while I am unaware of any evidence that Morgann ever returned the favor, the two men were certainly kindred spirits in their affection for Falstaff—and, by extension, for all those who might share their conception of him as first and foremost a jovial companion.[17] I would like, therefore, to return to Kenrick's delightful follow-up to *2 Henry IV*, *Falstaff's Wedding*, in order to take a more sustained look at how his practice as a reader both anticipates and complicates what Morgann would theorize more than two decades later.

Kenrick begins his preface to the 1760 version of the play by explaining that it was a closet drama "written in imitation of Shakespeare" some nine years before "when the author was young and giddy enough to amuse himself in a stuffed doublet, before a private audience, with an attempt at a personal representation of the humours of Sir John Falstaff."[18] The "striking excellencies of the character" left such "impressions" upon Kenrick that he felt compelled to compose the "present performance" as "a kind of poetical exercise" which might contribute "an hour's entertainment . . . concomitant with novelty" to the "reader of taste and judgment" who picked up his work (iv–vi). Despite these modest claims, however, Kenrick's text sprawls quite ambitiously across the gap between the close of *2 Henry IV* and the opening of *Henry V*. Consider only the basic contours of the plot: Scrope and Cambridge, the traitors discovered at the opening of *Henry V*, have devised a scheme to depose the newly crowned Hal and install Mortimer upon the throne (although Scrope, who is sleeping with Cambridge's wife, plans to betray both Cambridge and Mortimer in order to seize power for himself). They hire the banished Falstaff to assassinate the king at Southampton, where the English are assembling to invade France in the campaign that will culminate at Agincourt. Unbeknownst to them, Friar Paul, who serves as the guardian of Hal's sometime mistress, Eleanor Poins, has intercepted a letter from Cambridge to Scrope detailing their treachery and passed it on to the palace. Falstaff, who has been granted one final audience with Hal, confirms Friar Paul's account and betrays his would-be employers. And amid all this, as Kenrick's title suggests, Falstaff is scheming to marry Dame Ursula as a means of weaseling out of his £500 debt to her. As my summary should suggest, Kenrick presents what Garrick termed "Shakespeare's known characters" as nothing if not detachable into "a new performance."[19] It is not only Falstaff and Hal and their respective attendants who have migrated but also Shallow, Slender, and even the most minor of characters from *2 Henry IV*, such as Poins's "sister Nell" (2.2.109) or "old Mistress Ursula, whom I have weekly sworn to marry since I perceived the first white hair of my chin" (1.2.220–21), neither of whom manages to muster more than a single mention in the Shakespearean text. This is detachability with a vengeance. And as with Dorman and Morgann, the felt detachability of the characters seems to stem from their widespread dissemination, a dissemination which even reaches, Kenrick playfully suggests, to Eastcheap. One of Mistress Quickly's dunnings, for example, suggests considerable familiarity with Falstaff's sentiments concerning honor: "but then you know Sir John (no-body better) what honour is. It will buy neither coals nor candles; nor will my landlord take it for rent, nor the merchant for sack and sherry" (8). Now one could read this as simply a further fleshing out of Falstaff's life off-page: that is, the denunciation of honor which we get toward the close of *1 Henry IV* was but a rehearsing of ideas he had long held and no doubt expressed within Mistress Quickly's hearing. But the way in which Quickly's phrasing echoes that of Falstaff in its attempt to define honor through what it can accomplish—"Can honour set-to a leg? No. Or an arm? No. Or take away the grief of a wound? No" (5.1.130–33)—suggests the far more delicious possibility that Falstaff was so much "the idol of the English stage" and "ev'ry Body's Favourite," that even his Eastcheap companions have somehow either read or seen *1 Henry IV*.[20] If so, then surely his dissemination across the land of the living could go without saying. For Kenrick, it would seem, Falstaff has been so spread across the kingdom as to take on the placeless omnipresence of a figure like Sir Roger.

Of course, Kenrick's publication of *Falstaff's Wedding* did its part to extend Plump Jack's dissemination that much more. Kenrick's very choice of medium suggests that further adventures for Falstaff, despite his theatrical roots, might be best rendered through print. After all, he insists that *Falstaff's Wedding*, notwithstanding its origins in private performance and its dedication "to Mr. Quin, in return for the frequent pleasure received, by his representation of Sir John Falstaff" was nonetheless "never planned nor intended" for the stage (v). Now this may simply have been his making a virtue out of a necessity. Kenrick certainly complained in later life that Garrick tried to block *Falstaff's Wedding* from ever being staged (it was produced only once in Kenrick's lifetime, as a 1766 benefit for James Love). In *Love in the Suds*, for example, "Roscius" (a clear stand-in for Garrick) curses Kenrick: "Ne'er shall his Falstaff come again to life / . . . Ne'er will I court again his stubborn Muse, / But for a pageant would his play refuse. / While puff and pantomime will gull the town, / 'Tis good to keep o'erweening merit down."[21] But sour grapes or not, there does seem to be a certain logic both in Garrick's insistence that "I must be free enough to declare, that I could not venture to bring so many of Shakespeare's known characters upon the stage in a new performance" and in the decision to print that Garrick's rejection apparently forced.[22] That is, like Morgann, Kenrick presents a "stage Falstaff" who flourishes best in printed "poetical exercises." Hence even as we get further adventures which insist upon Falstaff's "guts, lyes and all"—act 2, scene 9 is nothing but an over-the-top description of how Falstaff's belly fared at the hands of a jeering mob—we are nonetheless unable to actually see Falstaff "wire-drawn between two stone-walls, as if they meant to make chitterlings of me" (30) or hear his response to an insolent "dried-eel's-skin of a fishmonger [who] ask'd me how I could complain of the crowd: 'Is a porpoise ill at ease . . . amidst a glut of sprats and herrings?'" (31). Rather, such scenes must be imagined and so can be readily made to conform to one's preexisting conception of Falstaff without any need to worry about potential incompatibility with an actor's conception of this "new performance." In short, for the purposes of character migration, the disembodiment of print offered more opportunities for the "stage Falstaff" than the competing embodiments of the theater.[23]

Kenrick meditates upon the implications of this seeming paradox in the most appropriate genre imaginable: the prologue and epilogue to the 1766 version of *Falstaff's Wedding* (the one which had been staged for James Love's benefit). Prologues and epilogues are, of course, the most ephemeral of all theatrical genres—because they would be abandoned after, at most, the first nine nights of a production. Yet they achieved an unusually enduring afterlife in print, being reprinted more or less verbatim in each successive edition of a play, even as the playtext itself was often revised to bring it into accordance with current performance practice. Hence the prologue and epilogue for a play that was staged only once within its author's lifetime, but which was repeatedly reissued "as it is acted," neatly recapitulate in their very genre Kenrick's argument that theatrical characters migrate best not into other performances but into print.

Kenrick's prologue turns upon the conceit that the audience is a jury empanelled to hear his trial for forging Shakespeare's signature on a writ which released "certain choice spirits, in theatrick shape" from Elysium, "the chief" of whom were Falstaff, Pistol, Dol Tearsheet, "the Widow Quickly," "Bardolph, Peto, Nym, and—several more; / link'd in a gang, each cut-purse with his crony, / All arrant thieves and Dramatis personae." According to Mercury, who serves as prosecutor, Kenrick's crimes extend beyond merely forging the writ to somehow unlawfully appropriating Shakespeare's characters: "poets having an exclusive right / To bring their mental progeny to light, / This right's invaded by the party peach'd; / Who *vi et armis,* hath th' old bard o'er-reach'd; / . . . With base design t'adopt them for his own, / Tho' Shakespeare's property, and his alone." By Mercury's reckoning, characters possess lives off-page, but our access to those lives lies wholly at the pleasure of their originary author. He alone has the right to disturb their Elysian pursuits; for anyone else to do so would constitute plagiarism and so would necessarily "prostitute to shame / Th' aforesaid Shakespeare's honour, name and fame." Literary characters, in this vision, are participants in an economy of scarcity, in which Kenrick's gain requires Shakespeare's loss.

The epilogue counters these charges in large part by denying their very validity. First off, Dame Ursula reminds her audience that her counterpart in the prologue "was no more Mercury, than I am / Queen Hecuba, the wife of Trojan Priam. / A messenger from Phoebus! He a god! / I can assure you all, 'Twas Mr. Dodd: / His dropping from the clouds, was all a sham; / And his pretended errand but a flam." Disbelief, it would seem, should not be too readily suspended when one is at the theater. It is worth keeping in mind as one watches a play that the assorted "heathen gods" who get trotted out are but "paste-board, made to fly / On hempen cords across the painted sky." All of this begs the question, of course, why the theater's use of "sham" gods descending from "canvas clouds" should render illegitimate the charges of forgery and plagiarism made out in the prologue. The answer seems to lie in the peculiarly appropriate intersection between James William Dodd's "flam" as Mercury and his "tale" which "tho' told so glib; . . . 'twas all a fib." That is, far from existing in an Elysian economy of scarcity, Falstaff and his crew

> dwell not with saints above, nor devils below:
> But, form'd th' imagination to engage,
> During their short-liv'd passage o'er the stage,
> As mere ideal characters exist,
> And stand as cyphers mark'd on Nature's list;
> To genius given a delegated power
> To form these transient beings of an hour;

Which, from this mimick world, when'er they go,
Are free to range in fancy's pimlico:
A limbo large and broad; which in the schools
Is call'd by some the Paradise of Fools.
Ferae naturae there, their preservation
Is purchas'd by no game association:
The poaching plagiary alone denied
A privilege, granted to each bard beside;
Who' tho' a cottager, to try his skill,
May shoot, or course, or hunt them down at will;
In his own paddock may the strays receive,
And scorn to ask a lordly owner's leave.

For such an ephemeral document, Kenrick's epilogue is extraordinarily rich in its implications for the study of character migration. Let us then take his points in turn, so as not to lose them amid the metaphorical tangle. First off, Dame Ursula insists that the lives of literary characters do extend off-page, but those lives are not lived "above" or "below" or in Elysium, but rather in "fancy's pimlico." Pinning down the location of the afterlife of characters is important to Kenrick because it enables him to refute the charge of plagiarism by denying its very possibility. That is, plagiarism might be an appropriate charge for someone with "base design t'adopt" Shakespeare's characters "for his own" if such characters really operated within an economy of scarcity. Elysium could be such an economy because it (like the Heaven and Hell presumably signaled by "above" and "below") involves bodily resurrection. If Falstaff is in Elysium, then he cannot at the same time be in Eastcheap. His movements are governed by all the usual laws of physics and so it makes sense to imagine him as a counter in a zero-sum game. If, however, Falstaff exists as a "mere ideal character," a "cypher . . . mark'd on Nature's list," then it becomes impossible for him to be expropriated and so for any charge of plagiarism to be sustained. Plagiarism is etymologically linked to kidnapping and one cannot kidnap a cypher.

Mercury's mistake, it would seem, was to imagine that the off-stage lives of Falstaff and his crew were governed by the same kinds of embodiment and scarcity as their on-stage lives. The epilogue argues that, quite to the contrary, whenever Falstaff and his friends are off-stage, they revert to an immateriality which gives them the freedom to "range in fancy's pimlico" as "*ferae naturae*" (beasts wild by nature and so incapable of becoming the objects of absolute property). While there they are no more capable of being monopolized by individual authors than *ferae naturae* were subject to the more than qualified control of a "game association," much less an individual landowner.[24] The force of this comparison is to suggest that literary characters are best regarded as legally akin to *ferae naturae* upon the commons, against which each "cottager" may "try his skill" in shooting, coursing, hunting, or enclosing within "his own paddock" without ever having "to ask a lordly owner's leave." That is, "each bard" may use the *ferae naturae* he catches as he or she sees fit, so long as he or she acknowledges their Shakespearean origin, and does not claim sole proprietorship as a "poaching plagiary" would do. Yet unlike the actual commons where scarcity and exhaustibility prevail, the textual commons of "mere ideal characters" can never be exhausted. "Each bard" may participate in the "universal promiscuous enjoyment" without ever diminishing the resources available to his or her fellow cottagers, thus giving the lie to Falstaff's own assertion that "I cannot last ever. . . . it was alway yet the trick of our English nation, if they have a good thing, to make it too common" (*2 Henry IV*, 1.2.194–96).[25] Accordingly, the game laws (and by implication the laws of literary property) do not apply, not only because dramatic characters are *ferae naturae* but also because there is no scarcity in "fancy's pimlico" and therefore no property in the ordinary sense.[26]

What sort of place can "fancy's pimlico" be, given the inexhaustibility and commonness of its inhabitants? Kenrick does not make it wholly clear, but it would seem that, like the actual Pimlico, it somehow combines the sociable pleasures of a pleasure garden with the sense of community attributed to the fast-disappearing (and increasingly idealized) village common upon which cottagers could graze their sheep and hunt *ferae naturae* for their dinners. Pimlico, like a number of outlying London suburbs in this period, offered an intriguing blend of the urban and the semi-rural (see Figure 3). On one hand, in 1762 "when the nearby Buckingham House [was] sold to George III, . . . much of the area was [still] taken up with osier beds, market gardens, and waste land" of the sort that often lay common.[27] Yet on the other hand, Pimlico was just down the road from Ranelagh and home to several taverns and pleasure gardens, most notably the Star and Garter (which offered "displays of fireworks and horsemanship") and Jenny's Whim. The latter "possessed, in addition to the usual bowers, alcoves and prim flowerbeds, a bowling-green, a grotto, a cock-pit and a ducking pond," not to mention "mechanical devices," including statues of Harlequin and the prophetess Mother Shipton, which "started up in the recesses of the garden when an unsuspected spring was trodden upon." There were also "huge fish and mermaids" which "rose at intervals from the water of the pond."[28] Extrapolating from this, it would seem that "fancy's pimlico" would function as a virtual equivalent to the actual Pimlico, offering an imaginary space wherein "bards" could not only receive stray characters into their own paddocks but also derive a sense of commonality and kinship from the knowledge that their fellow bards were doing the same. Like cottagers, they could make their own individual resources go further through the shared use of the commons than if they each confined themselves to what their own holdings afforded (that is, they could accomplish more with Falstaff and his crew than if they had to limit themselves to devising adventures for characters of their own invention). Yet, at the same time, like the habitués of Jenny's Whim, they could each focus upon the particular pleasures (or aspects of a character) of most specific interest to them, while still enjoying the frisson provided by the imagined throng milling about them. "Fancy's pimlico" is thus an instance, albeit a peculiarly spatialized one, of the widely held eighteenth-century fantasy of a republic of letters in which literary and class *ressentiment* might be suspended or even abolished through the collective experience of reading the same text. So long as readers are each "try[ing]" their skill upon a textual

Figure 3. Pimlico in the mid-eighteenth century. Courtesy of the Guildhall Library, Corporation of London.

common, they can all be imagined as "cottagers" coexisting in georgic tranquillity or fellow visitors to a place like Jenny's Whim, which at "its prime . . . seems to have been the resort of all classes"—from "the lower sort of people" on up to aristocrats like Lord Granby and Lady Fitzroy.[29] As a figure for the sort of virtual community-through-parallel-play that character migration enables, "fancy's pimlico" is evocative indeed.

It is also deeply appropriate, of course, that Kenrick should invoke the suburbs of imagination as justification for his "bring[ing] so many of Shakespeare's known characters" into "a new performance," as the Falstaff plays first achieved their social canonicity through repertory performance in the actual suburbs of London, where the pre-1642 theaters were housed. It was largely through these performances that Plump Jack came to be regarded as a figure sprawling enough for the *Shakspere Allusion-Book* to alter its usual procedures and catalog early seventeenth-century mentions of him separately: "for the purpose of this index Falstaff is treated as a work."[30] Yet, as Michael Dobson has shown, the consequence of all of these performances was that by Pepys's time the plays "belonged to the theatre more significantly than they belonged to Shakespeare."[31] From the very beginning, it would seem, social canonicity for the plays was curiously detached from their author's authority. As a name, Shakespeare would often receive quite extravagant obeisance, even as the work which supposedly guaranteed that name was regarded as but another constituent of our "Principal Old Stock Plays."[32]

Perhaps unsurprisingly, we can see a similar pattern of deference combined with a thorough undercutting of Shakespeare's authority in a "poetical exercise" like *Falstaff's Wedding*. To return to the plot of the 1760 version, for example, we can see how it offers up an explanation for one of the principal puzzles of *Henry V*: namely, how the king came to know of the plot against him. Shakespeare's text only asserts that "the King hath note of all that they intend, / By interception which they dream not of" (2.2.6–7); Kenrick's play specifies how that interception came about and attributes it to the quick wit and loyalty of Friar Paul and Falstaff, rather than the mysterious omniscience of kingship. *Falstaff's Wedding* thus affirms the veracity of *Henry V* (it remains true that Scrope "dream[s] not of" Falstaff's and Friar Paul's interventions), but at the cost of Shakespeare's authority. Shakespeare may well be correct in his chronicling of Hal's first weeks on the throne, but he has inexplicably failed to give proper credit for the preservation of the throne and in so doing has misrepresented the extent of Falstaff's "distinct and separate subsistence." As befits a "Historic Being," Falstaff's life goes on, despite the (admittedly ambivalent) efforts at the close of *2 Henry IV* to push him off-stage toward banishment, imprisonment, or death. Thus even as Dame Ursula, speaking on behalf of Kenrick in the epilogue, "begs leave submissively to say, / None more than he reveres great Shakespeare's name, / Or glows with zeal to vindicate his fame," the play nonetheless insists upon the ways in which Shakespeare's characters outstrip authorial control. As a result, Shakespeare's canonization is curiously divorced from the work which supposedly proves his greatness in the first place. It is in their migration to a non-Shakespearean "new performance" that "Shakespeare's known characters" most demonstrate the centrality and social value of Shakespeare's known plays. It is in their detachability, that is, that they most show their social canonicity.

* * *

Kenrick's insistence that he is demonstrating his reverence for Shakespeare through *Falstaff's Wedding* might seem a case of special pleading, were it not for the fact that once one starts to look for detachability in eighteenth-century discussions of literary character, it becomes nigh impossible to find instances which do not presume or comment upon its linkage to social canonicity. Put bluntly, any text from which a character migrates is likely to be, or be on the way toward becoming, a socially canonical text, not only because such texts are more attractive to readers so inclined but also (and just as importantly) because character migration exaggerates and so reveals the ways in which the processes of social canonization rely upon the same ontological paradoxes engendered by widespread dissemination as character migration itself. That is, the more material manifestations a text took, the less it was regarded as immanent in any particular manifestation, and hence the less it was constrained by that manifestation's necessary limitations. In other words, the more a text was disseminated (both in terms of number and variety of formats), the more potentially detachable its characters could seem. Social canonicity was thus, for many eighteenth-century readers, intimately intertwined with felt detachability—even when it never resulted in character migration.

Perhaps the best way into this puzzling state of affairs is first to examine the analogous world of reproductive prints, a world which, not surprisingly given its importance to print culture more generally, weighed heavily on the minds of many eighteenth-century readers. In an intriguing extension of Walter Benjamin's analysis of "The Work of Art in the Age of Mechanical Reproduction," John Brewer has argued that reproductive prints of Old

Master paintings "simultaneously debased the original image by increasing its circulation and enhanced its value by suggesting its uniqueness."[33] The alleged uniqueness to which he refers was largely a product of the discourse surrounding reproductive prints, a discourse which focused upon all of the qualities in the original paintings or drawings which could not be adequately reproduced, such as the texture of brushstrokes, the color of particular pigments, or "the *freedom* of the *manner.*"[34] In other words, as Hillel Schwartz shrewdly puts it, "it is within an exuberant world of copies that we arrive at our experience of originality."[35] Yet at the same time as the original was being debased and enhanced as a material artifact, the image which it bore often took on an allographic life of its own. That is, as a result of reproduction, especially widespread reproduction, a gap could open up between the image qua image and any particular manifestation it might take, including the original. Thus, for example, widely reproduced images like the Raphael cartoons at Hampton Court or Richard Wilson's *Niobe* (engravings of which sold 8,000 copies in their first year) took on a ghostly kind of existence apart from or at the interstices between their assorted manifestations, each of which could then potentially offer equal access to the image as image.[36] Indeed, for certain images, like Angelica Kauffmann's *Maria,* the original painting seemed to have been almost forgotten amid the flurry of reproductions. What remained—and what was important—was the image which "circulated all over Europe. In the elegant manufactures of London, Birmingham, etc., it assumed an incalculable variety of forms and dimensions, and was transferred to numerous articles of all sorts and sizes, from a watch case to a tea-waiter."[37] In the words of one observer, then, the appeal of reproductions was that they could "give us an Idea, and, as it were, the Possession of an infinite Number of Pictures, which it would require an immense Sum to purchase, and many of which cannot be purchased."[38] "Cosmetti" concurred with this sentiment, claiming that through reproductions, "fine pictures . . . may be circulated all over the world. This must give great satisfaction to the curious, who cannot afford to purchase fine pictures, and many others that would but cannot purchase them."[39] For these viewers, at least, actual possession of a painted canvas was largely beside the point, so long as one had access to its image. Reproduction, in other words, releases images from an economy of scarcity—where paintings sometimes cannot be had even by those with the means and desire to purchase them—in order to allow them to circulate in an economy of abundance, in which "the curious" have ready access to the images which catch their fancy. Yet at the same time, reproduction enhances the felt value of those images by including them in the "canon of great art," a canon which, as Brewer points out, was "largely shaped by what works were available in reproduction": "Raphael was 'divine' before engravings of his work were published after Dorigny, but he was more frequently invoked as *the* great artist thereafter" (460). If the logic here seems a bit circular, that is because it is: reproduction and social canonicity are locked into a feedback loop in which each reinforces the other.

I would like to suggest that a process somewhat analogous to what I have just been describing with respect to prints took place in the mid-eighteenth century with the increased printing and dissemination of certain key vernacular texts, most notably the boom in reprints of Shakespeare which began in the mid-1730s. As the result of a copyright dispute in 1734–35, for example, the entire Shakespearean canon suddenly became available in competing editions for far less than ever before, with the price of the entire oeuvre dropping almost sevenfold. The result, as Robert Hume has argued, was that "very abruptly, not only were all the plays within the reach of virtually any would-be buyer, but something like original texts were readily available to anyone," which "must have been a crucial factor in making Shakespeare much more widely and more truly known."[40] As even a glance at the English Short Title Catalog will reveal, similar competing editions and reprints were produced for almost every socially canonical text in the period, some by rival booksellers and some by the copyright holder seeking to offer his wares at multiple price points. This proliferation of editions and reprints, especially when set against the backdrop of the overall slump in British publishing in the second quarter of the eighteenth century, helped to ensure that the texts which they contained would seem more significant than previously thought, for, as Elizabeth Eisenstein has argued, a reader's sense of the familiar and notable is really a sense of what he or she keeps running into: "the more frequent . . . the encounter with the identical version . . . the deeper the impression it will leave."[41]

On its own, this point is hardly novel. John Guillory has been insisting for more than a decade that reproduction, what he calls the "continual reintroduction" of a work "to generations of readers," has always been a necessary if not sufficient part of canon formation.[42] What has gone less appreciated, though, is how the fact of multiple and competing reproductions could make the texts in question (and the characters which they contained) seem less tied to any particular manifestation they might take. Consider only the ways in which both sides of the literary property debate agreed upon the fundamental immateriality of the text, especially the socially canonical steady sellers which were at contest in most of the key lawsuits. For the advocates of perpetual copyright, like William Blackstone, "the identity of a literary composition consists intirely in the *sentiment* and the *language;* the same conceptions, clothed in the same words, must necessarily be the same composition; and whatever method [the author] takes of conveying that composition to the ear or eye of another, by recital, by writing, or by printing, in any number of copies, or at any period of time, it is always the identical work of the author which is so conveyed." The champions of limited, statutory copyright strenuously denied the conclusion which Blackstone drew from this assertion of a text's continuity across its manifestations—namely, that "no other man can have a right to convey, or transfer it, without [the author's] consent," regardless of how much time has transpired since its initial publication—but they readily concurred with his definition of a text's transmedial identity as stemming from its immateriality.[43] Indeed, they pointed to that very immateriality as evidence for the impossibility of an author's having a common-law right to his text as property: if texts are not coincident with their tangible material manifestations, then they can be, at best, "*quasi* property," since "*property* in a strict sense can no more be conceived without a *corpus,* than a parent can be conceived without a child."[44]

For many readers, then, Shakespeare was Shakespeare, regardless of whether one read him in the First Folio, an old quarto, a recent edition done by a prominent scholar or poet, or a cheap edition published in parts. This is not to deny that readers were often keenly aware of the differing claims being made for each edition; it is only to suggest that despite the widely followed public wrangling over the choices made by specific editors, readers seem to have felt that what they were getting *was* Shakespeare (or Swift or whoever else was the author in question). The canonical text, that is, was felt to transcend the specific forms taken by its myriad manifestations. Book collectors might prize certain volumes more than others; devotees of the theater might prefer plays published "as they are acted." But with rare exceptions, nonscholarly readers do not seem to have worried much about the inauthenticity of a given manifestation. As Stephen Orgel has shown,

> one of the most remarkable aspects of the theatrical medium is its ability to comprehend the widest variety of versions of a dramatic text within the concept of a single play. Davenant and Dryden's *Tempest* doesn't look much like *The Tempest* of the folio: it has a male ingenue parallel to Miranda named Hippolito, a young man who has never seen a woman; Miranda has been supplied with a sister, Dorinda; Sycorax has become Caliban's sister; Ariel has a girlfriend named Milcha; and only about a third of the dialogue bears any relation to the original text at all. This . . . was the standard performing version of *The Tempest* until 1832, and—despite howls of protest

from Gildon to Hazlitt—both it and the scholarly text on the bookshelf of every literate household were Shakespeare's *Tempest.*[45]

Nor was this capacious definition of the text something exclusive for Shakespeare. Peter Holland has argued that Restoration readers and theatergoers conceived "of the play as [a] separable entity . . . outside of the modes by which it was perceived."[46] Part of the burden of this chapter is to demonstrate how both Orgel's and Holland's observations are ultimately too modest: that is, it was not only plays which could be conceived of "separable entit[ies]," but socially canonical texts and characters more generally.

Here, obviously, the analogy between printed texts and reproductive prints falters. As Brewer points out, one of the consequences of the proliferation of prints was an emphasis by connoisseurs upon the unique materiality of the original painting, the ways in which it differed from (and was supposedly superior to) any of the other manifestations which that image might take. With printed texts, however, the primary outcome of increased reprinting and dissemination was an emphasis on the text's felt immateriality, the ways in which it transcended the necessary limitations and materiality of any given manifestation and so came off as fundamentally detachable. Indeed, where reproductive prints bestowed an "aura" upon their original as a unique material object worthy of preservation (or even veneration), printed books offered themselves as interchangeable and potentially superior surrogates for the original manuscript. To understand this difference in value, one needs only recall the typical printing-house practice of selling authorial foul papers to the rag man once type had been set. This would never have been done with a painting, even when, as with Hogarth's progresses, the painting was mostly an occasion for the engraving of reproductive prints. Thus, if anything, the allographic life of its own which a text could take on could exceed that of an image, which was still at least notionally tied to its material original.

Not surprisingly, given the logic of the feedback loop which characterizes so many of the phenomena we have been investigating, this gap between a text and its particular bibliographic manifestations only widened as the manifestations multiplied. The more disseminated and socially canonical a text became, the less sacrality any particular manifestation possessed. This helps to explain why Charles Lamb—in so many ways a citizen of the eighteenth century—could so confidently insist that "the possession" of a copy of Shakespeare or Milton "confers no distinction. The exterior of them (the things themselves being so common) . . . raises no sweet emotions, no tickling sense of property in the owner." This means that "in some respects, the better a book is, the less it demands from binding. Fielding, Smollet, Sterne, and all that class of perpetually self-reproductive volumes—Great Nature's Stereotypes—we see them individually perish with less regret, because we know the copies of them to be 'eterne.'"[47] That is, unlike "Banquo and his Fleance," in whom "nature's copy's not eterne" (*Macbeth,* 3.2.38–39), socially canonical texts cannot be murdered and so the loss of any particular copy is a matter for passing regret, not lasting lamentation. Like the cyphers in fancy's pimlico, the invulnerability of "Great Nature's Stereotypes" lies in their immateriality, which in turn stems from their widespread dissemination and testifies to their social canonicity (these are, after all, the "better" books).

But, of course, not all older texts nor all widely reproduced texts achieved social canonicity. Not everything old is revered, nor is everything widely disseminated held to be of lasting value (one need only remember the perennial jokes in the period concerning the ways in which the expansion of print culture had merely resulted in a proliferation of wastepaper). Thus even if social canonicity is in part a function of a text's being a "perpetually self-reproductive volume," reproduction and dissemination are not sufficient in themselves to render a text canonical. Plenty of schoolbooks and devotional works, such as *The Whole Duty of Man,* were reprinted in far greater numbers than any of the texts ever considered part of the vernacular canon. And, of course, most newspapers were produced and distributed in print runs that booksellers could only dream of, yet their appeal went hand-in-hand with their ephemerality. What sets the social canon apart—and so makes its characters likely candidates for migration—is the *kind* of reproduction its texts undergo, namely, a reproduction which emphasizes (or at least does not try to hide) the play of variation between versions: reproduction with a difference, so to speak.

It should shock no one at this point in my argument that the texts which constituted the social canon were also those which were most readily available in a host of different, and differing, reproductions. Indeed, it is hard to imagine how it could be otherwise. As Jonathan Miller has pointed out, mere replication does little in itself to canonize a work: "it is precisely because subsequent performances of Shakespeare's plays are interpretations, rather than copies [of the Elizabethan premiere], that they have survived."[48] This is because the production of straightforward facsimiles, whether on stage or in print, does not offer individual actors, viewers, or readers much of an opportunity to make a text or character their own. Obviously all copies differ from one another, if only by virtue of their sequence in the history of copying: "iteration alters, something new takes place."[49] But surely some iterations are newer than others and the difference seems lie in how ostentatiously they strive for "authentic" replication versus how many opportunities they extend for individual appropriation.[50] Without such opportunities, of course, it is almost impossible for a text or character to seem as if it belongs to all of us. To revert to Charles Churchill's terms, the very imaginability of something as "public property" depends upon its seeming somehow already "yours" and "mine." This helps to explain why readers like Kenrick and Lamb should, amid their fantasies of the textual commons, still insist upon the importance of individual ownership of books. Remember that Kenrick's cottagers still held their "own paddock[s]," despite the commonality of "fancy's pimlico." Similarly, even though Lamb argues that "the possession of [a Shakespeare] confers no distinction . . . the things themselves being so common," his understanding of their commonness depends upon each copy's having a different material history: "the sullied leaves and worn out appearance, nay, the very odour" of a particular volume can conjure up its former readers and so invoke "a community of feeling with my countrymen," a community whose sole link to one another is their shared reading of "those editions . . . which have been oftenest tumbled about and handled" (196–97). For both Kenrick and Lamb, then, the postulated commonness of the canonical text hinges upon an understanding that countless individual readers have already busied themselves hunting *ferae naturae* or handling their books in a fashion peculiar to them.

The felt publicity of the text, that is, stems from a reader's sense that there are other readers out there who are similarly laying claim to it and so collectively denying the possibility of sole proprietorship. Hence, even though, as I suggested earlier, most nonprofessional readers did not seem to worry much about the inauthenticity of a given manifestation—Shakespeare was Shakespeare—the mere fact that so many accusations of inauthenticity were tossed back and forth in the period helped to create the sense that if the text in question was the subject of multiple and potentially competing claims, then it was probably of value. It is in this way, I think, that we can best understand the cultural work being done by the incessant squabbling over the worth of various editions and reprints. Even as a bookseller was denouncing the wares of his rival as full of "Innumerable Errors" (or an editor was condemning his predecessors as philological dolts), he was nonetheless underscoring the worth of the text over which they were fighting.[51] The more claimants upon a text there were, the more attractive to readers it was likely to seem, if only because the sheer number of claimants would ensure that the text in question would feel common and detachable and so useable for one's own ends. Thus the very phenomenon about which a writer for *The Grub-Street Journal* complains—the arrogant encroachment of editors upon authors—helped to undo itself through the very proliferation of competing encroachments: one need not really worry that "it is no longer Bentley at the Tail of Horace, or Theobald at the Tail of Shakespear; but, as if the authors works were become their properties, they respectfully call them Bentley's *Horace*, or Theobald's *Shakespear*" if the market also contains Rowe's Shakespeare and Pope's Shakespeare and (within the next few decades) Sir Thomas Hanmer's Shakespeare, William Warburton's Shakespeare, Samuel Johnson's Shakespeare, and so on, not to mention the innumerable reprints which went without attribution.[52] As *The Monthly Review* put it, "the multiplicity of editions which his plays have undergone, in a few years" only underscores the "high esteem in which the writings of Shakespeare are held."[53] The result of such multiplicity, as Jonathan Bate has argued, is that every citation of a canonical text (which, of course, includes every claim made upon it) causes that text to take on "more of a force in the culture at large. And with each appropriation it becomes more difficult to occlude the 'afterlife' and recover the 'original.' The 'truth' of Shakespeare [and, I would add, his value] thus comes to reside in the very multiplicity of his manifestations."[54] Social canonicity, then, not only relies upon the widespread dissemination and felt detachability we have been examining, it also depends upon a perceived "multiplicity" which nonetheless reaffirms a text or character's essential cohesiveness. It relies, that is, upon reproduction with a difference.

It is in this context, I believe, that we best see how the deeply eccentric practice of character migration can nonetheless bring to light a far more widely held, yet rarely articulated conception of social canonicity as reproduction with a difference, for what is character migration, if not reproduction with a difference par excellence? Kenrick's Falstaff differs more from the Falstaff of the First Folio than any of the Falstaffs invented by Shakespeare's commentators, yet, for all that, he is still indisputably recognizable as a citation of the Shakespearean Falstaff and so contributes in the same way to Plump Jack's dissemination across the culture and beyond. Similarly, the Sir Roger de Coverly who stars in Dorman's playlet is hardly a facsimile of the Tory squire introduced in the second number of *The Spectator*, but he is nonetheless sufficiently identifiable as a version of that Sir Roger that he can enhance the squire's felt detachability that much more. And, while I have been unable to trace a copy, I would hazard a guess that William Dodd's

Sir Roger de Coverly (concerning which Arthur Murphy was consulted just a few months before Dodd's execution for forgery) would have had much the same effect upon its readers' sense of Sir Roger.[55] Character migration, one might say, not only speaks the unspoken presumptions surrounding social canonicity, it turns them up to eleven.

Indeed, I would like to propose that the ease with which characters could be imagined as detachable came to serve as a tacit criterion for social canonicity. Consider only the terms upon which Corbyn Morris takes up the by then century-old comparison of Ben Jonson to Shakespeare: "*Johnson* excellently concerts his Plots, and all his Characters unite in the one Design. *Shakespear* is superior to such Aid or Restraint; His Characters continually sallying from one independent Scene to another, and charming you in each with fresh Wit and Humour."[56] Proclaiming Shakespeare's superiority to Jonson was nothing new in 1744, and neither was the dismissal of intricate plotting as inferior to wit and humour. What is striking about Morris's comparison, though, is his praise of Shakespearean characters as "continually sallying from one independent Scene to another." Morris's choice of verbs suggests that not only are Shakespeare's scenes "independent" of plot, his characters are too. And if they can sally from scene to scene, then there is no obvious reason why they cannot migrate out of Shakespeare's scenes altogether. After all, Morris implies that his conception of Falstaff parts company with Shakespeare's: his account, while "chiefly extracted from . . . [the] 1st Part of King *Henry* the *Fourth*" omits those sinkings "into a *Cheat* or a *Scoundrel*" which mar him in that play and which represent him "greatly below his true character" in *The Merry Wives of Windsor* (xxviii). Yet at the same time, he contends that "your Attention is all call'd forth" by Falstaff's incongruities, with the result that "you are eager to watch him to the End of his Adventures; Your Imagination pointing out with a full Scope his future Embarrassments" (26). It would seem, then, that for Morris, no less than for Morgann or Kenrick, there is no necessary "End" to Falstaff's "Adventures," since both his "true character" and his "future Embarrassments" are more the products of "Your Imagination" than anything in the Shakespearean text. That is, Falstaff is not only characterized by his felt detachability—the ways in which he exceeds all of his Shakespearean iterations—he is also the common object of a potentially unlimited number of individual imaginings, each of which may carry with it a different sense of his "true character." As such, Morris's Falstaff seems remarkably reminiscent of Sir Roger-according-to-Dorman.

It should come as no surprise, then, that for Morris the true test of detachability (and implicitly social canonicity) was whether or not a character felt like an old friend. Morris appeals to his readers' memory of "that peculiar Delight, without any *Alloy,* which we all feel and acknowledge in *Falstaff*'s Company" and which makes "it . . . impossible to avoid *loving* him" or "to be tired or unhappy in his Company" (29). This delight stems from Falstaff's possession of "*such chearful and amiable* Oddities *and* Foibles, *as you would chuse in your own* Companions *in* real Life. . . . it being certain, that *whoever cannot be endured as an* accidental *Companion in* real Life, *will never become, for the very same Reasons, a* favorite comic Character *in the Theatre*" (30–31). Similarly, "you would be fond of Sir *Roger*'s Acquaintance and Company in *real Life,* as he is a Gentleman of *Quality* and *Virtue;* You love and admire him in the *Spectators* for the *same* Reasons; And for these also he would become, if he were rightly exhibited, a *favourite* Character in the *Theatre*" (32).[57] What is intriguingly obscured by Morris's repeated comparisons between beloved characters and "Companions *in* real Life" is, of course, the fact that characters are not inherently detachable "historic beings" but rather have their detachability and "true character" thrust upon them. That is, the "peculiar Delight . . . which we all feel and acknowledge in *Falstaff*'s Company" stems not so much from the "Oddities and Foibles" with which he first appears as from the "future Embarrassments" which individual readers can imagine for him and in so doing both adapt him to their own particular tastes and make him feel that much more detachable. Falstaff's appeal as a companion thus derives from the ways in which the "future Embarrassments" "your Imagination" invents for him can become self-fulfilling prophecies: "all the while as you accompany him forwards, he *heightens* your Relish for his future Disasters . . . so that at last when he falls into a Scrape, your Expectation is exquisitely gratify'd," which in turn "excites you the more to *renew* the Chace . . . thus yielding a perpetual *Round* of Sport and Diversion" (26–27).

Yet, as my extensive quotations have probably made clear, all this is being couched as a description of the practices of an indefinite "you." How do we get from the "you" who envisions Falstaff's "future Embarrassments" to the "we" who take pleasure "in Falstaff's Company"? How, in short, does the felt detachability of a character result in a virtual community forming around him? Morris obliquely suggests an answer to this puzzle in his argument that Don Quijote should be regarded as more than a burlesque buffoon: "you yourself, if he existed in real Life, would be fond of his Company at your own Table; which proves him, upon the whole to be an amiable Character; —— It is therefore no wonder that Signior *Don Quixote of La Mancha* has been so courteously receiv'd in every Country of *Europe*" (40). Morris's logic is slippery here—that dash is doing a lot of work—but it seems to go something like this: if "you" are fond of Don Quijote (or Falstaff or Sir Roger) after you have made him over to your taste and yet you see that others "in every Country in Europe" are similarly fond of him, then it only stands to reason that they must be somehow like you. Accordingly, all those who are fond of Don Quijote have a connection to one another which is triangulated through their mutual friend. Thus a virtual community forms around Don Quijote which in turn reaffirms his status as "an amiable Character" worthy of "our" friendship and the courteous reception which he has received. The proof of Don Quijote's social canonicity is thus to be found in the existence of a virtual community of those who are "fond of his Company."

This logic, such as it is, explains why it is not merely Quin's masterful performance of Falstaff which makes Samuel Foote claim that if, after seeing Quin, a spectator "does not express his Desire of spending an Evening with that merry Mortal, why, I would not spend one with him, if he would pay my Reckoning."[58] Rather, the very possibility of envisioning that evening stems from the ways in which Falstaff seems to possess an existence independent not only of Shakespeare but also of Quin or any other particular manifestation. A midcentury conjurer of "*Shakespeare*'s Ghost" suggests as much in his very grammar when he implores his audience to "let the true Falstaff give you mirth in Quin."[59] And as Foote's phrasing should suggest, the desirability with which one views the prospect of an evening with Falstaff could serve as a test of one's fitness to join a virtual community of his friends. Falstaff would then, of course, serve as the social glue binding its potentially disparate members into the "we" who Arthur Murphy asserts "love him, in Spight of his degrading Foibles, for his enlivened Humour and his companionable Qualities."[60] Indeed, on occasion, Falstaff's sheer companionability could transform a virtual community into actual, embodied sociability. Consider only Boswell's telling example of "a club in London at the Boar's Head in East-cheap, the very Tavern where Falstaff and his joyous Companions met; and the members of it all assume Shakespeare's characters. One is Falstaff, another Prince Henry, another Bardolph, and so on."[61] Boswell's account is sketchy, but I think we can safely conjecture that each future member of the club started out by regarding himself as a "joyous Companion" of Falstaff in a virtual space akin to "fancy's pimlico." It is unclear whether the club members were already drinking buddies, who fortuitously discovered their shared love for Shakespeare's "irregular humourists," or whether that discovery led to the formation of the club. Either way, however, their decision to pool their talents in the form of loose reenactments of the Eastcheap scenes testifies in its own peculiarly appropriate way to Falstaff's social canonicity. After all, what other fifteenth-century figure had a drinking club devoted to him more than three centuries later?

To return to the point with which we began, then, the reason why Morris finds Shakespeare superior to Jonson seems to hinge upon the greater availability of a virtual community of fellow friends of Falstaff. "After you have been *gratify'd* with [the] *Detection* and *Punishment*" of Jonson's characters, Morris claims, "you are quite tired and disgusted with their Company" (30). Shakespeare, on the other hand, "always supports his Characters in your *Favour*," never allowing them to grow tedious or despicable. Even the most Jonsonian of Shakespeare's characters, Ancient Pistol, "continues to threaten so well, that you are still desirous of his Company" (34). To revert to Morgann's terms, Jonson's characters must be considered as merely dramatic rather than historic beings, since, as a result of our fatigue and disgust, we do not have enough curiosity concerning their off-page lives to take pleasure in further imagining their company. Or, as Arthur Murphy puts it: "there is hardly any Thing in any of them, that would induce a Gentleman to spend an evening with them."[62] And in large part, we do not desire that evening because Jonson's characters do not sally forth from scene to scene; they do not seem "independent" or detachable. Felt detachability thus shapes the sense that readers had of what Samuel Johnson might have termed a character's "clubbability." And that sense in turn helped to determine his or her position in the social canon. For a reader like Morris, a character whose company is undesirable will necessarily be at best second rate, in much the same way as, for Foote, a highly successful and so potentially socially canonical figure like Captain Loveit from *Miss in her Teens* is ultimately doomed to ephemerality, since "I can't say I am fond of cultivating an Acquaintance with [Garrick's] Gentlemen" (45).

Foote's mention of Garrick in this context is strikingly prescient, for in many ways the reductio ad absurdum of social canonicity as felt detachability may be seen in Garrick's wildly successful afterpiece, *The Jubilee*. Written to capitalize upon (and recover the capital expended upon) the bicentennial celebration of Shakespeare's birth which Garrick helped organize, *The Jubilee* farcically depicts the reactions of various bumpkinish rustics and Irishmen to the emerging phenomenon of Bardolatry. Originally scheduled as the concluding triumph of the Jubilee in Stratford, but rained out, *The Jubilee* serves as a fitting emblem for a celebration which featured several other works by Garrick, but none by Shakespeare. After a series of misadventures which prevent the principal character, an Irish would-be wit, from ever seeing any of the Jubilee, Garrick's afterpiece concludes with a Pageant in which "the capital Characters of Shakespeare" parade across the stage for an hour and a half, while miming key scenes from their respective plays. Two prints published in *The Oxford Magazine* show the scene as it was intended for Stratford (Figures 4 and 5), while a third depicts the procession as actually done at Drury Lane (Figure 6).[63] While Garrick notes that "Every Scene in the different Plays represents some capital part of it in Action," the interactions between the various characters—including their singing two choruses written by Garrick and Isaac Bickerstaff (*pace* the engravings in *The Oxford Magazine,* these were the only words to leave their mouths)—suggest that far from merely serving as a pantomimic anthology, *The Jubilee* offers what Garrick had suggested ten years before "could not be venture[d]" with *Falstaff's Wedding:* namely, the "bring[ing] so many of Shakespeare's known characters upon the stage in a new performance."[64] Hence, depending on the night, audiences at Drury Lane could see either Benedick and Beatrice or Oberon and Titania dancing on the heels of the convicted Shylock, just as viewers of *The Oxford Magazine* engravings could see Slender quaking at the side of

Figure 4. The Procession as intended for the Stratford Jubilee, according to *The Oxford Magazine,* 1769. Courtesy of The Lewis Walpole Library, Yale University.

Caliban, while Tom o' Bedlam, Richard III, and Old Hamlet brought up the rear. One might even see two Pistols on stage at the same time (one parading downstage with the cast of *The Merry Wives of Windsor,* while the other was upstage being forced to eat Fluellen's leek). Kenrick, not surprisingly, was unimpressed and claimed that the extended dumb show was but the result of Garrick's own ineptitude : "when finding it difficult to make any of [the characters] speak with propriety, he contented himself with instructing them to bite their thumbs, screw up their mouths, and make faces at one another, to the great edification of the audience."[65] But Kenrick found himself in a distinct minority. According to the almost invariably candid prompter for Drury Lane, William Hopkins, "there never was an Entertainment produc'd that gave so much pleasure to all Degrees, Boxes, pit and Gallery."[66] Similarly, *The Town and Country Magazine* thought "the Pageant . . . gave universal satisfaction."[67] And the pleasure and camaraderie which the detachability of Shakespeare's characters could afford was sufficient, it would seem, to obviate the need for additional performance of the plays in which they initially appeared. For Garrick—and, according to *The St. James's Chronicle,* for "nine

Figure 5. A Continuation of the Procession as intended for the Stratford Jubilee, according to *The Oxford Magazine,* 1769. Courtesy of The Lewis Walpole Library, Yale University.

parts of every Audience" as well—felt detachability could serve as enough of an index to a text's social canonicity as to render further iteration of the text itself somewhat superfluous.[68]

* * *

Up until now, we have been investigating the ways in which character migration lays bare the importance of felt detachability to social canonicity. But detachability could also serve as a criterion for evaluating new works which were making a bid for canonicity. Hence, for example, Smollett's characters, along with those of Fielding and Sterne, were praised by *The Critical Review* as possessing the same kind of "independence" as Morris saw in Falstaff. The reviewer bemoans that most of "the poets of these days aim at nothing more than interesting the passions by the intricacy of their plots. . . . It is the

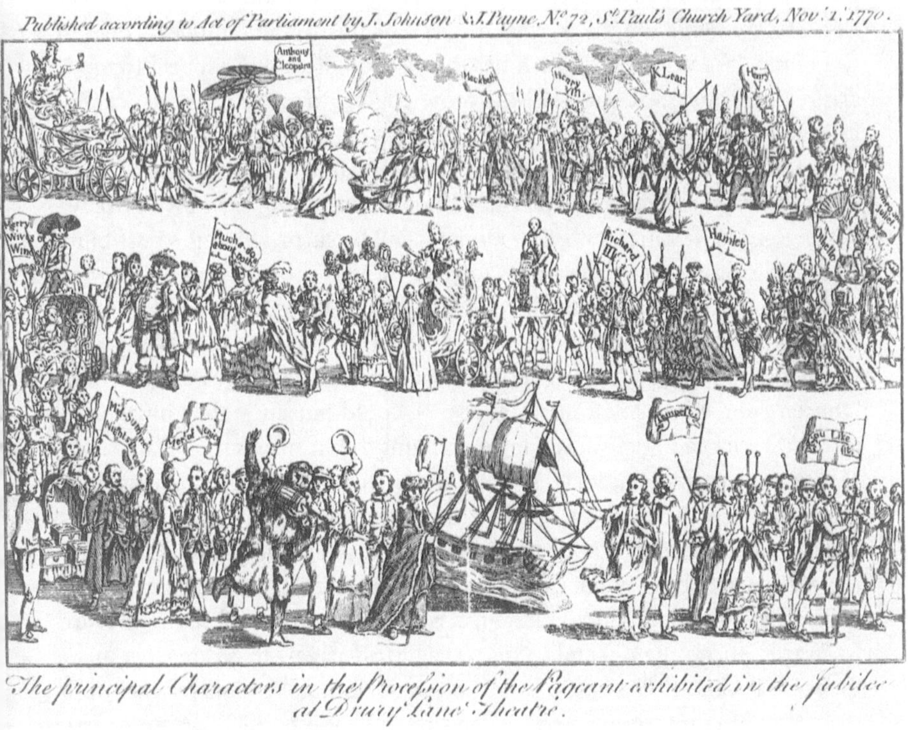

Figure 6. The Procession as actually staged at Drury Lane in 1770. By permission of the Folger Shakespeare Library.

suspense merely . . . that engages the reader's attention." Consequently, their works "are for ever laid aside after a single perusal: an engaging story will bear relating but once."[69] The novelistic personae of Smollett, Fielding, and Sterne on the other hand "will bear viewing repeatedly" because "each of these characters [Adams, Western, Bowling, Trunnion, and Uncle Toby] singly is complete; without relation to any other object they excite mirth; we dip with the highest delight into a chapter, and enjoy it without reflecting upon the contrivance of the piece, or once casting an eye toward the catastrophe" (428). For this reader, it would seem, closure may be indefinitely deferred in order to prolong our "mirth" and it is far from self-evident that those prolongations need come from the originary author. Indeed, he holds up the detachability of the characters—and by implication, their further iterability—as what will ensure their longevity and potential social canonicity: "the novels in which those characters are to be found . . . will furnish perpetual amusement" (428). Intriguingly, though, these pronouncements regarding the importance of detachability come in a review of Smollett's loose adaptation of *Don Quijote: Sir Lancelot Greaves.* For this reader, Smollett's debt to Cervantes (the very thing which has diminished the novel's appeal to modern readers) marks it out as all the more eligible to enter the social canon, as it is a sort of reproduction with a difference: Sir Lancelot and Crabshaw "resemble [Don Quijote and Sancho] without imitating, and remind us of what imparted exquisite enjoyment, without diminishing their own novelty" (428). Readers familiar with *Don Quijote* "will be surprised at the possibility of giving originality to characters formed on that model" (428). Given the widespread acclaim given to Cervantes's work as the quintessence of a certain kind of comedy, it would seem that inventing analogous characters who felt detachable and independent of plot, yet were intriguingly reminiscent of "those of the admirable Cervantes" (428), could put an author on the fast track to social canonicity. Even if we discount the enthusiasm of *The Critical Review* on account of Smollett's strong ties to that journal, it remains striking that the terms in which its reviewer describes what sets the best novelists apart from their competitors are the same as those employed to distinguish the vernacular canon of ancients from the heaps of merely old texts. Detachability, reproduction with a difference, ways of speaking and acting that are "characteristical" (428)—and so suggest a life off-page—these are what mark the socially canonical as such, as ancient in Sir Joshua Reynolds's sense of "a magazine of common property, always open to the publick, whence every man has a right to take what materials he pleases."[70]

Consider only the debate over Edward Moore's *The Foundling* which raged in the pages of *The Gentleman's Magazine* through the spring of 1748. Various correspondents of the magazine wrote in to register their thoughts concerning the morality of Moore's characters and the virtues of his play, which some hailed as the revival of a comic tradition killed off by the political excesses of the mid-1730s and the Licensing Act which followed. Now while it is striking that Moore's play should be discussed at all in the pages of *The Gentleman's Magazine* (the debate over *The Foundling* was only the second time "Mr. Urban" had published original criticism of a play), it is even more striking how the correspondents share a common conditional language, regardless of their sense of the play's merit. That is, whether hailing the play as "wrought up with many interesting incidents, great elegance of expression, delicacy of sentiment, and regard to the rules of the drama" or taking Moore to task for the improbability of his plot, the moral ambiguity of his hero, and the general lack of poetic justice in his ending, the correspondents shared a propensity to discuss the motivations and actions of Moore's characters in what Robert Newsom terms "probabilistic talk."[71] For example, H. G., a rather grumpy correspondent from Canterbury, claims that it is the "shame of being detected, rather than the sense of guilt, [which] first brings [Belmont] to think of marriage; without this circumstance he would have had no thoughts of repairing [Fidelia's] injuries."[72] An anonymous correspondent counters H. G.'s charges in the next issue: "it is not possible for any one absolutely to affirm, from Mr. *Belmont*'s character, that he would have acted the part of a villain, by ruining *Fidelia*, in case things could have taken such a turn as he expected." Rather, "it is possible he might have been reclaimed by her obstinacy in virtue, or diverted from his purposes, by her goodness." Similarly, far from it being improbable that Sir Charles Raymond would have left the infant Fidelia in the care of a nurse and never bothered to check up on her, he "might" easily have so left her "in the hurry and desperation of his affairs." Moreover, he "might have made an unsuccessful enquiry . . . tho' no notice is taken of it in the play." Indeed, this respondent prefaces a rebuttal to another one of H. G.'s objections with "Now, as it is carry'd on by the author. . . ," which suggests that it could readily be done otherwise.[73] As this conditional language should suggest, Moore's play is being represented as but a partial selection from the fictional archive. These "mights" and "withouts" imply other episodes not depicted, but capable of being imagined. They exist as what Gary Saul Morson calls "side-shadows," alternate possibilities the mere existence of which shades the perception of Moore's play.[74] Which is to say, they all presume a fundamental detachability or "Historic Being" for Moore's characters. While I have not come across any traces of characters migrating out of *The Foundling,* it seems likely, given the ways in which they were being discussed, that some readers may have at least speculated as to how Sir Charles would have made enquiries after Fidelia, or whether "*Fidelia* may be as fortunate in her yoke-fellow, as *Indiana* was happy in her *Bevil.*" After all, "from good sense and good humour on one side, and many more virtues on the other, we cannot help fancying, such a match as this to be fortunate and happy."[75] And as the allusion to the central couple in Steele's *The Conscious Lovers* (a staple on the 1740s stage) should suggest, the felt detachability of Moore's characters marked *The Foundling* out as a candidate for social canonicity.

The connections between potential canonicity and felt detachability emerge even more clearly out of the discourse swirling around Benjamin Hoadly's wildly popular *The Suspicious Husband*—the single most successful new comedy of midcentury. Hailed by Samuel Foote as the best comedy since Vanbrugh and Cibber's *The Provoked Husband* (twenty-one years previous) and praised by a correspondent to *The Gentleman's Magazine* as worthy of inclusion in "the treasure which you distribute so liberally among the public every month," Hoadly's play attracted particular attention for its depiction of Ranger, a genial and ultimately harmless rake.[76] Several readers and audience members profess to have been so entranced by Ranger as to forget he was only a character in a play. One "Sam. Riot," writing to *The Daily Gazetteer,* complains that Garrick "was so shamefully himself [i.e., in character], that I lost the entertainment of the stage, and imagined myself all the while upon the *Look-out* with him for midnight adventures."[77] Similarly, Foote recounts the reaction of a "a plain, honest, well-meaning citizen" sitting next to him at the first performance, "whose Imagination was strongly possessed by the Incidents of the Play": "at dropping of the Curtain, I could not help complaining to my Neighbour, that I was displeased at seeing *Ranger* go off as he came on. Could not, said I, the Author throw this Youth, in the Course of his Nocturnal Rambles, into some ridiculous Scene of Distress, which might, with Propriety, have reclaim'd him. But, as he now stands, who knows but the Rogue, after all the Pleasure he has given us, may spend the Night in a Round-House. By G—d! says the Cit, if it happen in my Ward, I'll release him; for I'm sure he is too honest a Fellow to run away from his Bail" (29). Obviously both Foote and the inventor of "Sam. Riot" are being more than a little sardonic, mocking the supposed credulity of their fellow audience members in order to establish their own credentials as proper judges of acting and playwriting. Despite this, however, they each call attention to Ranger's potential detachability in ways that seem wholly approving. "Sam.

Riot" may not like how immersed Garrick was in his character, but Riot's creator clearly intends it as a compliment that an audience member so reluctant to lose sight of the theatricality of his "entertainment" could nonetheless find himself wholly absorbed in envisioning himself as one of Ranger's unindicted co-conspirators "strolling about last Night,——upon the Look-out" and scaling the "Ladder of Ropes most invitingly fasten'd to [Jacintha's] Window."[78] In much the same way, Foote may be contemptuous of the cit's faith in Ranger's bail-worthiness, but he was the one who initially raised the issue of Ranger's life off-page by suggesting that "after all the Pleasure he has given us, [he] may spend the Night in a Round-House"—a place with which Ranger apparently already has some familiarity, given his assertion to Bellamy that "I believe I may have more interest there than you" (29). The author of *An Examen of the New Comedy, call'd The Suspicious Husband* would presumably take issue with Foote—he thinks Ranger's "Course of Pleasure was not yet run, he was in his full Career, and to have stopt him short, wou'd have been dangerous" (10)—but he too shares the sense that Ranger does not feel wholly immanent in Hoadly's play but is rather perpetually capable of sallying forth on new adventures. And the sign of his felt detachability was, not surprisingly, his capacity to serve as "my friend *Ranger*," who was "ever a good Companion."[79] Indeed, Ranger's companionability seems to have extended in even more directions than Falstaff's. Charles Ranger, the editorial persona for *The Gray's-Inn Journal*, responds in his third issue to readers' inquiries "after the Author" by telling them that he is "a near Relation to my Namesake in the Play."[80] Charles's guarded response may suggest that Ranger has a family somewhere with whom he is sufficiently close for them to name a child after him. Or perhaps Charles is Ranger's illegitimate son—after all, Mrs. Chatter, in Macklin's *The New Play Criticiz'd*, "think[s] Mr. Ranger . . . a charming Fellow! O lud! I protest I should not care to trust myself with him in his Chambers."[81] Indeed, one commentator even claimed that "Ranger was by nature formed to please the sex; and I believe there was scarce a woman off or on the stage who saw him, who did not wish to be Mrs. Strictland."[82] As all these jokes should suggest, the proof of Hoadly's fitness to join the social canon was the ease with which Ranger's life off-page could be both envisioned and enjoyed, an ease which allowed the overly literal but at times surprisingly insightful Sir Patrick Bashfull—from *The New Play Criticiz'd*—to presume that *The Suspicious Husband* was "one of Shakespear's" (54), even as Samuel Foote held the play up as evidence that "we are at least equal to the best of the *Roman* Comic Poets, *Terence*; and that is Reputation enough to satisfy our Ambition" (33–34).

* * *

Up until now we have been considering the links between felt detachability and social canonicity as they were experienced and articulated by various individual readers. However, as the remainder of my narrative will suggest, a number of canonically ambitious authors were eager to make these connections work to their advantage in a more rapid and controllable fashion than individual readers could be counted upon to provide and so set out to build opportunities for imaginative expansion (and evidence that others had already engaged in such) directly into their work. In my subsequent chapters, we will examine the quite elaborate strategies which Richardson, Sterne, and Scott adopted in their respective pursuits of the social canonicity which could accompany imaginative expansion. For the time being, however, I would like to close this chapter with a consideration of another author's bid for social canonicity, a bid which both relies upon and lays bare the connections between character migration, felt detachability, and a virtual community linked together through "old friends" which we have been tracing. I am thinking, of course, of Henry Fielding's *The History of the Adventures of Joseph Andrews, and of his Friend Mr. Abraham Adams,* which Richardson would famously denounce as a "lewd and ungenerous engraftment" of Pamela.[83]

For much of the past century, Joseph's alleged status as Pamela's brother has simply been interpreted as residual parody carried over from *An Apology for the Life of Mrs. Shamela Andrews.* By these accounts, which have been repeatedly pronounced to be discredited but nonetheless refuse to go away, Fielding originally intended to write a second *Shamela* (based upon the supposedly self-evident ridiculousness of a male Pamela), but got sidetracked into writing a novel in which the originally parodic character of Joseph took on a life of his own. In E. M. Forster's formulation—perhaps the single most influential of these accounts—"Fielding thought it would be fun to invent a brother to Pamela, a pure-minded footman, who should repulse Lady Booby's attentions just as Pamela had repulsed Mr. B.'s. . . . Thus he would be able to laugh at Richardson, and incidentally express his own views of life. Fielding's view of life however was of the sort that only rests content with the creation of solid round characters, and with the growth of Parson Adams and Mrs. Slipslop the fantasy ceases, and we get an independent work."[84] As a description of the chronology of *Joseph Andrews*'s composition, this may be true—we know almost nothing about it one way or another. As an account of the role played by Pamela in *Joseph Andrews,* however, it falls more than a little flat, perhaps most notably because it cannot explain why, if Joseph is ultimately not the child of the Andrews, Pamela and Mr. Booby should nonetheless remain key presences in the hectic dénouement of the final pages.

I would like to propose a counternarrative, one in which the presence of the Boobys in *Joseph Andrews* is not merely residual parody nor an occasion for some obvious jokes. Rather, Richardson was correct, perhaps more than he knew, when he claimed that "the Pamela, which [Fielding] abused in his Shamela, taught him how to write to please."[85] That is, in *Joseph Andrews* Fielding is making a bid for social canonicity by harnessing his characters to those of Richardson in order to suggest that his characters could also serve as detachable and sociable companions around whom a virtual community might form—indeed, they could do so better than Pamela and Mr. B. and so readers would be well advised to transfer their allegiances.

First of all, as is perhaps so obvious as to have gone without saying, all of the major characters in *Joseph Andrews* are connected in one way or another with the Booby household. Lady Booby is Squire Booby's aunt. Joseph begins the novel as her footman, Adams as her parson, and Fanny as her servant. Joseph is also supposedly Pamela's brother, and Fanny turns out to be Pamela's actual sister. And Pamela and Squire Booby, of course, have just driven down from the Lincolnshire of *Pamela* to the "Zumersetshire" of *Joseph Andrews.* Neither, of course, is an exact replica of Richardson's characters—Fielding's Pamela is a bit of an elitist prig, his Mr. Booby overly deferential to his aunt—but they are nonetheless clearly recognizable versions, reproductions with a difference, of the principals from *Pamela.* As such they participate in the proliferation of Pamelas which we will investigate in the next chapter. But, more importantly for our present purposes, they also presented an opportunity to import some of the luster of *Pamela*'s newfound social canonicity into the world of *Joseph Andrews.*

To understand Fielding's strategy, it is worth considering a somewhat more extravagant version of this same sort of opportunistic character migration: the masquerade ball toward the close of John Kidgell's *The Card.* Kidgell's narrator informs us that "many distinguished Personages composed this grand assembly; but as several of the Nobility and Gentry of the Bridegroom's *own Age and Nation* were then present, by an Accident equally agreeable and surprizing, I cannot meritoriously conceal an Affair of so much Consequence from the Reader's observation. The better to satisfy Curiosity, and pay a due Compliment to Merit, it may not be improper to represent them as distinguished by the Master of Ceremonies at the Ball." A guest list then follows: "*Roderick Random,* Esq; with Mrs. *Booby,* late Miss *Pamela*

Andrews. Joseph Andrews, Esq; Brother to Mrs. *Booby,* with Miss *Harriot Byron.* Mr. *Thomas Jones,* with Miss *Clarissa Harlowe. David Simple,* Esq; with Miss *Betsy Thoughtless.* And Sir *Charles Grandison,* Bart. With a Lady of an illustrious Family in *Spain,* distinguished by the Name of *Donna Dulcinea del Toboso*."[86] After this elaborate set-up, though, Kidgell does not really do anything that would require this all-star assemblage of novelistic characters: "*All the Ladies and Gentlemen set and changed Places; and set and changed Places again: — Then the first Couple cross'd over and turn'd; and Right Hand and Left all round.* The whole Entertainment was conducted with that Decency and Ease, which always accompanies true Politeness and Magnificence, and the Company retired extremely well satisfied and composed, excepting that Mr. *Thomas Jones,* in waiting on Miss *Harlowe* to her Chair, had the Impudence to be rude to her; and Sir *Charles Grandison,* for interposing, the Misfortune to *have his Ears boxed*" (2:296). Given the possibilities of this company, it seems extremely curious (and not a little disappointing) that all we get is dancing and one small altercation. But I suspect that to be disappointed is to miss the point. Kidgell is not bringing these characters in as a means of inventing further adventures for them. Rather he is "pay[ing] a due Compliment to Merit" and "satisfy[ing]" his readers' "Curiosity" in the hope that both merit and readerly curiosity will transfer over to his own characters. If these are the sort of people who come to Archibald's wedding, then surely there must be more to Archibald than might initially meet the eye. Like the hapless nerds in any number of teen movies, Kidgell is aiming for a sort of social canonicity by association.

The presence of the Boobys in *Joseph Andrews* seems best explicable if we consider it as a more thoroughgoing and successful version of the same strategy. That is, all roads lead to the Boobys in the hope that the detachability and social canonicity they have already begun to achieve in the *Pamela* craze will somehow prove contagious or transferable to Fielding's own—to his mind clearly more deserving—characters. This may seem a odd claim to make in the face of the novel's closing assertion that Joseph will not "be prevailed on by any Booksellers, or their Authors, to make his Appearance in *High-Life*," as Pamela had done.[87] One could simply interpret this as a final slap against Richardson, whose ignorance of the niceties of aristocratic life was an inexhaustible font of hilarity for a certain sort of high-born wit. But as a final sentence it seems so unmotivated and gratuitous in the context of the romance ending—the novel could very easily have closed with the narrator's "leav[ing] this happy Couple to enjoy the private Rewards of their Constancy" (343)—that it almost has to be doing more than just getting in a final jab. Indeed, the narrator goes out of his way to call his readers' attention to Joseph's decision to "imitate" his Parents "in their Retirement" as "particularly remarkable" (344). In light of the sheer ostentatiousness with which Joseph's retirement is presented, it seems far more promising to consider it as a gesture of deliberate withholding. That is, Joseph's life will continue off-page—he and Fanny "now live together in a State of Bliss scarce ever equalled" and Fanny is "extremely big with her first Child" (343–44)—but our access to that off-page life is going to be as strictly controlled as our access to their private moments has been throughout the narrative. There is more to Joseph than appears in *Joseph Andrews,* but the narrator presents himself as standing in the doorway of the fictional archive and deciding who may gain admission to which off-page materials. Hence he pointedly omits the "great deal of innocent Chat" which Joseph and Fanny engaged in at one of the alehouses along the road "as possibly, it would not be very entertaining to the Reader" (159–60). Yet he tantalizingly suggests a paragraph later that this is a pivotal moment in their courtship: "let it then suffice to say, that *Fanny* after a thousand Entreaties at last gave up her whole Soul to *Joseph,* and almost fainting in his Arms, with a Sigh infinitely softer and sweeter . . . she whispered to his Lips, which were then close to hers, 'O *Joseph,* you have won me; I will be yours for ever'" (160). If one wishes to learn more about that courtship, it seems that one must to submit to the narrator's authority. Accordingly, I would like to propose that the force of the final sentence is to suggest that Joseph *could* appear in high life, and if he did so, he would no doubt shine with more grace and politesse than Pamela was able to muster (after all, he—like Fielding himself—was a member of the gentry by birth, not just marriage). But the decision as to whether Joseph will ever so appear lies with Fielding, not with individual readers, "Booksellers, or their Authors." Fielding thus underscores Joseph's potential detachability while preventing him from actually going anywhere. And in so doing, he implies that Joseph is at least as worthy a candidate for social canonicity as Pamela, but that that social canonicity was best bestowed upon the terms he dictated—indeed, part of Pamela's problem may have been that by the time *Joseph Andrews* came out, she had made her "Appearance in *High-Life*" at the hands of several different writers.

Perhaps belatedly realizing the potentially counterproductive affront to readerly autonomy which this gesture of withholding might pose, Fielding spent the next few years repeatedly presenting Parson Adams as nothing if not detachable. Indeed, he crops up in no less than five additional texts within Fielding's later oeuvre. Note that in each case his appearance is framed in such a way as to underscore his companionability. Hence in the introduction to *A Journey from This World to the Next,* the fictional editor describes how he "communicated" the almost illegible manuscript from which the *Journey* has supposedly been printed "to my Friend Parson *Abraham Adams.*"[88] Not surprisingly, Adams is primarily concerned that the author of this manuscript, while clearly acquainted with Plato, may not have read him in the original. This invocation of the trope of friendship continues in the two letters Adams wrote to "My Worthy Friend," "the True Patriot," whose eponymous newspaper had been "inclosed in the Franks of my great and most honoured Patron," Squire Booby.[89] The first of these letters proffers what the True Patriot had described earlier as "a Letter, or rather Sermon, on the ensuing Fast [to solicit divine mercy in the midst of the '45], from our old Friend Mr. Abraham Adams."[90] As a sermon it is a wholly conventional diatribe against luxury. However, the argument is intriguingly interspersed with references to "these three last Years, during my sojourning in what is called the World, particularly the last Winter, while I tarried in the Great City" (154–55). Given that this number came out in mid-December 1745, it would seem that Adams's time in "the World" is synonymous with the forty-five months elapsed since the publication of *Joseph Andrews* and that he is willing to recount the observations he has made since the close of that novel to those who consider themselves his friends: after all, the entire letter is a response to the True Patriot's request for "something proper to be seen . . . by the Public" (152).[91] A few years later, Adams resurfaces as a contributor to *The Jacobite's Journal,* with John Trott-plaid explaining how "I know my Friend Mr. *Adams* so well, that I am convinced he will pardon the few Alterations I have made" in his submission.[92] We never learn what those alterations were, but Adams's letter does update us on the Boobys—among other things, we learn that Squire Booby keeps copies of *The Jacobite's Journal* "lying in his Hall-Window" (331)—and promises still further correspondence on "some other Opportunity" (335). I dwell on these post–*Joseph Andrews* iterations of Parson Adams because they each nicely rehearse the connections we have been tracing between character migration, felt detachability, and the trope of an "old friend" who binds together a virtual community. That is, each iteration offers a glimpse into Adams's life off-page within a frame which insists upon both his fundamental companionability—who else could be friends with both Squire Booby and John Trott-plaid?—and the ways in which he, like Trott-plaid, has taken on the placeless omnipresence of print and so may be found "all over the Kingdom at one and the same time," including in the Boobys' "Hall-Window." In general, as we have seen, social canonicity accrues as the result of a sense among readers that a given character was detachable, companionable, and capable of migration. Here it would seem that Fielding is attempting to short circuit that process by presenting a character already so infused with the migratory energies of the Boobys and so patently detachable and companionable that whatever social canonicity he might lack must be but a ridiculous oversight.

Presenting one's work as ready-made for admission to the social canon is a risky gambit, one which could very easily backfire. Yet the venture seems to have largely succeeded for Fielding, although not necessarily with as much obeisance as he would have liked. Parson Adams soon became the touchstone against which other English humourists were judged.[93] And the ease with which readers could imagine Adams's life off-page—an ease which, as we have seen, Fielding took great pains to create—seems to have become in turn transmissible to other members of his family. Consider only the reader of *The Gentleman's Magazine* who sent in a letter from Adams enclosing a Latin translation by "his little son Dick . . . of a favorite song of his worthy friend . . . Mr. Andrews."[94] This turns out to be "Say, Chloe, where must the Swain stray"—the song which Joseph had been singing when he and Fanny were reunited in Book II. Now since Dick was not present at Joseph's singing, there is no way to know whether his father repeated the song to him verbatim, Joseph reprised it on some later occasion, or Dick read about it in *Joseph Andrews.* Given Dick's triumphant invocation of textual authority later on in "The History of two Friends," the latter would offer the most delightful explanation, although it hardly matters, as all three scenarios equally require Dick to have a life which extends off-page, one in which he, unlike his father, gets the song's final double entendre. Highlighting Fielding's bawdry by translating it into Latin may hardly seem like a profitable endeavor. Yet for this reader—most likely a provincial clergyman or amateur scholar—it nonetheless seems to have served as a means of imagining himself as part of a larger virtual community comprised of those kindred souls who shared his affection for the Adams family and admiration for Sylvanus Urban.[95] And in so doing, he contributed in his own small way to furthering the felt detachability of Adams and little Dick, whom we can now imagine walking through the translation line by line, with Adams only concerned for his son's stylistic infelicities.

One final example should suffice as a testament to the success of Fielding's bid for social canonicity through felt detachability and companionability. In the autumn of 1742, Sir Dudley Ryder, then Attorney General, was retained by Fielding's bookseller, Andrew Millar, to get an injunction against an unauthorized reprint of *Joseph Andrews.* After a frustrating day in court arguing for this injunction, Ryder took a minute to write to his wife: "I have this Moment satt down after endeavouring to rescue Jos: Andrews & ye Parson Adams out of ye Hands of Pirates, but in vain for this time occasion'd by a Mistake in ye Attack. However another Broadside next week will do ye Business."[96] Literally, of course, Ryder is endeavoring to rescue *Joseph Andrews* out of the hands of literary pirates who would deprive Andrew Millar of his rightful profits. But his language teeters on the edge of character migration. Given the sheer number of rescues in *Joseph Andrews,* Ryder's phrasing suggests that he too imagined himself as something of a swashbuckling hero coming to the aid of his friends, much as Adams had come to the aid of the half-ravished Fanny on the Downs or Joseph had saved Adams from the Roasting Squire's dogs. In so doing, of course, he is inventing not just lives off-page for Joseph and Adams but ones offshore as well (it is difficult to get off "another Broadside" in the midst of Westminster Hall). Thus even as he is attempting to foil a certain sort of reproduction with a difference (Jacob Ilive's pirated edition), he is at the same time engaged in a far more outlandish and free-floating form of reproduction, one which underscores the social canonicity of Joseph and Adams, but in ways that Fielding probably never anticipated. Social canonicity, felt detachability, and a virtual community centered upon the further adventures of an "old friend" all thus coincide in the delightfully improbable site of the soon-to-be Chief Justice of England and his Walter Mitty-like fantasies.

Chapter 4
Lewd Engraftments and the Richardsonian Coterie Public

The first half of my narrative has been largely concerned with the textual commons as the invention of individual readers, often to the effacement or exclusion of authors. As my discussion of Henry Fielding at the close of the last chapter should suggest, however, many canonically ambitious writers were discontent with the ease with which their intentions and desires could be set aside by readers engaged in imaginative expansion. To better approximate the sheer contestedness of the literary field, then, I would like to consider the cases of three prominent authors—Samuel Richardson, Laurence Sterne, and (more briefly) Sir Walter Scott—who each attempted to assert his own centrality and authority while still striving to preserve some of the canonizing and community-inventing effects of imaginative expansion. In the present chapter, we will investigate the ways in which Richardson's practice of consulting extensively with his correspondents but ignoring most of their advice manifests itself as a peculiarly ambivalent stance toward imaginative expansion. On one hand, Richardson demanded an almost unprecedented control over his characters, denouncing migratory characters, such as those which appear in *Joseph Andrews*, as "lewd and ungenerous engraftment[s]," violations of both Pamela and his property.[1] On the other hand, both his correspondence and his novels are full of invitations to flesh out his already prolix narratives by imagining the contents of letters to which he, in his guise as editor, alludes but does not reproduce: the as yet unpublished portions of the fictional archive. And many readers accepted Richardson's invitations and deluged him—and the public more generally—with further letters and episodes, most of which were at odds with Richardson's manifest intentions. By tracing how Richardson solicited these contributions, only to ostentatiously ignore them, we can better discern how he endeavored to marshal the energies of imaginative expansion without having to relinquish authorial control by offering his characters—and himself—as the center of a virtual community modeled not on the commons but the coterie, with all the intimacy and personal authority which that ideal suggests. This chapter, then, will investigate how Richardson was both shaped by and attempted in turn to shape the practices of imaginative expansion which we have been tracing. It will reveal how a reading practice can not only affect the ways in which a text is read but also the ways in which it gets written in the first place, thus bearing out the force of Tony Bennett and Janet Woollacott's insight that "such inter-textual relations should not be construed as secondary phenomena but as determinations which actively press in upon and powerfully reorganize the specific texts which fall within the orbit of their activity."[2] Indeed, ultimately, this chapter, in conjunction with those still to come, will reveal the sheer extent to which canonically ambitious authors had to go in order to assert their now supposedly self-evident dominion over their own characters.

The practices of visualization and character migration which we have been examining separately came together with a vengeance in the frenzy which surrounded the publication of *Pamela*.[3] Consider only the language in which Aaron Hill urges Richardson to abandon his plans for an illustrated edition of the novel: "I am so jealous . . . in Behalf of our *inward* Idea of Pamela's *Person,* that I dread *any* figur'd Pretence to Resemblance. For it will be pity to look at an *Air,* and imagine it *Hers,* that does not carry some such elegant Perfection of Amiableness, as will be sure to find place in the *Fancy*."[4] Because Hill and his daughters are "jealous in Behalf of our inward Idea of Pamela's Person," he believes that any illustrations will necessarily disappoint. But how did they come to have such inward ideas of Pamela's person in the first place, and why should he be jealous on their behalf?

Perhaps not surprisingly, Hill was given to visualization along theatrical lines, and so was accustomed to making proprietary claims upon literary characters. He even professed to dream about Pamela: "if I lay the Book down, it comes after me.—When it has dwelt all Day long upon the Ear, It takes Possession, all Night, of the Fancy": "I admire, in it, the strong distinguish'd Variety, and picturesque glowing Likeness to *Life,* of the Characters. I know, hear, see, and live among 'em All: and, if I cou'd paint, cou'd return you their *Faces*."[5] Indeed, it seems he could paint far more than their faces: in another letter, Hill goes well beyond Richardson's text to detail exactly how Pamela's country habit hugs the contours of her body. In the course of defending Richardson's style, Hill drifts into rapture at how

> the *Thought* is every-where exactly *cloath'd* by the *Expression:* And becomes its Dress as roundly, and as close, as *Pamela* her Country-habit. Remember, tho' she put it on

with humble Prospect, of descending to the Level of her Purpose, it *adorn'd* her, with such unpresum'd *Increase* of Loveliness; sat with such neat Propriety of Elegant Neglect about her, that it threw out All her Charms, with tenfold and resistless Influence.—And so, dear Sir, it will be always found.—When modest beauty seeks to hide itself by casting off the *Pride* of *Ornament*, it but displays itself without a *Covering:* And so, becoming more distinguished, by its Want of *Drapery*, grows *stronger*, from its *purpos'd Weakness.*[6]

In envisioning Pamela's body in this manner, Hill imaginatively augments Miss Andrews in ways that are strongly reminiscent of the actors and readers we examined in Chapter 2: he invents "All her Charms" as part of envisioning what one of Garrick's correspondents had termed the "silent eloquence of gestures, looks, and pauses."[7] Pamela hardly moves a muscle in Hill's account and yet the roundness and closeness he ascribes to her costume allow her to appear with sufficient ideal presence that Fielding could parody Hill's ecstasy in *An Apology for the Life of Mrs. Shamela Andrews* with hardly a change of phrase: "Oh! I feel an Emotion even while I am relating this: Methinks I see *Pamela* at this instant, with all the Pride of Ornament cast off."[8] In so doing, of course, Hill stakes a proprietary claim upon Pamela such that, even as he is writing to Richardson, he can nonetheless still speak of "our *inward* Idea of Pamela's *Person*" as if it was both distinct from and as valid as Richardson's own ideas concerning Pamela's person. It is no wonder then that Hill should have been so provoked by the "too *tight-laced* Objection" of one of Richardson's anonymous critics, who thought that "the passage where the Gentleman is said to span the waist of *Pamela* with his Hands, is enough to ruin a Nation of Women by Tight-lacing." Hill cannot comprehend what this critic "could . . . find, to complain of, in a beautiful Girl of Sixteen, who was born *out of Germany*, and had not, yet, reach'd ungraspable *Roundness!*" because he was himself so fiercely devoted to Pamela's "roundness" as nothing if not graspable.[9] The test, for Hill, of whether one properly appreciated Pamela's "elegant Perfection of Amiableness" would thus seem to hinge upon the degree to which her graspable roundness had found "place in the *Fancy.*"

Hill was not unusual in his proprietary feelings toward Pamela, although few could match his effusion. Many readers staked similar claims, with the result that, as with the other characters we have been examining, Pamela rapidly came to seem detachable from Richardson's text, everywhere and therefore nowhere. And like the other characters, Pamela's felt detachability helped to make her the center of a virtual community. Hence it should come as no surprise that only two months after publication, *The Gentleman's Magazine* could claim that it was "judged in Town as great a Sign of Want of

Curiosity not to have read *Pamela,* as not to have seen the French and Italian Dancers" who were the hit of the current theatrical season.[10] Similarly, the mere fact that William Whitehead could ask "Who does not, *Pamela,* thy Suff'rings feel?" and expect the question to be understood as rhetorical suggests that in little more than three years Pamela had become so widely disseminated as to seem a plausible object of universal sympathy.[11] Yet, as should be apparent by this point in my narrative, the success of *Pamela* was not merely due to the irresistible charisma of Richardson's text. Rather, it was precisely those lewd and ungenerous engraftments that Richardson decried, "these Poachers in Literature," that gave her her place in the social canon and ensured that the heroine he called "my girl" would come to seem "our" girl too.[12]

* * *

Unlike some of the previous examples we have been considering, though, the response to *Pamela* did not completely efface Richardson as author, despite the novel's editorial fiction, which could easily have licensed such an erasure. Both Pamela's proponents and her foes kept Richardson at the center of the virtual community which was gathering around *Pamela.* The paradoxical result was that Richardson's readers granted him the centrality for which he hoped, but founded that centrality upon the very freedom which they took in their "Scandalous Attempts of Ingrafting upon his Plan."[13] That is to say, Richardson received more than the lip service given to Shakespeare, but the tribute was paid on terms other than—indeed quite contrary to—those he sought. Just as he insistently requested the advice of his correspondents, only to ignore most of what he received, so too did his readers seek him out only to disregard most of his strictures upon their reading practices.[14] In order to work out some of the implications of these paradoxes, and how they both responded to and shaped Richardson's own writing practices, let us consider, for a moment, the correspondence which poured into Salisbury Court in the wake of the publication of *Pamela.*

Much of Richardson's correspondence from this period offers up suggestions as to how he could usefully augment *Pamela.* For example, George Cheyne thought the proposed third and fourth volumes of *Pamela* (hereafter *Pamela . . . In her Exalted Condition*) could benefit from more incident:

a broken Leg, a disjointed Limb, a dangerous Fever, happening to a Husband and then the tender Care Vigilance and active Nursing of a loving Wife, and then she would have an Opportunity to insinuate all the noble religious and beautiful Sentiments to a rakish or unconverted [infidel], for such a Season is the Mollia Tempora Fandi. . . . The Death of a favourite Child, a sudden Conflagration of one's own, or his Neighbour's favourite Seat, an Epidemical Distemper, a severe Winter, a Famine etc., Quarrels among Neighbours or Friends, and the like great and unexpected Events, probably untied, always beget Attention in the Reader and calls naturally for Instruction.[15]

A few months later, Cheyne intimates that "perhaps I may add to another Edition or at least by some Additions and Alterations make them different Volumes of one Work."[16] As Cheyne's language should suggest, he was responding to an invitation from Richardson for "Hints" "regarding anything flagrantly amiss" in his work.[17] Yet despite Richardson's patent lack of interest in pursuing Cheyne's suggestions—he insisted that "I shall have no occasion [in the Two new Volumes] for such of the deep Scenes, as I believ'd necessary to the Story in two places in the former" and "only aimed to give the Piece such a Variety, as should be consistent with Probability"—Cheyne went on inventing still further ways in which to augment *Pamela.*[18] Thus a year later found him sketching out a project for giving "a Character and short Contents of all the Books in English or French that are fit to amuse, divert, or instruct the serious, virtuous Valetudinarians of whatever Kind. . . . This would come in very aptly with the Design of *Pamela* and might perhaps be called a Catalogue of her Library."[19] Now to most modern readers Cheyne's project would seem at some odds with "the Design of *Pamela.*" After all, Richardson had announced on the title page that he was writing "in order to cultivate the Principles of Virtue and Religion in the Minds of the Youth of Both Sexes," those readers Samuel Johnson would a decade later call "the young, the ignorant, and the idle."[20] There seems little reason to doubt that Richardson thought he was writing for the real-life equivalents of Pamela and B., not the valetudinarians at Bath to whom Cheyne administered. Why then should Cheyne characterize his plan as so "aptly" consistent with Richardson's "Design" that it might be fruitfully marketed by him under the name of Pamela?

Given the context of Cheyne's other correspondence with Richardson—most of which is taken up by prescriptions of "thumb vomits," "gentle Bleedings," and "low diets"—I suggest that what to us might seem like willful misreading is more an instance of Cheyne's feeling proprietary toward *Pamela* in the same way as he did toward his patients, including Richardson. That is, just as he redefines Richardson as a valetudinarian in need of physic, so too does he reenvision Richardson's "daughter" as a potential patient.

Pamela might not require any thumb vomits, but in seeking Cheyne's advice, Richardson had unwittingly brought her within Cheyne's sphere of influence, where she could be treated, if not as a valetudinarian, then as a helpmate-in-training to such, one who could benefit from Cheyne's vast insight and knowledge of the world. Indeed, it is striking just how many of his proposed "incidents" for *Pamela . . . In her Exalted Condition* revolve around just the sort of physiological crises—"dangerous fevers" and "epidemical Distempers"—in which Cheyne specialized. In redefining Pamela as a nurse and instructor of valetudinarians, then, Cheyne appropriates her through a kind of proleptic character migration (envisioning the incidents of Richardson's as yet unwritten sequel). In short, the reason why Cheyne could feel so confident only a year and a half after publication that *Pamela* "will be a classical Book" is that he is operating within the "yours," "mine," "public" logic which we have been tracing: he has already made it (and her) his own, and presumes that others have done the same, hence the work is destined to become "classical."[21]

Pamela's social canonicity thus emerges out of the collective mass of appropriations made by individual readers. Unlike most of the previous examples we have encountered, however, the majority of the expansions of *Pamela* addressed themselves to Richardson, placing him again and again at the center of a virtual community, even as the authority which would presumably justify his presence there was repeatedly effaced. Hence, amid Hill's detailing of the appropriations made by the members of his household, he alternates between referring to the novel's heroine as "your Pamela" and "our . . . Pamela."[22] As a living author jealous of his own property, Richardson could not simply be redefined—and hence dismissed—as a gloriously pliant authorizing ghost, in the way that Shakespeare often was. But neither were readers wholly willing to bow down before him and his conception of his work; to do so would be to deny the fantasy of commonality which underpins imaginative expansion.

In order to clarify this odd situation, let us consider another instance of the submission to Richardson of sketches for the continuation of *Pamela* which betray a strikingly unRichardsonian conception of its heroine. William Warburton reported to Richardson that he and Pope thought

> that one excellent subject of Pamela's letters in high life, would have been to have passed her judgment, on first stepping into it, on every thing she saw there, just as simple nature . . . dictated. The effect would have been . . . a most excellent and useful satire on all the follies and extravagencies of high life; which to one of Pamela's low station and good sense would have appeared as absurd and unaccountable as

> European polite vices and customs to an Indian. You can easily conceive the effect this must have added to the entertainment of the book; and for the use, that is incontestable. . . . when I have the pleasure of seeing you in town, we will talk over this matter at large; and, I fancy, you will make something extremely good of our hints.[23]

Now one could certainly argue that Pope and Warburton's idea of remaking Pamela into an ingénue straight out of Montesquieu fundamentally misinterprets Richardson's servant girl, and perhaps it does. Certainly Warburton's easy presumption that Richardson would be ready and willing to "make something extremely good of our hints" betrays his ignorance of Richardson's working habits. But be that as it may, it is striking how readily Warburton combines expressions of respect for Richardson and his work ("I have so true an esteem for you, that you may depend on any thing in my power") with a refusal even to acknowledge that Richardson might not want two more volumes of *Pamela* along these lines: "I have a great deal to say upon this subject, that, when we are together, you will . . . understand more perfectly" (1:133, 1:135). Richardson may have been present in his work for contemporary readers in a way that Shakespeare was not, but that did not prevent readers from taking the same liberties in sketching out further adventures for Pamela; it simply meant that they sent copies of those sketches to Salisbury Court.

Nor, indeed, did it prevent readers from besieging Richardson with fully formed scenes and letters ready for insertion into the next volume of *Pamela*. For example, Anthony Fulford submitted some poetry on behalf of a "learned Friend" that "may be of no disservice to your new Edition of Pamela."[24] Similarly, George Psalmanazar sent in a scene in which Lady Davers berates B.

> that if his Wife had not bewitch'd him into an utter Forgetfulness of what he was, and what Family he came from, he would rather have wished to see both her and me buried quick Seven Fathoms under-ground, than to take a Delight in seeing her debase herself [through her charitable visits] in such a manner as all the people of Quality are quite ashamed of, and to be so desirous that I should follow her Example. A fine Employment indeed . . . for Persons of our high Sphere, to go tuckt up and dancing after every tag-rag, and beggarly Crew that thinks fit to send for her, to be present at every Gossiping, not to mention some others of her condescending kind Offices, which I must own my squeamish Stomach turns at the very Thoughts of.[25]

Despite her initially "violent Passion," though, Psalmanazar's Lady Davers becomes a convert to Pamela's "Divine and Superabundant Goodness" as soon she actually witnesses the joy with which the cottagers gaze upon their benefactress.

While Richardson had solicited several of these contributions, including that of Psalmanazar, the only one he ever included in *Pamela . . . In her Exalted Condition* was Alexander Gordon's offering of "some thoughts on the opera" and even there he went out of his way to frame Gordon's words as a separate enclosure written hurriedly by B. at Pamela's request and sent to Lady Davers for further correction.[26] Psalmanazar's episode was dismissed out of hand in a marginal note as "ridiculous and improbable." Notwithstanding his persistent invitations, then, Richardson remained quite resistant to the prospect of collaboration: when the publisher of *Pamela's Conduct in High Life* suggested that they pool their resources and "join my [i.e., Richardson's] materials to those of their Author's and . . . let it come out under my Name," Richardson "rejected [the Proposal] with the Contempt it deserved" and "resolved to do it myself, rather than my Plan should be basely Ravished out of my Hands, and, probably my Characters depreciated and debased, by those who knew nothing of the Story, nor the Delicacy required in the Continuation of the Piece."[27] Why then did he continue to seek advice from his correspondents and why did they take such an interest in developing further adventures for Pamela, such that no less than Ralph Allen took the time to recommend the "genteel and generous Dismission of Mrs. Jewkes"?[28] Why, in short, did so many readers join Richardson's wife and their lodger, Elizabeth Midwinter, in wishing for "a little more of Pamela?"[29]

In approaching these questions, it is worth remembering that it was not only Richardson's loyal correspondents who were engaging in character migration and visualization, but also a much wider range of readers, most of whom were personally unknown to Richardson. For instance, several readers went out of their way to imagine Pamela's behavior in the bedroom subsequent to her marriage. Thus one J—— W—— closes his mock-epic, *Pamela: or, the Fair Imposter,* with a scene in which Sir Blunder catches Pamela in bed with Parson Williams: "Citations issu'd, and such Things of course, / Nor could the Law obtain him a Divorce. / Long Bills he fil'd, but broke his Heart with Grief, / Nor could his Riches purchase him Relief."[30] Similarly, the epilogue to Henry Giffard's *Pamela. A Comedy* pities "Unhappy *Belville!* What a Wife! — Protect her! / No doubt he'd often have a Curtain-Lecture: / Besides, a Girl, so over-fond of Grace, / Might be devout in an improper Place; / And pour forth Sermons from her fervent Mind, / When the poor Man's quite otherwise inclin'd."[31] Indeed, Giffard seems to have been consumed by the amorous possibilities of Pamela's life off-page: among other things, he invents a scene in which Parson Williams and the repentant John Arnold save Pamela from rape and thereby enable B.'s "Escape . . . from

Rage and violent Desire" and thus his conversion to Pamela's "transcendent Innocence" (52–53). Giffard also resolves the issue with which Ralph Allen had been wrestling by concocting a letter to Mrs. Jewkes left by Colbrand which reveals that he has tricked her into a bigamous marriage: "*I have told a you, plasieurs fois, dat you had great Beauti and Temtation about you; which, en verité, vas your Moné — And now I have got dat in my Possession, de rest of Madam* Jewkes *may allon au Diable . . . I have a very good Wife in my own Country, and tirteen little pretty Enfans, all like myself, which your good Guinea sal make alive fort bien. . . . you are a damn'd heretique old Vitch, and are more proper for Monsieur de Devil, dan for*" Colbrand. Lest anyone miss the point, Jack Smatter frames his reading of this letter with the pronouncement that Mrs. Jewkes's "punishment" is "justly inflicted" (67). And, of course, as we saw in the last chapter, the initial premise and much of the energy of Fielding's *Joseph Andrews* stem from the migration into that book of more or less the entire Booby household. All this is to say that perhaps even more than with the texts we have already considered, there seems to have been something in Richardson's work which called out for engraftment, even if it did not guarantee adherence to Richardson's terms.

* * *

Like most of the originary texts we have been considering, *Pamela* is ostentatious in its generic multiplicity, particularly the ways in which its heroine ultimately eludes the categories into which she might be placed and thereby hints at the untold possibilities of the fictional archive from which she is allegedly drawn. At various moments in the text, she seems "a Servant Maid," a "Farmer's Daughter," a "dutiful daughter," "an artful young Baggage," a self-assertive "saucebox," an almost-Lucretia, a Cinderella figure, a speculator on the marriage market, a hyperprolific correspondent, a patient Griselda, a model Christian woman, a damsel in distress. And yet none of these fully define her—a point underscored by the various Pameloid productions which attempted to do just that. Shamela may not much resemble the Pamela of *Pamela's Conduct in High Life* (the former is a dialect-spouting artful seductress, the latter a somewhat prim gentlewoman), yet they both recall aspects of Richardson's Pamela. And while Pamela herself takes the prize for generic multiplicity—a situation nicely figured within the text by B.'s pretense that the shy girl in a country habit over whom Hill was to wax rhapsodic was in fact "*Pamela*'s Sister, you are so like her" (56)—a similar complexity marks out most of her compatriots. More than a century ago, Austin Dobson noted that "Mr. B., the rake, comes out of the play-book; Mr. B, the reformed, out of the copy-book" and yet the two coexist within the boards of a single volume.[32] Analogous points could be made regarding most of the other principal characters. Mrs. Jewkes, for example, seems an odd conjunction of the predatory "old bawd" of coney-catching pamphlets with Ursula the pig-woman from *Bartholomew Fair.* Similarly, *Pamela Censured* tries to define "honest Mother *Jervis*" as but a country bumpkin, fit only to "marry *Jonathan,* and perhaps be promoted to a little Inn of Squire *B*'s in the Country, even that Mrs. *Pamela* stopp'd at in her Journey to the *Lincolnshire* Estate" (22). Yet within a few pages, the Censurer is talking about her as "a Woman of Discernment," "a Procuress," and a surrogate for the "young Gentleman who . . . wishes himself in [her] Place to *turn* Pamela *about and about and examine all her Dress to her under Petticoat*" (31, 36, 36). The effect of *Pamela*'s generic multiplicity, it would seem, was to highlight the sheer range of possibilities which its heroine and her fellow characters offered to the reader interested in making further forays into the fictional archive. Richardson thus offers up his text as a particularly promising object for imaginative expansion and so, at least potentially, social canonicity. But doing so necessarily risks exposing "my Pamela" and "my Plan" to "such scandalous Attempts of Ingrafting" as would render "all my Characters . . . likely to be debased, & my whole Purpose inverted."[33] What was a poor author to do? Was it possible "to claim authorship" without "exposing the author's text . . . to invasive forms of repetition . . . that may put in question the integrity of the original"?[34]

One answer may lie in the degree to which *Pamela* was always already steeped in the visual and theatrical. James Grantham Turner has provocatively cataloged the myriad ways in which readers of the novel, both friend and foe, seized upon the eroticized and dramatic "warm Scenes." Turner uses the reading practices he reconstructs to show how Richardson "assumes . . . that male and male-identified readers will project themselves into the 'room' created by the scene and then rewrite it more pornographically, unless forestalled by precisely the physical description that critics find objectionable" (82). Hence, Richardson's promise on the title page that *Pamela* "is intirely divested of all those Images, which, in too many Pieces calculated for Amusement only, tend to *inflame* the Minds they should *instruct*" is only partially fulfilled: *Pamela* may well be divested of "those Images . . . calculated for Amusement only" (as nothing in the novel could fit that criterion), but "it abounds with lively Images and Pictures" of all sorts, including ones which could inflame minds resistant to instruction.[35] Consider only the first of the "deep" or "warm" scenes: B's attempt upon Pamela in the summer-house.

Pamela describes the scene in considerable corporeal detail, noting how "I struggled, and trembled, and was so benumb'd with Terror, that I sunk down, not in a Fit, and yet not myself; and I found myself in his Arms, quite void of Strength, and he kissed me two or three times, as if he would have eaten me.—At last I burst from him, and was getting out of the Summer-house; but he held me back, and shut the Door" (23). Perhaps not surprisingly, this passage recalls the readerly visualizations we explored in Chapter 2, as well as the painterly and theatrical practices upon which they were modeled. Even those "inner" sensations which perhaps cannot be fully conveyed in any other genre—such as Pamela's not being herself—are described as if they were a rapid, visually legible series of pantomimic "hits": readers familiar with the stock repertoire of the passions could readily conjure up the Terror signified by a young woman's trembling and sinking down. The difference, of course, is that unlike the visualizations of the Inkle and Yarico story, here the gestural details are part and parcel of the originary narrative.

Lest we dismiss this likeness as simply a shared formal realism, it is worth remembering the context in which Pamela's description of the summer-house scene occurs: namely, her reconstruction of the "very long" letter which B. has apparently stolen (22). Her letters XI and XII supposedly reproduce the account given in that letter, but they do so "as briefly as I can" (22) and so suggest that the lost letter may have contained more than we have current access to. That is, the letters included in *Pamela* are but redactions of that "very long" letter which may still turn up. Yet at the same time, Pamela informs her parents that "I'll tell you all" (22) and so insinuates that the differences between the "very long" letter and her reconstruction of it ultimately do not matter: the latter is rich enough to conjure up the scene in "all" its plenitude.[36] In effect, these letters serve as surrogates for the practice of visualization, offering a previsualized account of the scene, one in which the gestures and expressions which readers would invent in order to lend the scene ideal presence were incorporated into the text before it ever left the printing house. The enriched text thus provided could both harness the canon-making and community-inventing energies of visualization and, at least in theory, obviate the need for further visualization by individual readers, even as it still called attention to the gap between the "very long" letter and what we actually get. In this way, Richardson could have his visualization and eat it too. He could try to lend his narrative the uncanny allure of the socially canonical without having to depend upon the lewd engraftments made by others. Of course, as I have been detailing, the latter part of this stratagem failed quite spectacularly. But Richardson's inability to forestall readerly engraftment need not indicate any other sort of failure. Indeed, I would like to contend that much of *Pamela*'s charisma is due precisely to the intertwining of previsualized detail, epistolary form, and the fictional archive which this example offers up.

Nor is the summer-house scene an isolated episode. An even more emphatic version of the same dynamic may be found in the next "warm scene": B.'s first attempt at raping Pamela. After B. forces his hand into Pamela's bosom, she faints, "and so, to be sure, I was [dead] for a time; for I knew nothing more of the Matter, one Fit following another, till about three Hours after, as it prov'd to be" (63–64). True to her word, we too know "nothing more of the Matter" for the rest of the paragraph, as Pamela's worried inquiries are simply shushed by Mrs. Jervis. But most readers at this point would presume that "worse" had happened, that the scene set by what the author of *Pamela Censured* calls "a Hundred little Actions, which every one's Fancy must help him to form" would naturally result in a rape, "however [Pamela] and Mrs. *Jervis* may endeavour to keep down the *Under Petticoat*" (41). And for a moment it seems as if Richardson is going to leave us to surmise what had happened: after all, Pamela "knew nothing more of the Matter," she "judg'd Mrs. *Rachel* knew nothing of the Matter" (64), B. has left the scene, and Mrs. *Jervis* is curiously reticent. We would be well within our rights to "guess the Matter to be bad enough," as the Maids do, "tho' they dare not say any thing" (64). Given the difficulties of "writing to the moment" while unconscious, it would seem that Richardson here relies upon his readers' fancies to visualize the scene (the narrative omission functioning something like a cinematic fade to black). Indeed, one could read Pamela's slight doubts regarding Mrs. Jervis's veracity as further invitation to speculate. If Pamela feels the need immediately to qualify her belief that "Mrs. *Jervis* saved me from worse" with "and she says she did, (tho' what can I think, who was in a Fit, and knew nothing of the Matter?)" then we might feel justified in sharing Pamela's suspicion that Jervis was somehow in on the plot and so is not fully to be trusted as our spectatorial deputy.

Yet Richardson is not simply handing the scene over to his readers to imagine. Rather, he immediately arranges for a summary of the events which transpired while Pamela was in "Fit after Fit": "it seems my wicked Master had, upon Mrs. *Jervis*'s second Noise on my going away, slipt out, and, as if he had come from his own Chamber, disturbed by the Screaming, went up to the Maids Room . . . and bid them go down and see what was the Matter with Mrs. *Jervis* and me" (64). Note that B. "slipt out" immediately after the last "Shriek" of Jervis's (which was in turn immediately after Pamela's fainting), so that there is nothing further in the scene to visualize, at least by the standards of the Censurer. Yet the summary of the events of three hours in a single paragraph begs for augmentation. Had Pamela been conscious, we would have gotten several pages out of this crisis; since she was not, we get just a bare skeleton of events upon which we could drape a visualization, yet we are also told that that visualization would not look like what we would naturally anticipate (that is, it would be a pathetic scene of Pamela in fits, rather than a further glimpse of her naked body). Not surprisingly, some hostile readers chose to disregard Richardson's efforts to delimit the scene: its equivalent in *Shamela,* for example, goes on at some length to detail the full extent of B.'s conquest: "our Hands, on neither Side, were idle in the Scuffle, nor have left us any Doubt of each other as to [the] matter" of B.'s potency or Shamela's "&c." (319).

Nevertheless, it is in this double move—prompting the visualizations of individual readers and then attempting to displace or deny their validity—that we can see Richardson's wish to harness the energies of visualization without conceding an inch to the engraftments which such appropriations required. In tracing the temporal sequence of these invitations and exclusions, then, we can discern Richardson's hope to defeat the kinds of pornographic imaginings that the Censurer and Fielding put forth, while still hanging on to the psychic investments which inspired such imaginings. As Lady Davers puts it in *Pamela . . . In her Exalted Condition,* "if you had not recited all you could recite, would there not have been Room for any one, who should have seen what you wrote, to imagine they had been still worse?----And how could the Terror be supposed to have had such Effects upon you, as to endanger your Life, without imagining you had undergone the worst that a vile Man *could* offer, unless you had told us, what that was which he *did* offer, and so put a Bound, as it were, to one's apprehensive Imaginations of what you suffered" (3:44). Had Pamela been "less particular in the Circumstances," that is, Lady Davers "should have judg'd [B.] had been still *worse,* and your Person, tho' not your Mind, less pure, than his Pride would expect from the Woman he should marry" (3:46). As it stands, though, Pamela's account has "convince[d] us all, that you have deserved the good Fortune you have met with, as well as all the kind and respectful Treatment he can possibly shew you" (3:44). Put simply, Richardson wants his readers to be every bit as "convinced" of Pamela's deserts as Lady Davers eventually becomes, but he wants them to do so without having to go through the "imagin[ing] . . . still worse" which prompted her initial disdain for Pamela. That is, he wants his readers to have the same possessive infatuation for Pamela as he does (which they can only have through the process of visualization), but he wants them to visualize her in exactly the same way and on exactly the same chaste terms as he does. Even for an aficionado like Hill, the conflicting demands are impossible to meet simply because each reader will flesh out different aspects of Richardson's heroine and so be convinced in his or her own way.

Thus far I have been focusing upon the "warm scenes" as particularly rich instances of Richardson's efforts to provide surrogates for readerly visualization in *Pamela.* And so they are, even when (as in the last example we discussed) the visualization suggested—the scene of Pamela in fits—is nowhere explicitly described. But almost any point in the novel could be shown to contain Richardsonian efforts to attract and control imaginative expansion of some sort because the entire narrative is founded upon the fiction of an archive of correspondence from which the anonymous editor has made a selection. With Gulliver or Macheath, of course, the archive was the invention of individual readers. Here it constitutes the very fabric of the novel. In the second sentence of the very first letter, after all, we are plunged into an ongoing correspondence between Pamela and her parents: "my good Lady died of the Illness I mention'd to you" (11). And time and time again throughout the novel, we are presented with summaries of letters which could not be transcribed, allusions to letters which have gone astray, and reminders of the editor's interventions and selections on our behalf. Hence, for example, Pamela "wrote to thank [Williams] most gratefully for his kind Endeavour" to interest Lady Darnford and Mr. Peters in her case, yet she "had not time to take a Copy of this Letter, I was so watch'd" (136). She does offer a fairly detailed précis, however, which recounts how the letter lamented

> the little Concern the Gentry had for my deplorable Case; the Wickedness of the World to first give way to such iniquitous Fashions, and then plead the Frequency of them against the Offer to amend them; and how unaffected People were to the Distresses of others. I recall'd my former Hint as to writing to Lady *Davers,* which I fear'd, I said, would only serve to apprize her Brother, that she knew his wicked Scheme, and more harden him in it, and make him come down the sooner, and to be the more determin'd on my Ruin; besides, that it might make Mr. *Williams* guess'd at, as a means of conveying my Letter; and being very fearful, that if that good Lady would interest herself in my Behalf, (which was a Doubt, because she both lov'd and fear'd her Brother) it would have no Effect upon him; and that, therefore, I would wait the happy Event I might hope for from his kind Assistance in the Key and the Horse, *&c.* I intimated my Master's Letter, begging to be permitted to come down; was fearful it might be sudden; and that I was of Opinion no Time was to be lost; for we might lose all our Opportunities, *&c.* telling him the Money-trick of this vile Woman, *&c.* (136)

Full as this summary may seem, Pamela's truncated phrases and repeated *et ceteras* nonetheless suggest that the letter which she "popt . . . under the Mould" (138) in the garden contained still more and that if we had proper access to the fictional archive we could discover exactly why she thought "no Time was to be lost" and how she described "the Money-trick" played by Mrs. Jewkes. The précis thus invites further augmentation even as it suggests that the account which it provides is sufficiently full that it will not be contradicted by the additional details one might discover in the archive. Indeed, Richardson goes out of his way to offer assurances as to Pamela's scrupulosity in these matters by having her repeatedly summarize "to the best of my Remembrance" (227) the parcels of her journal as they are seized by Mrs. Jewkes or requested by Mr. B. We, of course, have already read these parcels and so are in a position to appreciate the care with which Pamela "slightly touch[es] upon the Subject[s]" of those parcels for the benefit of her parents, in case she cannot "get them again for you to see" (236).

Similarly, the narrative periodically refers to letters which have gone astray or been destroyed and so cannot be included in the present volume. Thus, for example, one evening shortly before their marriage, Mr. B. "spoke with some Resentment" of "a Letter deliver'd me from [Lady Davers's] impertinent Husband, professedly at her Instigation, that amounted to little less than a Piece of insolent Bravery, on supposing I was about to marry you. I was so provok'd . . . that after I had read it, I tore it into a hundred Pieces, and scatter'd them in the Air, and bid the Man who brought it, let his Master know what I had done with his Letter" (328). Yet later that night he "wish[es] I had kept his Letter, that I might shew you how a Man that *acts* generally like a Fool, can take upon him to *write* like a Lord" (330). The letter in question has been ostentatiously ripped to bits, but B.'s description of it is full enough that readers of *Pamela* interested in reconstructing it may do so, albeit with the proviso that whatever they invent beyond the "insolent Bravery" and lordly style to which B. refers will necessarily be negligible. If Lord Davers's letter were sufficiently important that it had to be included in the present volume, then surely the editor would have devised some means of acquiring a copy as he does with the letter which Mr. Andrews manages to send via Parson Williams. Within the frame of the narrative, after all, there is no reason why Pamela should transcribe her father's epistle into her journal (as a physical artifact, the letter was already in her possession and her journal was being primarily kept for her parents, who could presumably remember what they had sent her under such extreme circumstances). Yet the editor deems this letter sufficiently important to insert it with a note:

"*N.B.* The Father's Letter was as follows" (159). The conclusion seems inescapable. With Lord Davers's missing letter, as with Pamela's various summaries or her mention of the "hundred tender Things [B.] express'd . . . that tho' they never can escape my Memory, yet would be too tedious to write down" (271), Richardson is offering an alluring glimpse of the depths of the fictional archive, yet doing so only to insist that further plumbing of those depths, while self-evidently delightful and improving, would nonetheless not yield anything to contradict or undercut what he has already provided.

As the vogue for *Pamela* took off, though, Richardson became increasingly proprietary toward the fictional archive, insisting that even the unwritten parts of *Pamela* were still subject to his authorial prerogative. Hence, for example, he denounced "certain Booksellers having in the Press a spurious Continuation of [his] Two Volumes"—namely, John Kelly's *Pamela's Conduct in High Life*—as "carrying on *against* his Consent, and without any other Knowledge of the story than what they are able to collect from the Two Volumes already printed."[37] Similarly, in the fifth edition, he alters his closing summary of Volume Two from "Here end the Letters of the incomparable Pamela" to "Here end, at present, the Letters of Pamela."[38] The implication seems clear: more letters are extant in the archive, and within Richardson's "Knowledge" and control. According to the preface to *Pamela . . . In her Exalted Condition,* the only reason why he had not published these additional letters at the outset was that he was "determined not to exceed" "the compass" of two volumes, despite so "great a Choice of Materials" (3:ii). Now, however, provoked by Kelly's alleged inclusion of all of "those Letters . . . written by *Pamela* to [Mrs. Jervis], Copies of others to different People, and Originals of several which [Jervis's niece] herself had receiv'd, sufficient to furnish a Volume, if not more, and to compleat her Life," Richardson was determined to "continu[e] the Work himself, from Materials, that, perhaps, but for such a notorious Invasion of his Plan, he should not have published."[39] Part of Kelly's provocation lay in his hint that despite having brought his narrative up to the moment of Pamela's death, he has not yet exhausted the archive: "the honourable Mrs. S—— and Mrs. B—— kept a close Correspondence; but as the Letters which passed between them for a Number of Years are intirely on Literature, and would be little entertaining to any but learned Readers, we have omitted them, though it is possible we may hereafter publish them under the Title of *Select Letters*" (2:314). This termination of Pamela's life, but not her writing, seems to have been the last straw for Richardson. In an advertisement at the close of the first four-volume set of *Pamela* (the octavo or so-called sixth edition), Richardson baldly announces that there being Reason to apprehend, from the former Attempts of some Imitators, who supposing the Story of Pamela a Fiction, have murder'd that excellent Lady, and mistaken and misrepresented other (suppos'd imaginary) Characters, that Persons may not be wanting, who will impose new Continuations upon the Publick: It is with a View to some Designs of this Nature, that the Editor gives this publick Assurance, by way of Prevention, That all the Copies of Mrs. *B.*'s Observation and Writings, upon every Subject hinted at in the preceding Four Volumes, and in particular those relating to *Devotion, Education, Plays,* &c. are now in *One Hand Only:* And that, *if ever* they shall be published, (which at present is a Point undetermined) it must not be, till after a certain Event, as unwished, as deplorable: And *then,* solely, at the Assignment of Samuel Richardson, of *Salisbury-Court, Fleetstreet,* the Editor of these Four Volumes of *Pamela: or, Virtue Rewarded.*

Still further possibilities for Pamela (including her actual death) thus lurk in the archive, but access to that archive is strictly controlled and all future installments will need to demonstrate their provenance before they may be accepted as authentic. No longer may readers simply "carry . . . on . . . without any other Knowledge of the story than what they are able to collect from the Two Volumes already printed."

Yet, as the mere existence of these advertisements should suggest, Richardson was far from the only one to play upon the fiction of the archive as a way to invite or justify imaginative expansion of *Pamela. Pamela's Conduct in High Life* advertised on its title page that it was "publish'd from her original papers" and its introduction is concerned with detailing the collection's provenance: the correspondence was assembled, along with "some loose Notes," by Mrs. Jervis's niece and successor as Pamela's housekeeper, one Mrs. Brenville, "mentioned by my Maiden Name, *Vaughan,* . . . after Mrs. *Jewkes* was dismiss'd" (1:v). These papers purport to provide a "more satisfactory" "Account of [Pamela's] Life" than had been offered "at the End of the second Volume of my Lady's Letters already publish'd" (1:vi). As such, they are more surrogates than supplements, corrections rather than engraftments. Similarly, the anonymous *Pamela in High Life* insists on its title page that it is "carefully extracted from Original Manuscripts, communicated to the Editor by her son," while *The Life of Pamela* goes so far as to insist that "whoever put together the other Account . . . was entirely misinformed of the Cause of Mr. *Andrews*'s Misfortunes . . . as will plainly appear in the following Sheets, for which we have the best grounded Authority from the original Papers now in the Hand of the Reverend Mr. *Perkins* of *Shendisford Abbey*" (2).[40] Even *Shamela* goes out of its way to trumpet on its title page its origin in "exact Copies of authentick Papers delivered to the Editor."

I submit that these archival fictions all play upon the same idea: that a certain indefinite number of Pamela's letters exist "out there" and that, despite Richardson's advertisements, they possess at least as much authority as those included in *Pamela.* Accordingly, the boundaries delimiting what constitutes *Pamela* are somewhat fluid: at the very least, the text includes Richardson's first two volumes, but at times it seems as if it also encompasses whatever else Pamela and her circle may have written, whether it be the further correspondence contained in Richardson's own continuation, or that published by others, or even the various letters and hints for letters sent into Salisbury Court. The felt capaciousness of *Pamela* is nicely figured by the now notorious Pamela waxworks, "at the Corner of Shoe-Lane, facing Salisbury-Court," which featured "above a hundred Figures in miniature" "representing the Life of that fortunate Maid, from the Lady's first taking her to her Marriage."[41] Richardson's *Pamela,* of course, begins several years after Pamela entered the B. household and so does not include Pamela's being "first tak[en]" into service. Such a scene does appear in *The Life of Pamela,* however (see Figure 7). For the waxworks artist, it would seem, the extant installments from the fictional archive were of equal weight (as indeed they were for the author of *The Life of Pamela,* who drew as freely upon Kelly's work as that of Richardson): what mattered was the availability of scenes "suitable to their Characters," rather than the authorship of such scenes.

Richardson himself seems to concede the attractiveness of this idea in his anxiety that "still more and more Volumes . . . so long as the Town would receive them would . . . generally accompany the Two I had written."[42] Richardson—and most bibliographers—would like to limit *Pamela* to "the Two [or four] I had written." Yet given his repeated appeals to readerly supplementation, it becomes rather difficult to police those textual boundaries. If an author anticipates that "when the Mind *begins* to be attach'd to Virtue, it will improve itself, and outstretch the poor Scenes which I intend only for a *first Attractive,*" then surely the contents of that outstretching belong to the same text as those "poor Scenes" themselves.[43] If "something . . . must be left to the Reader to make out," then that "something" must constitute a necessary, even integral part of the text. If he wishes "to interest the Readers so much in the Story, as to make them differ in Opinion as to the Capital Articles, and by Leading one, to espouse one, another, another, Opinion, make them all, if not Authors, Carvers," then the text must be capacious enough to accommodate those various carvings.[44] Otherwise it—and hence Richardson's "Scheme"—will simply fragment as each individual reader's engraftment pulls it in a different direction. Readers will become "carvers"

Figure 7. Lady B.'s first taking Pamela into service, as illustrated in *The Life of Pamela*, 1741. Courtesy of The Beinecke Rare Book and Manuscript Library, Yale University.

not only in Richardson's intended sense of "those that choose for themselves" but also in the more literal sense of "those wielding sharp implements," dividing the text into bite-size morsels.

The outstretchings made by individual readers, then, constitute part of the implicit archive from which *Pamela* is drawn—a situation neatly encapsulated by John Kelly in his condemnation of *Pamela Censured.* Kelly takes the Censurer to task for his attention to the ways in which Pamela was "stretch'd out at . . . length" when she fainted in her closet and asks indignantly "how can we fairly from the Words of *Pamela*'s Letter gather, that she fell in an indecent Posture? Well, but the Warmth of Imagination in this virtuous Censurer supplies the rest: He can't suppose that she could possibly fall but as he has painted her" and hence "contrives to give an Idea of *Pamela*'s hidden Beauties" (1:xiv). Kelly's point, obviously, is to condemn how "this virtuous Censurer [is] endeavouring to impress in the Minds of Youth that read his Defence of Modesty and Virtue, *Images* that may *inflame.*" Yet Kelly's language betrays him. In the midst of his diatribe, Kelly unwittingly suggests that the allegedly belated and spurious inventions of the Censurer may actually be chronologically prior to Richardson's text: "if the Letter has not discover'd enough, the pious Censurer lends a Hand, and endeavours to *surfeit your Sight* by lifting the Covering which was left by the Editor, and with the Hand of a boisterous Ravisher takes the Opportunity of *Pamela*'s being in a Swoon to ———" (1:xv). That is, by uncovering "*Pamela*'s hidden Beauties"—a phrase which neatly recalls the ways in which B.'s desire for Pamela's unseen body shaded into his desire for the unread letters which she had hidden about her body—the Censurer is revealing those beauties to be already extant, part of the archive, if not part of the published text. Indeed, Richardson admits as much when he revises this scene in the fifth edition to specify that Pamela fell on her face and so an uncovering would not reveal the breasts which B. so fetishized.[45] Kelly thus shares with his sworn enemy a sense of Pamela's body as if not "divested," then at least divestible "of the Drapery in which she is enclos'd, tho' not hid."[46] Richardson's editorial drapery, it would seem, was added after the fact and so, while it may be desirable, it may also be dispensed with if one wishes to view what lies beneath. Kelly may think the Censurer unfair because he "lays *Pamela* in a Posture, and particularizes her latent Charms and then charges his own luxurious Fancy on the Author" (1:xvi), yet those very practices are what Richardson's archival fiction invites. Indeed, such particularizing is what gave Pamela most of her charms in the first place by "permitting us to fill our Fancy" through "outstretching" Richardson's "poor Scenes"—scenes which, according to Aaron

Hill, themselves "stretch'd out this diminutive mere *Grain* of *Mustard-seed,* (a poor Girl's little, innocent, Story) into a Resemblance of That *Heaven,* which the Best of Good Books has compar'd it to."[47]

* * *

These outstretchings of individual readers into the archive came to serve as the foundation for an alternate mode of virtual sociability. In some ways, of course, the friends and admirers of Pamela resembled those surrounding any fictional character, such as the "old friends" of Falstaff whom we examined in the last chapter—consider only the nom de plume adopted by one of Richardson's correspondents: "Philopamela." But as I suggested above, the case of Pamela posed a significant difference in that Richardson was not nearly as readily effaced as the socially canonical (and safely dead) Steele or Shakespeare. Rather, he remained insistently, if intermittently, present to his readers, both in his ever failing, yet compulsively recurring role as guardian of *Pamela*'s textual boundaries and in his efforts to underscore the material differences between *Pamela* and the remainder of the fictional archive. This flickering yet tenacious authorial presence encouraged readers to envision themselves as part of a more intimate form of virtual community, one more akin to a coterie than to the commons or the playhouse.

Richardson, of course, had an actual, mostly female coterie in London. But he also came to serve as the center for a virtual coterie held together through readerly imaginings of further adventures (and even more importantly, further epistles) for his heroine and her compatriots. As in the flesh-and-blood coteries studied by Margaret J. M. Ezell, the members of this virtual coterie "used . . . writings to cohere social bonds among like-minded readers."[48] Unlike those embodied coteries, however, the virtual coterie of Pamela's admirers did not have to be comprised of persons known to one another, only those who could be presumed to be "like-minded." Similarly, the "writings" which helped social bonds to cohere did not need to actually circulate among the members of the virtual coterie, they had only to be imagined as capable of doing so.

To illustrate the differences between traditional coteries and what I would like to term the "coterie public," consider only the letter from Lady Davers to Pamela which an anonymous contributor sent to Richardson in October 1741. In a brief prefatory note, he or she asserts that the contribution is made "as a Friend to Virtue." The text of Lady Davers's letter makes clear, however, that being "a Friend to Virtue" is indistinguishable from being a Friend to the one whom Virtue has Rewarded. In this epistle, which recounts a surprise visit from Lord and Lady Wickam to the Davers and Lady Betty, Lord Wickam expresses surprise that Lady Davers and Lady Betty have become such converts to the cult of Pamela, given their previous hostility toward her. In order to explain their transformation, Lady Betty pulled out "our charming Pamela's journal" (which is to say, the most affecting portion of *Pamela*) and read from it, after which, Lady Davers reports, "every Soul sighed for you, every Eye wept for you, every Heart died for you, and every Tongue applauded you."[49] Indeed, Lady Wickam pleaded with Lady Davers to "secure me a Place in your amiable Sister's Breast, and let me be ranked in the number of her most sincere Admirers and Friends." Even the previously unrepentant Jackey pledged to "never draw his sword again, but in Defence of Virtue and Pamela"—a phrasing which suggests that they are one and the same. Lady Davers closes her letter with a reaffirmation of how she has become "as thorough a convert to your transcendent virtue, as my beloved Brother was."

Of course, this correspondent did not send Lady Davers's letter to Pamela, he or she sent it to Richardson in the hope that it might "be of . . . service to you in the Beginning of your 3d. Vol. (where it necessarily must come in, if at all)." In acting as a Friend of Virtue, it would seem, this correspondent hopes to serve other Friends of Virtue, including Virtue's local representative, Mr. Samuel Richardson, of Salisbury Court, Fleetstreet. Why else should this reader so insistently stage a scene in which "our charming Pamela's journal" serves to convert the doubting to her "transcendent virtue" and thereby transform them into "like-minded readers" of *Pamela?* This letter, that is, stages a coterie-like scene of reading, complete with tears and manuscript circulation, and so would seem a reaching out toward potential fellow participants, what Psalmanazar's version of Lady Davers had termed "converts . . . to this God-like Virtue."[50] However, it does not address those fellow converts directly but rather triangulates itself through the person of Richardson in the hope that he will insert this letter into the forthcoming *Pamela . . . In her Exalted Condition* and so allow this reader to connect, albeit indirectly, with Richardson's entire readership. Even though this letter was not ultimately included in Richardson's "3d. Vol.," the mere fact that it could be written and sent suggests that this "Friend to Virtue" suspects that he or she is not alone, that other Friends to Virtue might be available to participate in a coterie potentially coterminous with the public at large.

What is striking about all this, however, is that it positions Richardson in the place previously occupied only by the characters with whom readers might be old friends. Being a Friend to Virtue does not allow one to ignore Virtue's author in the way that Shakespeare might be ignored. Rather, if one is a Friend to Virtue in search of fellow converts, the virtual community one can imagine is organized not only around Pamela but also around Pamela's creator, whose intentions have to be acknowledged, if not always acquiesced to, in a way that was hitherto unnecessary. By virtue of his position as recipient and potential editor of all of these letters, Richardson—as much as Pamela—becomes the rallying point around which the coterie public can form. The anonymous contributor of Lady Davers's epistle acknowledges as much when he or she writes that "you have the Liberty of using it, with or without Alterations as it may best embrace your Design." Indeed, it could hardly be otherwise. If one wished to connect with other Friends to Virtue through the insertion of one's archival discoveries in a future edition of *Pamela,* one necessarily had to acknowledge the gatekeeper to that archive, what the title page to *Pamela . . . In her Exalted Condition* called "the Editor of the *Two* First" volumes. One had to pay a certain obeisance to the ultimate source of what Richardson would term "the pen and ink [which] . . . furnished the cement of our more intimate friendship."[51]

Richardson, characteristically, took considerable pains to draw quiet attention to his own centrality and necessity to the coterie public. Within his own correspondence, he often tried to represent himself as but a convenient postal drop, a harmless drudge simply increasing the efficiency of an already vibrant discourse. For example, when "two different ladies, who, unknown to, and but little acquainted with each other, sent me, the one, a letter, accusing Clarissa for a coquet; the other, taking her to task as a prude," Richardson sent "to each the other's letter for a full answer of her's."[52] Indeed, with *Sir Charles Grandison,* he went so far as to consider having "every one of my Correspondents, at his or her own Choice, assume one of the surviving Characters in the Story, and write in it; and . . . I shall pick and choose, alter, connect, and accommodate, till I have completed from them, the requested [further] Volume."[53] Yet even as both anecdotes strive to downplay Richardson's contribution to this discourse (he is merely forwarding or collating the contributions of others), they also rather tellingly underscore his role as a crucial intermediary without whom both the discourse and the coterie public more generally would collapse. Thus though Richardson's gambit with the "two . . . ladies" lost him "two correspondents, and what was worse, my two letters . . . the two ladies have ever since been well acquainted."[54] Their sociable debate concerning Clarissa's motives, far from being inevitable, was brought about through the agency of Richardson. Similarly, without Richardson's picking and choosing and altering and connecting and accommodating the contributions of his correspondents, those correspondents would be unable even to entertain the possibility of getting the further volume that they desired (at least under the imprimatur of Richardson), even though they would collectively be its authors. Despite his recurrent pose of modesty, then, Richardson repeatedly insisted that he was the nexus through which the coterie public imagined itself. He was the arborist charged with tending to the trunk upon which readers' various engraftments were being made.

Perhaps the most far-reaching way in which Richardson attempted to assert his centrality to the coterie public, though, was through the elaborate bibliographic games in which he engaged in order to highlight the material distinctions between Pamela's incessant scribblings and the form in which readers encountered them. That is, despite the fiction on the title page that *Pamela* was but "a series of Familiar Letters . . . Now first Published," Richardson repeatedly called attention to precisely those qualities of manuscript correspondence which defied transcription into print, thus underscoring the differences between the letters which supposedly comprise *Pamela* and *Pamela* itself, when considered as a material object. Indeed, in her very first letter Pamela marvels at how her "Eyes run" at the memory of the death of her mistress and advises her parents: "Don't wonder to see the Paper so blotted!" (11). A similar effort to draw her parents' attention to how her "miserable Scribble" is "all bathed and blotted with my Tears" follows on the heels of her moment of greatest despair: her pondside contemplation of suicide (175). In both cases, however, readers must take Pamela's word that her paper is so blotted. Their own copies of the pages containing those letters bear no such blottings (at least from the eyes of Miss Andrews) and so highlight the material distinctions to be drawn between Pamela's correspondence as it is employed within the text and that allegedly same correspondence as it is transcribed and printed in *Pamela.* Much the same effect is achieved by the attention which is paid to the appearance of handwriting. Thus B. is able to identity the writer of "the Gypsey Letter" warning Pamela of B.'s plan to dupe her into a sham-wedding by "the Setness of some of these Letters and a little Secretary Cut here and there, especially in that *c,* and that *r*": "it is the Hand of a Person bred in the Law-way . . . Why, *Pamela,* . . . 'tis old *Longman*'s Hand . . . !" (267). The italic c's and r's in this passage as printed, of course, are indistinguishable from those used throughout the novel. If we had full access to the archive, though, the fiction suggests that we could examine that "Billet" and see how its "Hand . . . seem'd disguised" (225).

The most dramatic and sustained way in which Richardson distinguishes between Pamela's manuscript scribblings and their printed transcription as *Pamela,* however, comes in the almost obsessive attention the narrative pays to the location of those writings. The printed *Pamela,* by virtue of its sheer success, could partake of the placeless omnipresence which readers attributed to widely disseminated print. Yet the manuscript text which it allegedly reproduced is repeatedly represented as both singular and highly locatable. Whether buried in the garden, concealed somewhere upon Pamela's person, or sent off in a packet to Mr. and Mrs. Andrews, Pamela's papers can only be in one place at a time. This scarcity seems to be part of their allure for the readers within the text. For B., of course, their inaccessibility is deeply intertwined with the similar inaccessibility of Pamela's body—a linkage made convincing by Pamela's incessant "thrust[ing]" of her correspondence "into my Bosom" (29) or "stitch[ing] them . . . in my Under-coat, next my Linen" "about my Hips" (131, 227).[55] Indeed, once B. begins to suspect that her "Written-papers" are concealed somewhere "about" her, he threatens "to strip my pretty *Pamela*" (233, 235) until he finds them, beginning by unpinning the handkerchief which covers the very bosom into which Pamela had so often thrust her correspondence—especially that with his perceived rival, Parson Williams—and which he had, of course, fondled in each of his attempted rapes. Given that this scene immediately follows his reading of that installment of Pamela's journal which lay "several Days under a Rose-bush"—not to mention his odd insistence that "I never undrest a Girl in my Life"—it would seem that the object of his desire here is not Pamela's bosom per se but what she has "written so far," which is shrouded, he thinks, by that handkerchief (234–35). Ultimately, of course, reading the papers which have been concealed around Pamela's body is what converts his desire for that body into an honorable uxorious flame. But even after B.'s conversion to virtue, the scarcity and singularity of Pamela's correspondence remains a textual concern. B. cannot read all of Pamela's journal at one sitting because it is physically dispersed, with some portions in Lincolnshire (which she further divides into various parcels) and some with Pamela's parents. Similarly, after Lady Davers asks for forgiveness, she requests that she be permitted to see Pamela's journal, which "will not only give me great Pleasure in reading, but will intirely reconcile me to the Step [B.] has taken. . . . When I can find, by your Writings, that your Virtue is but suitably rewarded, it will be not only a good Excuse for me, but for him, and make me love you" (454–55). Pamela readily assents in principle, but she cannot immediately grant the request as "my poor Father and Mother . . . have them in their

Hands at present; and your dear Brother has bespoken them, when they have done reading them" (455). Because of the journal's status as a unique manuscript, that is, Lady Davers has to get in line to read it in a way that few of the actual readers of *Pamela* had to do.

One might expect these repeated distinctions between the manuscript and printed texts of *Pamela* to weaken the authority of the printed *Pamela* by suggesting its inability to adequately testify to Pamela's sufferings: after all, the pages of the printed *Pamela* do not come preblotted with tears or stained with "the dry Mould in the Garden" (234). They are not even particularly scarce (there were six authorized editions in the first eighteen months, plus a piracy and apparent newspaper serialization). Given the ways in which the printed *Pamela* seems to fall short of its copy text, one might expect it to be regarded as an inadequate surrogate for Pamela's journal, one obviously incapable of bringing about the conversions to virtue that seem to follow the journal wherever it goes. Quite to the contrary, however, many of the most laudatory mentions of *Pamela* highlight its status as a printed book. Consider only Knightley Chetwood's pronouncement that "that if all the Books in England were to be burnt, this Book, next the Bible, ought to be preserved."[56] By yoking *Pamela* to the Bible in a speculative scenario involving the return of Marian book burning, Chetwood endows Richardson's text with an odd sacrality as an object. Like the Protestant martyrs who refused to surrender their English Bibles, readers of *Pamela* are here figured as not only recognizing the value of *Pamela* but perceiving that value as directly proportionate to its printed dissemination. Just as the success of the Reformation hinged upon the inability of the Catholic Church to ferret out every copy of the English Bible, so too, it would seem, the impact of *Pamela* hinged in part upon its ability as a book to escape the economy of scarcity within which its text putatively operates. That is, the authority of *Pamela* as object, far from being diminished by the differences between it and the manuscripts upon which it is allegedly based, seems to have been actually enhanced by its ability to reach widely dispersed readers at the same time. A book cannot become socially canonical if it only exists in one copy.

All this begs the question, though, of why so much attention should have been devoted to distinguishing Pamela's manuscripts from the printed *Pamela*, if the latter is not ultimately the worse for the comparison. The answer seems to lie in the way in which Richardson tacitly hints that the presence and power attributed to the manuscripts as traces of Pamela's suffering have been somehow transfused into the printed books so that they too might bring about the nigh-miraculous conversions attributed to Pamela's holograph journal. Witness only the lengths to which Richardson goes in the front matter to the second edition of *Pamela* to highlight the exemplary response of Harry Campbell, "a lively little Boy" in the Hill household, who has

> at once, become fond of his Book; which (before) he cou'd never be brought to attend to—that *he may read* Pamela, he says, *without stopping*. The first Discovery we made of this Power over so unripe and unfix'd an Attention, was, one Evening, when I was reading her Reflections at the *Pond* to some Company. The little rampant Intruder, being kept out by the Extent of the Circle, had crept under my Chair, and was sitting before me, on the Carpet, with his Head almost touching the Book, and his Face bowing down toward the Fire. . . . when, on a sudden, we heard a Succession of heart-heaving Sobs; which while he strove to conceal from our Notice, his little Sides swell'd, as if they wou'd burst, with the throbbing Restraint of his Sorrow. I turn'd his innocent Face, to look toward me; but his Eyes were quite lost, in his *Tears:* which running down from his Cheeks in free Currents, had form'd two sincere little Fountains, on that Part of the Carpet he hung over.[57]

Note how the Hill family's carpet has become tear-stained through a kind of displaced reenactment of the very tears with which Pamela "bathed and blotted" her journal as she wrote this scene. And as a result of this reenactment, little Harry "has, since, become doubly a Favourite—and . . . perhaps the youngest of *Pamela*'s *Converts*," thus preemptively sparing him the stages of aspersion and doubt which both B. and Lady Davers required before their respective conversions. Little Harry's tears would seem to suggest that the material differences between manuscript and print ultimately do not matter: that Pamela's contemplated suicide is sufficiently moving as to be equally capable of staining manuscript and printed pages, had only little Harry's head been "almost touching the Book" at a different angle.

This passage suggests that membership in the coterie public was potentially limitless and so could extend to include anyone with access to a copy of the printed *Pamela*. One did not need to be an intimate of the Richardsons or the Hills, so long as one was willing to follow the lead of little Harry. Yet even as this gesture potentially levels distinctions among Richardson's readers by insisting that the products of mechanical reproduction were every bit as efficacious as the tear-stained manuscripts of traditional coteries, it reinscribes Richardson's primacy within the coterie public. At the very moment when the gap between manuscript and print seems to close with the transformation of Aaron Hill's copy of *Pamela* into an object every bit as unique and poignant as Pamela's manuscript journal, it subtly reopens with a sly insistence that it nonetheless still matters whose tears are involved. No matter how moved little Harry may be, his tears will always be both belated and confined to that particular carpet, while the textual invocation of Pamela's tears will be disseminated in an ever-widening circle that reminds readers that they too will be at best reenacting the prior tears of their heroine. That is, the tears of individual readers will necessarily be both subsequent to and in imitation of those of Pamela and therein will lie both their glory and their limitation. Like little Harry's, their tears (and by implication, their response more generally) can only individuate a single copy of *Pamela,* whereas those of Pamela herself will exist as a sort of absent presence in every copy. Thus in an odd, but for many readers apparently compelling, logic, the printed *Pamela* takes on the authority of the unique manuscript such that despite its inability to show things like tearstains, it can nonetheless partake of their aura and sacrality—as can Richardson himself, who, unlike his readers, is allegedly in possession of those manuscripts and so curiously bathed in the presence which they radiate. Readers who wish to envision themselves as part of the coterie public may, like little Harry, be sufficiently moved by that presence as to attempt to replicate it, but their productions, whether verbal or lachrymal, will necessarily (according to the logic of these bibliographic games) have a more fraught and distanced relation to that presence. Try as he or she might, the Friend to Virtue's letter from Lady Davers to Pamela will not possess the same sacrality as those contained in the printed *Pamela,* unless Richardson deigned to include it in a subsequent edition (which, of course, would present its authority as stemming from its status as a unique manuscript within his control). The actual letter now preserved at the Victoria and Albert (see Figure 8) thus lacks the sacrality of the fictitious letters which supposedly served as Richardson's copytext. Hence the distinction between manuscript and print which has apparently been resolved within the frame of *Pamela* itself comes back with a vengeance to mark out the boundary between *Pamela* and the lewd engraftments of individual readers.

The felt sacrality which this displaced distinction could generate on behalf of the printed *Pamela* is brought out by another quintessentially Richardsonian gesture of what can only be described as hostile consultation. On several occasions, Richardson sent interleaved copies of his work to Hill and his daughters, Astraea and Minerva, accompanied by a request that they use the blank leaves for corrections and augmentations. When the interleaved and finely bound *Pamela* arrived, Astraea and Minerva thanked Richardson for his gift in quite extravagant language:

> It is not possible to have too much of Pamela: and therefore we took courage, and received her with less Confusion, tho' You sent her in splendor of her wedding

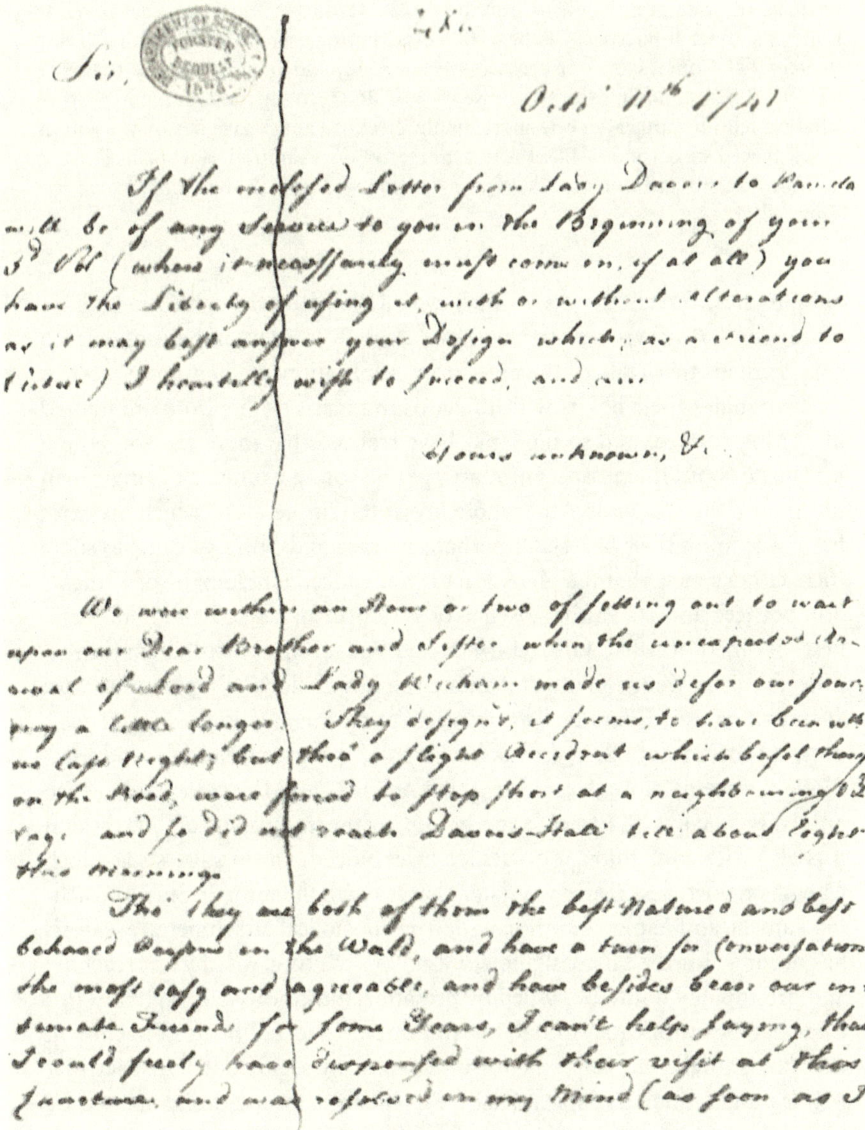

Sir,

Octr 11th 1741

If the inclosed Letter from Lady Davers to Pamela will be of any Service to you in the Beginning of your 3d Vol (where it necessarily must come in, if at all) you have the Liberty of using it, with or without Alterations as it may best answer your Design which (as a Friend to Virtue) I heartily wish to succeed, and am

Yours unknown, &c.

We were within an Hour or two of setting out to wait upon our Dear Brother and Sister when the unexpected Arrival of Lord and Lady W[illegible] made us defer our Journey a little longer. They design'd, it seems, to have been with us last Night; but thro' a slight Accident which befel them on the Road, were forced to stop short at a neighbouring [illegible] and so did not reach Davers-Hall till about Eight this Morning.

Tho' they are both of them the best Natured and best behaved Persons in the World, and have a turn for Conversation the most easy and agreeable, and have besides been our intimate Friends for some Years, I can't help saying, that I could freely have dispensed with their visit at this Juncture, and was resolved in my Mind (as soon as I

Figure 8. A letter from "Lady Davers" sent to Richardson, 1741. Courtesy of the Victoria and Albert Museum/V & A Images.

> Ornaments. Yet give us leave, to hope your Pardon, if we tell you, that no Dress can give this Charmer Beauties equal to her Natural ones — you know, she look'd most sweetly, in her honest Russet. And the only Wise and reasonable use we can presume to make of your permission to inscribe our Notes, upon those interleav'd White Emblems of her Innocence, will be to fill em with progressive memorandums of the Benefits her Conversation brings us, — How kind, and how instructive therefore have you been, good Sir, who (when we wanted Room to say the thousandth Part of what we felt for Pamela, in one short, single sheet of Paper) have bestow'd upon us a well-placed succession of Blank Pages, to receive our Admiration while its Force is new and warm: and our touch'd Hearts continue fill'd, with the whole Joy of the Impression.[58]

Despite these fervent thanks—which even Richardson thought "too high"—Astraea and Minerva seem to have never actually written in their interleaved copy. Perhaps they realized the indecorous implications of their final sentence, which equates their hearts with Richardson's blank pages: both are figured as writing surfaces and so they may have realized that there was something indelicate about the prospect of marriageable young women allowing a man not their father to peruse "the whole Joy of the Impression" which his work has made upon their hearts. Or perhaps Astraea and Minerva came to share their father's view that the blank leaves were indeed emblematic of Pamela's "Innocence" and so, in the absence of a reformed rake to annotate them, best "doomed" to what Aaron elsewhere termed an "unspotted virgin purity." Indeed, Aaron went so far as to equate the impressions of a pen with rape: "I must not, nay, I dare not, think of violating them."[59] Regardless of their motivations for not filling the book with their "progressive memorandums," though, it seems more than evident that Astraea and Minerva regarded even an ordinary copy of *Pamela* (one bound in the equivalent of "her honest Russet") with something approaching awe. Indeed, Aaron suggests as much when he reports, less than a year later, that his "daughters are in Surry, preaching Pamela, and Pamela's author, with true apostolical attachment."[60] *Pamela* has become, for the Hill daughters, a kind of scripture, worthy of preaching and presumably not to be sullied by profane hands incapable of giving "this Charmer Beauties equal to her Natural ones."[61] No doubt this attachment was not entirely the consequence of Richardson's gift, but I suspect that Astraea and Minerva's "apostolical" reverence was dramatically abetted by his gesture, with its daunting provision of blank leaves equal in bulk to the printed leaves, but not equal in quality (at least until filled up and perhaps not then), and never equal in appearance or dissemination.[62] That is, there is an implicit challenge in Richardson's gift: "here are the materials with which

Pamela produced the text which now comprises *Pamela*, can you write as well as her? If not, remember your place and pay homage to those who can." In the face of their almost certain inability to satisfy Richardson with their augmentations, Astraea and Minerva not only "wisely declined" to rise to the occasion but also, it would seem, were persuaded to grant the printed *Pamela* a reverence not unlike that accorded by another reader to Richardson's own correspondence: "tho' I am not Superstitious, I should regard a bit of Paper from your Hands, in the same manner as Bigots do Amulets and Relics of Saints."[63] In many ways, of course, the interleaved copy is an extreme case, but I suspect that a similar unwillingness to violate the blank spaces of *Pamela* (and so sully the text which wrought such amazing conversions) may help to account for the almost total lack of extant annotated copies, despite the intensity of the Pamela vogue.[64] Those who wished to expand upon *Pamela* through the invention of additional correspondence for her and her compatriots seem to have kept their expansions bibliographically separate from Richardson's work, thereby subtly reinforcing Richardson's distinctions regarding their comparative sacrality and so tacitly assenting to his claims to centrality among the coterie public.

Indeed, even when readers' engraftments were in specific competition with Richardson's version of *Pamela,* they still seem to have paid a certain backhanded compliment to the sacrality of *Pamela* as an artifact. Thus, for example, the advertisements for *Pamela's Conduct in High Life* go out of their way to specify that Kelly's collection is "*Printed on the same Letter as* Pamela, or Virtue Rewarded" as if to suggest that the similarity of the books as objects could guarantee other sorts of similarity as well.[65] Hence even as Kelly's text engages in what Richardson denounced as a "scandalous Attempt . . . of Ingrafting upon his plan," Kelly's two volumes pay a certain reluctant tribute to the numinous presence of both "Pamela, and Pamela's author," albeit without quite the "true apostolical attachment" of the Hill sisters. Richardson may not have been able to get his readers to outstretch his poor Scenes in the exact ways in which he hoped, but even his most serious competitors granted him much of the centrality for which he so yearned.

Similarly, even quite skeptical readers of *Pamela* seem to have found imagining themselves part of a coterie public with Richardson at its center an at least momentarily compelling prospect. Consider only a letter sent by William Shenstone to Richard Jago "in the Manner of Pamela." Shenstone begins by doing exactly what Aaron Hill dreaded. Rather than relying on "our inward Idea of Pamela's Person," Shenstone set out to illustrate the novel, to provide a "figur'd Pretence to Resemblance": "Well! and so I sate me down in my room, and was reading *Pamela*—one might furnish this book with several pretty decorations, thought I to myself; and then I began to design cuts for it, in particular places. For instance, one, where Pamela is forced to fall upon her knees in the arbor: a second, where she is in bed, and Mrs. Jewkes holds one hand, and Mr. B. the other: a third, where Pamela sits sewing in the summer-house, &c. So I just sketched them out, and sent my little hints, such as they were, to Mr. R———n."[66] Once his illustrations are complete, Shenstone slips into a parody of Pamela's "writing to the moment" which is so affectionate that it seems more akin to homage:

> As soon as I had sealed my letter, in comes Mrs. Arnold—'Well, Mrs. Arnold, says I, this Mr. Jago never comes—what can one do? I'm as dull as a beetle for want of company.' 'Sir, says she, the hen—' 'What makes you out of breath, says I, Mrs. Arnold, what's the matter?' 'Why, Sir, says she, the hen that I set last-sabbath-day-was-three-weeks has just hatched, and has brought all her eggs to good.' 'That's brave indeed, says I.' 'Ay, that it is, says she, so be and't please G–d an how that they liven, there'll be a glorious parcel of 'em. Shall I bring 'em up for you to see?' says she [a long conversation on the chickens then ensures] . . . 'Well, says I, Mrs. Arnold, you and your chicken may go down; I am going to write a letter.' So I sat down, and wrote thus far; scrattle, scrattle, goes the pen—why how now? says I—what's the matter with the pen? So I thought I would make an end of my letter, because my pen went scrattle, scrattle. Well, I warrant I shall have little pleasure when Mr. Jago *comes;* for I never fixed my heart much upon anything in my life, but some misfortune happened to balance my pleasure. — After all, thought I, it must be some very ill accident that outweighs the pleasure I shall take in seeing him. (29)

Stylistically, then, the bulk of the letter burlesques *Pamela,* faithfully capturing the inelegant language and quotidian concerns of Mrs. Arnold in order to gently mock the similar language and concerns of Pamela and Mrs. Jervis. Shenstone uses that parody, however, as a means of reconnecting with a distant friend through the mediation of *Pamela.* That is, Shenstone draws Jago's attention not only to Pamela as a correspondent—whose writings he elsewhere claims "would have made one good volume"—but also to *Pamela* as a printed book which could use "several pretty decorations" and which purports to be the transcription of manuscript correspondence very much like the letter Shenstone has just written.[67] The humor to be had at the heroine's expense only highlights the pleasures to be had from her book: surely among other things the epistle is a not so subtle invitation to Jago to request copies of Shenstone's "cuts" in order to extra-illustrate his own copy of *Pamela.* As such, Shenstone seems to be positioning himself and Jago as members of the coterie public, albeit members in less good standing than the Hill family. They are fellow readers of *Pamela;* their respective "want of company" may be relieved by the production of correspondence "in the Manner of Pamela"; and Shenstone's "pleasure when Mr. Jago *comes*" will be all the greater for their having shared both a sardonic grin at her expense and an appreciation of the possibilities of the "warm scenes" for actual visualization. Through what Richardson termed "the converse of the pen," which can make "distance, presence," their respective absences to one another—Shenstone's "want of company"—can be reimagined as a virtual sociability through the mediation of *Pamela* and the "pretty decorations" which she has inspired.[68] Or, to revert to the terms of my chapter title, Shenstone's engraftments—which Richardson no doubt found lewd and ungenerous—both testify to the allure of the coterie public and position Richardson at its center (after all, the "hints, such as they were" were sent to Richardson, not Jago). But they do so at the partial expense of Richardson's authority: if the coterie public is founded upon the power of correspondence to make absence presence, then the presence at the very heart of the coterie (Richardson's impressive bulk) was, paradoxically, curiously absent.

Chapter 5
Shandyism and the Club of True Feelers

If Richardson's readers positioned him at the center of the coterie public, they did so in ways which largely preserved their own readerly autonomy and thus implicitly thwarted his efforts to promote his own authority as final or even controlling. Two decades later, Laurence Sterne was not about to make the same mistake. Sterne was every bit as eager as Richardson to turn the canonizing and community-inventing effects of imaginative expansion to his own account. Unlike his predecessor, though, Sterne saw that the best way through which to write "not [to] be *fed*, but *famous*" was to cajole and flatter his readers into acceding to his authority over them, rather than attempting to render them superfluous.[1] As we have seen, most eighteenth-century readers were jealous of their own autonomy and so unlikely to respond well to bullying and preemption. If anything, they had to be convinced that the benefits which would accrue by submitting themselves to an author's authority were going to be more than worth the sacrifice. In this chapter, we will investigate how Sterne endeavored to make such obeisance a desirable and pleasurable prospect, one which seemed likely to bring about new forms of enjoyment and sociability, rather than merely a surrender of cherished readerly independence. Indeed, he went out of his way to convince his readers that not only did they not have to sacrifice their autonomy in any meaningful way, they might actually have new opportunities for its exercise if only they read his work in the proper manner. Yet amid the free-wheeling play of *Tristram Shandy* and *A Sentimental Journey* were a series of jokey yet powerfully insistent reminders that the pleasures which his readers had been enjoying and sharing with their fellows had not appeared out of thin air but rather been thoughtfully inserted for their benefit and the least they could do was to show a little gratitude. In so doing, Sterne modeled yet another form of virtual community: something akin to the uninhibited yet ultimately self-regulating clubs which were such a staple of eighteenth-century sociability.

Perhaps unsurprisingly, given his model, Sterne's gambit met with considerable success. The very idea of a virtual club, especially one comprised solely of "true feelers," seemed to have appealed to a broad spectrum of readers, including some who were otherwise hostile to Sterne's work.[2] Membership in such a club was not without its costs, however. By accepting Sterne's invitation to join a club of true feelers, readers also tacitly accepted a host of minor restrictions on their autonomy which collectively made it harder and harder to envision themselves as part of a public any broader than the necessarily restricted membership of the club, whose appeal, after all, lay in its exclusion of all those who were not "true feelers," however the latter might be defined. Thus the crazes which surrounded *Tristram Shandy* and *A Sentimental Journey* mark an important transition in the narrative we have been tracing. Those crazes helped to transform the authorial centrality which Richardson had sought into a real authority, one which ensured that readers would increasingly feel their strongest virtual attachments to authors, rather than to their fellow readers. Indeed, it is not too much to say that the intertwined affection toward authors and suspicion toward most of one's fellow readers which defines so much of nineteenth-century literary culture stems in considerable part from the chaotic, indecorous, but ultimately deferential sociability of Sterne's true feelers. This chapter, then, traces the Shandean gambits, both Sternean and otherwise, that made participation in a club of true feelers so compelling an option as to forever transform the balance of power between authors and readers.

* * *

More than any writer before him, Sterne built opportunities for imaginative expansion into his work. Indeed, in his conception of textuality, readers did at least as much work as authors: one of Sterne's most famous letters insists that "a true feeler always brings half the entertainment along with him. His own ideas are only call'd forth by what he reads, and the vibrations within, so entirely correspond with those excited, 'tis like reading *himself* and not the *book*."[3] This dictum echoes a pronouncement made by Toby in Volume Eight of *Tristram Shandy* (published three years earlier), when Trim was first attempting to tell "the Story of the king of Bohemia and his seven castles": to a merry tale, "a man should ever bring one half of the entertainment along with him."[4] In both formulations, proper reading is defined by the opportunities it offers a reader and the responsibilities which such opportunities incur. The "true feeler" can become almost a coauthor, matching his ideas and sympathetic vibrations to those already in the text and thereby doubling the "entertainment" which that text can afford. Yet if the text fails to entertain, the liability falls at least as much upon the reader as the author: it hints at a defect in "*himself* and not the *book*" and thus reveals him to be something other than a "true feeler," most likely yet another ruminant in "the *herd* of the *world*," among whom "there is so little true feeling." Obviously this sort of rhetoric shifting the onus of textual pleasure onto the individual reader dates back to antiquity. Traditionally, however, such rhetoric was merely paratextual: an empty threat flourished in a preface or prologue, rather than anything actually incorporated into the body of a text in any formal way. One of Sterne's chief innovations was to push this rhetoric to its logical conclusion by self-consciously providing opportunities for readers to furnish their share of the entertainment and so justify their title to true feeling.

Consider only the introduction of Dr. Slop. In the course of three paragraphs, Tristram repeatedly invites the reader to

> imagine to yourself a little, squat, uncourtly figure of a Doctor *Slop*, of about four feet and a half perpendicular height, with a breadth of back, and a sesquipedality of belly, which might have done honour to a Serjeant in the Horse-Guards. . . . Imagine such a one . . . coming slowly along, foot by foot, waddling thro' the dirt upon the vertebrae of a little diminutive pony,—of a pretty colour;---but of strength,---alack!——scarce able to have made an amble of it, under such a fardel, had the roads been in ambling condition,----They were not.—— Imagine to yourself, *Obadiah* mounted upon a strong monster of a coach-horse, prick'd into a full gallop, and making all practicable speed the adverse way. Pray, Sir, let me interest you a moment in this description. (2.9.121)

Tristram then narrates the near-collision between Obadiah and Slop "in the dirtiest part of a dirty lane" which results in Slop's "tumbling off [his pony] diagonally, something in the stile and manner of a pack of wool . . . with the broadest part of him sunk about twelve inches deep in the mire" where he was further "beluted, and . . . transubstantiated" by "an explosion of mud" from Obadiah's horse (2.9.122–23). Immediately thereafter, Slop enters the back-parlor at Shandy Hall like the ghost of Old Hamlet: "*unwiped, unappointed, unanealed,* with all his stains and blotches on him" (2.10.124), which apparently prompts Tristram to declare that

> writing, when properly managed, . . . is but a different name for conversation: As no one, who knows what he is about in good company, would venture to talk all;—so no author, who understands the just boundaries of decorum and good breeding,

would presume to think all: The truest respect which you can pay to the reader's understanding, is to halve this matter amicably, and leave him something to imagine, in his turn, as well as yourself. For my own part, I am eternally paying him compliments of this kind, and do all that lies in my power to keep his imagination as busy as my own. 'Tis his turn now;—I have given an ample description of Dr. *Slop*'s sad overthrow, and of his sad appearance in the back parlour;—his imagination must now go on with it for a while. Let the reader imagine then, that Dr. *Slop* has told his tale;——and in what words, and with what aggravations his fancy chooses:——Let him suppose that *Obadiah* has told his tale also, and with such rueful looks of affected concern, as he thinks will best contrast the two figures as they stand by each other: Let him imagine that my father has stepp'd up stairs to see my mother:—And, to conclude this work of imagination,—let him imagine the Doctor wash'd,—— rubb'd down,—condoled with,—felicitated,—got into a pair of *Obadiah*'s pumps, stepping forwards towards the door, upon the very point of entering upon action. (2.11.125–26)

There are a number of striking things about these passages, but surely the most significant has to be the way in which Tristram offers up the exact same sort of gestural detail as we saw readers inventing in Chapter 2, only to then explicitly invite his readers to carry on the visualization he has begun by further fleshing out the scene in various specific ways. And this shared responsibility for visualization supposedly exemplifies Tristram's "truest respect" for both his readers and "the just boundaries of decorum and good breeding." Imaginative expansion, at least when the mutual activity of both authors and readers, is here being held up as the quintessence of polite sociability. Obviously this is a rather odd claim to make, given both the scene in question—which is hardly decorous or well bred—and the sheer extent to which Tristram goes in instructing his readers how to imagine what is supposedly being left up to them (which might seem to belie his repudiation of an author's "think[ing] all"). Nonetheless, let us take Tristram's invitations seriously for a moment and consider some of the apparent effects and consequences for readers of sharing the visualization of these scenes.

Few readers were more gleeful in their acceptance of Tristram's invitations than John Hope, a columnist for *The Westminster Magazine* under the nom de plume of "The Leveller." Hope described for his readers the first time he read this scene:

I thought I saw before me the little fat Doctor, mounted on his diminutive poney that was waddling through the narrow dirty lane, at every step sinking to the knees in mire: I thought I saw the hasty Obadiah, mounted on a great unruly brute of a coach horse, galloping at his full speed: I thought I saw him, with this tremendous velocity, bounce upon the unsuspecting Doctor at the sudden turn of the garden

> wall: I painted to myself the terror and consternation of the Doctor's face; the vain attempts he would make, in the dirt, to turn his poney out of the way of Obadiah's horse: his crossing himself, like a good Roman-Catholic on the apprehension of inevitable death; his dropping his whip, through hurry and confusion, in crossing himself; his catching most naturally, and as if by instinct to recover his falling whip; his losing his stirrups in consequence thereof; his falling, like a windmill, with legs and arms extended; and then sticking, when he reached the earth, like a pack of wool in the mud; then the trepidation of Obadiah at the sight of the Doctor's dirty and dangerous state; the trouble he was at to stop his great, hard-mouthed, stiff-necked brute, which he could by no other means effect, than by pulling him round and round the prostrate Doctor, and bespattering him all with mud; the rueful face of Obadiah, and the aukward apologies he would make: All these, I say, with many other additional circumstances, painted themselves so strongly on my imagination, that I laughed most immoderately loud.[5]

A number of these details cannot be found in Sterne's text: the pony's sinking into the mud from the weight of his rider, Slop's splayed limbs extending like the sails on a windmill, the stiff neck of Obadiah's horse—these are all Hope's invention and it is striking how much they recall the "silent eloquence of gestures, looks, and pauses" we investigated in Chapter 2. Hope uses these additional details to flesh out the scene and render it sufficiently detailed as to seem ideally present when he reads it "in the company of two very sensible men," one of whose fancies was "tickled . . . as much as . . . mine, and he joined very heartily in the laugh." Shared visualization would thus seem to work in the way that Tristram had claimed it would. It prompts a laughter which furthers readerly sociability, even as it testifies to Hope's status as a true feeler characterized above all by his sincerity: "when I hear any thing very laughable, let it be in the Church, the Senate, or the Court, I can no more refrain from grinning, than I can from weeping at any affecting misery or distress of a fellow-creature. Every one must recollect some, among his acquaintances, whose risible faculties are as little under command as mine, and who stand as little in awe, as I do, of the censure of a superior" (33). And since the entire point of the essay is to counter Lord Chesterfield's "fashionable" insistence that laughter was the mark of "Folly and Ill-manners" with the argument that "*Laughter* is no more the characteristic of *Folly,* than *Gravity* is of *Wisdom,*" it seems more than coincidental that the passage which Hope invokes to make his point should be the very passage which Tristram had chosen to introduce his theory of writing as conversation which observes "the just boundaries of decorum and good breeding." The well-bred sociability which true feelers can forge with one another, far from necessitating a Chesterfieldian reserve, is actually undermined by the insincerity implicit in such politesse: "I can see no reason why the same serious, stupid face should be continued in a private company of friends; *Prudence* requires it no longer, among those to whom the rate of each other's understanding must be sufficiently known" (16). In the place of such false "sense and breeding" should be put the genuine sociability which arises from halving the matter amicably, both with one's fellow readers and with Tristram himself.

Thus far it would seem that Hope is serving as an almost ideal reader for Tristram in the ways in which he continues the visualization which Tristram had begun and thereby halves the matter amicably to the satisfaction of all involved, except his other companion who, "though a man of a good solid understanding, had neither a sprightly imagination, any taste for humour, nor the least turn for the burlesque" and so was no great loss (36). Yet it is worth noting that while Hope behaves as an exemplary reader in terms of *how* he approaches the scene, he quite insistently avoids the particular scenes which Tristram has designated. That is, he responds to Tristram's initial invitations to imagine Slop in the alley, rather than to the later indoor scene when readers' imaginations are more explicitly instructed to "go on with it for a while." One might be tempted to dismiss this as merely a personal predilection were it not for the fact that a similar recalcitrance describes all of the extant eighteenth-century illustrations of this episode. For example, George Romney painted only four scenes from the novel, a full half of which involved this incident: "The Entrance of Dr. Slop into the Parlour of Mr. Shandy" and "Obadiah Making his bow to Dr. Slop as the Doctor is falling in the Lane." Similarly, Henry William Bunbury chose "The Overthrow of Dr. Slop" as one of his four subjects from *Tristram Shandy*. Other artists drawn to the episode include Robert Dighton, who drew "Dr. Slop and Obadiah——meeting in the Dirty Lane——The Doctor thrown from his Pony" and John Nixon, who depicted Slop's arrival at Shandy Hall.[6] In each case, as with Hope, the images produced depict those scenes which Tristram had already described in considerable mock-heroic detail, rather than those ostensibly left open and available to readers. That is, these readers devoted their respective energies to further visualizing those scenes which Sterne privately feared might already be "Overloaded" with detail.[7] Why should this be and what might it reveal?

Surely part of an answer lies in the degree to which Tristram, as Tom Keymer has pointed out, quickly "contravene[s] his own theory" of reading as conversation "in a welter of bossy imperatives. . . . Within a few sentences, the relaxed convenor of collaborative meanings has mutated into a control freak" directing *how* readers are to imagine the scenes he has not described in full detail.[8] For a reader as devoted to his own autonomy as Hope (remember his self-description as one "who stand[s] . . . little in awe . . . of the censure of a superior"), there would almost necessarily be something irksome about accepting Tristram's guidance as to where to expand. Yet opting out of visualization would be self-defeating, for it would deprive him of the opportunity to prove himself a true feeler capable of genuine sociability. The compromise, it would seem, was to visualize along the lines of Tristram's invitation, but in places other than those specifically designated by him. Thus he could preserve his self-respect as a free-born Briton, while still participating in the Shandean sociability which halving the matter amicably could facilitate.

A similar dynamic seems to govern Bunbury's depiction of "The Overthrow of Dr. Slop" (Figure 9). Bunbury faithfully renders the scene as described by Tristram—right down to the sinking of "the broadest part of [Dr. Slop] . . . about twelve inches deep in the mire" (2.9.123)—but somewhat ostentatiously adds three rather Shandean details, as if to demonstrate his provision of half the entertainment. First off, and most conspicuously, a muddy dog is shown pouncing on the fallen Slop to add insult to the injury he has already sustained at the hooves of Obadiah's "strong monster of a

Figure 9. Henry William Bunbury, *The Overthrow of Dr. Slop*, 1773. Courtesy of The Lewis Walpole Library, Yale University.

coach-horse" and thereby help to ensure that Slop's name accurately signifies his true character. Together, these animals, both traditional emblems of hearty Englishness, help to underscore Slop's self-evident unworthiness—both as a Catholic and as a quack—to approach Mrs. Shandy's ****, much less deliver Tristram into this world or partake of his "properly managed" writing.[9] Indeed, Slop's exclusion from the world of Shandean sociability is further highlighted by Bunbury's decision to depict Obadiah's horse as bob-tailed and so akin to both Tristram and Toby in his symbolic eunuchry. And, of course, the sign indicating the way toward Shandy Hall takes the form of a pointing hand almost exactly like the printer's fist—☛—employed throughout *Tristram Shandy,* as if to suggest that the real reason one would go to Shandy Hall is for the pleasures it offers as a printed book, rather than the obstetric commissions it might afford. Collectively, these additions to Tristram's already "overloaded" scene position Bunbury as a reader much like Hope: appreciative of the opportunity to demonstrate his credentials as a true feeler capable of sustaining his half of the entertainment, but not cowed by Tristram's somewhat bullying instructions. As with Hope, the gesture seems to be not so much one of defiance as of self-assertion: an insistence that he is engaging in visualization because it pleases him, rather than because he has been instructed to do so.

I dwell upon Hope and Bunbury because they each nicely exemplify the dynamic between reader and author which Sterne's rhetoric seem to anticipate. That is, they each apparently conceive of their visualizations as a means toward participating in a raucous, seemingly irreverent, yet oddly respectful form of virtual sociability with both Tristram and their fellow readers. In so insistently staging their own readerly independence, they each offer up an image of themselves as fiercely devoted to liberty and even eccentricity. Yet in accepting Tristram's invitation to imagine, they are tacitly accepting his authority to at least broadly direct their attention, and so are implicitly surrendering a bit of their own autonomy in return for what he has to offer. This sort of voluntary submission to the authority of an ostensive equal is, of course, at the heart of the "associational world" of eighteenth-century club life. Just as actual club members repeatedly and loudly insisted upon the fiction that clubs were a space in which "all are equal and on the same level [and] no member shall assume a superiority over another," even as they organized themselves in often quite hierarchical and rule-bound ways, so too, it seems, the virtual sociability of the club of true feelers combined ostentatious gestures of autonomy with a tacit submission to Sterne's authority on the vast majority of matters which actually counted.[10]

That is, the "conversational liberty" implicit in gestures like Hope's and Bunbury's was not at all incompatible with a willing submission to the dictates of club officers, so long as those dictates promised to contribute to "the better regulation" of their mutual pleasures.[11]

Thus far we have been considering the readerly dynamics surrounding Tristram's explicit invitations to imagine particular vignettes. But similar dynamics also characterize those moments in which Sterne self-consciously exploits the possibilities of serial publication, which suggests that here too the matter is being halved with his readers, though again perhaps not quite as amicably as Tristram would have us believe. From rather early on, that is, Tristram displays a penchant for promising things that he cannot or will not deliver in the current installment of his *Life and Opinions.* For instance, amid his description of the midwife whom Elizabeth Shandy prefers, Tristram tries to indicate the breadth of her fame by earnestly

> fix[ing] it at about four or five miles, which not only comprehended the whole parish, but extended itself to two or three of the adjacent hamlets in the skirts of the next parish. . . . she was, moreover, very well looked upon at one large grange-house and some other odd houses and farms within two or three miles . . . from the smoke of her own chimney:----But I must here, once for all, inform you, that all this will be more exactly delineated and explain'd in a map, now in the hands of the engraver, which, with many other pieces and developments to this work, will be added to the end of the twentieth volume,---not to swell the work,—I detest the thought of such a thing;——but by way of commentary, scholium, illustration, and key to such passages, incidents, or inuendos as shall be thought to be either of private interpretation, or dark or doubtful meaning after my life and my opinions shall have been read over . . . by all the *world.* (1.13.39–40)

Clearly, Tristram is being more than a little ironic here: consider only how "swelling" a phrase follows his repudiation of swelling. Nor does understanding the geographical extent of the midwife's fame actually seem to require a map, much less one which would not arrive (at the current publication rate) until nine years hence. Yet, as is so often the case with Sterne, the joke makes a serious point. In a narrative as wandering and digressive as *Tristram Shandy* which is also being published in an undefined number of serial installments, it will not always be evident which aspects of the narrative might ultimately benefit from "commentary, scholium, illustration, and key," nor which of the assorted promises Tristram makes have any chance of being fulfilled. The circumference of the midwife's world *could* turn out to be significant. Tristram's account *could* run to twenty volumes. Neither is all that likely, but the point remains that serial publication, particularly of such an "odd" text, almost inevitably starts more hares than it follows and so each cryptic allusion or promised future pleasure is potentially available for readers to flesh out in anticipation. Perhaps their inventions will be countermanded by a subsequent installment; perhaps they will not. Regardless of the ultimate outcome, though, for the next year or more readers were free to invent whatever scenarios or glosses they pleased and to presume that the objects of their speculation were among the ways in which Tristram was halving the entertainment with them. After all, if he was so good a host as to leave "half a dozen places purposely open" for "your criticks and gentry of refined taste," then surely he would provide at least as many for "the rest of [his] guests" (2.2.96–97), given his proclivity for tantalizing them with the coy mention of such morsels as the significance of Toby's wound to his modesty: "which way could that effect it? The story of that, Madam, is long and interesting; ----but it would be running my history all upon heaps to give it you here. ——'Tis for an episode hereafter; and every circumstance relating to it in its proper place, shall be faithfully laid before you:----'Till then, it is not in my power to give further light into this matter, or say more than what I have said already" (1.21.75). Readers could wait until the fullness of time revealed that episode's "proper place." However, those "out of all patience for my uncle *Toby*'s character" (1.24.86) might well be tempted to take matters into their own hands, especially in the wake of Tristram's closing boast that

> you may conjecture upon [how Toby was bested in the debate over the proper way to deliver Tristram], if you please,—and whilst your imagination is in motion, you may encourage it to go on, and discover by what causes and effects in nature it could come to pass that my uncle *Toby* got his modesty by the wound he received upon his groin.—You may raise a system to account for the loss of my nose by marriage articles,——and shew the world how it could happen, that I should have the misfortune to be called Tristram, in opposition to my father's hypothesis, and the wish of the whole family, God-fathers and God-mothers not excepted.—These, with fifty other points left yet unravelled, you may endeavour to solve if you had time; but I tell you before-hand it will be in vain. . . . The reader will be content to wait for a full explanation of these matters until the next year,—when a series of things will be laid open which he little expects. (2.19.180–81)

The closing words of his first installment are thus an implicit dare from Tristram to his readers to see if they can come up with any "conjecture" or discovery as to what to do with the "places purposely [left] open" for them. It is a test, in short, of whether their share of the entertainment is up to snuff.

Similar dares may be found throughout *Tristram Shandy*, each one genially taunting readers to test their wits against those of Tristram in a game of character migration. Sometimes Tristram opens the door to readerly speculation only to shut it again immediately:

> When Susannah told the corporal the misadventure of the sash, with all the circumstances which attended the *murder* of me,—(as she called it)—the blood forsook his cheeks;—all accessories to murder, being principals,—*Trim*'s conscience told him he was as much to blame as *Susannah,*—and if the doctrine had been true, my uncle *Toby* had as much of the blood-shed to answer for to heaven, as either of 'em;—so that neither reason or instinct, separate or together, could possibly have guided *Susannah*'s steps to so proper an asylum. It is in vain to leave this to the Reader's imagination:——to form any kind of hypothesis that will render these propositions feasible, he must cudgel his brains sore,—and to do it without,—he must have such brains as no reader ever had before him.——Why should I put them either to tryal or to torture? 'Tis my own affair: I'll explain it myself. (5.18.450)

The answer, of course, lies in Toby and Trim's yet unnarrated pilfering of the sash weights and pulleys to make cannons for their military reenactments. The taunt here seems quite pointed: it would be a rare reader indeed who could devise such a "hypothesis," especially before his or her eyes fell upon the solution proffered in the following chapter. Yet given how many such enigmas were *not* immediately answered, it seems quite probable that some readers would have been at least tempted to pause and invent a scenario to "render these propositions feasible." After all, similar puzzles had been left hanging for multiple volumes. A year previous, for example, readers had been promised both "the catastrophe of my great uncle Mr. *Hammond Shandy,*——a little man,——but of high fancy:——he rushed into the duke of *Monmouth*'s affair" (3.10.198) and "a most minute account of every particular" of Uncle Toby's affair with Widow Wadman, including why, "after a series of attacks and repulses in a course of nine months," he "found it necessary to draw off his forces, and raise the siege somewhat indignantly" (3.24.246). Neither, despite Tristram's promise to provide at least the latter "in its proper place," had yet arrived and so both could potentially serve as opportunities for readerly invention, occasions through which to demonstrate oneself a true feeler by devising "a most minute account of every particular."

Yet, as with the Slop episode, readers embraced these opportunities to prove their title to true feeling, but did so by redefining them, as if to gesture toward playing the game more upon their own terms. Consider only the ways in which John Carr both takes up and sidesteps Tristram's teasing promise to explain Toby's modesty. Carr focuses not upon Toby's wound per se but rather upon what supposedly aggravated it: Walter's recurring allusions to Tristram's "great aunt Dinah, who, about sixty years ago, was married and got with child by the coachman, for which my father, according to his hypothesis of Christian names, would often say, She might thank her godfathers and godmothers" (1.21.73). According to Tristram, "the least hint of [the affair of my aunt Dinah] was enough to make the blood fly into [Toby's] face;---but when my father enlarged upon the story in mixed companies, which the illustration of his hypothesis frequently obliged him to do,----the unfortunate blight of one of the fairest branches of the family, would set my uncle *Toby*'s honour and modesty o'bleeding; and he would often take my father aside, in the greatest concern imaginable, to expostulate and tell him, he would give him any thing in the world, only to let the story rest" (1.21.76). Carr expands upon these fleeting mentions of Dinah in his *The Life and Opinions of Tristram Shandy . . . Vol. III* in order to make her a character in her own right: a disgruntled bluestocking who has been excluded from the birth of Tristram because of the affront her "frequent pregnancy" posed to the decency of the house (91). In Carr's version, the felt injustice of this exclusion bore so hard upon Dinah as to make her apparently take her own life amid the flurry of Tristram's birth. As a result, Slop, Toby, and Walter completely ignore the newborn Tristram in their zeal to conduct an autopsy: Slop because he was "positive many wonderful discoveries could be made" (93), Toby because he hoped "for the honour of the family" to discredit "an idle report . . . that *Dinah* was again pregnant" (102), and Walter because "if she was with child at this age, my system is as strong as the castle of *York!*" (102). The effect of this account of Dinah, including the multiplication of her liaison into "repeated transgressions" (91)—not to mention the further detailing of her initial seduction, which we now learn took place in a "green-house" (82)—is to make Toby's hypermodesty more credible. Few things could be more wounding to such a man than an aunt with such "ruinous decays of her character" (87) who nonetheless insisted on "speak[ing] without reserve her well-digested opinions concerning pregnant women" (76). Carr thus underscores Tristram's point that "the drawing of my uncle *Toby*'s character went on gently all the time [my aunt *Dinah* and the coachman came a-cross us] . . . so that you are much better acquainted with my uncle *Toby* now than you was before" (1.22.80). Yet he does so obliquely by taking up the passing mentions of Dinah, rather than the more ostentatious taunts that accompanied the mention of Toby's wound. Similarly, Carr implicitly reveals why "I should have the misfortune to be called Tristram, in opposition to my father's hypothesis" (2.19.180)—namely, Walter was too distracted by the prospect of dissecting Dinah to pay attention to the christening of his own son—but he does so indirectly through the invention of

Dinah's postmortem, rather by engaging head-on with Tristram's challenge. As with Hope and Bunbury, this obliqueness, in conjunction with his ventriloquizing of Tristram's voice, allowed Carr to maintain enough self-respect to position himself as an equal sharer in the entertainment, one wholly up to the task of solving the puzzles created by Tristram's games with serial publication. If Tristram proposes, then Carr disposes, with both fully capable of continuing their banter and raillery indefinitely: indeed, Carr's volume concludes with the properly Shandean gesture of an index to his yet unpublished Volume Seven. Among other things, this hints that patient readers will learn "why, on the coachman's death, [Dinah] took again the name of *Shandy*" (222).

* * *

Yet the example of Carr, like those of Hope and Bunbury, begs the question of why readers so apparently jealous of their own autonomy should have wanted to enter into Tristram's games in the first place. What was it, in short, that made it worthwhile to endure his taunts and practical jokes? Why should readers have wanted to join his entertainment at all, much less furnish half of it? The answer seems to lie, at least in considerable part, with the way in which Tristram represents himself as at heart but a fellow true feeler, an author who has magnanimously chosen not "to make use of the advantage which the fortune of the pen has . . . gained [him] over" his "gentle reader[s]" (7.6.584), but has instead confined himself to the egalitarian repartee of the club, "which stressed co-operation and the equality of speaker rights, informality, and spontaneity."[12] The answer lies, that is, in the degree to which Tristram—unlike, say, Richardson—seems to "get it," to be "one of us." And as with the members of actual clubs, those interested in participating in the virtual club of true feelers seem to have been willing to put up with and even enjoy pranks from their fellow club members that would have constituted a perhaps duel-worthy affront from anyone else.

Part of the supposed proof of Tristram's clubbability was the sheer extent to which his own narratorial pleasure stemmed from his indulgence in reading practices akin to those he was soliciting from the true feelers in his audience. For example, Tristram goes out of his way to make it clear that his "Plain Stories"—"those which . . . arose out of [his] journey across" the plains of Languedoc—constituted "the most fruitful and busy period of my life" (7.43.648). Traditionally, while "there is nothing more pleasing to a traveller . . . than a large rich plain," there is also nothing "more terrible to travel-writers . . . especially if it is without great rivers or bridges; and presents nothing to the eye, but one unvaried picture of plenty: for after they have once told you that 'tis delicious! or delightful! . . . they have then a large plain upon their hands, which they know not what to do with" (7.42.646). Tristram experiences no such difficulties because of the way in which he approaches the plain (and so the stories he can tell of it): "by stopping and talking to every soul I met who was not in a full trot—joining all parties before me—waiting for every soul behind—hailing all those who were coming through cross roads—arresting all kinds of beggars, pilgrims, fiddlers, fryars—not passing by a woman in a mulberry-tree without commending her legs, and tempting her into conversation with a pinch of snuff——In short, by seizing every handle, of what size or shape soever, which chance held out to me in this journey—I turned my *plain* into a *city*—I was always in company, and with great variety too" (7.43.648). As a result, Tristram, unlike other "travel-writers," can make the "Plain Stories" he is telling as pleasurable to his readers as the journey which inspired those stories had been for him. The mere "traces" of his pen, as he writes those stories, "are now all set o'vibrating together this moment" (7.43.648) and so true feelers, whose "vibrations within, so entirely correspond with those excited," may experience Languedoc without ever leaving home. But wherein does the difference between Tristram and those other travelers lie? Surely it is in the degree to which he brings the entertainment along with him in a manner remarkably akin to imaginative expansion. Indeed, in a letter to one of his dearest friends, Sterne described traveling in language unmistakably reminiscent of his theory of reading: "I shall spend every winter of my life [in London], in the same lap of contentment, where I enjoy myself now [in York]—and wherever I go—we must bring three parts in four of the treat along with us."[13] Like Carr, that is, Tristram hails what could be termed the minor characters of the journey—"those who were coming through cross roads"—and makes something out of them. Like Hope and Bunbury, Tristram pauses over what might seem to another traveler to be only momentarily engaging verisimilitude—the shapely legs of a woman in a mulberry tree—and works it up into a little vignette. And to ensure that his analogy between reading and traveling did not pass unnoticed, Tristram rather extravagantly puns upon "Plain Stories"—including giving the phrase its own line in far from unobtrusive capital letters—in order to make it clear that these are not only the stories occasioned by his journey across Languedoc but also a metonym for his *Life and Opinions* more generally. The latter, remember, were supposedly going more and more "straight forwards, without digression or parenthesis" (7.43.651) in the hope that they might ultimately be able to "go on even thus;

---

which is a line drawn as straight as I could draw it, by a writing-master's ruler, . . . turning neither to the right hand or to the left" (6.40.571–72). Hence, the pleasure to be had from "plain stories" (in both senses) lies not so much in the plains or stories per se—"pleasing" though they might be—but in what could be done with them, how they could be transformed into "cities" through the exertions of the traveler *cum* reader. By framing his "plain stories" this way, Tristram suggests that while he may have a head start, he is fundamentally but a fellow reader committed to the same pleasures as his club mates. Accordingly, he implies, his lead is both trustworthy and worth following, even if it means relinquishing a bit of independence along the way.

In a similar vein, Yorick marvels over "what a large volume of adventures may be grasped within this little span of life by him who interests his heart in every thing, and who, having eyes to see, what time and chance are perpetually holding out to him as he journeyeth on his way, misses nothing he can *fairly* lay his hands on."[14] As evidence for this claim, he points to how much narrative he has generated in "little more than a single hour in Calais" and suggests that he could do the same regardless of his location: "was I in a desert, I would find out wherewith in it to call forth my affections—If I could not do better, I would fasten them upon some sweet myrtle, or seek some melancholy cypress to connect myself to—I would court their shade, and greet them kindly for their protection—I would cut my name upon them, and swear they were the loveliest trees throughout the desert: if their leaves wither'd, I would teach myself to mourn, and when they rejoiced, I would rejoice along with them" (36–37). The ultimate test of true feeling, it would seem, is whether one can devise further adventures for even the most unpromising of characters (mute myrtles and cypresses) and use those inventions not merely for the "pleasure of the experiment" but also to forge an imagined sociability sufficiently satisfying that it can "call forth" all of one's "affections." Indeed, Yorick suggests that failure to at least aspire to such imaginings—which he readily attests have "kept my senses, and the best part of my blood awake, and laid the gross to sleep"—marks one out as an unfeeling member of "the *herd* of the *world*," like "the man who can travel from *Dan* to *Beersheba*, and cry, 'Tis all barren—and so it is; and so is all the world to him who will not cultivate the fruits it offers" (36). The alternative to true feeling, in other words, is traveling (and so implicitly reading) like "the learned Smelfungus," who returned from his journey "used worse than St. Bartholomew," and with "nothing but the account of his miserable feelings" to show for it (37). The choice seems clear: one may join Yorick in reading like a true feeler and so grasp "a large volume of adventures" out of almost any text—remember that at this point in the narrative Yorick has *done* remarkably little for a less feeling narrator to "lay his hands on"—or one may refuse to "cultivate the fruits" of one's reading and thereby condemn oneself to solitary bitterness. Surely those who aligned themselves with Mr. Yorick were likely to have more fun.

Tristram and Yorick do not confine themselves, however, merely to allegorizing the kind of reading in which they engage. They also each make a point of including what purport to be the material traces of their reading, as if to provide irrefutable evidence of their status as fellow members of the club of true feelers. The most ostentatious instance of this sort of trace is probably Tristram's facing-page translation of Slawkenbergius's Tale, which reveals at a glance that it includes far more gestural details than are present in the Latin original. For example, Tristram augments Slawkenbergius's rather spare "*quo facto, sinum dextram inserens*" [which done, putting his right-hand into his bosom] with "having uncrossed his arms with the same solemnity with which he crossed them, he took up the reins of his bridle with his left-hand" (4.Slawkenbergius's Tale.294–95). Similarly, when Slawkenbergius simply describes the stranger as "*manibus ambabus in pectus positis*" [laying both his hands upon his breast], Tristram makes it clear that they were "the one over the other in a saint-like position" (4.Slawkenbergius's Tale.292–93). The clear implication, it would seem, is that for Tristram, the pleasures of Slawkenbergius's Tale do not only lie in the "whimsical view of the involutions of the heart of woman" (4.1.326) it provides but also in the opportunities it affords to make the tale his own through the act of visualization. Such appropriation is attractive both for its own sake—the bawdy absurdity of Slawkenbergius's Tale is enhanced by solemnly augmenting it with precisely detailed postures—and because it drives home the irony of his noting that Slawkenbergius's "story-telling Latin is much more concise than his philosophic—and, I think, has more of Latinity in it" (4.Slawkenbergius's Tale.288). That is, it becomes a deliciously self-canceling endeavor to complain that Slawkenbergius's prolegomena is "not a little prolix," when one is simultaneously engaged in pumping up the prolixity of "the ninth tale of his tenth decad" and converting his "Latinity" into nasal farce (3.38.274, 3.42.286). Such jokes may seem pointless to us, but, as even a glance at the extant records of eighteenth-century clubs will suggest, there was an almost endless hunger among the clubbable for elaborate nonsense of this sort "as a kind of neutral language, free from political, religious, or class inflection."[15] By representing himself as a fellow visualizer, Tristram can make a claim to be providing his share of the entertainment, not only as an author, but also as a fellow reader devoted, like a good club member should be, to "the primacy of wit, the pursuit of pleasure, and the exercise of an all-encompassing raillery."[16]

An even more revealing, if less ostentatious instance of one of Sterne's narrators offering up the supposed traces of his reading as evidence of his own clubbability may be seen in Yorick's encounter with Maria of Moulines. Maria had, of course, been featured in Volume Nine of *Tristram Shandy* the previous year, where she appeared immediately on the heels of Tristram's invitation to "take my pen, and go on with the story" of Toby's romance with Widow Wadman, even though he had anticipated it would "be the choicest morsel of what I had to offer to the world" (9.24.779). Moreover, Maria's story, such as it is, is told by a postillion with "something in his face above his condition" (which Tristram would have "sifted out . . . had not poor Maria . . . taken such full possession of me") and it ends with a conclusion in which nothing is concluded: "Adieu, Maria!—adieu, poor hapless damsel!——some time, but not *now*, I may hear thy sorrows from thy own lips——but I was deceived; for that moment she took her pipe and told me such a tale of woe with it, that I rose up, and with broken and irregular steps walk'd softly to my chaise.———What an excellent inn at Moulins!" (9.24.783–84). Given this framing, it is not hard to imagine that even before Yorick got to her, readers attuned to Tristram's games might well have considered the possibility of further adventures for Maria, perhaps ones which would deliver a *verbal* account of her sorrows or reveal the identity of the mysterious postillion. Regardless of whether or not he had predecessors, though, Mr. Yorick certainly took the bait, telling his own readers how "the story [my friend, Mr. Shandy] had told of that disorder'd maid affect'd me not a little in the reading," with the result that "when I got within the neighborhood where she lived, it returned so strong into my mind, that I could not resist an impulse . . . to enquire after her" (149). These inquiries, while involving an allegedly flesh-and-blood encounter, are nonetheless framed as a Quixotic enterprise—"'Tis going, I own, like the Knight of the Mournful Countenance"—as if to suggest that what he learns is ultimately as much an extrapolation from his previous reading as anything else. That is, like Don Quijote, Yorick is determined in this scene to remain faithful to "the story [Mr. Shandy] had told," even when appearances might suggest that he should do otherwise. Accordingly, he frames his augmentations within a narrative of Maria's continuing life off-page: her father "died . . . of anguish, for the loss of Maria's senses about a month before," which "brought her more to herself" and so allowed her to give a coherent account of her sorrows, which included the loss of her goat, who "had been as faithless as her lover," along with a great deal of semi-conscious wandering. Indeed, since meeting Tristram, "she had . . . stray'd as far as Rome, and walk'd round St. Peter's once—and return'd back . . . alone across the Apennines—had travell'd over all Lombardy without money—and through the flinty roads of Savoy without shoes—how she had borne it, and how she had got supported, she could not tell" (150, 152). She has also slightly changed her appearance, such that now "her hair hung loose, which before was twisted within a silk net" (150). And, of course, "she had, superadded . . . to her jacket, a pale green ribband which fell across her shoulder to the waist" so that, in her recovering sanity, she might take a break from "never once [having] the pipe out of her hand" (9.24.782), but still keep it close "tied by a string to her girdle" (150). The point of all of this, surely, is to present Yorick as but a fellow reader of *Tristram Shandy,* one who, despite his having "but a few small pages left" (149) to tell his own tale, nonetheless takes the time to engage in the same sort of visualization and character migration as his readers.

Yet obviously there are important differences between the reading practices of Tristram and Yorick and those of Sterne's actual readers, most notably that Tristram and Yorick (both Sterne's own creations) confine themselves to reading other texts by Laurence Sterne. Such self-referential play is characteristically Shandean, of course: Tristram loudly insists at one point that he is "resolved never to read any book but my own, as long as I live" (8.5.661). But the self-referentiality takes on a slight edge in the context of clubbable imaginative expansion, an edge which implies that halving the matter between Slawkenbergius and Tristram or Tristram and Yorick just means that Sterne has taken on the responsibility of providing the whole entertainment, and so whatever pleasures readers have taken in these scenes should be regarded as a gift, an opportunity to sit back and relax without risking the loss of their respective titles to true feeling. Two corollaries readily stem from this insinuation: first, that readers should feel grateful for the way in which Sterne has shouldered their burdens without complaint, and second, that, given his provision of the entire entertainment, a modest amount of subordination to his authority may be in order. That is, Sterne may at heart be but a fellow true feeler, but, considering his labors and seniority, surely he is at least the *primus inter pares* of true feelers and so should be accorded at least as much respect as the president or founder of a club would receive.[17]

One of the principal means through which Sterne solicits this voluntary submission to his authority is by making it clear that his best jokes—those involving his books as material objects—will not work without it. As we have seen in previous chapters, readers' interest in and ability to engage in imaginative expansion typically relied upon the felt detachability of a given character, a detachability which in turn required a shared sense that the physical artifacts conveying those characters were more or less interchangeable. After all, the theory went, if a character could be said to be "public property" as the result of having been claimed as "yours" and "mine" enough times, then it went without saying that the particular editions and formats of the text containing that character could be safely regarded as merely contingent, rather than constitutive. Individual readers might have sentimental attachments to their own copies (or preferences for a specific edition), but an edition or format as such was unlikely to possess any particular sacrality. Sterne rejects this implied interchangeability, though, insisting instead that one of the preconditions for participation in the club of true feelers was having read his volumes as he intended them to appear.[18] Indeed, it has become something of a commonplace in modern scholarship that most of the "radical ways in which [*Tristram Shandy*] strained against the standards of the 'proper book'" lose their punch in any edition other than those personally supervised by Sterne.[19] Consider only the jocular taunt with which Volume One concludes: "what these perplexities of my uncle *Toby* were,——'tis impossible for you to guess;—if you could,—I should blush; not as a relation,—not as a man,—nor even as a woman,—but I should blush as an author; inasmuch as I set no small store by myself upon this very account, that my reader has never yet been able to guess at any thing. And in this, Sir, I am of so nice and singular a humour, that if I thought you was able to form the least judgment or probable conjecture to yourself, of what was to come in the next page,—I would tear it out of my book" (1.25.89). In the editions published in Sterne's lifetime, of course, that next page was a blank flyleaf and so no loss at all. Immediately after Sterne's death, though, publishers began collecting his work in sets of fewer than nine volumes, which meant that "the next page" was either the title page or the first chapter of Volume Two. This makes for a rather different punch line: far from being a knowing jest concerning traditional binding practices, Tristram's threat inadvertently becomes a puzzling fit of self-destructive pique. The joke only makes sense, that is, in the physical format endorsed and dictated by Sterne. Similarly, Tristram's tearing out of "a whole chapter" in Volume Four, which occasions "a chasm of ten pages . . . in the book" (4.25.372) marked by a jump in pagination from 146 to 156, becomes a hollow gesture in editions like the 1774 three-volume set offered by J. Murray which fail to register the consequences of this jump: namely, that the time-honored convention of placing even-numbered pages on the verso of a leaf is thrown out the window for the remainder of the volume.

Implicit in these bibliographic jokes, of course, is an understanding, shared between Sterne and his readers, that their humor turns upon treating things traditionally regarded as mere accidents of book production—pagination, number of volumes, perhaps even catchwords—as though they were every bit as substantive as the so-called main text.[20] Yet by ensuring that the jokes would only work in their authorized format, Sterne quietly insists upon his right to set the rules of the game in which he and his readers are engaged. Tristram might be halving the entertainment, but that did not mean that he was forgoing his rights as a host to direct the conversation or "order things" as he saw fit (2.2.96). Indeed, even in his most ostentatious bibliographic jokes—which do not as obviously depend upon the niceties of a particular format—Tristram nonetheless still pointedly insists upon the necessity for readers to "let me go on, and tell my story my own way" if "the slight acquaintance which is now beginning betwixt us" is to "grow into familiarity" and "terminate in friendship" (1.6.9). Consider the blank page for a moment. In order to convey what a temptation the Widow Wadman posed for Toby—"for never did thy eyes behold, or thy concupiscence covet any thing in this world, more concupiscible than widow *Wadman*" (6.37.565)—Tristram invites his "gentle reader" to sketch out his own private visualization: "to conceive this right,—call for pen and ink—here's paper ready to your hand.——Sit down, Sir, paint her to your own mind——as like your mistress as you can——as unlike your wife as your conscience will let you—'tis all one to me——please but your own fancy in it" (6.38.566). One might expect, given the habits we have been tracing, that readers would have jumped at this chance to lay claim to Widow Wadman by drawing her to their own minds. However, extensive investigation by several eminent Sterneans and historians of marginalia has been unable to turn up even a single copy in which the blank page is anything other than blank.[21] Obviously, arguing from absence is a tricky business, but in this case the absence seems quite striking and suggests that readers "got" the rather somber point implicit in Tristram's joke. That is, despite the seemingly open invitation to "paint her to your own mind" and Tristram's apparent rejoicing that his "thrice happy book" will "have one page, at least, within thy covers, which Malice will not blacken, and which Ignorance cannot misrepresent" (6.38.568), it is impossible to come up with a sketch of Widow Wadman that has any real chance of likeness. Quite simply, at this point in Tristram's narrative, readers have not been given the slightest inkling of what she looks like and so any "painting" in which they might engage is almost necessarily going to be wrong, given the sheer diversity of women that men have found "concupiscible" over the years. She might be old, she might be young, she might be fair, she might be dark . . . all we know is that she is a widow. Hence the sketches which would result from readers accepting Tristram's invitation are almost automatically going to be incapable of revealing anything other than the reader's own private (and no doubt maritally embarrassing) conception of ideal concupiscibility. Readers who pull out their pens at this point will simply betray that they do not get the joke and so are clearly not up to the task of providing half the entertainment. They will have nothing to show for their pains except a "crapped-up" book.[22] Those who get the joke, on the other hand, are implicitly admitted to the club of true feelers, but the price of their admission is a tacit acknowledgment of Tristram's right to set the rules of the game—which in this case means that the only ink allowed to appear on the page supposedly set aside for the use of individual readers is that left there by the printer in the form of a page number and the bleed-through from the verso of the leaf (see Figure 10). Membership in the club of true feelers is thus made attractive by tying it to bibliographic jokes which not all readers will necessarily get, but "getting it" requires a certain voluntary submission to Sterne's authority, a willingness to restrain one's impulses in the hope that such restraint will yield pleasures otherwise unavailable.

Indeed, as if to underscore the patent desirability of acquiescing to his authority, Sterne frames his most elaborate bibliographic joke—the marbled page—as the ultimate token of his "respect" for "the reader's understanding." Tristram introduces the marbled page (or, more properly, the marbled leaf) with one of his typical mock-scholastic taunts:

> And pray who was *Tickletoby*'s mare?—'tis just as discreditable and unscholar-like a question, Sir, as to have asked what year (*ab urb. Con*) the second Punic war broke out.—Who was *Tickletoby*'s mare!—Read, read, read, read, my unlearned reader! read,—or by the knowledge of the great saint *Paraleipomenon*—I tell you beforehand, you had better throw down the book at once; for without *much reading*, by which your reverence knows, I mean *much knowledge*, you will no more be able to penetrate the moral of the next marbled page (motly emblem of my work!) than the world with all its sagacity has been able to unraval the many opinions, transactions and truths which still lie mystically hid under the dark veil of the black one. (3.36.267–68)

As when he reproached Madam for being "so inattentive in reading" as to fail to comprehend "*that my mother was not a papist*" because "it was *necessary* I should be born before I was christen'd" (1.20.64–65), Tristram here berates the "unlearned reader" for allegedly not catching an allusion to an extremely minor episode in *Gargantua and Pantagruel.* Indeed, the allusion is only comprehensible at all if one has read Rabelais in translation: "Tickletoby" is Thomas Urquhart's rather free rendering of "Tappecoue." The passage thus implies that if readers wish to properly understand *Tristram Shandy* and so acquit themselves of the charge of being "unlearned," they must be willing to plumb similarly arcane depths by treating the marbled page as the "motly emblem of [his] work" whose moral must be painstakingly deciphered. That is, they must consider the marbled page as if it were a traditional

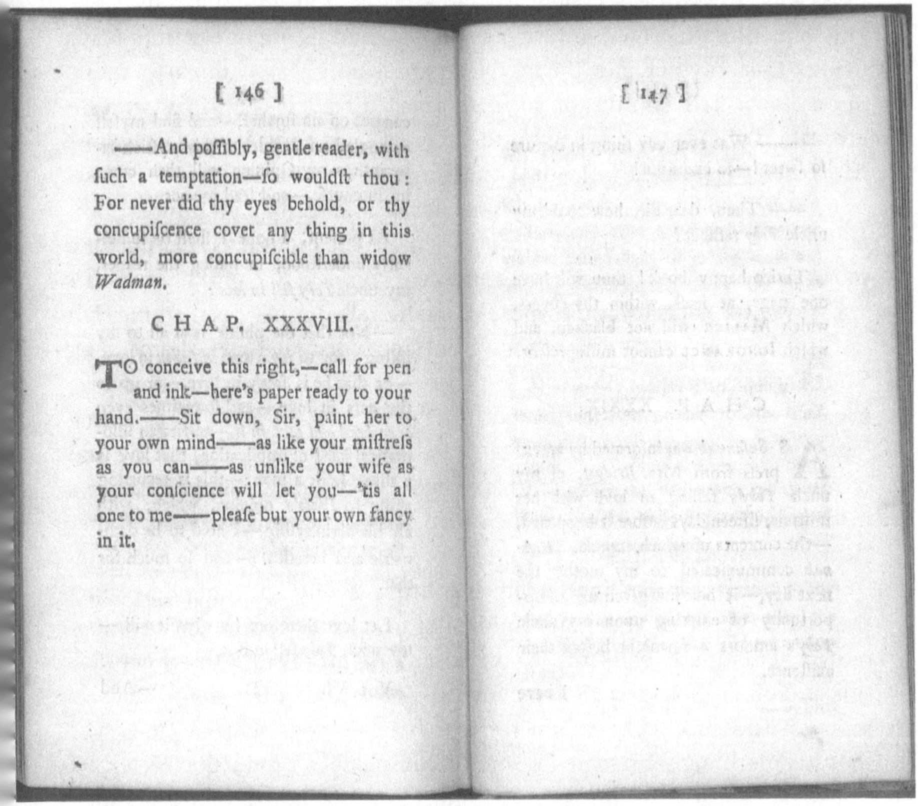

[146]

——And poſſibly, gentle reader, with ſuch a temptation—ſo wouldſt thou: For never did thy eyes behold, or thy concupiſcence covet any thing in this world, more concupiſcible than widow *Wadman*.

CHAP. XXXVIII.

TO conceive this right,—call for pen and ink—here's paper ready to your hand.——Sit down, Sir, paint her to your own mind——as like your miſtreſs as you can——as unlike your wife as your conſcience will let you—'tis all one to me——pleaſe but your own fancy in it.

[147]

Figure 10. The blank page in *Tristram Shandy,* 1762. Courtesy of The Rare Books and Manuscripts Library of The Ohio State University Libraries.

emblem, complete with motto and explanatory poem. The appearance of the marbled leaf, with its margins carefully echoing those of the facing printed pages, further hints at the notion that the marbling is somehow equivalent to text: the question is just a matter of "how?" Tristram even offers up a carrot to would-be emblematists: if they can solve the riddle posed by the marbled page, then they may congratulate themselves on having more "sagacity" than "the world" has hitherto demonstrated with regard to his previous foray into the world of the emblematic. But as the mention of the black page should suggest, especially in the context of metaphors of depth like "penetration" and "unraval[ling]," looking for "opinions, transactions and truths" in the marbled page is a wild-goose chase. The most remarkable thing about both pages is that, for all their unconventionality, they are still just pages in a book—with the same margins and pagination as any other page—and so possess no depth beyond a few millimeters. Penetration will only puncture the paper; unraveling will just rend its fibers. Far from being the key to all mythologies, the marbled page is pure play, with nary a moral to be drawn. Tristram tips off his truly learned readers to this jest with his invocation of the previously unheard-of "great saint *Paraleipomenon,*" whose name stems from the Septuagint's title for what Protestants term the Books of *Chronicles,* which recount additional details and further adventures omitted from the preceding Books of *Kings.* That is, the hint that searching for a moral in the marbled page is a fool's endeavor comes in the form of Tristram's swearing by a fictitious saint whose name literally means "[something] left out" of the main body of a narrative but appended later as a supplement. Saint Paraleipomenon is, of course, the perfect patron for the marbled page because it was not produced as part of the same sheet as its surrounding text but was rather inserted as a separate leaf at the time of stitching and binding. In other words, the marbled page is at its heart a supplement to a prior narrative, a furnishing of the other half of the entertainment, rather than any "mystically hid[den]" truth.

Yet there is something nonetheless fitting about Tristram's describing the marbled page as "the motly emblem of my work!" because the leaf does quite ostentatiously emblematize the sheer amount of work that went into this and other bibliographic jests. Any sort of marbling is a labor-intensive and expensive process, but Sterne seems to have gone out of his way to ensure that his marbling represented a sort of conspicuous production. Peter De Voogd has plausibly reconstructed the most likely method of producing such a leaf: "each individual octavo sheet must have been folded to form a kind of box [with the correct size margins], dipped in the marbling trough and, after drying, re-folded so as to prepare the *verso*."[23] Afterward, the page numbers were stamped on by hand. Lest the laboriousness of this process pass unnoticed, W. G. Day reminds us that "as there were approximately four thousand copies of the first edition the preparation of this one leaf involved eight thousand folding, marbling, sizing, and stamping operations. After each separate piece of marbling the surface in the trough would have had to be checked and if necessary skimmed. The colors would allow approximately eight-hundred marblings, so the run involved at least ten complete changes of color. The base solution of gum tragacanth and flea-seed would have needed changing at least four times, assuming that the operation took place in one trough."[24] The result was, of course, that each side of each leaf was unique in its particular pattern of spots and splatters and so no copy of *Tristram Shandy* was exactly like any other copy. The entire print run was, in effect, an *édition variée.* In the abstract, of course, this is true of any edition: bibliographers are fond of quipping that in the hand-press period every copy is an original, what with stop-press corrections, insufficient inking, broken type, and the like. But traditionally the variations between copies, if noticed at all, could be readily dismissed by most readers as merely the accidents of the printing process. Here those variations take center stage, with the result that readers, if they knew anything about marbling whatsoever, would be unable to regard their copies of *Tristram Shandy* as wholly interchangeable. The marbled page individuates each copy and thereby insinuates that these extraordinary labors have been undertaken in the service of forging a more intimate tie between readers and author than print culture usually afforded. That is, by providing a visual reminder that "the motley emblem of [his] work" took a different form in each copy, Tristram testifies to his commitment to ensuring that "the slight acquaintance which is now beginning betwixt us . . . will terminate in friendship" (1.6.9). Yet at the same time, he implicitly admonishes his readers to remember just *who* has taken such pains to provide them with an artifact unlike any other in the world and *who* has so flatteringly presumed that they at least would get his joke about "great saint *Paraleipomenon*" and so be able to distinguish themselves from "the *herd* of the *world*." Indeed, as the result of Tristram's unceasing labors, readers might even discover hitherto unknown forms of sociable exchange: after all, one of the great pleasures afforded by an *édition variée* is that of comparing the differences between copies with one's fellow readers or collectors. All that he asks in return is a little gratitude and respect: "I would go fifty miles on foot, for I have not a horse worth riding on, to kiss the hand of that man whose generous heart will give up the reins of his imagination into his author's hands,——be pleased he knows not why, and cares not wherefore" (3.12.214). All that he asks, that is, is that his readers willingly relinquish some of their cherished autonomy.

One final factor which may have contributed to the apparent willingness of many readers of the 1760s and 1770s to submit themselves to Sterne's authority in order to participate in the club of true feelers was the way in which he quite self-consciously intertwined "his own identity with that of his characters and present[ed] the undifferentiated amalgam to the public."[25] That is, one of the principal tactics adopted by Sterne in his avid pursuit of fame was his patent willingness "to take the part of the facetious Tristram Shandy or the benevolent parson Mr. Yorick," not only in his fiction, but also in his social performances as a newly minted celebrity whose movements, associations, and bon mots were the subject of considerable coverage in the newspapers.[26] Thus he cracked jokes, "talk[ed] nonsense," and in general "Shand[ied] it away" to whomever seemed likely to be responsive to such wit, even as he solicited subscriptions to *The Sermons of Mr. Yorick*, which, of course, conspicuously featured a frontispiece engraved after the Reynolds portrait of Sterne.[27] The effect, for many readers, of these "multiple and shifting roles" was an impression that there was no appreciable difference between Sterne and his narrators.[28] Thomas Gray, for example, reported to a friend that "Tristram Shandy is still a greater object of admiration, the Man as well as the Book. one is invited to dinner, where he dines, a fortnight beforehand. his portrait is done by Reynolds, & now engraving."[29] Similarly, a contributor to *The Grand Magazine* thought "the very sight of [friend *Tristy*] reviving—for his long sharp nose, and his droll look altogether, affect our risible faculties so strongly, that there is no looking at him without laughing. . . . Why, if he does but twist his nose on one side, there's humour in the distortion—and one cannot help laughing at the joke, even before he opens his mouth.—I only wish he was fatter."[30] These features, of course, match those of Sterne, as Thomas Patch's caricature of Tristram greeting Death "in so gay a tone of careless indifference . . . that he doubted of his commission" makes evident (7.1.576; see Figure 11). And never one to be outdone, the young James Boswell sent Sterne "A Poetical Epistle To Doctor Sterne, Parson Yorick, and Tristram Shandy," which recounts how "Poor Yorick" underwent an Ovidian metamorphosis into "Squire Tristram," concerning whom "a buzzing whisper flies about, / Where'er he comes they point him out; / Each waiter with an eager eye / Observes him as he passes by: / 'That there is he—do, Thomas, look!— / Who's wrote such a damn'd clever book.'"[31] I rehearse this now familiar evidence of the conflation of Sterne and his narrators because it

Figure 11. Thomas Patch, Tristram greeting Death, circa 1765. Courtesy of the Master and Fellows of Jesus College, Cambridge.

seems to illuminate a hitherto unexplored aspect of his desire to escape the fate of Richardson and other authors who found themselves and their authority effaced by their own readers. Put simply, if Sterne's principal characters were intertwined with his public persona, then whatever felt detachability they might possess would be accompanied—and probably offset—by a sense that "Sterne" had himself achieved a sort of placeless omnipresence that could not be nearly as readily disregarded. That is, like his characters, "Sterne" could be simultaneously everywhere—in that "he" was wherever Yorick and Tristram might be found—and nowhere, in that "his" identity could not be wholly pinned down to any single location, not even the tellingly entitled Shandy Hall in Coxwold. "Sterne" had, in effect, a sort of dispersed presence which made it far harder for readers to ignore or efface him than it had been with most other eighteenth-century authors. Every time Tristram or Yorick went away, they took a piece of Sterne with them, just as every time Sterne's exploits appeared in the newspapers, they offered an update on the current whereabouts of Tristram and Yorick. This desire to ensure his omnipresence—to make it clear that you can't play with Tristram or Yorick without inviting Sterne too—may help to explain his otherwise rather puzzling decision to sign the first text page of every copy of the first and second editions of Volume Five, the first edition of Volume Seven, and most copies of the first edition of Volume Nine, as if to guarantee their origin in the mind and pen of that composite being "*Tristram Shandy,* alias *Yorick,* alias the Rev. Mr. St****."[32] As with the marbled page, Sterne's signing many thousands of copies—the first edition of Volume Five alone required 4,000 autographs—represents an inordinate amount of labor, which his alleged fear of "imitation and forgery" does not satisfactorily explain.[33] Yet if one considers the signing not so much a gesture of authentication as an assertion of his lingering presence, then the autographs make a certain symbolic sense. Like the marbled page and Tristram's other bibliographic games, the autographs serve as reminders of just who has furnished the first half of the entertainment: not merely Tristram the disembodied character but also "L. Sterne," whose hand has touched the very page now in your possession and left its mark in the place traditionally reserved for ownership inscriptions (see Figure 12). It is as if every copy of those volumes was coming to its reader already second-hand.

* * *

We have no real way of knowing which of these various Shandean gambits convinced readers of the desirability of submitting to Tristram's authority in

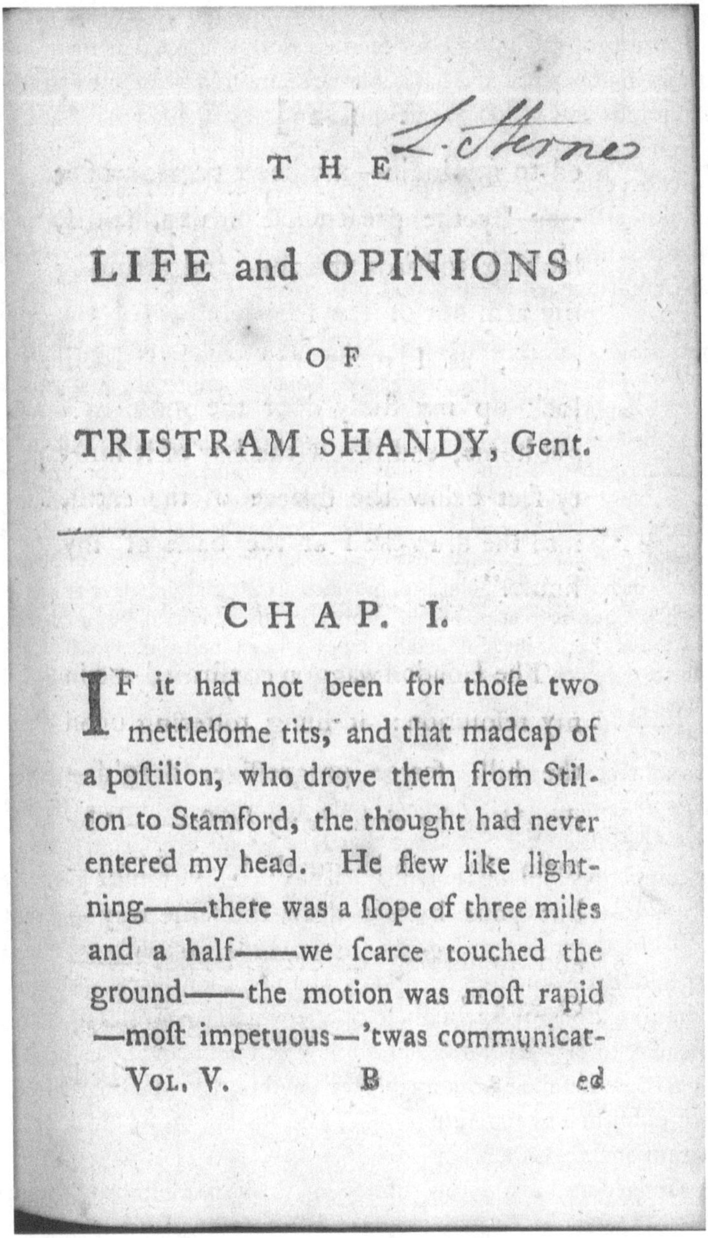

L. Sterne

THE

LIFE and OPINIONS

OF

TRISTRAM SHANDY, Gent.

CHAP. I.

IF it had not been for thoſe two mettleſome tits, and that madcap of a poſtilion, who drove them from Stilton to Stamford, the thought had never entered my head. He flew like lightning——there was a ſlope of three miles and a half——we ſcarce touched the ground——the motion was moſt rapid—moſt impetuous—'twas communicat-

VOL. V. B ed

Figure 12. Sterne's signature in Volume Five of *Tristram Shandy*, 1762. Courtesy of The Rare Books and Manuscripts Library of The Ohio State University Libraries.

order to join the club of true feelers, but the tone and underlying presumptions of much of the afterlife for Sterne's work suggest that many readers were more than persuaded. That is, Sterne seems to have loomed large in his readers' minds and virtual communities in a way that we have not previously seen. He was not only a figure of public interest but an acknowledged authority over his own work, one widely felt to be worthy of a certain playful but ultimately sincere deference in return for his pains. The jocular spirit of this deference is nicely captured by a mock-legal deposition signed by several Cambridge fellows and students:

> we whose names are underwritten have perused a book entitled & called The History of the life and opinions of Tristram Shandy Gent . . . and having well considered, weighed & examin'd the merit of the book or books aforesaid, do upon mature consideration, deliberation & examination of the same, think, and opine, and do hereby give it as our opinion, that the said book or books entitled &c— do or doth hold or contain & comprize the best & truest & most genuine original & new Humour, ridicule, satire, good Sense, good nonsense &&—&c.&c. — that hath been ever held, contained & comprized in any book or books hitherto put forth or published, or hereafter to be put forth or published, provided always that the said book or books hereafter to be put forth or published be not composed, written, put forth, or published by the Author of the aforesaid book or books entitled and called The History of the life & opinions of Tristram Shandy Gent . . . In witness whereof we sign our hands this 19th day of February 1760.[34]

In its use of repetitive legal formulae, the deposition recalls Elizabeth Shandy's marriage settlement, a single article of which took up eight pages in the first edition of Volume One. Yet where Tristram set up his narrative as a discourse competing with the law—after all, he can reduce those eight pages to "three words,——'My mother was to lay in, (if she chose it) in *London*'" (1.15.45)—the Cambridge fellows and students offered no parallel challenge to Sterne. Rather, if anything, their deposition positions itself as an homage to Tristram's parody of legal tautology, one which demonstrates their collective ability to play Tristram's game, but which pointedly holds back from any suggestion that their work might rival anything "composed, written, put forth, or published by the Author of . . . The History of the life & opinions of Tristram Shandy Gent."

A similar tone of bantering submission to Sterne's authority characterizes most of the extant efforts to provide further adventures for his characters. Far fewer genuine liberties were taken with his characters than with those we have previously examined, and those liberties which were taken were almost always accompanied by apparently heartfelt professions of reverence for Sterne's intentions. Consider only the ways in which the narrator of Leonard MacNally's *Sentimental Excursions to Windsor and Other Places* discusses Tristram's "book-debts" (5.8.434) with none other than Maria of Moulines:

> Had he filled his chapter upon button-holes, said I, it would have been delectable! ——He would have *filled* it in all probability, observed *Maria,* but poor fellow, you should recollect his misfortune—you should recollect he was grievously afflicted with a consuming *asthma,* the whole time he was composing his works——I see the force of your observation, said I, a man debilitated as he must have been . . . had something more material to employ his *mind,* and of course employ his *pen,* than such trifling subjects as *button-holes.* True, said *Maria,* but come, you appear in perfect health and spirits, so let me see what you can say upon the subject—here . . . is a blank page, continued *Maria,* taking Tristram Shandy out of my hand . . . come, I will have an immediate proof of your literary abilities——So saying, she brought pen and ink, and placing the blank chapter in Shandy before me on a table—write, write, said *Maria,* while I go order tea——.[35]

A meditation then follows on "A Button-hole!——what could *Sterne* possibly have said upon a *button-hole?*" until "having filled the blank leaf, I could proceed no further, so turned it down, that Maria might peruse it at her leisure" (169, 171). This passage is fascinating not so much for what it has to say about button-holes per se, but for the way in which it explicitly approaches the question in terms of "what would Sterne have done?" That is, MacNally has invented Maria's life off-page—somehow she has made it to Windsor where she has become a fierce opponent of the slave trade—but he has done so in the service of trying to reconstruct what Sterne would have written had his life not been tragically cut short. MacNally's allegiance, it would seem, is not to Maria so much as it is to Sterne, whom he has "always read . . . with delight" and whose "works . . . will be in the hands, and in the hearts of every man . . . of feeling; when the works of the *Smell-fungusses* and the *Mundungusses* of the age, will be lining trunks and band boxes" (60, 62). Rather than regarding Sterne's characters as the common link binding him to his fellow readers, MacNally appears to imagine Sterne as himself that link. Indeed, MacNally seems mildly contemptuous of most of his fellow readers. Whatever excellence "the imitators of Sterne" (a telling phrase in itself) may have is but a reflected glory—"the stile of Sterne is peculiar to himself"—and so the true feeler would do well to remember his place: "If I should exhibit any features bearing likeness to Sterne, I shall be proud of the similarity; but for this happiness I can scarcely hope" (61). What matters here is the "happiness" a "likeness to Sterne" can afford, not the joyous companionship of character migration in and of itself. Fellow true feelers may enjoy sharing their "happiness" with one another, but their felt camaraderie will always be triangulated through the figure of Sterne.[36]

An even more submissive relation between reader and author may be found in *Yorick's Sentimental Journey Continued,* which insists from the outset that "the following sheets are not presented to the Public as the offspring of Mr. Sterne's pen," but are nonetheless worthy of attention because "the intimacy which subsisted between Mr. Sterne and the Editor, gave the latter frequent occasion of hearing him relate the most remarkable incidents of the latter part of his last journey, which made such an impression on him, that he . . . has retained them so perfectly, as to be able to commit them to paper."[37] The result, while perhaps falling short of "his friend's stile and manner," was that "the work may now . . . be considered as complete; and the remaining curiosity of the readers of Yorick's Sentimental Journey, will at least be gratified with respect to facts, events, and observations" (3:v). This rather odd justification for the invention of further adventures intriguingly testifies to the sheer success of Sterne's gambits: the authority for the "facts, events, and observations" contained in this text does not derive from the felt detachability of the characters, but rather from Sterne's intentions as allegedly communicated to "Eugenius." The author, rather than the characters, is the one whose friendship matters. No doubt the supposed "intimacy which subsisted between" Yorick and "Eugenius" is every bit as fictional as any of the archives we have been examining, but the fact remains that where those previous invocations of the archive effaced their originary authors, *Yorick's Sentimental Journey Continued* leaves Sterne squarely at the center of attention.

Indeed, even when Eugenius's Yorick behaves in ways which would seem at considerable odds with the Yorick of *A Sentimental Journey,* the discrepancies between "these four volumes of Sentimental Travels" are implicitly explained away as merely the quirks of that amalgam being "Monsieur Yorick, or Monsieur Sterne," author of "the volumes of Tristram Shandy, together with his sermons" (4:122, 4:112). So, for example, Eugenius's Yorick watches through a keyhole as a *fille de joye* with whom he has been flirting (and perhaps more) has sex with her confessor in so exuberant a manner as to break the bed an hour before her next client is scheduled to appear. Clearly this pushes the delicately poised innuendo of *A Sentimental Journey* over into bawdy farce. Yet considering the ways in which the entire text is framed as an address to Eugenius, this episode seems wholly in keeping with, say, Tristram's habit of "telling Eugenius a most tawdry [story] . . . of a nun who fancied herself a shell-fish, and of a monk damn'd for eating a muscle" (7.1.576).

Given the apparent intertwining of Sterne, Tristram, and Yorick, that is, "Eugenius" seems to have thought it both desirable and appropriate to offer his version of Yorick as but a fleshing out of what, "if the author's life had been spared, the world would have received from his own hand" (3:iv). After all, he was only continuing a process begun by Sterne himself: in the later volumes of *Tristram Shandy*, "Mr. Sterne carries his readers through France, and introduces some scenes and characters which are afterwards taken up in his Sentimental Journey, particularly that of Maria: so that this may in some measure be considered as a continuation of the Life and Opinions of Tristram Shandy" (3:xvii–xviii). True feelers, it would seem, were not only eager to "give up the reins of [their] imagination[s]" (3.12.214), they were also willing to serve as somewhat jocular amanuenses for the dead. It is thus entirely fitting that Eugenius's account of Maria should have been incorporated, without citation, into *The Whole Story of the Sorrows of Maria, of Moulines. Selected from various works of the celebrated Sterne.* For the editor of this collection, the fictional archive of Maria's life is coterminous with the oeuvre of Sterne, regardless of its actual origin. Character migration has here resulted in the effacement, not of Sterne, but rather of Eugenius. Indeed, if anything, Eugenius's labors have only left Sterne all the more "celebrated" and authoritative.

But perhaps the ultimate testament to the sheer success of Sterne's gambits is that offered by his apparent critics, many of whom sparred with him in ways not readily distinguishable from the banter of his most loyal readers. Consider, for example, the fairly hostile account of Volumes Seven and Eight which appeared in *The Critical Review*. The reviewer takes Sterne to task for not better following the advice given in the *Critical*'s assessment of his last installment: "we have already done justice to all that was justifiable in the preceding volumes of this work, and wish that the author . . . had, in the two volumes before us, afforded the least field for the only pleasing part of our task, that of approbation."[38] Yet to drive this censure home, the *Critical*'s reviewer invents a dialogue between Toby, Trim, Walter, and Elizabeth Shandy regarding an invisible cock which Trim has paid to see. The point seems to be that "the seventh volume contains" nothing but "an unconnected, unmeaning, account of our author's journey to France" and so, like Trim, Tristram's readers have been taken in by a hoax (65). Yet, again like Trim, they cannot complain of having been "cheated; for they have been beforehand told [the cock] is invisible": "the author has pretended, from his commencement of authorship, neither to wit, taste, sense, nor argument" and so cannot be charged with any sort of fraud (66). His only desire has been to be in the public eye and the public has more than granted his wish: "*Videri vult et est*" (66).[39] Sterne's desire for fame may be disreputable, but his success in achieving that fame is undeniable. Indeed, this review does nothing if not further contribute to Sterne's social canonicity by admitting that "the best part of [the] joke"—Tristram's "manner"—is "a kind of . . . impassive object, upon which the artillery of criticism must be discharged in vain" (65). The rules of the game, that is, have already been set and so even the self-appointed regulators of taste must, if they wish to play at all, provide their share of the entertainment by performing their appointed roles as "your humble servants, the Reviewers of Breeches" (66). Tellingly, this is one of the groups of readers with whom Tristram had ostentatiously halved the entertainment: uncertain of the proper placement of his interjection "*Out upon it!*"—in one paragraph it could be a protest against cruelty to animals, in the next it could be a description of what happens to Tristram's "breeches pocket" after it has been "rent . . . in the most disasterous direction you can imagine"—Tristram has left the matter "to be settled by The Reviewers of My Breeches. which I have brought over along with me for that purpose" (7.32.632). The choice for the *Critical*'s reviewer, it would seem, was between exclusion from the club of true feelers and bantering submission to Tristram's authority. The reviewer might "advise him most heartily to consider the case of uncle Toby's red breeches," but he did so out of "love to Widow Wadman" and so was hardly in a position to be very scathing (66). The rewards of membership were apparently just too compelling to pass up.

So what, ultimately, were those rewards? What was the appeal of the club of true feelers? In a word, exclusivity without tears. Like most actual clubs, the virtual sociability of true feeling combined a rhetoric of extreme selectivity with a quite fluid and potentially capacious admissions policy. Thus while there are plenty of moments in *Tristram Shandy* when an invitation to visualize is combined with a ritual dismissal of "the *herd* of the *world*," it is almost always possible to separate oneself from that herd with minimal difficulty. For example, when Tristram recounts how his father told Toby to "make tea for yourself, brother *Toby* . . . taking down his hat—but how different from the sallies and agitations of voice and members which a common reader would imagine!—For he spake in the sweetest modulation—and took down his hat with the gentlest movement of limbs, that ever affliction harmonized and attuned together" (4.16.348–49), it remains perfectly easy to distinguish oneself from the misguided "common reader" while still preserving some of the cachet of being among the fit, though few, who could properly imagine the scene (which, after all, simply involves inverting

Walter's usual harsh tones and unwieldy gestures). For an age in which readers were growing increasingly suspicious toward one another, there could be few prospects more attractive. Indeed, it is not hard to imagine the entire reading public as potentially comprised of would-be true feelers defining themselves against the herd of common readers. Scapegoats need not exist in order to be effective.

Yet no matter how far the virtual sociability of the club of true feelers might extend, it still needed to maintain its felt exclusivity if it was going to preserve its allure. It is thus not surprising that a group of readers in Bath took steps to ensure the exclusion of "the *herd* of the *world*" by forming their own, nonvirtual Shandean Society, "consisting of about twelve or fourteen members, who wished to unite to the festivity of Anacreon, the humour of Prior, the harmony of Pope; and, above all, the sensibility and pleasantry of Sterne."[40] Each member was to "bring with him a volume of his favorite writer, and read such part aloud as he thought would most contribute to the amusement of the society" (28). When it came to be John Henderson's turn, he "produced a volume of Sterne, the god of his idolatry" and "entered so fully into the spirit of his author, so happily discriminated the characters, and so forcibly exhibited them, that his companions, finding more gratification in hearing him than themselves, which I believe will be acknowledged as strong a testimony of approbation as could be given by a society composed of reading men, constituted him reader to the club, and without an act of parliament confirmed his right to a name which had been given him by a friend a short time before; decreeing that from, and after that time, he should be distinguished by the name of Shandy" (29). These readings "threw new light upon many passages" and so helped establish Henderson's title to true feeling: "in the humorous passages, [he] called forth flashes of merriment, and drew tears from every eye in the pathetic" (29–30). Henderson and his fellows even invented a drinking game to enhance their opportunities to demonstrate their collective provision of half of the entertainment: each time they imbibed, rather than quaffing a potentially divisive "health to the political idol of the day," they were supposed to make a toast to "the memory of some departed genius," like Shakespeare, Rabelais, or Sterne, which contained "a sentiment which should have some allusion to . . . his writings, *and be new*" (27). But amid all their merriment, they took considerable pains to position themselves as an elite minority whose appreciation of Sterne was far from universally shared. Thus, for example, after Henderson's reading of "the story of Le Fevre . . . kindled a flame of admiration, and promoted a proposal to devote a day to the memory of the author, pour a libation over his grave, and speak a requiem to his departed spirit," Henderson was "appointed to select what he thought most fit for the occasion, and the next week produced an Ode" in which he excoriates the "unfeeling and cold blooded guest[s]" who

dar'd to violate [Sterne's] page;
In virtue barren, fruitful in their rage,
Vex'd, inly vex'd, that on inspection clear,
They search'd their hearts and found no Toby there. . . .
Some there arose who spurn'd the slavish tie,
And if they censur'd, would at least know why. . . .
To us belongs to vindicate his fame,
To pluck the nettle from his sacred grave, . . .
Oh! When ye hear his memory defam'd,
His wit misconstru'd, or his heart bely'd,
Loud be his warm benevolence proclaim'd,
'Till rage and error blushing turn aside.
Whate'er their motive, ignorance, or whim,
They slander'd nature when they slander'd him. (30–39)

The sociability afforded by the club of true feelers was, it would seem, inextricably tied to its felt exclusivity, which in turn was vigorously enforced through its members' repeated efforts to distinguish themselves from most of their fellow readers, whose "dull ignorance" and envy only underscored their inability to pursue Sterne's "daring flight" (33, 37). Only Henderson and his compatriots, as the self-constituted "friends of Sterne" (36), could properly "vindicate" Sterne's fame, because only they—as true feelers—understood both the truth and the desirability of Tristram's insistence that "'tis impossible" to "leave" him behind. Only the Shandean Society and its innumerable virtual equivalents, that is, could both see and embrace the felt inescapability of authors—"I must go along with you to the end of the work" (6.20.534)—which has marked literary culture ever since.

Scott's Parental Interest, an Afterword

At the outset of *The Case-Book of Sherlock Holmes,* Arthur Conan Doyle worries that Holmes, like "one of those popular tenors who . . . are still tempted to make . . . farewell bows to their indulgent audiences," may have overstayed his welcome. To console himself for the inevitability that Holmes "must go the way of all flesh, material or imaginary," Doyle muses that "one likes to think that there is some fantastic limbo for the children of imagination, some strange, impossible place where the beaux of Fielding may still make love to the belles of Richardson, where Scott's heroes may still strut, Dickens's delightful Cockneys still raise a laugh, and Thackeray's worldlings continue to carry on their reprehensible careers. Perhaps in some humble corner of such a Valhalla, Sherlock and his Watson may for a time find a place, while some more astute sleuth with some even less astute comrade may fill the stage which they have vacated."[1] As Doyle's little fantasia should suggest, the invention of further adventures for literary characters was hardly a practice confined to the eighteenth century. Yet there are important differences in kind between the practices with which we have been concerned and those characteristic of more recent centuries, differences which justify my *terminus ad quem* of 1825 (the year in which Sir Walter Scott's *Tales of the Crusaders* first appeared). Indeed, Doyle's very language underscores the most significant of these departures: namely, the sheer prominence and authority accorded to originary authors. Doyle writes of the "beaux of Fielding," rather than Joseph Andrews and Tom Jones; "Thackeray's worldlings," rather than Becky Sharp or Beatrix Castlewood. In Doyle's version of "fancy's pimlico," characters are linked to their authors by a proprietary language which signals a quite remarkable shift in readerly presumptions. Far from being largely irrelevant figures to be effaced through visualization and character migration, authors are here represented as the font of authority regarding those characters, including their lives off-page (after all, nowhere in the published work of either writer do "the beaux of Fielding . . . make love to the belles of Richardson"). So long as figures like

"Sherlock and his Watson" persist, it would seem, so too will their creators' proprietary control. But Doyle was hardly the first nineteenth-century author to suggest that this "fantastic limbo" was best left to the trained professionals who had created its inhabitants in the first place. In this brief afterword, we will survey the formation in the early nineteenth century of many of the presumptions which underpin Doyle's "fantastic limbo" and so mark the end of the sort of imaginative expansion with which we have been concerned. In so doing, we can begin to understand why nonauthorial imaginative expansion should now seem so eccentric and marginal, even as the genres and concepts it helped to invent—series fiction, the social canon, the very notion of virtual community—have become such obvious, self-sustaining, perhaps even seemingly inevitable features of our cultural landscape.

* * *

How did Doyle's "fantastic limbo" of proprietary authorship come to supplant Kenrick's vision of the textual commons? What can have brought this transformation about? Obviously, identifying causality in literary history is an extraordinarily difficult endeavor, but surely one of the principal factors undercutting the sustainability of imaginative expansion in its eighteenth-century forms was the collapse of the comparative domestic political stability which had enabled British readers to imagine themselves as part of a virtual community of readers not always already divided by politics and class. Such stability had always involved a certain willful blindness, of course, but prior to the 1770s and 1780s it had been relatively easy for most readers to imagine what Carol Kay has termed "a stable, nonpolitical realm, . . . a leisure space for reading and writing which could never be troubled by questions of power" and thus "made differences of opinion fun."[2] With the American War, and even more with the wars against revolutionary and Napoleonic France and the passionate agitation for reform which followed in their wake, fierce divisions opened up in the polity, open wounds which gave the lie to the putative liberty and suspension of difference afforded by the eighteenth-century public and so "forced [readers] to negotiate" the often considerable distance between their own political and class positions and their ideal of a broad virtual community of readers.[3] Many readers found it necessary to acknowledge that "the republic of letters," hitherto an "innocent cosmopolitanism," "has in truth almost as many divisions, with mutual jealousies and mutual ignorance, as the political relations which it comprehends" and so could no longer afford very many opportunities for play with one's fellow readers unless they already shared one's politics and social standing.[4] As a result of these deeply felt divisions, it became far easier to imagine oneself as part of what Jon Klancher terms a self-conscious "social audience" defining itself against other social audiences, than it was to sustain a vision of a single, cohesive reading public whose love for, say, Falstaff could suspend or even transcend the political differences dividing the nation.[5] Even when shared characters *could* serve as rallying points for much of the public (as Pickwick, Weller, Nickelby, and Little Nell were able to do in the 1830s and early 1840s), the center could not hold for long. Indeed, the more the reading public grew, the more readers of all sorts came to proleptically concur with Flora Poste that "one of the disadvantages of almost universal education was the fact that all kinds of persons acquired a familiarity with one's favourite writers. It gave one a curious feeling; it was like seeing a drunken stranger wrapped in one's dressing gown."[6] The intertwined affection toward authors and suspicion toward most of one's fellow readers which the club of true feelers had fostered back in the 1760s had come to full fruition by the early nineteenth century.

* * *

The increasing difficulty of imagining a virtual community of readers not always already divided against itself might seem counterintuitive, for one of the most striking features of Britain during this period was the sheer fervor and nigh-universality of its nationalism. Radicals and reactionaries may have despised one another, but, at least after the advent of the Terror, both defined themselves as strenuous proponents of all that was best about Britain (gone was the cosmopolitan, Francophile ideal of earlier decades). Why then should the virtual community of a reading public have been so hard to sustain when the imagined community of the nation was so incredibly compelling? The key seems to lie in the difference in rallying points. The "old friends" of a literary character organized themselves around a fictional, and so necessarily disembodied, being. The nation was able to fix upon the all-too-embodied king. As Linda Colley has pointed out, in the second half of George III's reign the monarchy became "more celebrated, more broadly popular and more unalloyedly patriotic than it had been for a century at least."[7] George III might himself seem trivial or pitiable, George IV a duplicitous scoundrel, but the "shift away from anger at the institution to mockery of individual royals and their foibles helped—as it still helps—to preserve it" and, indeed, to fuse the interests of the monarchy with those of the kingdom, "to argue that the monarchy was *the* uncontentious point of national union."[8] In order to be properly imaginable, it would seem, the community of the nation required a rallying point both corporeal and symbolic. It required, in short, the king's two bodies.[9]

Given this apparent need for an embodied national locus, it should come as no surprise that readers began to require similarly embodied rallying points if they were to sustain the fantasy of virtual community in the face of their patent differences and divisions. Particularly after Waterloo, when the threat of French invasion could no longer serve as a unifying fear and "the very *idea* of political opposition" intensified, it seemed imperative to preserve the public as an imaginable entity through any means possible.[10] Enter "The Author of Waverley," whose unprecedented combination of commercial success, critical acclaim, and mysterious identity enabled him to serve as the authorial equivalent of a monarch. As Ian Duncan has argued, it was only with Scott that "the cultural figure of the author achieves its modern canonical integrity, its monumental weight, in the public imagination. . . . Scott redefined the reading public in terms not only of magnitude but of quality, that is, social and political respectability." That respectability stemmed in turn from the vision which the sheer popularity of the Waverley novels afforded "of a unified public imagination—a society brought together in the act of reading the same book."[11] The "romance of an official national culture" which Duncan singles out as the source of Scott's prestige is crucial in marking the difference between what we have been examining and the changes of the early nineteenth century. Clearly the "'tis yours—'tis mine—'tis Public" logic we have been tracing presumes the possibility of a "society . . . reading the same book." What it did not presume—in large part because it did not have to do so—was the sheer improbability that such shared reading could actually bring a society together. In other words, it was necessary for the public to seem always already fragmented for "a unified public imagination" to appear a rare and desirable prospect, rather than a fairly ordinary occurrence. This shift in the comparative imaginability of a unified public is nicely captured by the astonishing catalog of Scott's readership which Harriet Martineau offers up as the supreme evidence of his genius. According to Martineau, Scott was

> eagerly listened to by the hundred thousand families, collected, after their daily avocations, under the spell of the northern enchanter; [with their] thumbed copies . . . in workshops and counting-houses, in the saloons of palaces, and under many a pillow in boarding schools. . . . [Scott] has exalted the tastes, ameliorated the tempers, enriched the associations, and exercised the intellects of millions. . . . If one

representative only of every class which have thus been benefited were to repair to his grave, the mourning train would be of a length that kings might envy. There would be the lisping child, weeping that there should be no more tales of the Sherwood Foresters and the Disinherited Knight; there would be the school-boy, with his heart full of the heroic deeds of Couer de Lion in Palestine; and the girl, glowing with the loyalty of Flora, and saddening over the griefs of Rebecca; and the artisan who foregoes his pipe and pot for the adventures of Jeanie Deans; and the clerk and apprentice, who refresh their better part from the toils of the counting-house amidst the wild scenery of Scotland; and soldier and sailor relieved of the tedium of barracks and cabin by the interest of more stirring scenes presented to the mind's eye; and rambling youth chained to the fireside by the links of a pleasant fiction; and sober manhood made to grow young again; and sickness beguiled, and age cheered, and domestic jars forgotten; and domestic sympathies enhanced.[12]

Young and old, male and female, aristocrat and artisan, sick and hale, all supposedly found common ground in the Waverley Novels. Yet this felt commonality was not a shared affection for a particular character—girls apparently preferred Flora MacIvor, while artisans liked Jeanie Deans—but rather a shared experience of reading the same author. The possibility of social reunification lay in their collective gratification at the hands of The Author of Waverley, the ways in which his work, almost regardless of its specific content, could be confidently expected to provide "holidays for the whole kingdom."[13]

The fervor with which monarchic authors were embraced as the public's last best hope only intensified as the century progressed. A reviewer for *Fraser's Magazine*, for example, hailed Dickens as "one who has done more . . . for the promotion of peace and goodwill between man and man, class and class, nation and nation, than all the congresses under the sun": "Boz, and men like Boz . . . sweep away the prejudices of class and caste, and disclose the common ground of humanity which lies beneath facticious, social, and national systems. They introduce the peasantry to the peerage, the grinder at the mill to the millionaire who owns the grist."[14] Indeed, the public seemed hardly imaginable except as triangulated through him: "there is not a fireside in the kingdom where the cunning fellow has not contrived to secure a corner for himself, as one of the dearest, and by this time, one of the oldest friends of the family. In his company the country squire shakes his jolly sides, the City merchant smoothes his care-wrinkled forehead—as he tells his tale to misses in their teens, mammas, grandmammas, and maiden aunts" (698). Note how it is the monarchic author, rather than any of his characters, who is here the "old friend" capable of binding together disparate readers into what another reviewer terms a "communion" which is "continual, confidential, something like personal affection."[15] Apparently, the public, like the nation, could only hang together if it rallied around "a national writer," one who could bring "the worker for his daily bread into constant fellowship and communion with thousands of his fellow creatures."[16]

Indeed, if we are to believe Wordsworth, it could be no other way: "every author, as far as he is great and at the same time *original,* has had the task of *creating* the taste by which he is to be enjoyed." Since "to create taste is to call forth and bestow power" upon those souls intelligent enough "to be passive to a genuine poet," and since such passivity means "judging . . . by [one's] own feelings genuinely, and not by reflection upon what will probably be the judgments of others," it stands to reason that any already constituted body of readers will necessarily be inadequate to the task.[17] Only through a new abstraction centered on the charismatic and proprietary author—what Wordsworth terms "the People, philosophically characterised"—could genuine social reunification come about.[18] Only by repudiating any consideration of one's fellow readers which was not filtered through what William Harrison Ainsworth tellingly termed "the throne of letters" could virtual community be ensured.[19]

* * *

Yet in order to be perceived as possessing the necessary charisma to bind together a virtual community, authors needed first to be granted a proprietary, monarchic authority over their own creations. Toward this end, nineteenth-century readers actively collaborated in the enclosure of the textual commons, even when it meant abandoning their own claims upon a given character. This is not to say that imaginative expansion necessarily waned in the period—one needs only remember the fifteen installments of *The Girlhood of Shakespeare's Heroines*—but readers so inclined seem to have been drawn to characters not on the basis of their felt commonness but rather on that of their distinguished provenance. If, in the eighteenth century, the invention of afterlives for a character helped to boost that character's originary author into the social canon, by the nineteenth century those afterlives aided in the ratification of those authors' already established canonicity and proprietary control. In part, this newfound assent to proprietary authorship was simply an outgrowth of "the extreme impatience" with which "by the 1780s both law and political economy regarded co-existent properties" more generally.[20] The very idea of the commons, whether real or metaphorical, seemed increasingly untenable. If property needed a single owner and sustainable virtual community required an embodied monarchic author, then it only stood to reason that the author in question should be granted sole proprietorship over his or her own creations. Otherwise he or she would lack the necessary authority to serve as a rallying point for the public. Indeed, for many readers, this authority extended well beyond an author's published texts to encompass in some hazy way his or her characters' entire lives, both on- and off-page. Consider only the very revealing deference shown to Jane Austen in this area. According to her nephew, Austen "took a kind of parental interest in the beings whom she had created" and

> would, if asked, tell us many little particulars about the subsequent career of some of her people. In this traditionary way we learned that Miss Steele never succeeded in catching the Doctor; that Kitty Bennett was satisfactorily married to a clergyman near Pemberley, while Mary obtained nothing higher than one of her uncle Philips' clerks, and was content to be considered a star in the society of Meriton; that the "considerable sum" given by Mrs. Norris to William Price was one pound; that Mr. Woodhouse survived his daughter's marriage, and kept her and Mr. Knightley from settling at Donwell, about two years; and that the letters placed by Frank Churchill before Jane Fairfax, which she swept away unread, contained the word "pardon."[21]

In the case of the Austen family, much of this deference is probably attributable to the affection with which Austen's nieces and nephews regarded their aunt. But the proprietary language—"her people"—which J. E. Austen-Leigh uses here nonetheless powerfully testifies to the shift in readerly presumptions which I have been sketching. Austen is presumed to know more about "the subsequent career of . . . her people" than anyone else could and so her "parental interest in the beings . . . she had created" was self-evidently worth respecting and revering. Hers was what David Riede has described as the desideratum of Romantic authorship more generally: "an authority apparently beyond argument."[22]

Once again enter The Author of Waverley, who, more than anyone else, seems to have helped to position these new presumptions at the very core of nineteenth-century literary culture. In 1820, Scott was at the height of his popularity. His novels were appearing in editions of ten to twelve thousand copies, often to be immediately reprinted to satisfy the mania with which "everybody is tearing [them] out of each other's hands, and talking of nothing else."[23] Moreover, these reprints—especially when collected as the *Novels and Tales of the Author of Waverley*—insisted upon their filiation with one another as a coherent oeuvre whose "sequence and interconnection" set them apart from their competitors on the market.[24] It thus makes a certain sense that when the integrity of that oeuvre was challenged by the advertisement of an unauthorized fourth series of *Tales of My Landlord,* Scott should not only have taken steps to "assure . . . the public, that this Author has no concern whatever with the catchpenny publication" but also to "guarantee . . . the Public" that his next novel, *Ivanhoe,* which he had planned to bring out as the work of "Laurence Templeton," was in fact "written by The Author of Waverley."[25] Indeed, as if to "affirm . . . his absolute proprietorship over the fictional world he has created," Scott introduced *Ivanhoe* with a lengthy "Dedicatory Epistle to the Rev. Dr. Dryasdust," in which "Templeton" alludes to Dryasdust's "learned northern friend, Mr. Oldbuck of Monkbairns" and Sir Arthur Wardour, both of whom had first appeared four years earlier, along with Dryasdust, in *The Antiquary.*[26] This sort of character migration within a single author's oeuvre was hardly unprecedented—in addition to the examples we have already considered, several figures from *Ferdinand, Count Fathom* show up in *Humphry Clinker*—but Scott's version, particularly as it unfolded over the next five years in a series of increasingly elaborate front matter, went well beyond anything we have seen in the ways in which it insisted upon his "absolute proprietorship" over his own characters.[27]

The sheer depth and bravura of Scott's "parental interest" in his characters comes out in the epistolary exchange between Captain Clutterbuck and The Author of Waverley which prefaces Scott's next novel, *The Monastery.* Clutterbuck, a half-pay officer and amateur antiquarian, has written to The Author of Waverley to see if he might be interested in editing a memoir of pre-Reformation Scotland which Clutterbuck has acquired. If so, Clutterbuck proposes that they split the profits and the credit on the title page. The Author of Waverley answers with a quite astonishing denunciation of Clutterbuck's cheek which hinges upon a complete rejection of the presumptions undergirding imaginative expansion in its eighteenth-century forms. That is, according to The Author of Waverley, Clutterbuck is utterly unsuitable to serve as a coauthor because of his patently disembodied fictionality: he hails from "the province of Utopia" (24), "whose unsubstantial species . . . permits them to assume all manner of disguises" (26). Like MacDuff, he is "not born of woman, unless, indeed, in that figurative sense, in which the celebrated Maria Edgeworth may be termed mother of the finest family in England" (27).[28] And like his fellow "Editors of the land of Utopia"—"the sage Cid Hamet Benengeli, the short-faced president of the Spectator's Club, poor Ben Stilton"—Clutterbuck is not to be trusted, precisely because

> the Editors of your country are of such a soft and passive disposition, that they have frequently done themselves great disgrace by giving up the coadjucators who first brought them into public notice and public favour, and suffering their names to be used by those quacks and imposters who live upon the ideas of others. Thus I shame to tell how the sage Cid Hamet Benengeli was induced by one Juan Avellaneda to play the Turk with the ingenious Miguel Cervantes, and to publish a second part of the adventures of his hero the renowned Don Quixote, without the knowledge or co-operation of his principal aforesaid. It is true, the Arabian Sage returned to his allegiance, and thereafter composed a genuine continuation of the Knight of La Mancha, in which the said Avellaneda of Tordesillas is severely chastised. . . . Yet, notwithstanding the *amende honorable* thus made by Cid Hamet Benengeli, his temporary defection did not the less occasion the decease of the ingenious Hidalgo Don Quixote. . . . Cervantes put him to death, lest he should again fall into bad hands. Awful, yet just consequence of Cid Hamet's defection! (27–29)

Clutterbuck's felt detachability, his capacity for "defection," thus disables him and makes it imperative, under penalty of death, that he not allow his name to be used by anyone other than his originary author. In fact, to drive the point home, The Author of Waverley professes himself "sorry to observe my old acquaintance Jedediah Cleishbotham has misbehaved himself so far as to desert his original patron, and set up for himself" in the unauthorized fourth series of *Tales of My Landlord*: "I am afraid the poor pedagogue will take little by his new allies, unless the pleasure of entertaining the public, and, for ought I know, the gentlemen of the long robe, with disputes about his identity" (29). A note then follows that "I am since more correctly informed, that Mr Cleishbotham died some months since at Gandercleugh, and that the person assuming his name is an imposter. . . . Hard! that the speculators in print and paper will not allow a good man to rest quiet in his grave!!!" (29). The threat in all of this is scarcely veiled: Clutterbuck had better not participate in any adventures off-page which do not appear under the aegis of The Author of Waverley, lest he risk the fate of Don Quijote and Jedediah Cleishbotham. The paths of character migration lead but to the grave:

> I will . . . put my own buist upon my own cattle, which the attorney tells me will be a crime to counterfeit, as much as it would to imitate the autograph of any other empiric—amounting, as advertisements upon little vials assure us, to nothing short of felony. If, therefore, my dear friend, your name should hereafter appear on any title page without mine, readers will know what to think of you. I scorn to use either arguments or threats; but you cannot but be sensible, that, as you owe your literary existence to me on the one hand, so, on the other, your very all is at my disposal. I can at pleasure cut off your annuity, strike your name from the half-pay establishment, nay actually put you to death, without being answerable to any one. (29)

I quote so extensively from The Author of Waverley's "Answer" to Clutterbuck because it so completely rejects the underlying readerly presumptions we have been tracing. Far from enabling the common use of a character, immateriality is here presented as what should ensure sole proprietorship: a character without a body has his "very all" at his creator's "disposal." Similarly, the social canonicity of a character, far from being the result of his having been claimed by myriad individual readers, is here depicted as, if anything, diminished by such disgraceful misuse. After all, the Jedediah Cleishbotham of the unauthorized fourth series will be unable to entertain the public with anything but "disputes about his identity" quite simply because he is appearing in what Scott's publisher denounced as a "spurious work."[29]

As the very notion of "disputes about [Cleishbotham's] identity" should suggest, The Author of Waverley is pinning his claim to authority over his own characters upon the idea that some further adventures are legitimate and others spurious and that the difference lies in their respective provenance. Most of the readers we have been examining would have rejected this concept, if they even recognized it, and sided instead with William Fearman, the apparent author of the unauthorized fourth series of *Tales of My Landlord,* in his belief that fictional beings were incapable of being spurious: "Jedediah Cleishbotham is notoriously a fictitious name, and belongs to no one. To say that there is anyone of that name having property in any thing, is a *fraudulent* assertion. It is open to any body to assume it."[30] That is, "the *Fourth Series* . . . is no more *spurious* than the *First,* the *Second,* or the *Third*" because Cleishbotham does not really exist and so cannot be falsified or monopolized: "that Jedediah will prosecute Jedediah, because Jedediah's stores have happily furnished a Fourth Series, is as little to be believed as feared."[31] The Author of Waverley, on the other hand, saw his characters' disembodiment and fictionality as precisely what justified his title to "put my own buist on my own cattle": namely, that "I have never seen, and never will see, one of their faces . . . yet I am better acquainted with them than any man who lives" (30). His "parental interest," in other words, was what made them "his people."

As if to further demonstrate his absolute authority, Scott returned to these games two years later in *The Fortunes of Nigel* and *Peveril of the Peak.* Together, the front matter in these novels stage a lengthy exchange between Clutterbuck and Dryasdust in which they each brag about their comparative access to The Author of Waverley. Clutterbuck begins by reminding Dryasdust that they are siblings of a sort: "we may indeed esteem ourselves as come of the same family, or, according to our country proverb, as being all of one man's bairns."[32] But given his status as a literary celebrity—"the share which I had in introducing . . . The Monastery . . . to public notice, has given me a sort of character in the literature of our Scottish metropolis"—Clutterbuck found it only fitting that he should be the first to behold "the Eidolon, or Representative Vision, of the Author of Waverley!" and hail him, out of "filial instinct," "with the classical salutation of, *Salve, magne parens!*" (1:ii; 1:vii). Dryasdust in turn scoffs at Clutterbuck's priding himself upon a mere "fortuitous rencontre" with their "great progenitor" when *he* had had a lengthy "interview . . . marked with circumstances in some degree more formally complaisant than those which attended your meeting with him," including "the communication of a large roll of papers, containing a new history, called Peveril Of The Peak."[33] Dryasdust professes to be unmoved by this distinction, but his modesty is far from convincing: "Heaven forbid I should glory or set up any claim of superiority over the other descendants of our common parent, from such decided marks of his preference—*Laus propria sordet.* I am well satisfied that the honour was bestown not on my person, but my cloth—that the preference did not elevate Jonas Driasdust over Clutterbuck, but the Doctor of Divinity over the Captain. *Cedunt arma togae*—a maxim never to be forgotten at any time, but especially to be remembered when the soldier is upon half-pay" (1:iv). As with actual monarchs, it would seem, proximity and access are everything. Indeed, like good courtiers, Clutterbuck and Dryasdust spend their time off-page endlessly gossiping about the activities of their monarchic "common parent." Thus, Dryasdust knows that The Author of Waverley has been elected a member of "that Society of select Bibliomaniacs," the Roxburghe Club, before The Author tells him, because Clutterbuck "wrote to me . . . that such a report was current among the Scottish antiquaries" (1:xvi). And much of their respective letters, after the initial jockeying for position, are spent detailing for one another The Author of Waverley's point-by-point rebuttals of various commonplace criticisms of the Waverley Novels, such as their allegedly loose plotting and historical sloppiness.

Clutterbuck and Dryasdust thus seem to have been granted further adventures by their "venerable senior" (1:iii) only insofar as they can reinforce his authority and social canonicity. Far from being "Historic . . . beings" whose "roundness and integrity" gave "them an independence" from their Author, they exist solely at his pleasure, as the tour-de-force Introduction to *Tales of the Crusaders* makes clear. This text purports to be the minutes, surreptitiously taken by an Edinburgh reporter, of a closed "general meeting of the shareholders designing to form a joint-stock company, united for the purpose of writing and publishing the class of works called the Waverley Novels" (1:i). The Author of Waverley proposes to the various attendees—including Jonathan Oldbuck, "a son of Dandie Dimont," Laurence Templeton, Dryasdust, Clutterbuck, "the worthy minister of Saint Ronan's Well," and several unnamed others—that they incorporate in order to become "a *persona standi in judicio,* with full power to prosecute and bring to conviction all encroachers on our exclusive privilege" (1:v, 1:xii, 1:vi). He also thinks that the introduction of machinery invented by "the ingenious Mr. Dousterswivel" from *The Antiquary* may enable them to become more efficient in the production of "those parts of the narrative which are at present composed out of commonplaces, such as the love-speeches of the hero, the description of the heroine's person, the moral observations of all sorts, and the distribution of happiness at the conclusion of the piece" (1:vi, 1:viii–ix). To his surprise, the assembled characters stage a pseudo-Luddite revolt at the prospect of being supplanted "by the use of steam" (1:viii). Oldbuck even charges The Author of Waverley with seeking "a despotic authority, inconsistent with our freedom," over his fellow shareholders (1:xx). In response, The Author of Waverley threatens his characters with annihilation: "I will discard you—I will unbeget you . . . I will vindicate my own fame with my own right-hand, without appealing to such halting assistants, 'whom I have used for sport, rather than need' . . . in a word, I will write History" (1:xxiv–xxv). And true to his word, the assembled characters never again appear in Scott's oeuvre, while The Author of Waverley shifts genre and goes on to produce his promised "Life of Napoleon Buonaparte" (1:xxvii).

The Introduction to *Tales of the Crusaders* thus enacts what The Author of Waverley had long been threatening: the exercise of his Cervantine right to put his characters to death, lest they should fall into bad hands and threaten the "spirit of subordination, highly necessary to success in every enterprize where joint wisdom, talent, and labour, are to be employed" (1:xviii). Yet far from diminishing his social canonicity, this slaughter of the fictional serves as perhaps the ultimate testimony to Scott's monarchic authority. Back in the Introductory Epistle to *The Fortunes of Nigel,* The Author of Waverley had insisted that what Clutterbuck regarded as The Author's greatest liability—his astonishing rate of production—was in fact what grounded his social canonicity. His "poor family" might perish in a Malthusian nightmare, but he, as The Author of Waverley, would only profit from their loss:

> like many a poor fellow, already overwhelmed with the number of his family, I cannot help going on to increase it—"'Tis my vocation, Hal."—Such of you as deserve

oblivion—perhaps the whole of you—may be consigned to it. At any rate, you have been read in your day, which is more than can be said of some of your contemporaries, of less fortune and more merit. They cannot say but that you *had* the crown. As for myself, I shall always deserve, at least, the unwilling tribute which Johnson paid to Churchill, when he said, though the fellow's genius was a tree which bore only crabs, yet it was prolific, and had plenty of fruit, such as it was. It is always something to have engaged the public attention for seven years. Had I only written Waverley, I should have long since been, according to the established phrase, "the ingenious author of a novel much admired at the time." I believe, on my soul, that the reputation of Waverley is sustained very much by the praises of those, who may be inclined to prefer that tale to its successors. . . . It is some consolation to reflect that the best authors in all countries have been the most voluminous; and it has often happened, that those who have been best received in their own time, have also continued to be acceptable to posterity. I do not think so ill of the present generation, as to suppose that its present favor necessarily infers future condemnation. (1:xliii–xlv)

The Author of Waverley's social canonicity and his ability to bind the public together through their shared "attention" to his work are thus not the result of any of his characters per se, but rather of the sheer breadth of his oeuvre, the way in which he is continually producing new characters to replace those "as deserve oblivion." The very overproduction that would have insured misery and starvation in the realm of political economy is here revalorized as the source of The Author of Waverley's continuing allure. Characters come and go; the only thing which can lastingly hold "public attention" is the monarchic author, who might well provide further adventures for particularly beloved characters (indeed, he resurrects Jedediah Cleishbotham for an authorized fourth series of *Tales of My Landlord*), but was under no obligation to do so. Character migration was part of "our exclusive privilege," not to be trespassed upon by lowly "encroachers." Only The Author of Waverley, could "shake . . . hands with [his characters] as his oldest and best acquaintances . . . and having performed the duties of a hospitable and intellectual host, seat . . . himself down with his companions in the evening . . . and never quit . . . them till he has given them some idea of his own greatness, and impressed them with a higher sense of their own capabilities."[34] Everyone else had to confine themselves either to waiting for the next installment from "the Author of the Scotch Novels" or to endlessly replaying what he had already published, consoling themselves that "Oldbuck still dwells amid his antiquities and his potteries, his pedantry, and his woman kind, and is perpetually reminding his nephew of the unfortunate accident with the Phoca."[35]

* * *

In many ways, we still live in Sir Walter's world. Following his example, both directly and as filtered through that of Balzac, Trollope, Doyle, and countless other novelists, series fiction has established a hold on the public which has never been shaken off. So too, for the most part, has Scott's conception that an author's power to "put my own buist upon my own cattle" amounts to a moral and quasi-legal right to monopolize their afterlives. Guided by a widely held, if not wholly correct sense that copyright and trademark law now extends to govern not only specific kinds of derivative works but the "total concept and feel" of an originary text, most present-day readers and viewers with an interest in seeing "more" of a given character are faced with a rather stark set of alternatives.[36] On one hand, they could choose to wait, however impatiently, for the originary author or studio to provide further adventures for that character. In so doing, of course, they would tacitly legitimate proprietary claims like those asserted by Lucasfilm: "we love our fans. We want them to have fun. But if . . . somebody is using our characters to create a story unto itself, that's not in the spirit of what we think fandom is about. Fandom is about celebrating the story the way it is."[37] In this conception of literary culture, the authorized version, no matter how much it may have entered "inescapably into common consciousness" and become an "icon . . . of popular culture," must be protected against all "plundering by free riders."[38] A reader's place is but to sit back and admire.

Readers discontent with such all-encompassing authorial control could, of course, choose to plunge ahead and devise their own further adventures, but they do so knowing full well that they will be regarded by most of the culture as at best eccentric and more likely transgressive or even "plundering." Indeed, for many postmodern writers and devotees of "slash fiction," this transgressiveness is precisely the point. The pleasure they take in reading and writing such further adventures is directly proportionate to the degree to which it seems to undercut the intentions and proprietary control of the originary author. Often such rewritings are done in the name of what "really happened": thus *The Wind Done Gone* purports to be the diary of a slave in the household of Scarlett O'Hara, while many of the Star Trek slash fictions narrate various homoerotic dalliances which Gene Roddenberry was too supposedly cowardly to broadcast. But even when there is no explicit rebuke toward the originary author, such work still suggests that there is something which that author failed to do properly, if only by virtue of how he or she attempted to direct readerly attention. As in the world of Scott's parental interest, the relationship between authors and readers is here envisioned as a contestatory zero-sum game: the text is a finite resource whose use as a commons will only result in its depletion.

One of the principal goals of this study has been to show how our current ways of thinking about characters as participants in an economy of scarcity have not always been as dominant or as seemingly self-evident as they are today. The corollary which emerges from this inquiry, of course, is that these ways of thinking need not (and, to my mind, should not) continue indefinitely. I thus find it heartening to see the glimmerings of a genuine if perhaps necessarily limited alternative to the economy of scarcity, one in which certain characters, at least, can operate in something approximating the economy of abundance which we have been tracing.

Perhaps the best example of this emerging alternative conception of literary property is Alan Moore and Kevin O'Neill's series of graphic novels, *The League of Extraordinary Gentlemen,* in which a host of popular nineteenth-century characters—including Allan Quartermain, Captain Nemo, Mina Harker (née Murray), Edward Hyde, and the Invisible Man—are brought together to defend Britain from various pulp-fiction threats. What distinguishes *The League of Extraordinary Gentlemen* from most of its postmodern competition is Moore and O'Neill's patent lack of interest in subverting or displacing the originary texts in which these characters first appeared. This is not to say that Moore and O'Neill do not have fun at some of those characters' expense: the League visits a boarding school in which Rebecca of Sunnybrook Farm and Pollyanna have been mysteriously impregnated, while Olive Chancellor is getting her "independent American ways" thrashed out of her by Katy Carr.[39] But *King Solomon's Mines* is no worse off today than it was before *The League of Extraordinary Gentlemen.* It may even have gained some new readers intent on catching Moore and O'Neill's elaborate allusions. Instead of engaging in the zero-sum game I have been describing, Moore and O'Neill use the established reputations of these characters—all of whom have, rather tellingly, read about one another—as a springboard in order to construct an alternate universe in which their previous exploits have the status of history. The circa 1898 Britain of *The League of Extraordinary Gentlemen* is thus a particularly knowing and self-conscious descendent of a place like "fancy's pimlico." Within its confines, the originary versions of these characters simply serve as back story: Mina's encounter with Dracula, like Professor Moriarty's standing as "the Napoleon of Crime," are but points of departure for their respective current ventures in what Moore has termed the "enormous technicolor playground" of "literature."[40]

Figure 13. Mina Murray, Auguste Dupin, and Allan Quartermain's first encounter with Mr. Hyde. *The League of Extraordinary Gentlemen* is ™ and © Alan Moore and Kevin O'Neill.

Consider only the panel in which we first encounter Mr. Hyde (Figure 13): the elderly Auguste Dupin steadies himself upon Mina Murray as they gaze up at Hyde, who has just burst through the door clutching Allan Quartermain. Readers familiar with these characters' previous appearances will realize that the scarf Mina is wearing around her neck must be to conceal the wounds left by Dracula. Similarly, the cane Hyde is wielding is presumably the one he used to kill Sir Danvers Carew. And, of course, Quartermain's frame still shows how physically powerful he must have been in his prime. But in each case, readers can also see that time has not stood still: the now-divorced Mina is wearing a dress of which Jonathan Harker would never approve (she is working undercover as a *demimondaine*), while Hyde has grown well beyond his size at the close of Stevenson's tale and Quartermain has evidently more than met his match: he defeats Hyde by pouring laudanum down his throat, rather than through any muscular Christian fisticuffs. None of these characters (not even Dupin, who has come out of retirement to investigate the murder of Anna Coupeau) are constrained or limited by their originary appearances. Indeed, as if to underscore the playful counterfactuality of this entire world, the junction box on the wall suggests that Thomas Edison and Nikola Tesla have been able to reconcile their fierce differences in order to market the Edison Teslaton to landlords in the Rue Morgue.

Similar effects are produced, albeit on a quieter scale, in an engraved portrait of a previous version of the League (Figure 14) which Mina studies in the British Museum, while her colleagues discuss who might have stolen the gravity-defying material known as cavorite, which initially appeared in

Figure 14. The League of Extraordinary Gentlemen as of 1787. *The League of Extraordinary Gentlemen* is ™ and © Alan Moore and Kevin O'Neill.

H. G. Wells's *The First Men in the Moon.* The print depicts Lemuel Gulliver (with a Lilliputian bull at his feet), The Scarlet Pimpernel and his wife, Doctor Syn (from Russell Thorndike's eponymous novels), Fanny Hill, and Natty Bumppo. Chronologically, this grouping seems extremely implausible, if we consider their respective publication dates: Gulliver first appeared in the world in 1726, while Doctor Syn did not show up until 1915. By this logic, neither would be obviously available for a portrait dated 1787. As with the panel we have already considered, however, the effect of bringing these characters together is to underscore the delightful counterfactuality of it all, the self-evident folly of trying to distinguish between eighteenth-century characters and characters from later historical fiction set in the eighteenth century. All are equal participants in what Moore terms "the endless, bottomless intricacy" of his and O'Neill's "literary Sargasso."[41] The only justification they require for their appearance together is that given by Nemo in his confession that "if I'm honest, I'm here because I wanted another adventure," to which Quartermain replies "Yes. It's hard to just stop, isn't it?" (45). I can only hope that as the afterlife of character continues, other readers will abandon their self-defeating commitments to the economy of scarcity and, like Moore and O'Neill, set out to devise those further adventures.

Notes

Cottagers upon the Textual Commons

1. Montagu, *The Complete Letters of Lady Mary Wortley Montagu*, 3:68.

2. Castle, *Masquerade and Civilization*, 134.

3. I borrow the phrase "imaginative expansion" from Eric Rothstein ("'Ideal Presence' and the 'Non Finito,'" 312), but as my investigation has itself expanded, the phrase has, quite appropriately, taken on a life of its own. For Rothstein, "imaginative expansion" simply means "reader-created content, stimulated . . . by descriptive excellence and sometimes continuing . . . after the poem has come to an end" (308). The primary purpose of such reading was to induce what Lord Kames called "ideal presence," a condition in which the reader is "thrown into a kind of reverie; in which state, forgetting that he is reading, he conceives every incident as passing in his presence, precisely as if he were an eye-witness" (*Elements of Criticism*, 1:112). It is not my wish to quarrel with Rothstein's description of imaginative expansion; so far as it goes, it is a significant contribution to intellectual history and an important attempt to show that "this critical position probably represents real reading behavior, as well as a fashion of expressing enthusiasm" (310). But Rothstein's account, concerned as it is with aesthetic theory, cannot really accommodate individual readers, like Lady Mary, whose practices were far from systematic or philosophically coherent, nor can it adequately deal with readings like hers. Moreover, Rothstein concerns himself only with imagined tableaux and so has nothing to say about the invention of afterlives for characters, which my own research suggests was the predominant form taken by imaginative expansion.

4. Carey, *Shakespeare's Jubilee*, 14.

5. Knights, *How Many Children Had Lady Macbeth?*, 6–7.

6. Berger, "What Did the King Know and When Did He Know It?," 823.

7. Thompson, *The Making of the English Working Class*, 12.

8. Gallagher, *Nobody's Story*, 168–69; Hume, *A Treatise of Human Nature*, 319.

9. Lynch, *The Economy of Character*, 4–5.

10. Freeman, *Character's Theater*, 8.

11. Revel, "Microanalysis and the Construction of the Social," 495.

12. Lynch may well be correct that "it is romantic-period characters who first succeed in prompting their readers to conceive of them as beings who take on lives of their own and who thereby escape their social as well as their textual contexts" (8), but the accuracy of her assertion hinges upon the word "prompting." As we shall see, readers were busy inventing lives off-page for characters by the mid-1720s; the characters just may not have actively "prompted" such a response. Similarly, Freeman is

completely right to insist that there are important ontological differences between the disembodied nobodies of the novel and the all-too-embodied roles of the theater. What my own research suggests, however, is that many eighteenth-century playgoers were more than willing to overlook that difference and so were not nearly as "*precluded* [from] the kind of proprietary relationship . . . crucial to the experience of the 'realist' novel" as Freeman would have us believe (18).

13. Piozzi, *Anecdotes of the late Samuel Johnson*, 332.

14. DeMaria, *Samuel Johnson and the Life of Reading*, xv.

15. Darnton, "First Steps Toward a History of Reading," 157; Brewer, "Cultural Consumption in Eighteenth-Century England," 369.

16. Slawinski, "Reading and Reader in the Literary Historical Process," 538.

17. See Chartier, "The *Bibliothèque bleue* and Popular Reading."

18. See Ginzburg, *The Cheese and the Worms*; Darnton, "Readers Respond to Rousseau"; Brewer, "Reconstructing the Reader"; Jardine and Grafton, "Studied for Action"; and Sharpe, *Reading Revolutions*.

19. Here, obviously, I do not share James Raven's confidence that "questions of readership and reading strategies" are "best approached from the basis of a careful accumulation of a series of case-studies of readers and their memoirs of reading" (*Judging New Wealth*, 6). Case studies are invaluable, but something more than mere "accumulation" is necessary if we are going to be able to answer such questions with any satisfaction. As Siegfried Kracauer has powerfully argued, the relationship between micro- and macrohistory is "incommensurable" and "nonhomogeneous" and so one cannot simply assume that the amassing of case studies, no matter how "careful," will result in a cohesive overall picture ("The Structure of the Historical Universe," 126–27).

20. Levi, "On Microhistory," 109. The phrase "normal exception" (sometimes translated as "exceptional normal") comes from the work of Edouardo Grendi. For a fuller discussion of the "normal exception," and of the use of evidence in microhistory more generally, see Muir's "Introduction," especially xiv–xxi.

21. Ginzburg, "Microhistory," 33; Levi, 109.

22. Ginzburg and Poni, "The Name and the Game," 8. Even some of microhistory's fiercest critics grant that when faced with "the scarcity of available documentation or the impossibility of using traditional means for making that documentation speak out," attention to the normal exception can be a "fascinating but undeniably risky methodological skeleton key" capable of yielding legitimate and "productive" insights (Ferrone and Firpo, "From Inquisitors to Microhistorians," 522). Cf. Kracauer's proposal that "the vast knowledge we possess should challenge us not to indulge in inadequate syntheses but to concentrate on close-ups and from them casually range over the whole, assessing it in the form of aperçus. The whole may yield to such lightweight skirmishes more easily than to heavy frontal attack" (134–35).

23. Ginzburg, "Clues," 124.

24. Eco, *The Limits of Interpretation*, 7.

25. See Genette, *The Work of Art*. My thinking here has also been influenced by Catherine Gallagher's provocative meditations on "the ways materiality ceases to matter but is nevertheless indispensable," especially her contention that "the more identical copies of a text there were, the less that text seemed to occupy any particular location, and the less it seemed the physical emanation of any body" (xxiii, 62).

26. Stern, "*Tom Jones* and the Economies of Copyright," 436.

27. Simon Stern, 435.

28. *An Enquiry into the Nature and Origin of Literary Property*, 4.

29. Rose, "The Comedy of the Commons," 140. My sense of what is at stake in Kenrick's analogy has also been significantly shaped by Thompson, "Custom, Law, and Common Right."

30. Blackstone, *Commentaries on the Laws of England*, 2:2, 2:32.

31. *The Spectator* 411 (3:538).

32. Rev. W. K. Riland Bedford, *Three Hundred Years of a Family Living, being a History of the Rilands of Sutton Coldfield*, quoted in Thompson, "Custom, Law, and Common Right," 158.

33. Carol Rose, 125, 138.

34. Warner, *The Letters of the Republic*, 40. Cf. his insistence that "a public is always in excess of its known social basis. . . . It must include strangers" (*Publics and Counterpublics*, 74).

35. Carol Rose, 141.

36. Carol Rose, 147.

37. I use the term "virtual communities," rather than Benedict Anderson's celebrated "imagined communities," to help signal that the kinds of readerly communities I am interested in are not for the most part coterminous with the nation. Nonetheless, they too are communities mediated through writing (and often print-capitalism), and so are in an important way "imagined communities" premised upon the "deep, horizontal comradeship" (7) which comes with a shared interest in devising further adventures for a beloved character.

38. Churchill, *The Apology. Addressed to the Critical Reviewers*, in *The Poetical Works of Charles Churchill*, 42.

39. *An Enquiry into the Nature and Origin of Literary Property*, 5.

40. Reynolds, *Discourses on Art*, 107.

41. Carol Rose cites an 1833 case, *Rex v. Leake*, as evidence for the "English doctrine of acceptance, which . . . held that the general public could turn a passageway into a public road by its mere use. . . . Once the public had acted in this way, local officials had no choice in the matter" (118). But Edward Young's choice of metaphors suggests that the doctrine was well known at least sixty years earlier: "while the true Genius is crossing all publick roads into fresh untrodden ground," the writer who fails to know and reverence his own originality is "up the knees in Antiquity . . . treading the sacred footsteps of great examples" (*Conjectures on Original Composition*, 55). Those texts which have become public through repeated use are thus muddy roads into which hapless travelers may sink; "true Genius" lies in blazing a new trail across "fresh untrodden ground." Young is, of course, a champion of the economy of scarcity, but his language nonetheless captures the inverse relation between public use and felt private ownership.

42. Like his hero Samuel Johnson, DeMaria seems to presume that readers and writers operate in an economy of scarcity, such that if "there never was a time, in which men of all degrees of ability, of every kind of education, of every profession and employment, were posting with ardour so general to the press," then that must mean that "writers will, perhaps, be multiplied, till no readers will be found, and

then the ambition of writing must necessarily cease" (Johnson, *The Adventurer* 115, in *The Idler and The Adventurer,* 457, 459). Clearly, the phenomenon we are dealing with suggests otherwise.

43. Guillory, *Cultural Capital,* vii, ix.

44. See, for example, Brewer, *The Pleasures of the Imagination*; Kramnick, *Making the English Canon*; and Trevor Ross, "Copyright and the Invention of Tradition."

45. For evidence of how the felt value of these characters continued into the nineteenth century, see Jonathan Rose, *The Intellectual Life of the British Working Classes.*

46. Moretti, "The Slaughterhouse of Literature," 209–11.

47. Guillory does grant that "the entire domain of intertextuality, or response to earlier by later writers, is a powerful agency for the preservation of these writers," but he immediately undercuts the force of his observation by insisting that since "authors learn whom to read and how to judge in the schools," writers must pass "into school curricula in order for one to speak of canonicity" (355–56 n67).

48. Bennett and Woollacott, *Bond and Beyond,* 48. While I have not done the work necessary to substantiate this claim, I suspect that this devotion to characters even carried over into the realm of lyric poetry. Certainly many, if not all, of the poems most widely and intensely beloved in the eighteenth century—including Pope's "Eloisa to Abelard," Gray's "Elegy Written in a Country Churchyard," and the songs of "Ossian"—feature strong personae whose utterances both presume and hint at ongoing lives off-page.

49. Morgann, *Shakespearian Criticism,* 169n; Bennett and Woollacott, 13.

50. Gramsci, *Selections from Cultural Writings,* 350.

51. Habermas, "Further Reflections on the Public Sphere," 425.

52. Mah, "Phantasies of the Public Sphere," 166.

53. Michael Warner, *Publics and Counterpublics,* 11–12.

54. Morgann, 215; Foote, *The Roman and English Comedy Consider'd and Compar'd,* 41; Morris, *An Essay Towards Fixing the True Standards of Wit, Humour, Raillery, Satire, and Ridicule,* 26.

55. Kermode, *Forms of Attention,* 62.

56. Newsom, *A Likely Story,* 11.

57. Morgann, 148.

58. Davies, *Dramatic Micellanies,* 1:249.

59. Mah, 168.

60. Shields, *Civil Tongues and Polite Letters in British America,* xvi.

61. Hunter, *Before Novels,* 158.

62. Domestic political stability began to deteriorate in the 1760s, in large part because of the ability of John Wilkes to organize previously inchoate discontent.

63. Kay, *Political Constructions,* 11, 222.

64. Kevin Sharpe and Steven Zwicker argue that "it was the Whigs' construction of an aesthetic as well as political culture that secured their dominance. What sustained Whig hegemony and the appearance, to some degree the reality, of stability was not merely the political arts of patronage and management but the construction of a new culture of commerce and politeness and a new aesthetic of refinement and taste. There were strains and divisions in this society, but the culture long glossed and contained them" ("Introduction," 5–6).

65. See, for example, Brean S. Hammond, *Professional Imaginative Writing in England*; Kewes, *Authorship and Appropriation*; Loewenstein, *The Author's Due*; and Saunders and Hunter, "Lessons from the 'Literatory.'" Together, this work provides a powerful corrective to the overly legalistic accounts of Mark Rose and Martha Woodmansee.

66. Pocock, *Virtue, Commerce, and History*, 115.

67. Trevor Ross, 8.

68. Loewenstein, 229.

69. Certeau, *The Practice of Everyday Life*, 174.

Chapter 1

1. Zwicker, *Lines of Authority*, 202. For an intriguing meditation upon the difference it makes when historical events pass from living memory and have "to be reconstituted . . . as secondary effect," see Phillips, *Society and Sentiment*, 33–34.

2. For a useful discussion of "application," see Zwicker, "Reading the Margins."

3. Gallagher, *Nobody's Story*, 124.

4. It seems worth noting that my account of imaginative expansion follows roughly the same chronological trajectory as that charted out by H. J. Jackson in her history of marginalia. Jackson divides her narrative into three periods: the Kingdom of Competition (prior to 1700), the Kingdom of Subjectivity (after 1820), and the Kingdom of Sociability, which dominated literary culture between 1700 and 1820 (*Marginalia*, 44). Sociable marginalia were "typically . . . personal, and designed to be shared" (54–55). Indeed, "at every level the personal element in eighteenth-century marginalia can be linked to their social function" (61), much like the further adventures for beloved characters we will be investigating, which were aimed at fostering new forms of virtual sociability, despite their patent idiosyncrasy. Prior to the eighteenth century, Jackson claims, most marginalia was combative (as perhaps the high stakes of political and religious turmoil demanded). After 1820 or so, "readers retreated into themselves, and annotation became predominantly a private affair, a matter of self-expression" (73), rather than communal sharing.

5. Marcus, *Puzzling Shakespeare*, 37.

6. On such crises, see McKeon, *The Origins of the English Novel*, 124.

7. Addison, *A Discourse on Ancient and Modern Learning*, 2.

8. Young, *An Apology for Princes*, 372.

9. Pope, *A Key to the Lock*, 26.

10. Zwicker, "Reading the Margins," 104.

11. *The Spectator* 512 (4:318). This number offers an account of the pleasures afforded "in the reading of a Fable," a category which, for Addison, includes texts like *Absalom and Achitophel.*

12. The copy in question is Clark *PR 3506 .H94 M3.

13. Zwicker, "Reading the Margins," 109, 108.

14. Breval, *A Compleat Key to the Non-Juror*, 25.

15. Gay and Pope to Swift, 7 November 1726, in *The Correspondence of Jonathan Swift*, 3:47. Hereafter this collection will be cited as *Correspondence.*

16. Pope to Swift, 16 November 1726, in *Correspondence,* 3:52.

17. Swift to Pope, 17 November 1726, in *Correspondence,* 3:56.

18. Gay to Swift, 2 December 1728, in *Correspondence,* 3:204.

19. For a shrewd assessment of the nature and extent of the "particular reflections" in these texts, see Downie, "The Political Significance of *Gulliver's Travels*" and "Gay's Politics."

20. Swift to Pope, 29 September 1725, in *Correspondence,* 2:606. Presumably aware of the thin ice on which he was skating, Benjamin Motte seems to have altered a number of passages from Swift's manuscript in order to soften or obscure the available "reflections."

21. Gay, *Polly,* in *Dramatic Works,* 2:70.

22. Swift to Pope, 16 July 1728, in *Correspondence,* 3:189.

23. Hammond, "Introduction," 13.

24. Swift, *Gulliver's Travels,* 5. I have chosen to use this edition, rather than the standard *Prose Works of Jonathan Swift,* because it is based upon the 1726 text, which would have been the only version available to most of the readers whom we will be considering.

25. Hume to unknown correspondent, in Goldgar, "A Contemporary Reaction to *Gulliver's Travels,*" 2. Cf. Colin Nicholson's contention that "as more and more details of political topicality are brought to light, the more apparent it becomes that *Gulliver's Travels* is teasing the reader by merging character and event into fictional contours and by constantly shifting its ground to create serial and overlapping senses of fleeting recognition and partial apprehension . . . that should and should not relate to any determining picture of actuality" (*Writing and the Rise of Finance,* 108).

26. Rawson, *Gulliver and the Gentle Reader,* 9.

27. Cavallo and Chartier, "Introduction," 35.

28. James Hume, in Goldgar, "A Contemporary Reaction to *Gulliver's Travels,*" 2.

29. In addition to the passages just enumerated, see the "Proofs of my prodigious Strength" with which Gulliver "obliged" the curiosity of the Blefuscan ambassadors, although he "shall not trouble the Reader with the Particulars" (44–45), the repetition of his intention to publish "a particular Treatise" describing "this Empire" (47), his wish "not [to] trouble the Reader with the particular Account of my Reception" at the Blefuscan court "which was suitable to the Generosity of so great a Prince," but was attended with "Difficulties . . . for want of a House and Bed, being forced to lie on the Ground, wrapt up in my Coverlet" (62), and "the certain Accident" by which he "discovered" that the King of Blefuscu "was very glad of my Resolution" to go home "and so were most of his Ministers" (64). I confine myself to examples from Part I, since that voyage seems to have been of greatest interest to the readers with whom we shall be concerned, but Parts II through IV are chock-full of similar passages.

30. See, for example, Gulliver's coyness in recounting the use made of him by "the handsomest among [the Brobdingnagian] Maids of Honor," who "would sometimes set me astride upon one of her Nipples, with many other Tricks, wherein the Reader will excuse me for not being over particular" (99).

31. Boswell, *Life of Johnson,* 595.

32. *The Devil to Pay at St. James*['] *s,* 13.

33. I owe this clever formulation to Bogel, *The Difference Satire Makes*, 22.

34. Pope, *Minor Poems*, 278. All subsequent citations from the "Verses Explanatory and Commendatory" will be made parenthetically from this edition, despite the uncertainty of the poems' authorship.

35. In Lord Oxford's transcript of "The Lamentation," Glumdalclitch also angrily asks herself "Why did I not suspect Hippina's Muff, / And search the shag of Thighatira's Ruff. / These filthy Sluts, their Jordans ne'er abscond / To them a piss-pot, but to thee a pond" (271).

36. *Applebee's Original Weekly Journal*, 13 April 1728.

37. Swift, "The Life and Character of Dr. Swift," in *The Complete Poems*, 485.

38. Morson, *Narrative and Freedom*, 150.

39. Garrick, *The Plays of David Garrick*, 1:107–8. Cf. the similarly playful—and utterly unverifiable—claim that Gulliver was "mistaken" when he "mentions but two Kingdoms which the *Lilliputians* called the two great Empires of the World, I suppose upon account only of being the most powerful; for my Friend has often assured me, there were divers other Monarchies and Republicks composed of the same sort of Men, and among whom he lived many Years" (*A Cursory View of the History of Lilliput*, vi).

40. Rawson, *Gulliver and the Gentle Reader*, 27.

41. *Two Lilliputian Odes*, 11; Hunter, "*Gulliver's Travels* and the Later Writings," 226–27.

42. Rawson, "Gulliver and Others," 484.

43. Barthes, *S/Z*, 67.

44. Hunter suggests that "it is a safe guess that more than 20,000 copies of *Gulliver's Travels* were circulating among London's half-million people by the end of December [1726]—almost seven times the number of copies of *The Spectator* that Addison claimed would reach 60,000 readers—and the book's fame spread quickly throughout both England and Ireland" ("*Gulliver's Travels* and the Later Writings," 216).

45. For readers' "sensitivity to variant editions . . . with sophisticated appreciation of the mutability of the text" and "a sense of contingency . . . attributed both to material variations of the texts and to different reception circumstances," see Raven, "New Reading Histories, Print Culture, and the Identification of Change," 283. Further examples, including William Shenstone's insistence that tall authors shouldn't be published in squat formats like the quarto, may be found in Stoddard, "Morphology and the Book." And cf. the broader point made by David McKitterick that "most . . . readers" accepted "that the printed book not only was, but necessarily was, subject to change from copy to copy" (*Print, Manuscript, and the Search for Order*, 111).

46. John Arbuthnot to Swift, 5 November 1726, in *Correspondence*, 3:45. Cf. Pope's claim that "what you call your Couzen's wonderful Book . . . is *publica trita manu* [well worn by the hand of the public]" (Pope to Swift, 16 November 1726, in *Correspondence*, 3:52). The perception that the *Travels* were "universally read" was hardly limited to the Scriblerians: see, for example, *The Blunder of all Blunders* which describes how "poor Lemuel's laid upon the Table, / And every one, as he is able, / In blust'ring Words and smart Orations, / Begins to vent his Observations."

47. Gay and Pope to Swift, 7 November 1726, in *Correspondence*, 3:47. This

letter also describes how the *Travels* have "pass'd Lords and Commons, *nemine contradicente;* and the whole town, men, women, and children are quite full of it" (3:48).

48. Genette, *The Work of Art,* 88.

49. *The Penny London Post,* 25 November 1726, in Teerink, *A Bibliography of the Writings of Jonathan Swift,* 203.

50. French, "The Swift-Gulliver Litigation," 52.

51. Wilson, *Theaters of Intention,* 219.

52. French, 52.

53. Luke Wilson, 219.

54. Lady Bolingbroke to Swift, circa late February 1727–28, in *Correspondence,* 3:159 (my translation); Morson, 150.

55. Gay, *The Beggar's Opera,* in *Dramatic Works,* 2:4. All subsequent citations will be made parenthetically, giving first the act and scene number.

56. *Mist's Weekly Journal,* 19 June 1725.

57. *The Country Journal,* 17 February 1728.

58. *The Country Journal,* 17 February 1728.

59. "An excellent New Ballad, call'd, *A Bob for the C——t,*" in *The Country Journal,* 28 December 1728.

60. Winton, *John Gay and the London Theatre,* 195–96 n30.

61. *The Senator,* 16 February 1728, in *The Beggar's Opera,* 84.

62. I am here indebted to Bogel's suggestion that "Gay's *Opera* . . . refuses a rhetoric built upon sheer rejection and sheer embrace in favor of one that commingles and problematizes" the terms of a given comparison in the same way that a simile does. Hence, "*The Beggar's Opera* is *like* an opera" (138–39).

63. Cook, *Memoirs of Charles Macklin,* 54.

64. Donaldson, *The World Upside-Down,* 196.

65. Swift to Gay, 26 February 1728, in *Correspondence,* 3:162; *The Senator,* quoted without citation in Goldgar, *Walpole and the Wits,* 72.

66. Donaldson, 163.

67. Brewer, *The Pleasures of the Imagination,* 439.

68. Holland, *The Ornament of Action,* 118.

69. Penelope Darves to Ann Granville, 14 March 1728, in *The Autobiography and Correspondence of Mary Granville,* 1:163.

70. Advertisement for 24 June 1728, quoted in Robert D. Hume, *Henry Fielding and the London Theatre,* 37.

71. Swift and Thomas Sheridan, *The Intelligencer* 3 (63). Cf. Pope's description of how "the vast success of [the opera] was unprecedented, and almost incredible. . . . *Sophocles* and *Euripides* were less follow'd and famous" (*The Dunciad,* 190).

72. Robert D. Hume, *Henry Fielding and the London Theatre,* 37.

73. *The Grub-Street Journal,* 25 November 1736.

74. *St. James's Chronicle,* 8 August 1781, quoted in Schultz, *Gay's Beggar's Opera,* 79. For an extreme example of a novelty staging, consider the performance "at Barnstaple in Devonshire, when Macheath had but *one eye;* Polly but *one arm;* the songs supported in the orchestra by a man who whistled to the tunes, whilst the Manager could not read" (Cook, 62)

75. Schultz, 352.

76. *Mist's Weekly Journal*, 6 July 1728. The Congress was a diplomatic gathering at Soissons, which Fenton's lover, the Duke of Bolton, was scheduled to attend.

77. Gay to Swift, 20 March 1728, in *Correspondence*, 3:166; Gay, *Polly*, in *Dramatic Works*, 2:83.

78. Gay, *Polly*, in *Dramatic Works*, 2:71–72.

79. Sutherland, "'Polly' among the Pirates," 291.

80. *The Female Faction*, 4.

81. Cervantes, *The History of that Ingenious Gentleman, Don Quijote de la Mancha*, 733. *Macheath in the Shades* was offered at Covent Garden in 1735 but never printed. For a brief account, see the letter "John Gay" sent from the Elysian Fields to *The Prompter* lambasting the play as "a spurious degenerate issue, a hydra-offspring of the author's own brain" (45). Given the neo-Aristotelian bent of the rest of the letter, this may suggest that the play's appeal lay in the ways in which the "new medley" further multiplied Macheath's already hydra-headed maze of possibilities.

82. *The Flying Post*, 12 April 1729.

Chapter 2

1. Felsenstein, "Introduction," 1.

2. Spence, *An Essay on Pope's Odyssey*, 2. Austin Wright suspects that Philypsus is an autobiographical projection (*Joseph Spence*, 17).

3. Rogerson, "The Art of Painting the Passions," 70.

4. McKenzie, *Certain, Lively Episodes*, 5. For more on the origins and persistence of this repertoire, see Barnett, *The Art of Gesture*, Jennifer Montagu, *The Expression of the Passions*, Roach, *The Player's Passion*, and Smart, "Dramatic Gesture and Expression in the Age of Hogarth and Garrick."

5. Wilkes, *A General View of the Stage*, 132–33; *Thesaurus Dramaticus*, s.v. "Dying."

6. Wilkes, 114.

7. Kames, *Elements of Criticism*, 1:112.

8. Kames, *Elements of Criticism*, 3:174.

9. *The Spectator* 11 (1:48).

10. Davis, *The Problem of Slavery in Western Culture*, 10–11.

11. Wollstonecraft, *A Vindication of the Rights of Woman*, 215; Bellamy, *Miscellanies in Prose and Verse*, 2:9.

12. Stedman had hoped to purchase the woman in order to educate and marry her, but she rejected him with such nobility that he thought it worth embarrassing himself in order to recount the anecdote. As part of doing so, he apologizes, presumably for displaying such a feeling and antimercantile heart, to "those alone who have read the history of *Inkle* and *Yarico* . . . with pleasure and *approved* of that Gentleman's conduct" (*Narrative of Five Years Expedition against the Revolted Negroes of Surinam*, 98). Cf. the scene in Arthur Murphy's *The Citizen*, in which two merchants take turns praising Inkle for exemplifying "the very spirit of trade" and "calculation" (12). The use of Inkle as a touchstone continues at least as late as 1860, when George Eliot uses him to certify the acuity of David Faux's surname: David had "read some novels from

the adjoining circulating library, and . . . even bought the story of 'Inkle and Yarico', which had made him feel very sorry for poor Mr. Inkle" (*Brother Jacob*, 50).

13. Lawrence Marsden Price, *Inkle and Yarico Album*, 32.

14. Burke, *Popular Culture in Early Modern Europe*, 169.

15. Marina Warner, *Joan of Arc*, 7; Lawrence Price, 32.

16. Hertford, "An Epistle from Yarico to Inkle," in *English Trader, Indian Maid*, 96. Unless otherwise specified, all Inkle and Yarico materials will be hereafter cited parenthetically from this collection.

17. Wilkes, 125.

18. *Thesaurus Dramaticus*, s.v. "Despair."

19. Kames notes that "the reflection that a story is a pure fiction, will indeed prevent our sympathy; but so will . . . the reflection that the persons described are no longer existing. It is present distress only that moves my pity" (*Elements of Criticism*, 1:115). Ideal presence "admits not any time but the present" (*Elements of Criticism*, 1:111).

20. *Thesaurus Dramaticus*, s.v. "Compassion" and "Falling in Love."

21. Being "levell'd low . . . prone and dumb" is a classic sign of mourning, while a "fault'ring Tongue" was one of the conventional symptoms of amazement (*Thesaurus Dramaticus*, s.v. "Grief" and "Astonishment")

22. See, for example, the lovers' initial meeting in Stephen Duck's *Avaro and Amanda: A Poem in Four Canto's, Taken from 'The Spectator,' Vol. I, No. XI.* Here Yarico (curiously renamed Amanda) "fix'd in amaze, a-while she list'ning stood; / Then swift approach'd him, rushing thro' the wood. / Th'affrighted merchant rose with gazing eyes, / And tim'rous looks, that testify'd surprise: / Backwards he starts; the dame, with equal fears, / Recedes as fast, and wonders what appears" (130). Wild starts and frozen limbs were among the usual ways of designating Astonishment and Wonder. In much the same way, Edward Jerningham's *Yarico to Inkle: An Epistle* closes by imagining a Dido-like suicide for Yarico in which "extended on the crimson floor: / These temples clouded with the shades of death, / These lips unconscious of the ling'ring breath: / These eyes uprais'd (ere closed by fate's decree) / To catch expiring one faint glimpse of thee" as her "fault'ring voice" fades into silence (162). Similarly upturned eyes and failing speech, especially when delivered from a prone position, were stock conventions for the Dying. As the century wore on, these passions could be more and more telegraphically expressed, thus Charles James Fox's "Yarico to Inkle" has its Yarico simply describe how "I left you fixt in attitude of woe; / And, slow retreating, saw your fearful eye / Pursue my steps, and heard the bursting sigh" (250). The exact gestures and expressions that constitute an "attitude of woe" presumably went without saying.

23. Wilkes, 125, 112; Hill, *An Essay on the Art of Acting*, in *The Works of the late Aaron Hill*, 4:366.

24. Wilkes, 121.

25. Le Brun, *A Method to learn to Design the Passions*, 42.

26. Wilkes, 121.

27. Aaron Hill, 4:361.

28. In addition to the examples we have already considered (and those cited in note 22), see William Pattison's "Yarico to Inkle: An Epistle," John Winstanley's "Yarico's

Epistle to Inkle: A Poem, Occasion'd by Reading *Spectator,* Vol. I, No. 11," the "Yarico to Inkle" by "Amicus" and that by "Peter Pindar," the four-letter exchange between Inkle and Yarico written by W. Smith and John Webb which appeared in *The Lady's Magazine,* Paul Methuen's *An Epistle from Yarico to Inkle,* and Anna Maria Porter's "Epistle from Yarico to Inkle," all of which are either reprinted or fully cited in *English Trader, Indian Maid* (although it should be noted that the epistle by "Amicus" originally appeared in *The Farmer's Magazine* 3 [1778]: 366–68). James Beattie wrote a fragmentary "complaint" for Yarico "on being abandoned by Inkle . . . which is in the epistolary form," but left it "uncorrected" (*Essays and Fragments in Prose and Verse,* 59).

29. Farrell, "Reading and Writing the *Heroides,*" 323.

30. Ovid, "Dido to Aeneas," in Dryden, *Poems,* 134.

31. Pope, "Eloisa to Abelard," in *The Rape of the Lock and Other Poems,* 328, 344.

32. Beer, "'Our unnatural No-voice'," 133.

33. Beer, 133. Reuben Brower insists that this familiarity is constitutive of the genre itself: "a heroic epistle always assumes that the facts are well known to the reader" (*Alexander Pope,* 65).

34. Beer, 138.

35. Hiffernan, "Inkle and Yarico. Taken from the *Spectator,* Vol. I, No. XI," in *Miscellanies in Prose and Verse,* 152, 147.

36. Kennedy, "Epistolarity," 225. Stephen Duck nicely exploits these ironies by having his Inkle (renamed Avaro) pledge that "so shall our future Race of Children see / A constant Proverb made of you and me: / When *British* Youths shall court the doubting Dame, / And want Expressions equal to their Flame; / Then, strongly to attest it, shall be said, / '*True, as Avaro to the Indian Maid*'" (*Poems on Several Occasions,* 114–15). This passage is not included in the excerpts from Duck which appear in *English Trader, Indian Maid.*

37. Knox, *Essays Moral and Literary,* 1:5, 1:126.

38. Blair, *Lectures on Rhetoric and Belles Lettres,* 1:408.

39. G. O., "To the Author of an Epistle from Yarico to Inkle, lately publish'd," *The London Magazine* 5 (1736), 215.

40. Gay, *The Present State of Wit,* in *Poetry and Prose,* 455. As a young law student, Dudley Ryder was shown "some letters that were sent to Mr. Steele when he wrote the *Spectators* which he had not made use of" (*The Diary of Dudley Ryder,* 183).

41. Sherman, *Telling Time,* 143. Cf. Charles A. Knight's point that "perhaps the most universal communal feature of literate men and women in 1711–12 was that they read and discussed the *Spectator.* Addison and Steele sought to find, through the medium of print, the equivalent of a common oral culture" ("Bibliography and the Shape of the Literary Periodical in the Early Eighteenth Century," 247).

42. Sherman, 114.

43. Collet to Elisabeth Collet, 26 August 1714, in *The Private Letter Books of Joseph Collet,* 100.

44. Knox recommends that "the boy's library consist of such books as Rollin's History, Plutarch's Lives, and the Spectators; and, together with the improvement of his morals and understanding, which he must derive from reading them, he will have

it in his power to spend his vacant time in such mental amusements as are truly and permanently delightful" (1:71). Such boys were, of course, among the most devoted patrons of the supposedly far less improving circulating libraries.

45. Michael Warner, *Publics and Counterpublics,* 96.

46. Hulme, *Colonial Encounters,* 259.

47. A clue to the tale's general reputation may be gleaned from the presence of "urns devoted to Potiphar's wife and the Ephesian widow" in the meeting place of the Medmenhamite Brotherhood, Francis Dashwood's club of *über*-rakes (Paulson, *Hogarth,* 273).

48. Guillory, *Cultural Capital,* 97.

49. Scott, *Minstrelsy of the Scottish Border,* 1:8.

50. Bickerstaff's lost *Inkle and Yarico* is briefly chronicled in Tasch, *The Dramatic Cobbler,* 123–24.

51. Price, *Theatre in the Age of Garrick,* 4–5.

52. Davies, *Dramatic Micellanies,* 1:305; Clive, in *The London Daily Post,* 19 November 1736.

53. *A Statement of the Differences Subsisting Between the Proprietors and Performers of the Theatre-Royal,* 62.

54. "The Occasional Prompter," *The Daily Journal,* 3 January 1737.

55. Bellamy, *An Apology for the Life of George Anne Bellamy,* 1:100.

56. On the division of the pre-Restoration repertory, see Robert D. Hume, "Securing a Repertory." Hume explains that prior to 1728, "new plays belonged exclusively to the company that first performed them . . . but this appears to have been a matter of private co-operation" (*Henry Fielding and the London Theatre,* 19). Shirley Strum Kenny clarifies the status of older but post-Restoration plays by noting that the "perennial favorites" of circa 1700—Congreve, Vanbrugh, Cibber, Farquhar, and Steele—"spread to more than one house when parts no longer seemed to belong to a single player" as a result of the originating actor's death ("Perennial Favorites," S8).

57. A "part" meant both the role in question and "a roll of paper containing [the actor's] lines and minimal cues. . . . When, on an actor's death or retirement, the parts were redistributed, the process involved the physical handing over of the manuscript parts" (Holland, *The Ornament of Action,* 65). This helps to account for why "when she was unable to perform," "Laetitia Cross sent her part in to the theatre . . . so that someone else could read it" (Tiffany Stern, *Rehearsal from Shakespeare to Sheridan,* 212 n70).

58. Tiffany Stern, 284.

59. Neville, *Diary,* 45. Cf. George Saville Carey's "Lecture on Mimicry" which featured a host of "characters imitated" along the lines of the actors most closely associated with them: e.g., "Othello, Mr. Barry. Jane Shore, Mrs. Hartley. Waterman, Mr. Bannister" (quoted in Highfill, "Performers and Performing," 175). Carey's mimicry included some roles "in the Manner of" actors no longer among the living.

60. On the Macklin riots, see Kinservik, "A Sinister *Macbeth.*" Cf. the hissing of "the lovely Mrs. Horton . . . for taking over a part at Drury Lane which had formerly been 'the property' of Mrs. Younger" (Clinton-Baddeley, *All Right on the Night,* 177).

61. Robert D. Hume, *Henry Fielding and the London Theatre,* 105.

62. Lynch, *Box, Pit, and Gallery,* 17. *Tamerlane* was offered in competing

performances every November 5, just as, until 1751 when Garrick abolished the custom, *The London Cuckolds* would be performed by both houses every Lord Mayor's Day (14).

63. Robert D. Hume, *Henry Fielding and the London Theatre,* 240 n103. Cibber thought that the Restoration division of the repertory ensured that "the Stage was supply'd with a greater variety of Plays, than could possibly have been shewn, had both Companies been employ'd at the same time, upon the same Play; which Liberty too, must have occasion'd such frequent Repetitions of 'em, by their opposite Endeavours to forestall and anticipate one another, that the best Actors in the World must have grown tedious and tasteless to the Spectator." For Cibber, competition led only to "a daily Contention which shall soonest surfeit you with the best Plays" (*An Apology for the Life of Colley Cibber,* 56).

64. Kinservik, *Disciplining Satire,* 107–8.

65. This is a common phenomenon in "highly traditional and articulate theatre[s]" with a limited repertory: within such a milieu, the "actor-as-performer . . . catches our interest" more than the "actor-as-character," with the result that "audiences tend to be more cognizant of the performing features or surface" (Beckerman, "Theatrical Perception," 162).

66. Burnim, *David Garrick,* 131; Holland, "The Age of Garrick," 78.

67. Gentleman, *The Dramatic Censor,* 1:189.

68. *The Gentleman's Magazine* 20 (1750), 438.

69. Stone, "The Making of the Repertory," 205.

70. *Restoration and Georgian England,* 341, 162. A good example of this presumption would be Betterton's performance of Henry VIII, "he being Instructed in it by Sir *William* [Davenant], who had it from Old Mr. *Lowen,* that had his Instructions from Mr. *Shakespear* himself" (Downes, *Roscius Anglicanus,* 55). Cf. Cibber's account of his meticulous reproduction of Thomas Doggett's performance of Fondlewife (114–16).

71. "Mediator Poenitus," letter to "The Occasional Prompter," *The Daily Journal,* 23 December 1736.

72. Brewer, *The Pleasures of the Imagination,* 337.

73. *The London Chronicle,* 19–21 December 1758, reprinted in *Restoration and Georgian England,* 422. I quote only what is excerpted in this anthology, as the available microfilm for this issue reproduces a copy in which Murphy's essay has been clipped out.

74. Barthes, "Baudelaire's Theater," 26.

75. Freeman, *Character's Theater,* 34.

76. Worthen, *The Idea of the Actor,* 72. Michael S. Wilson concurs with this description, noting that "hits" served as "touchstones for comparative judgment" ("Garrick, Iconic Acting, and the Ideologies of Theatrical Portraiture," 379).

77. Unknown correspondent to Garrick, quoted without citation in Tiffany Stern, 256.

78. John Hill, *The Actor,* 177, 249.

79. Cibber, 63.

80. Locke, *Two Treatises of Government,* 306.

81. Locke, 306.

82. Locke, 305.

83. Brewer, *The Pleasures of the Imagination*, 390.

84. *An Enquiry into the Nature and Origin of Literary Property*, 10.

85. "The Occasional Prompter," in *The Daily Journal*, 6 December 1736. The performance rights to unpublished plays remained the property of their author or his or her assignees. For a discussion of Macklin's defense of these rights, see Kinservik, "*Love à la Mode* and Macklin's Return to the London Stage in 1759," 17. Cf. his account of Samuel Foote's sale of such rights in "Satire, Censorship, and Sodomy in Samuel Foote's *The Capuchin*," 656.

86. John Hill, 177.

87. Hill to Booth, 25 December 1732, in *The Works of the late Aaron Hill*, 1:118.

88. Churchill, *The Apology. Addressed to the Critical Reviewers*, in *The Poetical Works of Charles Churchill*, 42–44.

89. Warner, *Publics and Counterpublics*, 68.

90. *Theatrical Biography*, 1:vi.

91. For a host of examples of the audience being figured as a representative political body, see Hughes, *The Drama's Patrons*, 3–11. Cf. Arthur Murphy's modification of this rhetoric: in Garrick's time, "the theatre engrossed the minds of men to such a degree, that it may now be said, that there existed in England a *fourth estate*, King, Lords, and Commons, and *Drury-Lane play-house*" (*The Life of David Garrick*, 2:201).

92. Theophilus Cibber, *Two Dissertations on the Theatres*, quoted in Pedicord, *The Theatrical Public in the Time of Garrick*, 118–19.

93. Ralph, *The Case of Authors by Profession or Trade*, 23.

94. Boaden, *Memoirs of the Life of John Philip Kemble*, 1:93.

95. Murphy, in *The Morning Chronicle*, 30 October 1773.

96. *An Epistle from Yarico to Inkle, Together With their Characters, as related in the Spectator*, 7.

97. Weddell, *Incle and Yarico*, 36–37.

98. Calasso, *The Marriage of Cadmus and Harmony*, 281.

99. Downes, 94.

Chapter 3

1. By calling the practice "migration" I hope to emphasize the ways in which these characters stray from their originary texts and authors. For revivals within a given oeuvre (a common practice in the series fiction of the nineteenth and twentieth centuries), John Updike's concept of "character resurrection" might be more appropriate ("Recurrent Characters," 9).

2. My principal predecessor in this inquiry has been J. Paul Hunter, whose "Serious Reflections on Farther Adventures" offers an intriguing discussion of "mobile characters" as a sign "that novelistic narratives do not really end, as individual texts may suggest or presume, but that stories are interwoven, seamless, continuous, and relatively endless" (282). As my quotation should suggest, however, Hunter is primarily concerned with how this might illuminate "resistance" to closure "as a standard,

widespread feature" of the eighteenth-century novel (279). Accordingly, his work goes in a significantly different direction from my own.

3. Dorman, *Sir Roger de Coverly*, 5.

4. *The Spectator* 34 (1:142).

5. *The Spectator* 116 (1:475).

6. Aikin, in *The Monthly Magazine* 9 (1800), 3; Knox, *Essays Moral and Literary*, 1:5. George Justice notes that "in terms of popularity and influence, the papers concerning Sir Roger gained from the beginning a disproportionate share of attention and praise" (*The Manufacturers of Literature*, 55).

7. Franklin, *Poor Richard, 1736. An Almanack*, in *The Papers of Benjamin Franklin*, 2:136.

8. Fielding, *The Jacobite's Journal* 1 (5 December 1747), in *The Jacobite's Journal and Related Writings*, 96.

9. Murphy, *The Gray's-Inn Journal* 1 (21 October 1752), in *The Gray's-Inn Journal*, 1:1–2.

10. Justice, 55.

11. Shiells and Cibber, *The Lives of the Poets of Great Britain and Ireland*, 3:312.

12. Morgann, *Shakespearian Criticism*, 169n.

13. Davies, *Dramatic Micellanies*, 1:249–50, 1:252.

14. Davies, *A Genuine Narrative of the Life and Theatrical Transactions of Mr. John Henderson*, 56, 55.

15. For Charke's puppetry, see Speaight, *The History of the English Puppet Theatre*, 104.

16. Davies, *Dramatic Micellanies*, 1:249.

17. Kenrick, *London Review* 6 (1777), quoted in Daniel A. Fineman, "Biographical Introduction," 16.

18. Kenrick, *Falstaff's Wedding, . . . Being a Sequel to the Second Part of the Play of King Henry the Fourth*, v. Unless otherwise noted, all quotations will be drawn from this version of Kenrick's play, rather than the somewhat pared down acting text published in 1766.

19. Garrick to Richard Berenger?, 5 July 1759, in *The Letters of David Garrick*, 1:311.

20. Richard Cumberland, *The Observer* 86, in *The Observer*, 3:244; *A Letter to Colley Cibber*, 13. For other allegations of Falstaff's universal appeal, consider only Nicholas Rowe's assertion that "*Falstaff* is allow'd by every body to be a Masterpiece" ("Some Account of the Life &c. of Mr. *William Shakespear*," xvii) or Thomas Davies's proclamation seventy-five years later that "it is confessed, by all the world, that there is an uncommon fame and versatility in the mirth of Falstaff which is superior to all that dramatic poetry has hitherto invented" (*Dramatic Micellanies*, 1:237).

21. Kenrick, *Love in the Suds*, 21.

22. Garrick to Berenger?, 5 July 1759, in *The Letters of David Garrick*, 1:311.

23. It is worth noting, though, that Thomas Davies hoped that with the death of Garrick and the advent of John Henderson as "an admirable representer of the jolly knight . . . *Falstaff's Wedding* will be restored to the public" as a theatrical piece (*Memoirs of the Life of David Garrick*, 2:104).

24. For more on *ferae naturae*, see *The Dictionary of English Law*, s.v. "Animals ferae naturae," and Munsche, *Gentlemen and Poachers*, 3–6.

25. The phrase "universal promiscuous enjoyment" comes from a decision by Lord Loughborough against gleaning as a common-law right. Loughborough thought the claim indefensible, as it was "incapable of enjoyment, since nothing which is not inexhaustible, like a perennial stream, can be capable of universal promiscuous enjoyment" (quoted in Thompson, "Custom, Law and Common Right," 139). As Thompson details, the exhaustibility of the actual commons was frequently cited as an argument against them.

26. Intriguingly, the analogy of *ferae naturae* crops up in Justice Yates's famous dissent in *Millar v. Taylor,* the main opinion of which "upheld the author's common-law right and the perpetuity of literary property" (Mark Rose, *Authors and Owners,* 78). Key to Yates's argument is "the maxim . . . that nothing can be an object of property, which is not capable of a sole and exclusive enjoyment. . . . without that power [of excluding others], the right will be insignificant: it will be in vain to contend that 'that is your own,' which you cannot prevent others from sharing in. . . . But how can an author, after publishing his work, confine it to himself?" A published text—and its characters—are like "wild animals. . . . They are yours, while they continue in your possession; but no longer. So, from the time of publication, the ideas become incapable of being any longer a subject of property: all mankind are equally intitled to read them; and every reader becomes as fully possessed of all the ideas, as the author himself ever was. . . . Every purchaser of a book is the owner of it: and, as such, he has a right to make what use of it he pleases" (*The English Reports,* 98:233–34).

27. *The London Encyclopedia,* s.v. "Pimlico." It is worth noting that Kenrick is referring to "the area immediately south west of Buckingham Gate (then St James's Street) . . . known for two hundred years, from the 1620s, as Pimlico." The present-day Pimlico is "south west of the original area" (Watson, *Westminster and Pimlico Past,* 31).

28. Wroth, *The London Pleasure Gardens of the Eighteenth Century,* 220, 222–24.

29. Chancellor, *The Pleasure Haunts of London,* 368.

30. *The Shakspere Allusion-Book,* 2:536.

31. Dobson, *The Making of the National Poet,* 18–19.

32. Downes, *Roscius Anglicanus,* 24.

33. Brewer, *The Pleasures of the Imagination,* 460.

34. Gilpin, *An Essay upon Prints,* 245. For more on this discourse, itself largely an eighteenth-century invention, see Karpinski, "The Print in Thrall to its Original."

35. Schwartz, *The Culture of the Copy,* 212.

36. For the "wide variety of forms" through which "all levels of society" "might have . . . seen" the Raphael Cartoons, see Clayton, *The English Print,* 49–52.

37. Joseph Moser, quoted without citation in Whitley, *Artists and their Friends in England,* 1:373.

38. *Sculptura-Historico-Technica,* vi–vii.

39. "Cosmetti," *The Polite Arts,* 26–27.

40. Hume, "Before the Bard," 54. For a broader survey of the competing editions, see Andrew Murphy, *Shakespeare in Print,* 57–141.

41. Eisenstein, *The Printing Revolution in Early Modern Europe,* 89.

42. Guillory, *Cultural Capital,* 28.

43. Blackstone, *Commentaries on the Laws of England,* 2:406.

44. Kames, *Remarkable Decisions of the Court of Session,* 157–58.

45. Orgel, "The Authentic Shakespeare," 14.

46. Holland, *The Ornament of Action,* 118.

47. Lamb, "Detached Thoughts on Books and Reading," in *Elia and the Last Essays of Elia,* 196–97.

48. Miller, *Subsequent Performances,* 55.

49. Derrida, "Limited, Inc," 175.

50. I am not denying, of course, that—as Stephen Orgel has shown—the notion of "authenticity" is "profoundly time bound" (3) and so at least in theory every bit as subject to individual taste and connoisseurship as the most outlandish imaginative expansion. The variants between putatively "authentic" iterations, however, tend to be quieter than those with which we have been concerned.

51. The phrase quoted comes from one of William Chetwood's advertisements castigating, on behalf of Jacob Tonson whose copyright had lapsed, Richard Walker's reprint edition of Shakespeare. It is reproduced in Ford, *Shakespeare,* 44–45.

52. *The Grub-Street Journal* 220 (14 March 1734).

53. *The Monthly Review* 49 (1773), 419.

54. Bate, *Shakespearean Constitutions,* 36–37.

55. See Dunbar, *The Dramatic Career of Arthur Murphy,* 311.

56. Morris, *An Essay Towards Fixing the True Standards of Wit, Humour, Raillery, Satire, and Ridicule,* 34.

57. It is unclear from Morris's phrasing whether he is unaware of Dorman's play or simply thinks it not an example of right exhibition.

58. Foote, *The Roman and English Comedy Consider'd and Compar'd,* 41. Cf. Elizabeth Montagu's claim that "a person must be ill-natured, as well as dull, who does not join in the mirth of this jovial companion" (*An Essay on the Writings and Genius of Shakespeare,* 106).

59. "*Shakespeare's* Ghost," *The London Magazine* 19 (1750), 279.

60. Murphy, in *The London Chronicle,* 25–27 January 1757.

61. Boswell, *Boswell's Journal of a Tour to the Hebrides with Samuel Johnson,* 209.

62. Murphy, *The Gray's-Inn Journal* 38 (7 July 1753), in *The Gray's-Inn Journal,* 1:244.

63. For a full description of the procession, see Deelman, *The Great Shakespeare Jubilee,* 282–86, and Stochholm, *Garrick's Folly,* 160–71. George Colman included a rival procession in his *Man and Wife; or, the Shakespeare Jubilee,* as did George Saville Carey in *Shakespeare's Jubilee, A Masque.*

64. The first quotation comes from a marginal note in one of the manuscripts of *The Jubilee* (*The Plays of David Garrick,* 2:115n).

65. Kenrick, *Love in the Suds,* 21. Cf. Samuel Foote's quip that "to solemn sounds see sordid scene-men stalk / And the great Shakespeare's vast creation—walk!" (prologue spoken at the Haymarket, 16 January 1770, quoted in Deelman, 285).

66. Hopkins, diary entry for 26 October 1769, quoted in Deelman, 284–85.

67. *The Town and Country Magazine* 1 (1769), 549.

68. *The St. James's Chronicle,* quoted without citation in Deelman, 285.

69. *The Critical Review* 13 (1762), 427–28.

70. Reynolds, *Discourses on Art,* 107

71. "Character and plot of the *Foundling," The Gentleman's Magazine* 18 (1748), 51; Newsom, *A Likely Story,* 11.

72. "Remarks on the Foundling," *The Gentleman's Magazine* 18 (1748), 116.

73. "Remarks on the Foundling, in Answer to those in March, p. 114," *The Gentleman's Magazine* 18 (1748), 209, 207, 209. Cf. the similar presumptions made by a reader of *The Tatler* who took up the Political Upholsterer's case, explaining that he "did not Ruin himself (as [Bickerstaff] would Insinuate to the world) by turning politician, but for want of his Just debts, due to him from persons of Quality, which was the Occasion of his takeing so many turns in the park, to avoid the Sight of his Constant Dunners" (Thos. Hope to Mr. Bickerstaff, 22 May 1710, in *New Letters to the Tatler and Spectator,* 125).

74. With "sideshadowing," "we see . . . the image of what else could have happened. Sideshadows conjure the ghostly presence of might-have-beens or might-bes" with the result that "the hypothetical shows through the actual and so achieves its own shadowy kind of existence in the text" (Morson, *Narrative and Freedom,* 118).

75. "Remarks upon the Foundling in Answer to those in March, p. 114," *The Gentleman's Magazine* 18 (1748), 258, 259.

76. "Account of the Suspicious Husband," *The Gentleman's Magazine* 17 (1747), 133. Only a few weeks prior to its debut, when the script was submitted to the Licenser, *The Suspicious Husband* was still entitled "The Rake"—an appellation which better highlights its real center of interest for most theatergoers. As the author of *An Examen of the New Comedy, call'd The Suspicious Husband* notes, "*Ranger* . . . is the Life and Soul of the whole" (9). It is also worth pointing out that when Sylas Neville read the play at dinner prior to seeing it performed, he only read "Ranger's part" (*Diary,* 9).

77. The letter to *The Daily Gazetteer* is reprinted in *The Gentleman's Magazine* 17 (1747), 79–80.

78. Hoadly, *The Suspicious Husband,* 76.

79. Foote, 31; Arthur Murphy, in *The London Chronicle,* 3–5 February 1757.

80. Arthur Murphy, *The Gray's-Inn Journal* 3 (4 November 1752), in *The Gray's-Inn Journal,* 1:15.

81. Macklin, *The New Play Criticiz'd,* 48.

82. *Dialogue in the Shades Between the Celebrated Mrs. Cibber, and the no less Celebrated Mrs. Woffington,* quoted in Stone and Kahrl, *David Garrick,* 735 n46.

83. Richardson to Lady Bradshaigh, late November or early December 1749, in *Selected Letters of Samuel Richardson,* 133.

84. Forster, *Aspects of the Novel,* 119.

85. Richardson to Lady Bradshaigh, late November or early December 1749, in *Selected Letters of Samuel Richardson,* 133.

86. Kidgell, *The Card,* 2:294–95.

87. Fielding, *Joseph Andrews,* 344.

88. Fielding, *A Journey from This World to the Next,* in *Miscellanies by Henry Fielding,* 4.

89. Fielding, *The True Patriot* 7 (17 December 1745), in *The True Patriot and Related Writings,* 151.

90. Fielding, *The True Patriot* 6 (10 December 1745), in *The True Patriot and Related Writings*, 376.

91. Adam's second letter to the True Patriot appeared in number 13 (28 January 1746) and mostly concerns a young profligate whom he and Mr. Wilson had met at a dinner. Incensed by the wastrel's effrontery, Adams attempted to strike him, but only succeeded in giving a bloody nose to "a Jackanapes" who "whipt my Peruke from my Head" (205). Tellingly for our purposes, Adams signs this letter "your hearty Friend and Well-wisher" (207).

92. Fielding, *The Jacobite's Journal* 32 (9 July 1748), in *The Jacobite's Journal and Related Writings*, 330.

93. See Tave, *The Amiable Humorist*, 144–45. This success may account for the comparatively relaxed and casual tone with which Fielding presents his final iteration of Adams: "But in [Thwackum's] stead, Mr. *Allworthy* hath lately taken Mr. *Abraham Adams* into his House, of whom *Sophia* is grown immoderately fond, and declares he shall have the Tuition of her Children" (*The History of Tom Jones*, 980).

94. *The Gentleman's Magazine* 16 (1746), 268.

95. On the sociability afforded provincial readers by *The Gentleman's Magazine*, see Barker, "Poetry from the Provinces."

96. Ryder to Anne Ryder, 23 October 1742, quoted in Battestin with Battestin, *Henry Fielding*, 359.

Chapter 4

1. Richardson to Lady Bradshaigh, late November or early December 1749, in *Selected Letters of Samuel Richardson*, 133. Hereafter this collection will be cited as *SL*.

2. Bennett and Woollacott, *Bond and Beyond*, 91.

3. Unlike many of the cases we have been investigating, the *Pamela* vogue has received a great deal of critical attention. I have benefited most from Eaves and Kimpel, *Samuel Richardson*; the various introductions in *The Pamela Controversy*; and Turner, "Novel Panic."

4. Hill to Richardson, 9 February 1741. Extracts from this letter were printed as part of the front matter to the second edition of *Pamela*. Wherever this is the case, I will quote from Appendix One of Keymer and Wakely's edition of *Pamela*, rather than the various collections of Richardson's or Hill's correspondence, in large part because I am interested in how Hill's response itself became part of the *Pamela* craze. Here my quotation is from *Pamela*, 517–18.

5. Hill to Richardson, 17 December 1740, in *Pamela*, 506.

6. "Abstract of a second Letter from the same Gentleman," in *Pamela*, 508.

7. Unknown correspondent to Garrick, quoted without citation in Tiffany Stern, *Rehearsal from Shakespeare to Sheridan*, 256.

8. Fielding, *An Apology for the Life of Mrs. Shamela Andrews*, 311. Hereafter this text will be cited as *Shamela*.

9. Hill to Richardson, 6 January 1741, in *Pamela*, 511–12. The anonymous gentleman's objection appears on 509.

10. *The Gentleman's Magazine* 11 (1741), 56.

11. Whitehead, *On Nobility,* 6.

12. Ralph Courtville to Richardson, 8 June 1741, quoted in *The Pamela Controversy,* 1:xiii; Richardson to George Cheyne, 31 August 1741, in *SL,* 47.

13. Richardson to James Leake, August 1741, in *SL,* 44. Richardson seems to have been fond of describing expansions of his work in these terms. In addition to the phrase just quoted, and the famous description of *Joseph Andrews* as "a lewd and ungenerous engraftment," an advertisement in *The Daily Gazetteer* ironically describes the "*pretended Continuation*" of *Pamela*—John Kelly's *Pamela's Conduct in High Life*—as a "*worthy Ingraftment*" (30 May 1741).

14. For a useful survey of Richardson's "compulsive desire for literary consultation," see Sabor, "Richardson and his Readers."

15. Cheyne to Richardson, 7 July 1741, in *The Letters of Doctor George Cheyne to Samuel Richardson,* 67–68. Hereafter, this collection will be cited as *LCR.* Richardson refers scornfully to these suggestions in a late 1741 letter to Stephen Duck: "an excellent Physician was so good as to give me a Plan to break Legs and Arms and to fire Mansion Houses to create Distresses; But my Business and View was to aim at Instruction in a genteel and usual Married Life." He will, however, include "a strong Jealous Scene" (*SL,* 52–53).

16. Cheyne to Richardson, 10 January 1742, in *LCR,* 82.

17. Richardson to Cheyne, circa 1742, in *SL,* 55. Cf. Richardson's request to Duck "to point out *particular* Faults" (*SL,* 52).

18. Richardson to Cheyne, 31 August 1741, in *SL,* 50; Richardson to Cheyne, circa 1742, in *SL,* 54.

19. Cheyne to Richardson, 5 September 1742, in *LCR,* 109–10.

20. Johnson, *The Rambler* 4 (31 March 1750), in *The Rambler,* 21.

21. Cheyne to Richardson, 2 May 1742, in *LCR,* 93.

22. Hill to Richardson, 29 December 1740, in *The Correspondence of Samuel Richardson,* 1:55; Hill to Richardson, 9 February 1741, in *Pamela,* 518. Hereafter the former collection will be cited as *Correspondence.*

23. Warburton to Richardson, 28 December 1742, in *Correspondence,* 1:134–35.

24. Fulford to Richardson, 25 January 1742, in Richardson, Correspondence, Forster Collection Manuscripts XVI.I, f. 82. Hereafter this collection will be cited as *FM.*

25. Psalmanazar to Richardson, *FM* XVI.I, ff. 27–33.

26. Richardson, *Pamela . . . In her Exalted Condition,* 4:86–88. For Gordon's original, see *FM* XVI.I, f. 12.

27. Richardson to Leake, August 1741, in *SL,* 43.

28. Richardson to Ralph Allen, 8 October 1741, in *SL,* 51. This is a reply to a no longer extant letter of Allen's.

29. Richardson to Hill, circa late 1741, in *SL,* 41.

30. *Pamela: or, the Fair Imposter,* 55. This poem may provide a surrogate for the "much longer" letter promised at the close of *Shamela,* which ends with a reference to how "Mr. *Booby* hath caught his Wife in bed with *Williams;* hath turned her off, and is prosecuting him in the spiritual Court" (344).

31. Giffard, *Pamela. A Comedy,* 69.

32. Austin Dobson, *Samuel Richardson,* 35.

33. Richardson to Leake, August 1741, in *SL,* 43–44.

34. William B. Warner, *Licensing Entertainment,* 283 n3.

35. The last phrase quoted comes from Jean Baptiste de Freval, "To the Editor of the Piece intitled, Pamela; or Virtue Rewarded," in *Pamela,* 5.

36. Fielding may be parodying this technique (as well as Richardson's prolixity) when he has the editor of *Shamela* note that Booby's letter to her "with a large Number of Promises" "as well as the next which *Shamela* wrote, and which contained an Account of all the Proceedings previous to her Marriage" and which only "left off at our sitting down to Supper on our Wedding-Night" are "unhappily lost" (334). Indeed, early in her next letter she reminds her mother about "Mr. *Williams,* who, as I informed you in my last, is released, and presented to the Living, upon the Death of the last Parson" (334–35).

37. Richardson, in *The Daily Gazetteer,* 7 May 1741.

38. On this change, see Eaves and Kimpel, *Samuel Richardson,* 134–35.

39. Kelly, *Pamela's Conduct in High Life,* 1:iii; Richardson, in *The Daily Gazetteer,* 7 May 1741.

40. So far as I can figure out, Shendisford is a wholly fictional locale, as would befit the archive supposedly housed there. I can find no mention of it in any gazetteer, nor on any map of Britain. Tom Hothem has pointed out to me that "the *OED* defines . . . 'shend' . . . first as 'to put to shame or confusion; to confound, disgrace'; then, third, 'to destroy, ruin, bring to destruction'." Either etymology would be quite appropriate for a spurious provenance which sends would-be investigators on a wild-goose chase.

41. *The Daily Advertiser,* 23 April 1745, reprinted in *The Pamela Controversy,* 2:xlvi.

42. Richardson to Leake, August 1741, in *SL,* 44.

43. Richardson to Cheyne, 31 August 1741, in *SL,* 47.

44. Richardson to Lady Bradshaigh, 25 February 1754, in *SL,* 296. This edition suggests "carpers" as an emendation. Tom Keymer argues quite forcefully, however, that "the MS . . . clearly reads 'Carvers', an archaism in the eighteenth century but frequent in seventeenth-century writers such as Joseph Hall . . . whose casuistry Richardson knew" (*Richardson's Clarissa and the Eighteenth-Century Reader,* 74 n202). My eyes concur with Keymer's reading of the word in question as "carvers."

45. For this change, see Eaves and Kimpel, "Richardson's Revisions of *Pamela,*" 67.

46. *Pamela Censured,* 25.

47. "Permitting us to fill our fancy" is from *Pamela Censured,* 34; Hill to Richardson, 17 December 1740, in *Pamela,* 506.

48. Ezell, *Social Authorship and the Advent of Print,* 42.

49. Unknown correspondent to Richardson, 11 October 1741, *FM* XVI.I, ff. 69–72.

50. Psalmanazar to Richardson, *FM* XVI.I, ff. 27–33.

51. Richardson to Anne Granville Dewes, 15 December 1756, in *Correspondence,* 4:110–11.

52. Richardson to Lady Bradshaigh, circa February or March 1751, in *Correspondence,* 6:82.

53. Richardson to Lady Bradshaigh, 30 May 1754, in *SL,* 306.

54. Richardson to Lady Bradshaigh, circa February or March 1751, in *Correspondence* 6:82–83.

55. Pamela also hoards "what [blank paper] I was about in my Bosom" (122), thereby highlighting both the scarcity and the allure of the materials out of which she crafts her correspondence.

56. Chetwood, as forwarded by Ralph Courtville, 27 January 1741, *FM* XVI.I, f. 43.

57. Hill to Richardson, 29 December 1740, in *Pamela*, 515.

58. Astraea and Minerva Hill to Richardson, 30 December 1740, *FM* XIII.II, f. 34. I am grateful to Christine Gerrard for providing me with a transcript of this letter, when the available microfilm proved illegible.

59. Aaron Hill to Richardson, 7 January 1745, in *Correspondence* 1:100, referring to an interleaved draft of *Clarissa*.

60. Hill to Richardson, 15 October 1741, in *Correspondence*, 1:79.

61. Other readers may have shared some version of this "apostolical attachment." The Philadelphia printer William Bradford, for example, included *Pamela* "in a list of religious books for sale" (Wolf, *The Book Culture of a Colonial American City*, 188).

62. H. J. Jackson suspects "that interleaved volumes often go this way: annotators begin enthusiastically, but after a while the prospect becomes discouraging—all those blank leaves still to fill—and unless the book is very important to them, or the task quite imperative, they give up" (*Marginalia*, 34).

63. Anonymous correspondent to Richardson "only a few months after the publication of *Pamela*," quoted without citation in Downs, *Richardson*, 47. "Wisely declined" is Eaves and Kimpel's description for Astraea and Minerva's behavior with respect to the interleaved *Pamela* (*Samuel Richardson*, 120).

64. The only exception to this unwillingness of which I am aware is that of Lady Bradshaigh, although her copy of *Pamela* has gone missing. See, however, the probabilistic and thoroughly unabashed marginalia in her copy of *Clarissa* (now at Princeton and conveniently reproduced in *The Annotations in Lady Bradshaigh's Copy of Clarissa*) and her copy of *Sir Charles Grandison*, now at the Huntington.

65. *Commonsense* 225 (30 May 1741).

66. Shenstone to Jago, 22 July 1741, in *The Letters of William Shenstone*, 28. The title phrase "in the Manner of Pamela" was given to the letter by Shenstone's first editor, James Dodsley.

67. Shenstone to Richard Graves, 1743, in *Letters of William Shenstone*, 82.

68. Richardson to Sophia Westcomb, circa 1746, in *SL*, 65.

Chapter 5

1. Sterne to Dr. *****, 30 January 1760, in *Letters of Laurence Sterne*, 90. Hereafter this collection will be cited as *Letters*.

2. Sterne may have himself participated in a virtual club—the Demoniacs—during the years leading up to *Tristram Shandy*. According to Arthur H. Cash, it is not difficult to believe that the Demoniacs got together to drink and read Rabelais, but there is no specific evidence to suggest that their existence was ever more than a shared figment of the imagination ("Sterne, Hall, Libertinism, and *A Sentimental Journey*, 299–300).

3. Sterne to John Eustace, 9 February 1768, in *Letters*, 411.

4. Sterne, *The Life and Opinions of Tristram Shandy*, 682. All subsequent citations will be made parenthetically, giving first the volume and chapter numbers.

5. The Leveller, "His Defense of Laughter, Against Lord Chesterfield's unwarrantable Attack," *The Westminster Magazine* 3 (January 1775), 35.

6. For details, see, respectively, Eaves, "George Romney," De Voogd, "Henry William Bunbury," De Voogd, "Robert Dighton's Twelve *Tristram Shandy* Prints," and McKitterick, "*Tristram Shandy* in the Royal Academy."

7. Sterne to unknown correspondent, summer 1759, in *Letters*, 77.

8. Keymer, *Sterne, the Moderns, and the Novel*, 35.

9. For the irreproachable Englishness of dogs and horses, see Paulson, *Popular and Polite Art in the Age of Hogarth and Fielding*, 57–60.

10. Devon Record Office manuscript 337B/76/98, quoted in Clark, *British Clubs and Societies*, 195. My understanding of club solidarity and hierarchy is deeply indebted to Clark.

11. Shields, *Civil Tongues and Polite Letters in British America*, 207, 200.

12. Clark, 229. Clark notes that "jests and conundrums, riddles, rebuses and anagrams, even in some circles, puns, were an important part of this repartee." For more on the centrality of "play and free conversation" to club life, see Shields, 175–208.

13. Sterne to Robert Foley, 16 November 1764, in *Letters*, 234.

14. Sterne, *A Sentimental Journey through France and Italy*, 36.

15. Clark, 229.

16. Shields, 189.

17. On the importance of seniority to clubs, see Clark, 253–54.

18. Sterne's concern with the look and format of his work is well known. See, for example, his letters to Robert Dodsley offering *Tristram Shandy* first as "a Volume in Oct^{vo} of about the Size of the Essay upon ingenious Tormenting . . . allowing the same Type & Margin" (23 May 1759, in *Letters*, 74) and later as "a lean edition, in two small volumes, of the size of Rasselas, and on the same paper and type" (October 1759, in *Letters*, 80).

19. Moss, "Sterne's Punctuation," 183.

20. For an intriguing speculation that Sterne may have deliberately manipulated his text so that the catchwords would duplicate certain key terms, such as Walter's "Humph!," for comic effect, see Fanning, "On Sterne's Page," 444–45.

21. Peter J. De Voogd's conclusion that "the page has remained disappointingly blank in all the copies I have seen" ("*Tristram Shandy* as Aesthetic Object," 384) has been privately echoed to me by Elizabeth Harries, Heather Jackson, Tom Keymer, Melvyn New, and Roger Stoddard.

22. I take this delightful phrase from a 1996 lecture at Berkeley by Maurice Sendak. Sendak explained that he had stopped doing book signings after a boy, who was evidently at one of his signings under duress, blurted out when his turn came: "Please don't crap up my book!"

23. De Voogd, "Laurence Sterne, the Marbled Page, and 'the Use of Accidents,'" 284–85.

24. Day, "*Tristram Shandy*," 145.

25. Donoghue, *The Fame Machine*, 71.

26. Ian Campbell Ross, *Laurence Sterne,* 6.

27. Sterne to David Garrick, 19 March 1762, in *Letters,* 157.

28. Briggs, "Laurence Sterne and Literary Celebrity in 1760," 256.

29. Gray to Thomas Wharton, 22 April 1760, in *Correspondence of Thomas Gray,* 670–71.

30. "Animadversions on *Tristram Shandy,*" *The Grand Magazine* 3 (April 1760). This particular issue is not included in the available microfilm, and so I have quoted from *Sterne: The Critical Heritage,* 64–66.

31. Boswell, "A Poetical Epistle to Doctor Sterne, Parson Yorick, and Tristram Shandy," in *Boswell's Book of Bad Verse,* 136.

32. "An Account of the Rev. Mr. ST****, and his Writings," in *The Grand Magazine* 3 (1760), 309.

33. Ian Campbell Ross attributes the signing to a desire "to protect himself against imitation and forgery" (269). Cf. Arthur H. Cash's theory that "Sterne was probably worried about a pamphlet which had appeared just three days before, *The Life and Amours of Hafen Slawkenbergius, Author of the Institute of Noses,* which, said the advertisement in the *London Chronicle,* was printed 'in the Size and Manner of Tristram Shandy, in order that so valuable a Supplement may be preserved by being bound at the End of the Sixth Volume.'" (*Laurence Sterne,* 113). But neither biographer explains why Sterne should be suddenly worried about such things, given his previous delight in "a shilling pamphlet wrote against Tristram.—I wish they would write a hundred such" (Sterne to Stephen Croft, circa 1 May 1760, in *Letters,* 107).

34. The deposition was included in a letter from Thomas Twining to Daniel Twining, 19 February 1760, and is transcribed in Bandry and Santovetti, "Thomas Twining Reads *Tristram Shandy.*"

35. MacNally, *Sentimental Excursions to Windsor and Other Places,* 165–66. The "blank chapter" refers to the misplaced Chapters 18 and 19 of Volume Nine, which initially appeared as the recto and verso of the same leaf.

36. It thus seems telling that when Anna Seward invokes the tropes of ideal presence and "old friends," she does so as a testament to Sterne's "originality" and "all-atoning wit": "there is an immense superiority [to the Scriblerians] in the vividness with which he has coloured [Walter] Shandy; in the dramatic spirit he has infused into the character; in the variety of situations in which he has placed the hypothesis-monger,—all natural, probable, and exquisitely humourous. We see and hear the little domestic group at Shandy-hall; nor can we help an involuntary conviction, not only that they all existed, but that they had been of our acquaintance" (Seward to George Gregory, 5 December 1787, in *Letters of Anna Seward,* 1:375–77). Cf. her insistence that Walter "Shandy's pedantries and systematic absurdities are natural living manners—he is of our acquaintance;—we sit at table with him. Every personage in his family, down to the fat scullion, lives—and they are, by those happy characteristic touches, that mark the hand of genius, brought to our eye, as well as to our ear" (Seward to Gregory, 30 October 1788, in *Letters of Anna Seward,* 2:184–85).

37. *Yorick's Sentimental Journey Continued,* 3:iii–v. As the pagination of my citation should suggest, this collection offered itself as a surrogate for the third and fourth volumes promised by Sterne in an insert to the subscription copies: "the Author begs leave to acknowledge to his Subscribers, that they have a further claim

upon him for Two Volumes more than these delivered to them, and which nothing but ill health could have prevented him, from having ready along with these. The Work will be compleated and delivered to the Subscribers early the next winter" (quoted in *A Sentimental Journey through France and Italy*, xxx).

38. *The Critical Review* 19 (1765), 65.

39. The Latin phrase is a clever adaptation of Martial's epigram 8.19: "*Pauper videri Cinna vult; et est pauper*" or "Cinna wishes to appear a poor man. And he is a poor man" (*Epigrams*, 2:174–75). Presumably Sterne's wish to appear at all is evidence of a sort of metaphorical poverty.

40. John Ireland, *Letters and Poems by the late Mr. John Henderson*, 26. The existence of this society nicely confirms and extends David Shields's observation that "the virtual sociability of the framing club of a periodical (in which each subscriber was a 'corresponding member') did not supplant the arenas of conversational sociability; rather, it popularized clubbing, company keeping, and personal communication by enhancing the mystique of private society" (xxx).

Scott's Parental Interest

1. Doyle, *The Case-Book of Sherlock Holmes*, 3.

2. Kay, *Political Constructions*, 11, 203.

3. Klancher, *The Making of English Reading Audiences*, 8.

4. *The Edinburgh Review* 1 (1803), 253.

5. Klancher, 44. Part of this felt disintegration of the reading public may be attributable to the strains experienced by one of its principal models: the theatrical public. Gillian Russell has argued that John Philip Kemble's 1809 raising of ticket prices at Covent Garden—the principal grievance against which the sixty-six nights of Old Price riots were directed—"threatened the idea of theatre as a representative assembly. His opponents interpreted the raising of prices as suggesting that admission was a matter of capacity to pay rather than a recognition of a right to entertainment at a price one could afford. Implicitly this right was also a political right to a place within the national theatre of Britain, expressed by the slogan-like status of the phrase 'box, pit, and gallery'. The riots only served to confirm that the culture's confidence in this formulation was in crisis: the experience of the 1790s and the French wars had caused 'box, pit, and gallery' to split apart" ("Theatre," 227–28).

6. Gibbons, *Cold Comfort Farm*, 129.

7. Colley, *Britons*, 195.

8. Colley, 210–11.

9. Intriguingly though, as Kevin Gilmartin has shown, many radicals imagined that the public would magically reunify as soon as parliamentary reform was enacted, thereby presumably obviating the need for a monarchic center ("Popular Radicalism and the Public Sphere," 555–56).

10. Chandler, "'Wordsworth' after Waterloo," 107.

11. Duncan, *Modern Romance and Transformations of the Novel*, 178.

12. Martineau, "The Achievements of the Genius of Scott," *Tait's Edinburgh Magazine* 10 (1833), 446–48.

13. Sydney Smith to Archibald Constable, 25 December 1819, in *The Letters of Sydney Smith,* 1:342. Cf. Catherine Cuthbertson's proclamation that "the whole world, from the learned heads of universities to the ragged pupils of our national schools, consume their leisure hours in reading the works of one prolific novelist; he who supersedes the pursuit of old black letter literature; he from whose heroines our fair ones form their manners; he whose muse supplies the patriot with strains for melodies to whet their courage and their sword" (*The Hut and the Castle,* quoted in Cruse, *The Englishman and His Books in the Early Nineteenth Century,* 229).

14. *Fraser's Magazine* 42 (1850), 700, 698.

15. *Fraser's Magazine* 29 (1844), 167.

16. *The North British Review* 13 (1850), 371. I take the phrase "a national writer" from the citation presented to Dickens at an 1853 banquet in his honor given by the citizens of Birmingham. For details, see Dickens, *The Speeches of Charles Dickens,* 154.

17. The first three phrases are from the "Essay, Supplementary to the Preface," in *The Prose Works of William Wordsworth,* 3:80, 3:82, 3:66. The final quotation comes from the "Preface" to *Lyrical Ballads,* in *Prose Works,* 1:154.

18. Wordsworth, "Essay, Supplementary to the Preface," 3:84.

19. Ainsworth to Hugh Beaver, 24 December 1838, in Ellis, *William Harrison Ainsworth and His Friends,* 1:346.

20. Thompson, "Custom, Law and Common Right," 162.

21. Austen-Leigh, *A Memoir of Jane Austen,* 118–19. Another family memoir records that "Jane Fairfax survived her elevation only nine or ten years" (251 n119).

22. Riede, *Oracles and Hierophants,* 29.

23. Lady Louisa Stuart to Scott, 11 August 1818, in Lockhart, *Memoirs of the Life of Sir Walter Scott,* 3:266.

24. Millgate, *Walter Scott,* ix.

25. John Ballantyne, in *The Morning Chronicle,* 28 October 1819; Scott, *Ivanhoe,* 3.

26. Alter, *Partial Magic,* 17; Scott, *Ivanhoe,* 5. Alter's phrase describes Cervantes's inserting himself into the narrative of *Don Quijote* in order to insist that "these fictional materials . . . however lifelike, however absorbing, have been assembled in the imagination of the writer, who is free to reassemble them in any number of ways, or to put them aside and tell his own story directly, and the fictional materials have no existence without the writer" (17–18). As my next paragraph will show, the precedent set by Cervantes was very much on Scott's mind in these years.

27. At the home of 'squire Burdock, Matthew Bramble and his family meet Renaldo and Serafina de Melville, who are "on their way to Scotland" (Smollett, *The Expedition of Humphry Clinker,* 161). Soon afterward the Melvilles' coach is held up by highwaymen and they are rescued by "a country apothecary, called Grieve" (161), who turns out to be Ferdinand, Count Fathom, now "a sincere convert to virtue" (166) and husband to Elinor. The Countess de Melville later takes Fathom's daughter to the Hunter's Ball in Edinburgh, where she "attracted all eyes" and "the agreeable miss Grieve . . . made many conquests" (216).

28. Scott underscores Clutterbuck's fictionality a few years later by revealing his address to be "Fairy-Lodge, Near Kennaquhair, N. B." (*Peveril of the Peak,* 1:i). "Kennaquhair" is, of course, Scots for "know not where" and so a clever transliteration of "Utopia."

29. Ballantyne, in *The Morning Chronicle,* 28 October 1819.

30. Fearman, "A Letter in Reply to the ridiculous Threats of Mr. John Ballantyne . . . Addressed to the Editors of the Daily Papers, but too long for insertion," in *Tales of My Landlord,* xiv.

31. Fearman to Ballantyne, in *Tales of My Landlord,* xi–xii.

32. Scott, *The Fortunes of Nigel,* 1:i.

33. Scott, *Peveril of the Peak,* 1:ii-iii.

34. "On the Living Novelists," *The London Magazine and Monthly Critical and Dramatic Review* 2 (1820), 267.

35. "On the Living Novelists," 269.

36. For the legal developments, see Vaidhyanathan, *Copyrights and Copywrongs,* 81–116.

37. Jim Ward, quoted in Amy Harmon, "'Star Wars' Fan Films Come Tumbling Back to Earth," *The New York Times,* 28 April 2002, section 2.

38. Dmitri Nabokov, "On a Book Entitled Lo's Diary," ix.

39. Moore and O'Neill, *The League of Extraordinary Gentlemen,* 43.

40. Moore, "Interview," 221.

41. Moore, "Introduction," 12.

Bibliography

An Account of the State of Learning in the Empire of Lilliput. Together with the History and Character of Bullum the Emperor's Library-Keeper. London, 1728.

Addison, Joseph. *A Discourse on Ancient and Modern Learning . . . Now first published from an Original Manuscript.* London, 1739.

Alter, Robert. *Partial Magic: The Novel as a Self-Conscious Genre.* Berkeley: University of California Press, 1975.

Anderson, Benedict. *Imagined Communities: Reflections on the Origin and Spread of Nationalism.* Rev. ed. London: Verso, 1991.

Austen-Leigh, J. E. *A Memoir of Jane Austen and Other Family Recollections.* Ed. Kathryn Sutherland. Oxford: Oxford University Press, 2002.

Bandry, Anne, and Olivia Santovetti. "Thomas Twining Reads *Tristram Shandy.*" *The Shandean* 11 (1999–2000): 135–46.

Barker, Anthony D. "Poetry from the Provinces: Amateur Poets in the *Gentleman's Magazine* in the 1730s and 1740s." In *Tradition in Transition: Women Writers, Marginal Texts, and the Eighteenth-Century Canon,* ed. Alvaro Ribeiro and James G. Basker, 241–58. Oxford: Clarendon, 1996.

Barnett, Dene. *The Art of Gesture: The Practices and Principles of Eighteenth-Century Acting.* Heidelberg: C. Winter, 1987.

Barthes, Roland. "Baudelaire's Theater." In *Critical Essays.* Trans. Richard Howard. Evanston, Ill.: Northwestern University Press, 1972.

———. *S/Z.* Trans. Richard Miller. New York: Hill and Wang, 1974.

Bate, Jonathan. *Shakespearean Constitutions: Politics, Theatre, Criticism, 1730–1830.* Oxford: Clarendon, 1989.

Battestin, Martin C., with Ruthe R. Battestin. *Henry Fielding: A Life.* London: Routledge, 1989.

Beattie, James. *Essays and Fragments in Prose and Verse.* Edinburgh, 1794.

Beckerman, B. "Theatrical Perception." *Theatre Research International* 4 (1979): 157–71.

Beer, Gillian. "'Our unnatural No-voice': The Heroic Epistle, Pope, and Women's Gothic." *The Yearbook of English Studies* 12 (1982): 125–51.

The Beggar's Opera. Ed. J. V. Guerinot and Rodney D. Jilg. Hamden, Conn.: Archon Books, 1976.

Bellamy, George Anne. *An Apology for the Life of George Anne Bellamy.* 2d ed. London, 1785.

Bellamy, Thomas. *Miscellanies in Prose and Verse.* 2 vols. London, 1795.

Benjamin, Walter. *Illuminations.* Ed. Hannah Arendt. Trans. Harry Zohn. New York: Harcourt, Brace, and World, 1968.

Bennett, Tony, and Janet Woollacott. *Bond and Beyond: The Political Career of a Popular Hero.* Houndsmills, Basingstoke: Macmillan Education, 1987.

Berger, Harry, Jr. "What Did the King Know and When Did He Know It? Shakespearean Discourses and Psychoanalysis." *South Atlantic Quarterly* 88 (1989): 811–62.

Blackstone, William. *Commentaries on the Laws of England: A Facsimile of the First Edition of 1765–1769.* Chicago: University of Chicago Press, 1979.

Blair, Hugh. *Lectures on Rhetoric and Belles Lettres.* 2 vols. London, 1783.

The Blunder of all Blunders, On the Wonder of all Wonders. Or, Gulliver devour'd by Butterflies: Or, the Fops Observation on Lilliput. Dublin, 1726.

Boaden, James. *Memoirs of the Life of John Philip Kemble, Esq.* 2 vols. London, 1825.

Bogel, Fredric V. *The Difference Satire Makes: Rhetoric and Reading from Jonson to Byron.* Ithaca, N.Y.: Cornell University Press, 2001.

Boswell, James. *Boswell's Book of Bad Verse (A Verse Self-Portrait); or, "Love Poems and Other Verses by James Boswell."* Ed. Jack Werner. London: White Lion Publishers, 1974.

———. *Boswell's Journal of a Tour to the Hebrides with Samuel Johnson, L.L.D. 1773.* Ed. Frederick A. Pottle and Charles H. Bennett. New ed. New York: McGraw-Hill, 1961.

———. *Life of Johnson.* Ed. R. W. Chapman. Oxford: Oxford University Press, 1980.

Bradshaigh, Lady Dorothy. *The Annotations in Lady Bradshaigh's Copy of Clarissa.* Ed. Janine Barchas and Gordon D. Fulton. Victoria: English Literary Studies, University of Victoria, 1998.

Breval, John Durant. *A Compleat Key to the Non-Juror. Explaining the Characters in that Play, with observations thereon.* 2d ed. London, 1718.

Brewer, John. "Cultural Consumption in Eighteenth-Century England: The View of the Reader." In *Frühe Neuzeit–Frühe Moderne? Forschungen zur Vielschichtigkeit von Übergangsprozessen,* ed. Rudolf Vierhaus, 366–91. Göttingen: Vandenhoeck and Ruprecht, 1992.

———. *The Pleasures of the Imagination: English Culture in the Eighteenth Century.* New York: Farrar Straus Giroux, 1997.

———. "Reconstructing the Reader: Prescriptions, Texts and Strategies in Anna Larpent's Reading." In *The Practice and Representation of Reading in England,* ed. James Raven, Helen Small, and Naomi Tadmor, 226–45. Cambridge: Cambridge University Press, 1996.

Briggs, Peter M. "Laurence Sterne and Literary Celebrity in 1760." *The Age of Johnson* 4 (1991): 251–80.

Brower, Reuben Arthur. *Alexander Pope: The Poetry of Allusion.* Oxford: Clarendon, 1959.

Burke, Peter. *Popular Culture in Early Modern Europe.* New York: Harper and Row, 1978.

Burnim, Kalman A. *David Garrick, Director.* Pittsburgh: University of Pittsburgh Press, 1961.

Calasso, Roberto. *The Marriage of Cadmus and Harmony.* Trans. Tim Parks. New York: Knopf, 1993.

Carey, George Saville. *Shakespeare's Jubilee, A Masque.* London, 1769.

Carr, John. *The Life and Opinions of Tristram Shandy, Gentleman, Vol. III.* London, 1760.

Cash, Arthur H. *Laurence Sterne: The Later Years.* London: Methuen, 1986.

———. "Sterne, Hall, Libertinism, and *A Sentimental Journey*." *The Age of Johnson* 12 (2001): 291–319.

Castle, Terry. *Masquerade and Civilization: The Carnivalesque in Eighteenth-Century English Culture and Fiction*. Stanford, Calif.: Stanford University Press, 1986.

Cavallo, Guglielmo, and Roger Chartier. "Introduction." In *A History of Reading in the West*, ed. Guglielmo Cavallo and Roger Chartier, trans. Lydia G. Cochrane, 1–36. Amherst: University of Massachusetts Press, 1999.

Certeau, Michel de. *The Practice of Everyday Life*. Trans. Steven F. Rendall. Berkeley: University of California Press, 1984.

Cervantes Saavedra, Miguel de. *The History of that Ingenious Gentleman, Don Quijote de la Mancha*. Trans. Burton Raffel. New York: Norton, 1995.

Chancellor, E. Beresford. *The Pleasure Haunts of London during Four Centuries*. London: Constable, 1925.

Chandler, James. "'Wordsworth' after Waterloo." In *The Age of William Wordsworth: Critical Essays on the Romantic Tradition*, ed. Kenneth R. Johnston and Gene W. Ruoff, 84–111. New Brunswick, N.J.: Rutgers University Press, 1987.

Chartier, Roger. "The *Bibliothèque bleue* and Popular Reading." In *The Cultural Uses of Print in Early Modern France*, trans. Lydia G. Cochrane, 240–64. Princeton, N.J.: Princeton University Press, 1987.

Cheyne, George. *The Letters of Doctor George Cheyne to Samuel Richardson (1733–1743)*. Ed. Charles F. Mullett. Columbia: University of Missouri Press, 1943.

Churchill, Charles. *The Poetical Works of Charles Churchill*. Ed. Douglas Grant. Oxford: Clarendon, 1956.

Cibber, Colley. *An Apology for the Life of Colley Cibber, with an Historical View of the Stage during his own Time*. Ed. B. R. S. Fone. Ann Arbor: University of Michigan Press, 1968.

Clark, Peter. *British Clubs and Societies, 1580–1800: The Origins of an Associational World*. Oxford: Clarendon, 2000.

Clayton, Timothy. *The English Print, 1688–1802*. New Haven, Conn.: Yale University Press for the Paul Mellon Centre for Studies in British Art, 1997.

Clinton-Baddeley, V. C. *All Right on the Night*. London: Putnam, 1954.

Collet, Joseph. *The Private Letter Books of Joseph Collet*. Ed. H. H. Dodwell. London: Longmans, Green and Co., 1933.

Colley, Linda. *Britons: Forging the Nation, 1707–1837*. New Haven, Conn.: Yale University Press, 1992.

Cook, William. *Memoirs of Charles Macklin, Comedian, with the Dramatic Characters, Manners, Anecdotes, &c. of the Age in which he lived: forming an History of the Stage during almost the Whole of the last Century*. London, 1804.

Cosmetti. *The Polite Arts*. London, 1767.

Cruse, Amy. *The Englishman and His Books in the Early Nineteenth Century*. New York: Thomas Y. Crowell, 1930.

Cumberland, Richard. *The Observer: Being a Collection of Moral, Literary, and Familiar Essays*. 5 vols. London, 1786–90.

A Cursory View of the History of Lilliput for these last forty three Years, Containing Some Remarks upon the Origin, Nature and Tendency of the Religious and Political Disputes which exist among the Subjects. London, 1727.

Darnton, Robert. "First Steps Toward a History of Reading." In *The Kiss of Lamourette: Reflections in Cultural History*. New York: Norton, 1990.

———. "Readers Respond to Rousseau: The Fabrication of Romantic Sensitivity." In *The Great Cat Massacre and Other Episodes in French Cultural History*. New York: Basic Books, 1984.

Davies, Thomas. *Dramatic Micellanies: Consisting of Critical Observations on several Plays of Shakspeare: With a Review of his Principal Characters, and those of Various Eminent Writers, as represented by Mr. Garrick, and Other Celebrated Comedians*. 3 vols. London, 1784.

———. *A Genuine Narrative of the Life and Theatrical Transactions of Mr. John Henderson*. London, 1777.

———. *Memoirs of the Life of David Garrick, Esq*. 2 vols. London, 1780.

Davis, David Brion. *The Problem of Slavery in Western Culture*. Ithaca, N.Y.: Cornell University Press, 1966.

Day, W. G. "*Tristram Shandy:* The Marbled Leaf." *The Library* 5th ser. 27 (1972): 143–45.

Deelman, Christian. *The Great Shakespeare Jubilee*. London: Michael Joseph, 1964.

DeMaria, Robert, Jr. *Samuel Johnson and the Life of Reading*. Baltimore: Johns Hopkins University Press, 1997.

Derrida, Jacques. "Limited, Inc. abc . . ." *Glyph* 2 (1977): 162–254.

The Devil to pay at St. James[']s: Or, a full and true Account of a most horrid and bloody Battle between Madam Faustina and Madam Cuzzoni. London, 1727.

De Voogd, Peter J. "Henry William Bunbury, Illustrator of *Tristram Shandy*." *The Shandean* 3 (1991): 138–44.

———. "Laurence Sterne, the Marbled Page, and 'the Use of Accidents'." *Word and Image* 1 (1985): 279–87.

———. "Robert Dighton's Twelve *Tristram Shandy* Prints." *The Shandean* 6 (1994): 86–98.

———. "*Tristram Shandy* as Aesthetic Object." *Word and Image* 4 (1988): 383–92.

Dickens, Charles. *The Speeches of Charles Dickens*. Ed. K. J. Fielding. Oxford: Clarendon, 1960.

The Dictionary of English Law. Gen. ed. Earl Jowitt. Ed. Clifford Walsh. London: Sweet and Maxwell, 1959.

Dobson, Austin. *Samuel Richardson*. New York: Macmillan, 1902.

Dobson, Michael. *The Making of the National Poet: Shakespeare, Adaptation and Authorship, 1660–1769*. Oxford: Clarendon, 1992.

Donaldson, Ian. *The World Upside-Down: Comedy from Jonson to Fielding*. Oxford: Clarendon, 1970.

Donoghue, Frank. *The Fame Machine: Book Reviewing and Eighteenth-Century Literary Careers*. Stanford, Calif.: Stanford University Press, 1996.

Dorman, Joseph. *Sir Roger de Coverly, or the Merry Christmas. A Dramatic Entertainment of Two Acts*. London, 1740.

Downes, John. *Roscius Anglicanus*. Ed. Judith Milhous and Robert D. Hume. London: Society for Theatre Research, 1987.

Downie, J. A. "Gay's Politics." In *John Gay and the Scriblerians*, ed. Peter Lewis and Nigel Wood, 44–61. London: Vision Press, 1988.

———. "The Political Significance of *Gulliver's Travels*." In *Swift and His Contexts*, ed. John Irwin Fischer, Hermann J. Real, and James Wooley, 1–19. New York: AMS Press, 1989.

Downs, Brian W. *Richardson*. London: Routledge, 1928.

Doyle, Arthur Conan. *The Case-Book of Sherlock Holmes*. Ed. W. W. Robson. Oxford: Oxford University Press, 1993.

Dryden, John. *Poems, 1649–1680*. Ed. Edward Niles Hooker and H. T. Swedenberg Jr. Berkeley: University of California Press, 1956.

Duck, Stephen. *Poems on Several Occasions*. London, 1736.

Dunbar, Howard Hunter. *The Dramatic Career of Arthur Murphy*. New York: MLA, 1946.

Duncan, Ian. *Modern Romance and Transformations of the Novel: The Gothic, Scott, Dickens*. Cambridge: Cambridge University Press, 1992.

Eaves, T. C. Duncan. "George Romney: His *Tristram Shandy* Paintings and Trip to Lancaster." *Huntington Library Quarterly* 7 (1944): 321–26.

Eaves, T. C. Duncan, and Ben D. Kimpel. "Richardson's Revisions of *Pamela*." *Studies in Bibliography* 20 (1967): 61–88.

———. *Samuel Richardson: A Biography*. Oxford: Clarendon, 1971.

Eco, Umberto. *The Limits of Interpretation*. Bloomington: Indiana University Press, 1990.

Eisenstein, Elizabeth L. *The Printing Revolution in Early Modern Europe*. Cambridge: Cambridge University Press, 1983.

Eliot, George. *The Lifted Veil* [and] *Brother Jacob*. Ed. Helen Small. Oxford: Oxford University Press, 1999.

Ellis, S. M. *William Harrison Ainsworth and His Friends*. 2 vols. London: John Lane, The Bodley Head, 1911.

The English Reports. 176 vols. Edinburgh: W. Green and Sons, 1900–1932.

English Trader, Indian Maid: Representing Gender, Race, and Slavery in the New World: An Inkle and Yarico Reader, ed. Frank Felsenstein. Baltimore: Johns Hopkins University Press, 1999.

An Enquiry into the Nature and Origin of Literary Property. London, 1762.

An Epistle from Yarico to Inkle, Together With their Characters, as related in the Spectator. Marblehead, 1792.

Ezell, Margaret J. M. *Social Authorship and the Advent of Print*. Baltimore: Johns Hopkins University Press, 1999.

Fanning, Christopher. "On Sterne's Page: Spatial Layout, Spatial Form, and Social Space in *Tristram Shandy*." *Eighteenth-Century Fiction* 10 (1998): 429–50.

Farrell, Joseph. "Reading and Writing the *Heroides*." *Harvard Studies in Classical Philology* 98 (1998): 307–38.

Fearman, William. *Tales of My Landlord, New Series, Containing Pontefract Castle*. London, 1820.

Felsenstein, Frank. "Introduction." In *English Trader, Indian Maid: Representing Gender, Race, and Slavery in the New World: An Inkle and Yarico Reader*, ed. Frank Felsenstein, 1–51. Baltimore: Johns Hopkins University Press, 1999.

The Female Faction: or, The Gay Subscribers. London, 1729.

Ferrone, Vincenzo, and Massimo Firpo. "From Inquisitors to Microhistorians: A Critique of Pietro Redondi's *Galileo eretico*." *Journal of Modern History* 58 (1986): 485–524.

Fielding, Henry. *An Apology for the Life of Mrs. Shamela Andrews.* In *The History of the Adventures of Mr. Joseph Andrews and of his Friend Mr. Abraham Adams and An Apology for the Life of Mrs. Shamela Andrews.* Ed. Douglas Brooks-Davies. Rev. Thomas Keymer. Oxford: Oxford University Press, 1999.

———. *The History of Tom Jones, a Foundling.* Ed. Fredson Bowers. Middletown, Conn.: Wesleyan University Press, 1975.

———. *The Jacobite's Journal and Related Writings.* Ed. W. B. Coley. Middletown, Conn.: Wesleyan University Press, 1975.

———. *Joseph Andrews.* Ed. Martin C. Battestin. Middletown, Conn.: Wesleyan University Press, 1967.

———. *Miscellanies by Henry Fielding, Esq.: Volume Two.* Ed. Hugh Amory. Middletown, Conn.: Wesleyan University Press, 1993.

———. *The True Patriot and Related Writings.* Ed. W. B. Coley. Middletown, Conn.: Wesleyan University Press, 1987.

Fineman, Daniel A. "Biographical Introduction." In Maurice Morgann, *Shakespearian Criticism: Comprising An Essay on the Dramatic Character of Sir John Falstaff, Extensive Revisions of the Essay, A Commentary on The Tempest, Miscellaneous Comments,* ed. Daniel A. Fineman. Oxford: Clarendon, 1972.

Foote, Samuel. *The Roman and English Comedy Consider'd and Compar'd. With Remarks on the Suspicious Husband.* London, 1747.

Ford, Herbert L. *Shakespeare, 1700–1740: A Collation of the Editions and Separate Plays, with Some Account of T. Johnson and R. Walker.* Oxford: Oxford University Press, 1935.

Forster, E. M. *Aspects of the Novel.* New York: Harcourt, Brace, and World, 1927.

Franklin, Benjamin. *The Papers of Benjamin Franklin.* Ed. Leonard W. Labaree et al. 36 vols. New Haven, Conn.: Yale University Press, 1959–2001.

Freeman, Lisa A. *Character's Theater: Genre and Identity on the Eighteenth-Century English Stage.* Philadelphia: University of Pennsylvania Press, 2002.

French, David P. "The Swift-Gulliver Litigation." *Notes and Queries* n.s. 11 (1964): 52–53.

Gallagher, Catherine. *Nobody's Story: The Vanishing Acts of Women Writers in the Marketplace, 1670–1820.* Berkeley: University of California Press, 1994.

Garrick, David. *The Letters of David Garrick.* Ed. David M. Little and George M. Kahrl. 3 vols. Cambridge, Mass.: Belknap Press of Harvard University Press, 1963.

———. *The Plays of David Garrick.* Ed. Harry William Pedicord and Frederick Louis Bergmann. 7 vols. Carbondale: Southern Illinois University Press, 1980–82.

Gay, John. *Dramatic Works.* Ed. John Fuller. 2 vols. Oxford: Clarendon, 1983.

———. *Poetry and Prose.* Ed. Vinton A. Dearing. Oxford: Clarendon, 1974.

Genette, Gérard. *The Work of Art: Immanence and Transcendence.* Trans. G. M. Goshgarian. Ithaca, N.Y.: Cornell University Press, 1997.

Gentleman, Francis. *The Dramatic Censor; or, Critical Companion.* 2 vols. London, 1770.

Gibbons, Stella. *Cold Comfort Farm.* London: Longmans, Green and Co, 1933.

Giffard, Henry. *Pamela. A Comedy.* London, 1742.

Gilmartin, Kevin. "Popular Radicalism and the Public Sphere." *Studies in Romanticism* 33 (1994): 549–57.

Gilpin, William. *An Essay upon Prints, containing Remarks upon the Principles of picturesque Beauty, the Different Kinds of Prints, and the Characters of the most noted Masters; Illustrated by Criticisms upon particular Pieces; to which are added, Some Cautions that may be useful in collecting Prints.* London, 1768.

Ginzburg, Carlo. *The Cheese and the Worms: The Cosmos of a Sixteenth-Century Miller.* Trans. John and Anne Tedeschi. London: Routledge, 1980.

———. "Clues: Roots of an Evidential Paradigm." In *Myths, Emblems, Clues,* trans. John and Anne C. Tedeschi, 96–125. London: Hutchinson Radius, 1990.

———. "Microhistory: Two or Three Things That I Know about It." *Critical Inquiry* 20 (1993): 10–35.

Ginzburg, Carlo, and Carlo Poni. "The Name and the Game: Unequal Exchange and the Historiographic Marketplace." In *Microhistory and the Lost Peoples of Europe,* ed. Edward Muir and Guido Ruggiero, 1–10. Baltimore: Johns Hopkins University Press, 1991.

Goldgar, Bertrand A. "A Contemporary Reaction to *Gulliver's Travels.*" *The Scriblerian* 5, no. 1 (1972): 1–3.

———. *Walpole and the Wits: The Relation of Politics to Literature, 1722–1742.* Lincoln: University of Nebraska Press, 1976.

Gramsci, Antonio. *Selections from Cultural Writings.* Ed. David Forgacs and Geoffrey Nowell-Smith. Trans. William Boelhower. Cambridge, Mass.: Harvard University Press, 1985.

Granville, Mary. *The Autobiography and Correspondence of Mary Granville, Mrs. Delany.* Ed. Lady Llanover. 3 vols. London, 1861.

Gray, Thomas. *Correspondence of Thomas Gray.* Ed. Paget Toynbee and Leonard Whibley, with corrections and additions by H. W. Starr. Oxford: Clarendon, 1971.

Guillory, John. *Cultural Capital: The Problem of Literary Canon Formation.* Chicago: University of Chicago Press, 1993.

Habermas, Jürgen. "Further Reflections on the Public Sphere." In *Habermas and the Public Sphere,* ed. Craig Calhoun, 421–61. Cambridge, Mass.: MIT Press, 1992.

———. *The Structural Transformation of the Public Sphere: An Inquiry into a Category of Bourgeois Society.* Trans. Thomas Burger and Frederick Lawrence. Cambridge, Mass.: MIT Press, 1989.

Hammond, Brean S. *Professional Imaginative Writing in England, 1670–1740: "Hackney for Bread."* Oxford: Clarendon, 1997.

Hammond, Paul. "Introduction." In *Selected Prose of Alexander Pope,* ed. Paul Hammond, 1–18. Cambridge: Cambridge University Press, 1987.

Haywood, Eliza. *Memoirs of a Certain Island Adjacent to the Kingdom of Utopia. Written by a Celebrated Author of that Country. Now translated into English.* 2d ed. London, 1726.

Hiffernan, Paul. *Miscellanies in Prose and Verse.* London, 1755.

Highfill, Philip H., Jr. "Performers and Performing." In *The London Theatre World, 1660–1800,* ed. Robert D. Hume, 143–80. Carbondale: Southern Illinois University Press, 1980.

Hill, Aaron. *The Works of the late Aaron Hill, Esq.* 4 vols. London, 1753.

Hill, John. *The Actor, a Treatise on the Art of Playing.* London, 1750.

Hoadly, Benjamin. *The Suspicious Husband. A Comedy.* London, 1747.

Holland, Peter. "The Age of Garrick." In *Shakespeare: An Illustrated Stage History,* ed. Jonathan Bate and Russell Jackson. New York: Oxford University Press, 1996.

———. *The Ornament of Action: Text and Performance in Restoration Comedy.* Cambridge: Cambridge University Press, 1979.

Hughes, Leo. *The Drama's Patrons: A Study of the Eighteenth-Century London Audience.* Austin: University of Texas Press, 1971.

Hulme, Peter. *Colonial Encounters: Europe and the Native Caribbean, 1492–1797.* London: Methuen, 1986.

Hume, David. *A Treatise of Human Nature.* Ed. L. A. Selby-Bigge. 2d ed. rev. by P. H. Nidditch. Oxford: Clarendon, 1978.

Hume, Robert D. "Before the Bard: 'Shakespeare' in Early Eighteenth-Century London." *ELH* 64 (1997): 41–75.

———. *Henry Fielding and the London Theatre, 1728–1737.* Oxford: Clarendon, 1988.

———. "Securing a Repertory: Plays on the London Stage, 1660–65." In *Poetry and Drama, 1570–1700: Essays in Honour of Harold F. Brooks,* ed. Antony Coleman and Antony Hammond, 156–72. London: Methuen, 1981.

Hunter, J. Paul. *Before Novels: The Cultural Contexts of Eighteenth-Century English Fiction.* New York: Norton, 1990.

———. "*Gulliver's Travels* and the Later Writings." In *The Cambridge Companion to Jonathan Swift,* ed. Christopher Fox, 216–40. Cambridge: Cambridge University Press, 2003.

———. "Serious Reflections on Farther Adventures: Resistances to Closure in Eighteenth-Century English Novels." In *Augustan Subjects: Essays in Honor of Martin C. Battestin,* ed. Albert J. Rivero, 276–94. Newark: University of Delaware Press, 1997.

Ireland, John. *Letters and Poems by the late Mr. John Henderson. With Anecdotes of his Life.* London, 1786.

Jackson, H. J. *Marginalia: Readers Writing in Books.* New Haven, Conn.: Yale University Press, 2001.

Jardine, Lisa, and Anthony Grafton. "'Studied for Action': How Gabriel Harvey Read his Livy." *Past and Present* 129 (November 1990): 30–78.

Johnson, Samuel. *The Idler and The Adventurer.* Ed. W. J. Bate, John M. Bullitt, and L. F. Powell. New Haven, Conn.: Yale University Press, 1963.

———. *The Rambler.* Ed. W. J. Bate and Albrecht B. Strauss. New Haven, Conn.: Yale University Press, 1969.

Justice, George. *The Manufacturers of Literature: Writing and the Literary Marketplace in Eighteenth-Century England.* Newark: University of Delaware Press, 2002.

Kames, Lord. *Elements of Criticism.* 3 vols. Edinburgh, 1762.

———. *Remarkable Decisions of the Court of Session, from the year 1730 to the year 1752.* 1766. Excerpted in *English Publishing, the Struggle for Copyright, and the Freedom of the Press: Thirteen Tracts, 1666–1774.* New York: Garland, 1975.

Karpinski, Caroline. "The Print in Thrall to its Original: A Historiographic Perspective." In *Retaining the Original: Multiple Originals, Copies, and Reproductions,* ed. Kathleen Preciado, 101–9. Washington: National Gallery of Art, 1989.

Kay, Carol. *Political Constructions: Defoe, Richardson, and Sterne in Relation to Hobbes, Hume, and Burke.* Ithaca, N.Y.: Cornell University Press, 1988.

Kelly, John. *Pamela's Conduct in High Life. Publish'd from Her Original Papers.* 2 vols. London, 1741.

Kennedy, Duncan F. "Epistolarity: The *Heroides.*" In *The Cambridge Companion to Ovid,* ed. Philip Hardie, 217–32. Cambridge: Cambridge University Press, 2002.

Kenny, Shirley Strum. "Perennial Favorites: Congreve, Vanbrugh, Cibber, Farquhar, and Steele." *Modern Philology* 73, no. 4 (1976): S4-S11.

Kenrick, William. *Falstaff's Wedding, A Comedy. Being a Sequel to the Second Part of the Play of King Henry the Fourth. Written in Imitation of Shakespeare, by Mr. Kenrick.* London, 1760.

———. *Falstaff's Wedding, A Comedy: As it is acted at the Theatre-Royal in Drury Lane.* London, 1766.

———. *Love in the Suds; A Town Eclogue. Being the Lamentation of Roscius for the Loss of his Nyky.* In *A Letter to David Garrick, Esq. From William Kenrick, LL.D.* 3rd ed. London, 1772.

Kermode, Frank. *Forms of Attention.* Chicago: University of Chicago Press, 1985.

Kewes, Paulina. *Authorship and Appropriation: Writing for the Stage in England, 1660–1710.* Oxford: Clarendon, 1998.

Keymer, Tom. *Richardson's Clarissa and the Eighteenth-Century Reader.* Cambridge: Cambridge University Press, 1992.

———. *Sterne, the Moderns, and the Novel.* Oxford: Oxford University Press, 2002.

Kidgell, John. *The Card.* 2 vols. London, 1755.

Kinservik, Matthew J. *Disciplining Satire: The Censorship of Satiric Comedy on the Eighteenth-Century London Stage.* Lewisburg, Pa.: Bucknell University Press, 2002.

———. "*Love à la Mode* and Macklin's Return to the London Stage in 1759." *Theatre Survey* 37, no. 2 (November 1996): 1–21.

———. "Satire, Censorship, and Sodomy in Samuel Foote's *The Capuchin* (1776)." *Review of English Studies* n.s. 54 (2003): 639–60.

———. "A Sinister *Macbeth:* The Macklin Production of 1773." *Harvard Library Bulletin* n.s. 6 (1995): 51–76.

Klancher, Jon P. *The Making of English Reading Audiences, 1790–1832.* Madison: University of Wisconsin Press, 1987.

Knight, Charles A. "Bibliography and the Shape of the Literary Periodical in the Early Eighteenth Century." *The Library* 6th ser. 8 (1986): 232–48.

Knights, L. C. *How Many Children Had Lady Macbeth?: An Essay in the Theory and Practice of Shakespeare Criticism.* Cambridge: Gordon Fraser, Minority Press, 1933.

Knox, Vicesimus. *Essays Moral and Literary.* New ed. 2 vols. London, 1782.

Kracauer, Siegfried. "The Structure of the Historical Universe." In *History: The Last Things Before the Last.* New York: Oxford University Press, 1969.

Kramnick, Jonathan Brody. *Making the English Canon: Print-Capitalism and the Cultural Past, 1700–1770.* Cambridge: Cambridge University Press, 1998.

Lamb, Charles. *Elia and The Last Essays of Elia.* Ed. Jonathan Bate. Oxford: Oxford University Press, 1987.

Le Brun, Charles. *A Method to learn to Design the Passions, Proposed in a Conference on their General and Particular Expression.* Trans. John Williams. London, 1734.

A Letter to Colley Cibber, Esq; on his Transformation of King John. London, 1745.

Letters in Prose and Verse to the Celebrated Polly Peachum: From the most Eminent of her Admirers and Rivals. London, 1728.

Levi, Giovanni. "On Microhistory." In *New Perspectives on Historical Writing,* ed. Peter Burke, 93–113. University Park: Pennsylvania State University Press, 1991.

The Life of Pamela. London, 1741.

A little more of that Same: or, A Recollection of sundry Material Passages omitted in a late Treatise, entituled, The Devil to Pay at St. James's. London, 1727.

Locke, John. *Two Treatises of Government.* Ed. Peter Laslett. 2d ed. Cambridge: Cambridge University Press, 1970.

Lockhart, John Gibson. *Memoirs of the Life of Sir Walter Scott.* 5 vols. Boston: Houghton Mifflin, 1901.

Loewenstein, Joseph. *The Author's Due: Printing and the Prehistory of Copyright.* Chicago: University of Chicago Press, 2002.

The London Encyclopedia, ed. Ben Weinreb and Christopher Hibbert. Bethesda, Md.: Adler and Adler, 1986.

Lynch, Deidre Shauna. *The Economy of Character: Novels, Market Culture, and the Business of Inner Meaning.* Chicago: University of Chicago Press, 1998.

Lynch, James J. *Box, Pit and Gallery: Stage and Society in Johnson's London.* Berkeley: University of California Press, 1953.

Macklin, Charles. *The New Play Criticized: Or, the Plague of Envy.* Los Angeles: William Andrews Clark Memorial Library, 1967.

MacNally, Leonard. *Sentimental Excursions to Windsor and Other Places.* London, 1781.

Mah, Harold. "Phantasies of the Public Sphere: Rethinking the Habermas of Historians." *Journal of Modern History* 72 (2000): 153–82.

Marcus, Leah. *Puzzling Shakespeare: Local Reading and Its Discontents.* Berkeley: University of California Press, 1988.

Martial. *Epigrams.* Trans. D. R. Shackleton Bailey. 3 vols. Cambridge, Mass.: Harvard University Press, 1993.

McKenzie, Alan T. *Certain, Lively Episodes: The Articulation of Passion in Eighteenth-Century Prose.* Athens: University of Georgia Press, 1990.

McKeon, Michael. *The Origins of the English Novel, 1600–1740.* Baltimore: Johns Hopkins University Press, 1987.

McKitterick, David. *Print, Manuscript, and the Search for Order, 1450–1830.* Cambridge: Cambridge University Press, 2003.

———. "*Tristram Shandy* in the Royal Academy: A Group of Drawings by John Nixon." *The Shandean* 4 (1992): 85–110.

Memoirs Concerning the Life and Manners of Captain Mackheath. London, 1728.

Memoirs of the Court of Lilliput. Written by Captain Gulliver. Containing an Account of the Intrigues, and some other particular Transactions of that Nation, omitted in the two Volumes of his Travels. London, 1727.

Miller, Jonathan. *Subsequent Performances.* London: Faber and Faber, 1986.

Millgate, Jane. *Walter Scott: The Making of the Novelist.* Toronto: University of Toronto Press, 1984.

Montagu, Elizabeth. *An Essay on the Writings and Genius of Shakespeare.* London, 1769.

Montagu, Jennifer. *The Expression of the Passions: The Origin and Influence of Charles*

Le Brun's Conférence sur l'expression générale et particulière. New Haven, Conn.: Yale University Press, 1994.

Montagu, Lady Mary Wortley. *The Complete Letters of Lady Mary Wortley Montagu.* Ed. Robert Halsband. 3 vols. Oxford: Clarendon, 1965–67.

Moore, Alan. "Introduction" and "Interview." In Jess Nevins, *Heroes and Monsters: The Unofficial Companion to The League of Extraordinary Gentlemen,* 11–14 and 207–39. Austin, Texas: MonkeyBrain, 2003.

Moore, Alan, and Kevin O'Neill. *The League of Extraordinary Gentlemen,* vol. 1. La Jolla, Calif.: America's Best Comics, 2000.

Moretti, Franco. "The Slaughterhouse of Literature." *Modern Language Quarterly* 61 (2000): 207–27.

Morgann, Maurice. *Shakespearian Criticism: Comprising An Essay on the Dramatic Character of Sir John Falstaff, Extensive Revisions of the Essay, A Commentary on The Tempest, Miscellaneous Comments.* Ed. Daniel A. Fineman. Oxford: Clarendon, 1972.

Morris, Corbyn. *An Essay Towards Fixing the True Standards of Wit, Humour, Raillery, Satire, and Ridicule. To which is Added, an Analysis of the Character of an Humourist, Sir John Falstaff, Sir Roger de Coverly, and Don Quixote.* London, 1744.

Morson, Gary Saul. *Narrative and Freedom: The Shadows of Time.* New Haven, Conn.: Yale University Press, 1994.

Moss, Roger B. "Sterne's Punctuation." *Eighteenth-Century Studies* 15 (1981–82): 179–200.

Muir, Edward. "Introduction: Observing Trifles." In *Microhistory and the Lost Peoples of Europe,* ed. Edward Muir and Guido Ruggiero, vii–xxviii. Baltimore: Johns Hopkins University Press, 1991.

Munsche, P. B. *Gentlemen and Poachers: The English Game Laws, 1671–1831.* Cambridge: Cambridge University Press, 1981.

Murphy, Andrew. *Shakespeare in Print: A History and Chronology of Shakespeare Publishing.* Cambridge: Cambridge University Press, 2003.

Murphy, Arthur. *The Citizen: A Farce.* London, 1763.

———. *The Gray's–Inn Journal.* 2 vols. London, 1756.

———. *The Life of David Garrick, Esq.* 2 vols. London, 1801.

Nabokov, Dmitri. "On a Book Entitled Lo's Diary." In Pia Pera, *Lo's Diary,* trans. Ann Goldstein, vii–x. New York: Foxrock, 1999.

Neville, Sylas. *Diary, 1767–1788.* Ed. Basil Cozens-Hardy. London: Oxford University Press, 1950.

New Letters to the Tatler and Spectator. Ed. Richmond P. Bond. Austin: University of Texas Press, 1959.

Newsom, Robert. *A Likely Story: Probability and Play in Fiction.* New Brunswick, N.J.: Rutgers University Press, 1988.

Nicholson, Colin. *Writing and the Rise of Finance: Capital Satires of the Early Eighteenth Century.* Cambridge: Cambridge University Press, 1994.

Orgel, Stephen. "The Authentic Shakespeare." *Representations* 21 (winter 1988): 1–25.

Pamela Censured: In a Letter to the Editor. London, 1741.

The Pamela Controversy: Criticisms and Adaptations of Samuel Richardson's Pamela, 1740–1750. Ed. and intro. Thomas Keymer and Peter Sabor. 6 vols. London: Pickering and Chatto, 2001.

Pamela in High Life; or, Virtue Rewarded. London, 1741.

Pamela: or, the Fair Imposter. A Poem in Five Cantos. By J—— W——, Esq. Dublin, 1743.

Paulson, Ronald. *Hogarth.* Vol. 3, *Art and Politics, 1750–1764.* New Brunswick, N.J.: Rutgers University Press, 1993.

———. *Popular and Polite Art in the Age of Hogarth and Fielding.* Notre Dame, Ind.: University of Notre Dame Press, 1979.

Pedicord, Harry William. *The Theatrical Public in the Time of Garrick.* New York: King's Crown Press, 1954.

Phillips, Mark Salber. *Society and Sentiment: Genres of Historical Writing in Britain, 1740–1820.* Princeton, N.J.: Princeton University Press, 2000.

Piozzi, Hester Lynch. *Anecdotes of the late Samuel Johnson LL.D. during the last twenty years of his life.* In *Johnsonian Miscellanies,* ed. George Birkbeck Hill, 1:141–351. Oxford: Clarendon, 1897.

Pocock, J. G. A. *Virtue, Commerce, and History: Essays on Political Thought and History, Chiefly in the Eighteenth Century.* Cambridge: Cambridge University Press, 1985.

Pope, Alexander. *The Dunciad.* Ed. James Sutherland. 3d ed. London: Methuen, 1963.

———. *A Key to the Lock. Or, a Treatise proving, beyond all Contradiction, the dangerous Tendency of a late Poem, entituled, The Rape of the Lock, to Government and Religion.* London, 1715.

———. *Minor Poems.* Ed. Norman Ault and John Butt. London: Methuen, 1954.

———. *The Rape of the Lock and Other Poems.* Ed. Geoffrey Tillotson. 3d ed. London: Methuen, 1962.

The Present State of the Stage in Great-Britain and Ireland. And the Theatrical Characters of the Principal Performers in both Kingdoms, Impartially Considered. London, 1753.

Price, Cecil. *Theatre in the Age of Garrick.* Oxford: Basil Blackwell, 1973.

Price, Lawrence Marsden. *Inkle and Yarico Album.* Berkeley: University of California Press, 1937.

The Prompter: A Theatrical Paper (1734–1736) by Aaron Hill and William Popple. Ed. William W. Appleton and Kalman A. Burnim. New York: Benjamin Blom, 1966.

Ralph, James. *The Case of Authors by Profession or Trade, Stated. With Regard to Booksellers, the Stage, and the Public.* London, 1758.

Raven, James. *Judging New Wealth: Popular Publishing and Responses to Commerce in England, 1750–1800.* Oxford: Clarendon, 1992.

———. "New Reading Histories, Print Culture, and the Identification of Change: The Case of Eighteenth-Century England." *Social History* 23 (1998): 268–87.

Rawson, Claude. "Gulliver and Others: Reflections on Swift's 'I' Narrators." In Jonathan Swift, *Gulliver's Travels,* ed. Albert J. Rivero, 480–99. New York: Norton, 2002.

———. *Gulliver and the Gentle Reader: Studies in Swift and Our Time.* London: Routledge, 1973.

Restoration and Georgian England, 1660–1788. Comp. David Thomas and Arnold Hare. Theatre in Europe: A Documentary History. Cambridge: Cambridge University Press, 1989.

Revel, Jacques. "Microanalysis and the Construction of the Social." In *Histories: French Constructions of the Past*, ed. Jacques Revel and Lynn Hunt, trans. Arthur Goldhammer, 492–502. New York: New Press, 1995.

Reynolds, Sir Joshua. *Discourses on Art*. Ed. Robert R. Wark. San Marino, Calif.: Huntington Library, 1959.

Richardson, Samuel. Correspondence. Forster Collection Manuscripts, Victoria and Albert Museum, London. Wakefield: Micro Method, 1969. Microfilm.

———. *The Correspondence of Samuel Richardson, Author of Pamela, Clarissa, and Sir Charles Grandison*. 6 vols. London, 1804.

———. *Pamela; or, Virtue Rewarded*. Ed. Thomas Keymer and Alice Wakely. Oxford: Oxford University Press, 2001.

———. *Pamela: or, Virtue Rewarded. In a Series of Familiar Letters from a Beautiful Young Damsel to her Parents: And afterwards, In her Exalted Condition, Between Her, and Persons of Figure and Quality, Upon the Most Important and Entertaining Subjects, in Genteel Life. The Third and Fourth Volumes*. London, 1742.

———. *Selected Letters of Samuel Richardson*. Ed. John Carroll. Oxford: Clarendon, 1964.

Riede, David G. *Oracles and Hierophants: Constructions of Romantic Authority*. Ithaca, N.Y.: Cornell University Press, 1991.

Roach, Joseph R. *The Player's Passion: Studies in the Science of Acting*. Newark: University of Delaware Press, 1985.

Rogerson, Brewster. "The Art of Painting the Passions." *Journal of the History of Ideas* 14 (1953): 68–94.

Rose, Carol M. "The Comedy of the Commons: Custom, Commerce, and Inherently Public Property." In *Property and Persuasion: Essays on the History, Theory, and Rhetoric of Ownership*. Boulder, Col.: Westview Press, 1994.

Rose, Jonathan. *The Intellectual Life of the British Working Classes*. New Haven, Conn.: Yale University Press, 2001.

Rose, Mark. *Authors and Owners: The Invention of Copyright*. Cambridge, Mass.: Harvard University Press, 1993.

Ross, Ian Campbell. *Laurence Sterne: A Life*. Oxford: Oxford University Press, 2001.

Ross, Trevor. "Copyright and the Invention of Tradition." *Eighteenth-Century Studies* 26 (1992): 1–27.

Rothstein, Eric. "'Ideal Presence' and the 'Non Finito' in Eighteenth-Century Aesthetics." *Eighteenth-Century Studies* 9 (1976): 307–32.

Rowe, Nicholas. "Some Account of the Life &c. of Mr. *William Shakespear*." In *The Works of Mr. William Shakespear*. London, 1709.

Russell, Gillian. "Theatre." In *An Oxford Companion to the Romantic Age: British Culture, 1776–1832*, ed. Iain McCalman, 223–31. Oxford: Oxford University Press, 1999.

Ryder, Dudley. *The Diary of Dudley Ryder, 1715–16*. Ed. William Matthews. London: Methuen, 1939.

Sabor, Peter. "Richardson and his Readers." *Humanities Association Review* 30 (1979): 161–73.

Saunders, David, and Ian Hunter. "Lessons from the 'Literatory': How to Historicise Authorship." *Critical Inquiry* 17 (1991): 479–509.

Schultz, William Eben. *Gay's Beggar's Opera: Its Content, History, and Influence.* 1923. Reprint. New York: Russell and Russell, 1967.

Schwartz, Hillel. *The Culture of the Copy: Striking Likenesses, Unreasonable Facsimiles.* New York: Zone Books, 1996.

Scott, Sir Walter. *The Fortunes of Nigel. By the Author of 'Waverley, Kenilworth,' &c.* 3 vols. Edinburgh, 1822.

———. *Ivanhoe.* Ed. Graham Tulloch. Edinburgh: Edinburgh University Press, 1998.

———. *Minstrelsy of the Scottish Border.* Ed. T. F. Henderson. 4 vols. Edinburgh: William Blackwood, 1902.

———. *The Monastery.* Ed. Penny Fielding. Edinburgh: Edinburgh University Press, 2000.

———. *Peveril of the Peak. By the Author of 'Waverley, Kenilworth,' &c.* 4 vols. Edinburgh, 1822.

———. *Tales of the Crusaders. By the Author of 'Waverley, Quentin Durward,' &c.* 4 vols. Edinburgh, 1825.

Sculptura-Historico-Technica: or the History and Art of Ingraving. London, 1747.

Seward, Anna. *Letters of Anna Seward.* 6 vols. Edinburgh, 1811.

Shakespeare, William. *The Norton Shakespeare: Based on the Oxford Edition.* Ed. Stephen Greenblatt et al. New York: Norton, 1997.

The Shakspere Allusion-Book: A Collection of Allusions to Shakspere from 1591 to 1700. 2 vols. London: Oxford University Press, 1932.

Sharpe, Kevin. *Reading Revolutions: The Politics of Reading in Early Modern England.* New Haven, Conn.: Yale University Press, 2000.

Sharpe, Kevin, and Steven N. Zwicker. "Introduction: Refiguring Revolutions." In *Refiguring Revolutions: Aesthetics and Politics from the English Revolution to the Romantic Revolution,* ed. Kevin Sharpe and Steven N. Zwicker, 1–21. Berkeley: University of California Press, 1998.

Shenstone, William. *The Letters of William Shenstone.* Ed. Marjorie Williams. Oxford: Basil Blackwell, 1939.

Shields, David S. *Civil Tongues and Polite Letters in British America.* Chapel Hill: University of North Carolina Press for the Institute of Early American History and Culture, 1997.

Shiells, Robert, and Theophilus Cibber. *The Lives of the Poets of Great Britain and Ireland.* 5 vols. London, 1753.

Sherman, Stuart. *Telling Time: Clocks, Diaries, and English Diurnal Form, 1660–1785.* Chicago: University of Chicago Press, 1996.

Slawinski, Janusz. "Reading and Reader in the Literary Historical Process." Trans. Nina Taylor. *New Literary History* 19 (1988): 521–39.

Smart, Alastair. "Dramatic Gesture and Expression in the Age of Hogarth and Reynolds." *Apollo* 82 (1965): 90–97.

Smith, Sydney. *The Letters of Sydney Smith.* Ed. Nowell C. Smith. 2 vols. Oxford: Clarendon, 1953.

Smollett, Tobias. *The Expedition of Humphry Clinker.* Ed. O. M. Brack Jr. Athens: University of Georgia Press, 1990.

Speaight, George. *The History of the English Puppet Theatre.* 2d ed. Carbondale: Southern Illinois University Press, 1990.

The Spectator. Ed. Donald F. Bond. 5 vols. Oxford: Clarendon, 1965.

Spence, Joseph. *An Essay on Pope's Odyssey: In which Some particular Beauties and Blemishes of that Work are consider'd.* London, 1726.

A Statement of the Differences Subsisting Between the Proprietors and Performers of the Theatre-Royal, Covent-Garden, given in the Correspondence which has passed between them. London, 1800.

Stedman, John Gabriel. *Narrative of Five Years Expedition against the Revolted Negroes of Surinam.* Ed. Richard Price and Sally Price. Baltimore: Johns Hopkins University Press, 1988.

Stern, Simon. "*Tom Jones* and the Economies of Copyright." *Eighteenth-Century Fiction* 9 (1997): 429–44.

Stern, Tiffany. *Rehearsal from Shakespeare to Sheridan.* Oxford: Clarendon, 2000.

Sterne, Laurence. *Letters of Laurence Sterne.* Ed. Lewis Perry Curtis. Oxford: Clarendon, 1935.

———. *The Life and Opinions of Tristram Shandy, Gentleman.* Ed. Melvyn New and Joan New. Gainesville: University Presses of Florida, 1978.

———. *A Sentimental Journey through France and Italy and Continuation of the Brahmine's Journal.* Ed. Melvyn New and W. G. Day. Gainesville: University Press of Florida, 2002.

Sterne: The Critical Heritage. Ed. Alan B. Howes. London: Routledge, 1974.

Stochholm, Johanne M. *Garrick's Folly: The Shakespeare Jubilee of 1769 at Stratford and Drury Lane.* London: Methuen, 1964.

Stoddard, Roger E. "Morphology and the Book." In *A Library-Keeper's Business.* New Castle, Del.: Oak Knoll Press, 2002.

Stone, George Winchester, Jr. "The Making of the Repertory." In *The London Theatre World, 1660–1800,* ed. Robert D. Hume, 181–209. Carbondale: Southern Illinois University Press, 1980.

Stone, George Winchester, Jr., and George M. Kahrl. *David Garrick: A Critical Biography.* Carbondale: Southern Illinois University Press, 1979.

Sutherland, James R. "'Polly' among the Pirates." *Modern Language Review* 37 (1942): 291–303.

Swift, Jonathan. *The Complete Poems.* Ed. Pat Rogers. London: Penguin, 1983.

———. *The Correspondence of Jonathan Swift, D.D.* Ed. David Woolley. 4 vols. Frankfurt am Main: Peter Lang, 1999–.

———. *Gulliver's Travels.* Ed. Albert J. Rivero. New York: Norton, 2002.

Swift, Jonathan, and Thomas Sheridan. *The Intelligencer.* Ed. James Woolley. Oxford: Clarendon, 1992.

Tasch, Peter A. *The Dramatic Cobbler: The Life and Works of Isaac Bickerstaff.* Lewisburg, Pa.: Bucknell University Press, 1971.

Tave, Stuart M. *The Amiable Humorist: A Study in the Comic Theory and Criticism of the Eighteenth and Early Nineteenth Centuries.* Chicago: University of Chicago Press, 1960.

Teerink, H. *A Bibliography of the Writings of Jonathan Swift.* 2d ed. Philadelphia: University of Pennsylvania Press, 1963.

Theatrical Biography: or, Memoirs of the Principal Performers of the Three Theatres-Royal. 2 vols. Dublin, 1772.

Thesaurus Dramaticus. Containing all the Celebrated Passages, Soliloquies, Similies, Descriptions, and other Poetical Beauties in the Body of English Plays, Antient and Modern, Digested under Proper Topics. London, 1724.

Thompson, E. P. "Custom, Law and Common Right." In *Customs in Common.* New York: Free Press, 1991.

———. *The Making of the English Working Class.* New York: Pantheon, 1963.

Travels into Several Remote Nations of the World. By Capt. Lemuel Gulliver. Vol. III. London, 1727.

Turner, James Grantham. "Novel Panic: Picture and Performance in the Reception of Richardson's *Pamela.*" *Representations* 48 (fall 1994): 70–96.

Two Lilliputian Odes: The First, On the Famous Engine with which Captain Gulliver Extinguish'd the Flames in the Royal Palace . . . The Second, Inviting a Bookseller, to a Coffee-House, where the Author was. London, 1727.

Updike, John. "Recurrent Characters." *Inside Borders* (November 1998): 8–9.

Vaidhyanathan, Siva. *Copyrights and Copywrongs: The Rise of Intellectual Property and How It Threatens Creativity.* New York: New York University Press, 2001.

Warner, Marina. *Joan of Arc: The Image of Female Heroism.* London: Weidenfeld and Nicolson, 1981.

Warner, Michael. *The Letters of the Republic: Publication and the Public Sphere in Eighteenth-Century America.* Cambridge, Mass.: Harvard University Press, 1990.

———. *Publics and Counterpublics.* New York: Zone Books, 2002.

Warner, William B. *Licensing Entertainment: The Elevation of Novel Reading in Britain, 1684–1750.* Berkeley: University of California Press, 1998.

Watson, Isobel. *Westminster and Pimlico Past: A Visual History.* London: Historical Publications, 1993.

Weddell, Austin. *Incle and Yarico: A Tragedy, of Three Acts. As it was intended to have been Performed at the Theatre-Royal, in Covent-Garden.* London, 1742.

Whitehead, William. *On Nobility: An Epistle.* London, 1744.

Whitley, William T. *Artists and their Friends in England, 1700–1799.* 2 vols. 1928. Reprint. Bronx, N.Y.: Benjamin Blom, 1968.

The Whole Story of the Sorrows of Maria, of Moulines. Selected from various works of the celebrated Sterne. 2d ed. Boston, 1793.

Wilkes, Thomas. *A General View of the Stage.* London, 1759.

Wilson, Luke. *Theaters of Intention: Drama and the Law in Early Modern England.* Stanford, Calif.: Stanford University Press, 2000.

Wilson, Michael S. "Garrick, Iconic Acting, and the Ideologies of Theatrical Portraiture." *Word and Image* 6 (1990): 368–94.

Winton, Calhoun. *John Gay and the London Theatre.* Lexington: University Press of Kentucky, 1993.

Wolf, Edwin, II. *The Book Culture of a Colonial American City: Philadelphia Books, Bookmen, and Booksellers.* Oxford: Clarendon, 1988.

Wollstonecraft, Mary. *A Vindication of the Rights of Woman.* Ed. Miriam Brody. London: Penguin, 1992.

Woodmansee, Martha. *The Author, Art, and the Market: Rereading the History of Aesthetics.* New York: Columbia University Press, 1994.

Wordsworth, William. *The Prose Works of William Wordsworth.* Ed. W. J. B. Owen and Jane Worthington Smyser. 3 vols. Oxford: Clarendon, 1974.

Worthen, William B. *The Idea of the Actor: Drama and the Ethics of Performance.* Princeton, N.J.: Princeton University Press, 1984.

Wright, Austin. *Joseph Spence: A Critical Biography.* Chicago: University of Chicago Press, 1950.

Wroth, Warwick. *The London Pleasure Gardens of the Eighteenth Century.* London: Macmillan, 1896.

Yorick's Sentimental Journey Continued. To which is prefixed, some Account of the Life and Writings of Mr. Sterne. London, 1769.

Young, Edward. *An Apology for Princes; or the Reverence due to Government.* In *The Works of the Author of the Night-Thoughts,* 5:302–72. New ed. London, 1767.

———. *Conjectures on Original Composition. In a Letter to the Author of Sir Charles Grandison.* London, 1759.

Zwicker, Steven N. *Lines of Authority: Politics and English Literary Culture, 1649–1689.* Ithaca, N.Y.: Cornell University Press, 1993.

———. "Reading the Margins: Politics and the Habits of Appropriation." In *Refiguring Revolutions: Aesthetics and Politics from the English Revolution to the Romantic Revolution,* ed. Kevin Sharpe and Steven N. Zwicker, 101–15. Berkeley: University of California Press, 1998.

Index

Acknowledgments

I always read acknowledgments first, in large part to see how a scholar has dealt with his or her own belatedness in such a hyperconventionalized genre. I doubt I can provide much formal innovation, but it is one of the great pleasures of my life as a writer finally to record the debts I have been so shamelessly accruing over the years.

I continue to marvel at how many of my interests were formed by my undergraduate mentors: John Smyth, Richard Tristman, and Rush Welter. As an institution, the Bennington I knew was purged out of existence more than a decade ago; as an ideal, it remains ever with me. In more recent years, my habits of thought have been shaped in important and multifarious ways by Cathy Gallagher, Susan Hegeman, Carla Hesse, Peter Sahlins, and James Turner. I have also benefited greatly from the timely encouragement and smart questions of Jim Chandler, Helen Deutsch, Ian Duncan, Frank Felsenstein, Bob Griffin, Nick Howe, Paul Hunter, Matt Kinservik, Jayne Lewis, Jim Phelan, Steven Zwicker, and the virtual community of c-18l. While I have never had the good fortune to meet Gérard Genette, Franco Moretti, or Carol Rose, this book would have been conceptually far thinner (and perhaps not even possible) without the sparks thrown off by their provocative and far-reaching ideas. Finally, I am grateful to Jerry Singerman, Leah Price, and another still anonymous reader for the University of Pennsylvania Press for the care with which they ensured that my work would not appear before it had been fully cooked.

The warmth, wit, and bartending skills of my friends (who often double as colleagues) have collectively enabled me to avoid a surprisingly large number of anxieties endemic to academic life. If of making books there is no end, there is also no end to the friendships (and Homeric catalogs of friendships) which book-making can create. Thanks are especially due to Lawrie Balfour, Alison Beck, Brad Berens, Kathi Inman Berens, Caroline Bicks, Larry Chernikoff, Cate Corcoran, Frank Donoghue, Jared Gardner, Kevis Goodman, Beth Hewitt, Craig Huntley, Robin Judd, Seb and Janette Knowles, Larry Kutchen, Marlene Longenecker, Sandra Macpherson, Diana Maltz, Craige Roberts, Edye Sanford, Maura Spiegel, Kenny Steinman, Simon

Stern, Karl and Heather Thiel, Roxann Wheeler, Luke Wilson, and Gary Wolf. Whenever I write, I keep my mother-in-law, Mary Morton, at the back of my mind in an attempt to ensure that the stakes of my argument will be readily apparent to smart readers outside the academy. And the commitment of my parents, Don and Sue Brewer, both to me and to higher education more generally, has never been anything short of remarkable. Indeed, their generous support, along with that of the University of California, Berkeley, the William Andrews Clark Memorial Library, the Mabelle McLeod Lewis Fund, and The Ohio State University, has granted me the rare privilege of having almost enough time to write.

The generic requirements of the acknowledgments page mandate that, like the wine at Cana, the best be saved for last. I can do no more than to refer the gentle reader to my dedication. My life is incalculably sweeter because of my darling wife and children, my every moment devoted to devising our further adventures together.

www.ingramcontent.com/pod-product-compliance
Lightning Source LLC
LaVergne TN
LVHW091517200926
848483LV00005B/436/J

* 9 7 8 0 8 1 2 2 3 8 6 4 8 *